W9-DFR-181

(continued on back)

THE PERSONAL LIFE
OF THE PSYCHOTHERAPIST

The Personal Life
of the Psychotherapist

James D. Guy

Associate Professor
Rosemead School of Psychology
Biola University

JOHN WILEY & SONS

New York • Chichester • Brisbane • Toronto • Singapore

ISBN 0-471-84854-9

Printed in the United States of America

10 9 8 7 6 5 4 3 2 1

*To Margaret,
my wife and friend*

Foreword

James D. Guy, Jr., in his exploration of *The Personal Life of the Psychotherapist,* has made a wonderful contribution to the literature on who we are as therapists. Therapists have functioned since the 1920s, but minimal attention has been paid to the impact on our personal and professional lives as a consequence of the work we do.

In this book, with ample space given to an excellent bibliography, we are requested to begin to look at who we are, why we chose this profession, as well as what are the gratifications and liabilities in our therapeutic journey.

Guy begins with a discussion of the satisfactions of being a psychotherapist, which include independence, financial rewards, recognition, prestige, intellectual stimulation, and personal fulfillment. It is no mean feat to enter one of the many roads that lead to a career in psychotherapy. The road may lead through the fields of psychology, psychiatry, social work, psychiatric nursing or counseling, but each requires two to eight years of graduate school and training. As the process moves along, the psychotherapist begins to feel the impact of training either through personal therapy, supervision, or schooling. Some of us are better suited than others for this field. Others seek to find personal answers for their complex life difficulties; while still others have a sincere desire to contribute and to help. For whatever reasons, whether suited or not for this field, we apply and seek to work in this profession.

Once one has graduated, the beginning impact of our work is subtly felt. As Guy points out, the building of a practice has its initial rewards and frustrations but start we must. (Along with the work in the practice a beginning sense of isolation, degrees of loneliness, fatigue, the need for emotional control, one-way intimacy and setting aside personal concerns make themselves felt.)

It is important to note that the book expounds, in Chapter 4, on the impact of psychotherapeutic practice on personal relationships. Having been in psychoanalytic practice for 30 years, I can vouch for the importance of relating to one's spouse and children in spite of feeling drained, spent, and fatigued at the end of a hectic day. It is precisely because we may feel drained that our family, significant others, friends, colleagues, and others in our social relationships become "life savers." The more we isolate ourselves, the more the propensity for impairment and burnout may occur.

We, the healers, have had a difficult time in acknowledging that we may have become impaired and might need to turn to others for help. It is difficult to recognize and admit that years of professional life make themselves felt in ourselves, our office, and in our home. Guy clearly indicates that mental illness, suicide, substance and sexual abuse may become forks in the road for some colleagues.

We also need to recognize that each phase of our lives, from early adulthood to middle and late adulthood, promote issues that may be of a very personal nature. These issues may be illness, disability, death of a loved one, divorce, or just plain aging. Each issue requires our understanding and recognition.

Each phase of our life brings with it degrees of career satisfaction and a potential for burnout. An understanding of the process of how this may occur and the reality of stating to each other that the possibilities for impairment are real may serve as beginning steps for diminishing this potentially depleting process.

Guy offers many suggestions throughout the book as to what we can do. He speaks of tending to oneself through self-care, seeking further personal therapy or supervision, reducing stress related to clinical practice, meeting with colleagues, participating in seminars or workshops, and turning to our loved ones.

This book offers much to the graduate student, the teacher, and the practitioner. Many of us have traveled the trial-and-error journey without the assistance of a wonderful book such as this one. However, I end with a hopeful note. The very fact that a book such as this has been written strongly suggests that if we can look at ourselves in a forthright fashion, then most assuredly the anguish and despair of our present colleagues and our future generations of young therapists, one of whom is my daughter Lisa, will be significantly diminished.

HERBERT J. FREUDENBERGER

April 1987
New York

Series Preface

This series of books is addressed to behavioral scientists interested in the nature of human personality. Its scope should prove pertinent to personality theorists and researchers as well as to clinicians concerned with applying an understanding of personality processes to the amelioration of emotional difficulties in living. To this end, the series provides a scholarly integration of theoretical formulations, empirical data, and practical recommendations.

Six major aspects of studying and learning about human personality can be designated: personality theory, personality structure and dynamics, personality development, personality assessment, personality change, and personality adjustment. In exploring these aspects of personality, the books in the series discuss a number of distinct but related subject areas: the nature and implications of various theories of personality; personality characteristics that account for consistencies and variations in human behavior; the emergence of personality processes in children and adolescents; the use of interviewing and testing procedures to evaluate individual differences in personality; efforts to modify personality styles through psychotherapy, counseling, behavior, therapy, and other methods of influence; and patterns of abnormal personality functioning that impair individual competence.

IRVING B. WEINER

University of Denver
Denver, Colorado

Preface

The interpersonal relationship between the therapist and the patient is typically both the subject and the mode of psychotherapy, regardless of the theoretical orientation of the psychotherapist (Henry, Sims, & Spray, 1973). For the past several decades, a substantial amount of research has focused on the consequences of this relationship for the patient. It has now been generally established that the psychotherapy relationship has a positive, even curative, impact on most patients, particularly when the therapist is caring, competent, and experienced (Garfield & Bergin, 1978).

Until recently, however, very little was known about the impact of this relationship on the therapist. In fact, little consideration was given to the effects of conducting thousands of hours of psychotherapy on the personal life and relationships of the psychotherapist.

There seems to be an increasing realization that psychotherapists are often deeply impacted by the therapeutic relationships that they form with patients. It can no longer be assumed that the therapist remains unaffected by the time he or she spends with these individuals, hour after hour, day after day, year after year.

Recent research suggests that the private life of the therapist is often significantly impacted by psychotherapeutic practice in a wide variety of ways. In some cases, the impact is positive and growth enhancing (Burton, 1975; Farber, 1983a; Farber & Heifitz, 1981). For others, the consequences of psychotherapeutic practice can be rather negative and destructive (Cray & Cray, 1977; Farber, 1983b; Henry, et al., 1973). In most cases, there seems to be an interactive effect between the hazards inherent in the practice of psychotherapy and the individual, personal dynamics of the therapist.

The purpose of this book is to examine in depth the multitude of factors which contribute to the impact of psychotherapeutic practice on the therapist. In addition to exploring the elements of clinical practice which affect the life of the therapist both negatively and positively, special attention will be given to the interaction between these factors and the personality characteristics and significant events which occur in the natural course of the therapist's lifetime.

xi

It is hoped that such an examination and discussion will enable psychotherapists reading this book to enhance the positive impact of their work upon their private life, while reducing or eliminating the potentially negative consequences of clinical practice. While admittedly grandiose, it is the author's hope and expectation that thoughtful consideration of these issues will improve not only the quality of patient care, but also the quality of the therapist's overall life satisfaction.

May we all enjoy long, satisfying careers as psychotherapists, and fulfilling, meaningful lives with friends and family as a result.

JAMES D. GUY, JR.

South Pasadena, California
April 1987

Acknowledgments

A project of this size can never be accomplished in isolation. It requires the input, assistance, and support of many people. It is out of extensive discussion, reflection, and interaction that these ideas and formulations have emerged. I wish to thank the many psychotherapists who contributed to the thinking behind this book over the past several years, through our direct and indirect interaction.

I wish to thank the faculty at Fuller School of Psychology, my internship supervisors at Milwaukee County Mental Health Complex and Northwestern University Institute of Psychiatry, and my colleagues at the Rosemead School of Psychology, Biola University, for providing me with the clinical training which has made it possible for me to practice the psychotherapy that I have come to so enjoy.

I also wish to thank my research assistants Gary Liaboe, M.A., Janet Souder, M.A., and Miriam Stark, M.A., for their tireless efforts in helping me conduct the research and data gathering which provided the foundation for this book.

Finally, I would like to express special appreciation to Margaret Guy, M.S.W., for her many hours of reading and discussion during the preparation of this work. She has been both my most loyal supporter and toughest critic.

J.D.G.

Contents

THE PERSONAL LIFE
OF THE PSYCHOTHERAPIST

CHAPTER 1

Factors Leading to the Career Choice of Psychotherapist

Society reserves a special place of honor for its "healers." As Henry (1966) points out, such individuals have always been treated as privileged persons who are permitted legitimate access to the hidden and the mysterious, using "tools" of healing which are more internal than external, more private than public, and which are exempt from the scrutiny of others. The "cures" obtained are more often dependent on faith and belief than on evidence or logic. Theirs is a profession surrounded by a certain mystique and aura which elicits both respect and fear in the layperson. Rather than being regarded as a desirable profession, it is seen as a "calling" which brings great rewards, such as wealth and prestige, at high personal cost.

Healers or shamans are thought to be best suited for their profession because of the extent of their own personal wounds (Goldberg, 1986). Their private pain is thought to give them insight and empathy into the distress of others, while their survival or victory over their afflictions gives them great power and authority over those of others. The archetypal "wounded healer" has universal appeal. They are worthy of almost unquestioning trust and respect. As Bugental (1964) states, in every age humans have turned to the shaman for help in contending with the unknown aspects of life. Invariably, those to whom they turn have been invested with supranormal vision and potency. Such individuals are seen as filling a role which is alternately blessed and cursed, but above all, necessary.

The psychotherapist is often regarded as the latest descendant of a long line of healers which can be traced back to prehistoric times (Bugental, 1964). The psychotherapist's ancestors include the witch doctor, wizard, priest, and family doctor. Such individuals have traditionally been assigned the task of bringing relief to both individual and community suffering. Currently, it is the psychotherapist who is expected to unlock the mysteries of human pain. This is not only true for those infirmities typically seen as emotionally based, such as some forms of depression and psychosis, but also for some forms of illness previously thought to have a purely physical etiology, such as cancer, cardiac

1

problems, and ulcers. Recent advances in psychosomatic research and the increasing popularity of the holistic health movement have placed the psychotherapist in a position of prominence in the battle against distress of all kinds.

As true of the ancestoral shamans, psychotherapists are afforded a special position in our society. Some individuals regard the therapist as a saint, worthy of great respect and admiration (Guy & Liaboe, 1986a). In the case of these individuals the psychotherapist is sought out for advice and guidance, as well as for the healing of psychic pain. Fees are gratefully paid, and the therapist receives both high status and prestige in the community. He or she is regarded as "gifted" and "special," and a valued family resource. On the other hand, some regard the psychotherapist as "a member of a marginal professional group, a bearer of bad news, someone to consult as a last resort, or a person with near extrasensory powers who can see through their defenses at will" (Guy & Liaboe, 1986a, p. 113). As such, both conversation and eye contact are to be avoided, and the psychotherapist is regarded with suspicion and fear. Regardless of how people choose to react, psychotherapists are seen by nearly everyone as serving a necessary role in our society. However, this role is rarely coveted by those respecting its importance. It is also safe from elimination by those regarding its usefulness with suspicion.

It is interesting to note the manner in which the role of psychotherapist is portrayed in the popular media. During an informal telephone interview with the supervisor of dramatic series development of ABC television in Hollywood, three sources of information were identified for determining how psychotherapists are portrayed (Liaboe & Guy, in press). These were: the producer's or writer's personal conceptualizations, editorial research of newspapers, magazines, and other publications, and direct observation or interviews. As noted by Eber & O'Brien (1982), a host of movies have portrayed the therapist and the process of psychotherapy in a stereotypical fashion. Films such as *Ordinary People* (1981), *Lady in the Dark* (1944), *Spellbound* (1945), *The Mark* (1962), *Bob & Carol & Ted & Alice* (1969), *Blume in Love* (1973), *An Unmarried Woman* (1978), *David & Lisa* (1963), *I Never Promised You a Rose Garden* (1979), and *Equus* (1977), in addition to television shows such as "Bob Newhart," "Mash," "St. Elsewhere," "Cheers," and "Growing Pains," create a certain public image of the psychotherapist and the nature of the therapeutic encounter. For the most part, the therapist is portrayed as the tireless sleuth who attempts, often by rather unconventional means, to uncover the single repressed traumatic event which underlies the emotional distress, thereby resulting in seemingly instant cure. Although entertaining, this rendition tends to be rather "simplistic, sentimentalized, and romanticized " (Eber & O'Brien,1982, p. 120). It depicts the psychotherapist as the neurotic or sometimes comic hero or heroine, who almost inadvertently brings about a sudden, dramatic cure through prompting of the patient's insight and recall. Farber (1983a) points out that the media also caricatures the psychotherapist at times as humorless, controlled, impersonal, and egotistical, with personal idiosyncracies surpassing those of his or her patients. Yet, regardless of the questionable authenticity of such descriptions, the public is presented with the notion that psychotherapists are, indeed, the shamans of our society, concurrently loved and hated, respected and feared, credible and yet suspect.

As a contemporary shaman, the psychotherapist serves a necessary and often vital function in relieving the pain and distress of millions of individuals annually. A recent National Institute of Mental Health (NIMH) study (Seligmann, 1984) revealed that nearly 20% of the American population received a psychiatric diagnosis during a one year period. Few would dispute that the training and experience of most psychotherapists make them well-suited for providing comfort and relief for such individuals.

Many roads lead to a career in psychotherapy. Among the total number of persons practicing psychotherapy in the United States are approximately 29,000 psychiatrists, 26,000 clinical psychologists, 31,000 psychiatric social workers, 10,000 psychiatric nurses, and 10,000 plus counselors of various types, representing a variety of graduate degrees such as MD, PhD, PsyD, EdD, MSW, MFCC, MS, and MA (Goldberg, 1986). The formal training required varies from two to more than eight years, plus the several thousand hours of postgraduate supervised experience necessary to qualify for state licensure or registration. Practicing psychotherapists represent a wide array of theoretical orientations and approaches, ranging from the cognitive and short-term to the psychoanalytic and long-term models. The practice of psychotherapy occurs within a variety of work settings. Sessions may take place in a private office, clinic, counseling center, or hospital. They may be part of an inpatient or outpatient treatment program. Therapy sessions may involve only the individual patient, or they may include the spouse, family, or a group of several patients. The cost of therapy may be borne entirely by the patient, or partially or fully covered by an insurance policy, employer, or family member. In more indirect ways, psychotherapists also provide help to individuals in distress by means of telephone, television, radio, and printed books and materials. Psychotherapists function in a wide variety of ways, in many different settings, to provide assistance, advice, and relief from distress. The curriculum requirements of graduate programs, and the postgraduate requirements necessary for eventual licensure or certification, are constantly fluctuating in an attempt to provide a wide assortment of psychotherapists who are able to address the changing needs of a complicated society.

What do these diverse groups of clinicians have in common? More importantly, what factors led to their decision to practice psychotherapy? A review of the literature suggests that factors inherent in the role of psychotherapist, as well as a variety of personal factors, interact to attract individuals to this career choice. This chapter will examine the many benefits and satisfactions associated with being a psychotherapist. It will also discuss the functional and dysfunctional personal motivations for entry into this career. Finally, the role of the family of origin in predisposing the individual towards becoming a psychotherapist will be explored. Suggestions will be made as to how these various factors influence the decision to enter this field.

SATISFACTIONS OF BEING A PSYCHOTHERAPIST

There are a number of factors inherent in the role of psychotherapist that may attract individuals to this career choice. Many of these "fringe benefits" and sources of satisfaction are widely known and may serve to motivate some individuals to choose this occupation.

Independence

At a practical level, becoming a psychotherapist provides a high degree of professional independence (Tryon, 1983a). Whether the therapist chooses to practice within a clinic, hospital, group practice, or in an independent private practice, the work is typically conducted in isolation and independent of direct supervision and evaluation. Thus the therapist is able to adopt a unique personal style of practice.

Therapists typically have a great deal of control over the scheduling of work hours, allowing for a valued flexibility uncharacteristic of many other careers. Not only are they able to decide when to schedule appointments, but they are often in a position to decide how many appointments to schedule within a given day or week, particularly in the case of the private practitioner. In addition, psychotherapy is one of the few professional careers which can be undertaken successfully on a part-time basis (Norcross, Nash, & Prochaska, 1985). The training required for a career in psychotherapy provides opportunities for greater diversity as well, allowing the therapist to engage in teaching, research, supervision, and consultation, in addition to direct clinical services.

Psychotherapists are often in a position to decide which patients to accept into psychotherapy, allowing for specialization in terms of age, sex, and diagnosis of patients regarded as appropriate and desirable to the particular therapist (Burton, 1975). The clinician can also choose to be a generalist, or can change specialties at any time, with the required additional training. In short, the therapist is often able to work only with those types of individuals that he or she enjoys. Such independence allows the therapist to have a sense of control over the way he or she spends time in professional pursuits.

Financial Rewards

As Marston (1984) points out, one of the rewards of a career in psychotherapy is the opportunity to earn a considerable amount of money. While certainly not the most lucrative of professional careers, psychotherapists typically earn a comfortable income well above the mean income of the general population, particularly for those working full-time in private practice (Tryon, 1983b). In addition, therapists are able to determine, within some limits, what size income to earn during a given period of time, due to the flexibility and diversification inherent in the profession. It is also possible to supplement one's income with additional independent private practice, regardless of the primary work setting, enabling the clinician to charge professional fees according to his or her own preference and needs, within acceptable limits. Most would agree that the financial rewards of psychotherapeutic practice are quite adequate (Burton, 1975).

Variety

Few occupations provide the endless variety, surprises, and challenges found in the practice of psychotherapy. Within the context of the consulting office, the therapist enters freely into the world of a wide array of individuals, from the uneducated and impoverished to the extremely wealthy and famous. As Greben (1975) and Burton (1975) point out, the psychotherapist becomes intimately acquainted with an astonishing variety of human endeavors, experiences, world views, emotions, and behaviors by means of psychotherapeutic relationships. In a very real way, the psychotherapist has a "front row seat" in the lives of musicians, scientists, movie stars, blue collar laborers, politicians, doctors, salespeople, lawyers, and vagrants. Bugental (1964) asserts that the therapist is privileged to participate with unique immediacy in the business of life itself, participating in the heights of elation and self-affirmation as well as the depths of confusion and madness. Those encountered represent all races, ages, and walks of life. As a result, therapists are exposed to people and events which would not likely be encountered in their own private life and social arena. In this way, no two patients are alike and each new encounter provides the clinician with a unique individual with whom to work.

There is also variety in the types of problems which each patient brings to the clinician. Over the course of a professional career, the therapist will encounter nearly every type of emotional disorder imaginable. While some individuals will present with symptoms of depression, others will present with thought disorders or anxiety. Because of the interaction which occurs between symptoms and life events, each patient presents with a uniquely different form of psychopathology or emotional distress. Thus the variety of symptoms and problems encountered seems almost endless.

Recognition and Prestige

The role of the psychotherapist, and the training and education required for this vocation, bring a certain amount of prestige and recognition from family, friends, and the wider community (Farber & Heifetz, 1981; Tryon, 1983a). As described by Marston (1984), there is a certain notoriety associated with a career in psychotherapy. Many individuals respect the advanced degrees earned by the therapist, recognizing the motivation, intelligence, and commitment required for such an achievement. Our society has traditionally valued education, and the therapist is esteemed for his or her accomplishments in this regard.

There is also a special status afforded to those regarded as a "professional," a ranking for which the psychotherapist clearly qualifies. Both Farber and Heifetz (1981) and Tryon (1983a) report that therapists enjoy a special honor and respect due to community recognition of their position as mental health professionals.

They are regarded as highly trained experts belonging to the larger medical profession, which itself has a special status in American society .

In addition to valuing the required education and training, a career in psychotherapy has a certain mystique to it. Many individuals have an intuitive sense that the psychotherapist belongs to a unique fraternity of special individuals capable of encountering and absorbing a great deal of human pain and suffering with few apparent ill effects. There is a persistent belief that psychotherapists do something terribly important for the larger society, a task which cannot be accomplished by anyone else (Burton, 1975). They, therefore, receive the admiration of the layperson who ascribes special qualities, gifts, and abilities to those who are able to practice psychotherapy successfully, and by definition fill these unique roles in the community.

There is also a certain natural curiosity associated with a career in psychotherapy. The general public seems to recognize that the therapist seeks to find answers to the existential questions that plague humankind. There may be the resultant belief that the psychotherapist has answers for the many and varied problems associated with daily life. Thus the clinician is afforded a special respect and honor by those who feel far less enlightened and informed (Guy & Liaboe, 1986a).

All of these factors combine to create a distinctive prestige and professional status enjoyed by most psychotherapists, making this an attractive career choice for those so inclined.

Intellectual Stimulation

Inherent in the practice of psychotherapy is a high degree of intellectual stimulation and growth for the therapist (Goldberg, 1986). This is due to both the types of people who enter therapy as patients, and the problems that they bring for consideration.

Those choosing to enter psychotherapy as a patient are often verbal, intelligent, and motivated. Depending on the person, they may also be insightful, stimulating, and provocative. As a result, the psychotherapist may spend many hours interacting intimately and intensely with individuals who are very intellectually stimulating. The ideas discussed, the issues considered, and the very quality of the interaction in the relationship can provide regular and significant intellectual gratification for both participants. Patients are often among the most interesting people encountered during the therapist's lifetime. The myriad of world views, perspectives, and experiences disclosed by patients expand the therapist's own repertoire of knowledge and insights, a very exciting by-product of this career endeavor.

The patient problems, symptoms, and difficulties confronting the practicing psychotherapist are themselves intellectually stimulating. The therapist continually generates hypotheses about the presenting symptoms, as pointed out by Burton (1975), and moves to hypothesis testing and eventual confirmation of fact. In this way, the therapist conducts a type of ongoing research concerning human behavior and development (Kohut, 1977). In much the same way as a detective searches for clues, formulates hunches, and then uncovers facts to provide the details of a given event, the psychotherapist labors to understand the etiology of psychopathology, thereby facilitating a cure. The fact that continued suffering (or even suicide or homicide) may ride on the outcome of this undertaking adds a sense of urgency and importance to the task. Whether this endeavor is regarded as scientific research, a holy calling, or creative artistic expression, the discovery of the etiology of a given constellation of symptoms, and/or the cure of same, results in an intellectual stimulation of the highest order.

Indeed, few careers provide the intellectual challenge, variety, and stimulation inherent in the practice of psychotherapy. As noted by Bugental (1964), there is no other career which allows the individual to immerse himself or herself in the workings of psychological processes in their natural condition to the same degree.

Emotional Growth and Satisfaction

The work of the psychotherapist provides a certain amount of emotional growth and satisfaction for the therapist. For many, this seems to be one of the most attractive motivators for entering the profession (Goldberg, 1986; Guy, Stark, & Poelstra, 1987; Marston, 1984). This is the natural result of the factors involved in providing clinical care, as well as a by-product of the therapeutic relationship itself.

Therapists report that they experience significant emotional growth through years of clinical practice (Farber, 1983b; Farber & Heifetz, 1981). They note an increase in assertiveness, self-assurance, self-reliance, psychological mindedness, introspection, self-reflection, and sensitivity in their own personal lives, as a consequence of promoting similar changes in the lives of their patients. It's as though the therapist is able to internalize the guidance, help, and encouragement provided for the patient in facilitating his or her own personal growth. Regardless of theoretical orientation, this continued focus on growth, change, and increased sensitivity has an impact on the therapist's own functioning.

It may also be that emotional growth occurs for the therapist because of the challenge presented by conducting therapy with someone who may have some insights and depth not possessed by the therapist in a particular area. Psychotherapists regularly come in contact with patients who have mastered a particular problem, attained insight into an issue, or explored in depth a specific feeling which has eluded the therapists themselves. As a result, some emotional growth occurs in the therapist, who inadvertently benefits from what the patient has to teach him or her about life. As described by Bugental (1964), the interactive nature of the therapeutic relationship provides numerous opportunities for therapists to increase their own realization of their potential. While this is obviously not the purpose of the relationship, it is sometimes a highly gratifying natural by-product. Although there are dysfunctional aspects associated with entering the profession because of a desire for personal growth, as will be discussed later in this chapter, the potential for this growth to occur is certainly an attractive feature of a career in psychotherapy.

Finally, the psychotherapist experiences emotional satisfaction as a result of relating on a deep, intimate level with many people (Farber & Heifetz, 1981). Experiencing caring for and from patients, over the years, is extremely satisfying and meaningful for the therapist. It is also inspiring to encounter the depth of courage, integrity, and sincerity of some individuals as they struggle to live out their destiny. The psychotherapist is in a privileged position to witness this battle, to share in the pain of defeat and the joy of victory.

Personal Enrichment and Fulfillment

Some individuals are drawn to a career in psychotherapy because of a desire to help people, serve society and humankind, and improve the quality of life for others (Farber & Heifetz, 1981; Henry, Sims, & Spray, 1971; Tryon, 1983a). Indeed, in one recent survey psychotherapists identified this wish to help others as the primary reason for entering a career in psychotherapy (Guy, Stark, & Poelstra, 1987). As described by Bugental (1964), perceiving oneself as successful in this noble endeavor brings a deep sense of personal satisfaction and fulfillment. Participating in a patient's "emergence" can be a profoundly moving experience. Relieving human suffering and promoting personal growth make the therapist feel worthwhile and useful. In fact, some therapists report that they have a sense of "calling" which empowers them to pursue this career (Burton, 1975). Through the practice of psychotherapy, they receive a sense of worth and accomplishment beyond that associated with many other careers.

Successfully promoting growth in others, maintaining contact with patients formally or informally over the years, and meeting their friends and family members by way of referral, allows the psychotherapist the rare satisfaction of seeing the fruits of his or her labor. Longitudinal contacts of this sort provide an ongoing sense of fulfillment as the therapist witnesses the impact of a successful course of treatment on the present and future life and relationships of patients. The lasting respect, caring, and attachment that develop in such cases provide a special sense of personal enrichment for the therapist.

Summary

Factors inherent in the practice of psychotherapy make it a very desirable career choice. As a result, for example, during the last decade organized human service and independent clinical practice have become the fastest growing and most frequently selected primary work settings for psychologists (Pion, 1986). As its visibility has increased through media exposure and societal acceptance, it may be that many are motivated towards a career in psychotherapy because of the independence, financial rewards, variety, recognition and prestige, intellectual stimulation, emotional growth and satisfaction, and personal enrichment and fulfillment to be derived from it.

It should be noted that there are many liabilities associated with a career in psychotherapy, in addition to the aforementioned fringe benefits. Factors such as a highly variable and undependable income, intense isolation, emotional fatigue, frustration resulting from intense interactions with very disturbed and demanding people, grave ethical and legal responsibilties, public criticism of the mental health field, secret doubts about the efficacy of therapy, and many other negative aspects associated with psychotherapeutic practice sometimes have a detrimental impact on practicing psychotherapists. While these liabilities may be apparent to individuals contemplating entry into the profession, the preponderance of benefits seem to outweigh the liabilities for most people. However, as will be discussed in more detail in this chapter, some of the negative aspects of therapeutic practice are often overlooked or minimized, by both those in the profession and the general public. As a result, those attracted to the practice of psychotherapy because of their conclusion that the benefits far outweigh the disadvantages may eventually decide that they were misinformed and change their assessment at a later time. At any rate, for the purpose of this discussion, it is assumed that the benefits outweigh the liabilities for those choosing to become psychotherapists, thereby making it an attractive career option.

In view of the desirable features of a career in psychotherapy, why is such a choice pursued by so relatively few people? Obviously, it is not an appropriate career for everyone, and the general public seems to know this. Who, then, is best suited to become a psychotherapist? Or, perhaps more to the point, what motivates those who choose to become a therapist?

PERSONAL FACTORS LEADING TO BECOMING A PSYCHOTHERAPIST

It seems reasonable to assume that there is a self-selection process at work which leads certain individuals to enter the profession of psychotherapy. These personal motivations go beyond the desire to enjoy the benefits of the profession as outlined previously. There are both conscious and unconscious motivations which, in some cases, promote eventual professional success and personal satisfaction, and in other cases, sabotage attempts to achieve them.

Functional Motivators

Curious and Inquisitive

There are several personal characteristics which motivate individuals to pursue a career as a psychotherapist and make them well-suited to this profession. Perhaps the most obvious quality is a natural interest in people (Storr, 1979). Inherent in their personality is a curiosity about human behavior and an attraction to the world of the personal versus the impersonal. Such individuals typically enjoy the artistic, expressionistic aspects of life, rather than the mechanistic, scientific dimensions (Dent, 1978). As a result, they are attracted to the creative aspects of psychotherapeutic cure rather than the scientific features. As Szalita (1985) puts it, such individuals have a deep interest in people and a natural curiosity about themselves and others. While this is obviously a tenuous generalization, it makes both intuitive and objective sense. An interest in people, and a natural curiosity about the way they live their lives, are obvious assets to successful psychotherapeutic endeavors. Related to this quality is a natural inquisitiveness regarding human emotions and motivations. Someone inquisitive about the many permutations and variations in human behavior is likely to be attracted to the profession of psychotherapy. Marston (1984) describes this as a desire for discovery, an inner drive toward deeper realizations about life and human experience.

Able to Listen

People who are drawn to becoming psychotherapists are often good listeners. As described by Fromm-Reichmann (1960), the ability to listen is the therapist's primary curative instrument. While Rogers (1951) has demonstrated that the ability to listen accurately and helpfully can improve with practice, those attracted to this profession often possess a seemingly natural ablility to do so. More than that, such people seem to enjoy listening to others talk about themselves. Rather than finding this exercise tedious and tiresome, they find it to be stimulating, even exhilarating.

Comfortable with Conversation

In contrast to the ability to listen, and yet inexorably linked to it, is the ability to be easily talkative. Since the early writings of Freud (1949), it has been established that talking is the manner and means by which psychotherapy takes place. It is therefore necessary that the therapist be advanced in his or her verbal skills. The psychotherapist must be somewhat of a natural conversationalist if the endeavor is to be enjoyable and successful. As Marston (1984) describes it, therapists typically enjoy talking, find good conversation to be rewarding and reinforcing, and sometimes marvel that they get paid for doing what they enjoy most. While there may be a great degree of variation among therapists, it is unlikely that someone who finds talking terribly adversive and uncomfortable will be attracted, much less suited, to a career as a psychotherapist.

Empathic and Understanding

Possessing the capacity for empathy and understanding is another desirable personal characteristic of those attracted to this profession. Such individuals are able to enter into the world of others, not only by listening, but by a deep understanding and empathy, enabling them to form alliances with others which are often helpful to both parties (Storr, 1979). It may be the realization of being in possession of this ability that draws some to a profession which regards it as central to the task at hand. While it has been demonstrated that empathic skills can be enhanced, or sometimes even learned (Rogers, 1951), those who already possess them prior to making this career choice obviously have an advantage. Farber (1985a) describes this empathic quality as "psychological-mindedness," a trait which has at its core the ability to reflect on the meaning and motivation of behavior, thoughts, and feelings in oneself and others. This trait is thought by Farber to be the result of a complex interaction of genetic endowment and a number of environmental influences. It is a gift, a way of being and understanding, that is generally present in those who are attracted to psychotherapy as a profession.

Emotionally Insightful

It is also helpful to be very familiar and comfortable with the wide range of human emotions; one's own as well as those of others'. By being aware of one's emotions, an individual is able to more freely enter into an interactive, reciprocal relationship with others, such as is required in the practice of psychotherapy. Comfort and familiarity with one's own feelings promotes a naturalness, a genuiness which has been shown to promote growth and psychotherapeutic cure in others (Rogers, 1961). This will also enable the person to be comfortable with the emotional expression of others, a valuable asset in psychotherapeutic work. An individual drawn to becoming a psychotherapist will find it necessary to display an unusual tolerance for the wide range of emotions that patients are likely to experience and express, such as sorrow, anger, joy, disappointment, shock, rage, and so on (Storr, 1979). Not only will it be necessary to tolerate their expression, but it may also be important to facilitate and encourage their emergence. This requires a comfort which needs to be developed, either prior to or after entry into the profession.

Introspective

Many individuals who choose to become therapists seem to possess a natural tendency to be introspective. Not only will this enable the psychotherapist to accept and understand the feelings of the patient, but it will also help him or her to more freely enter into the relationship with an openness, genuineness, and comfort that enhances the self-exploration of the patient (Rogers, 1951). As mentioned earlier, Farber (1985a) identifies this ability to be introspective as one aspect of the psychological mindedness found in most therapists.

Capable of Self-denial

Those individuals who have a capacity for self-abnegation, and the ability to deny personal gratification are well-suited for the practice of psychotherapy. Since the focus of the therapeutic encounter is on the needs and interests of the patient, the therapist is forced to hold back much of himself or herself, requiring the ability to set aside personal needs in order to better focus of those on the patient (Storr, 1979). The therapist is typically immersed in one-way relationships in which the patient is encouraged to self-disclose while the therapist only minimally self-discloses, if at all (Greben, 1975). Those individuals who are unable to tolerate this are ill-suited to this career option and are not likely to be attracted to becoming a psychotherapist.

Tolerant of Ambiguity

Related to this capacity for self-denial is the ability to tolerate ambiguity and to resist premature closure. This requires that the individual be reluctant to give quick answers, take over and exert control, and assume an authoritarian posture in the face of patient confusion and frequent crisis (Storr, 1979). Due to the subjective, intuitive nature of the therapeutic endeavor, "answers" to existential questions and the resolution of life issues are often illusive and unclear. The therapist must be comfortable living with the unknown, partial answers, and incomplete explanations. He or she must be able to resist the temptation to give easy answers and directives, and focus, instead, on encouraging the patient to find his or her own solutions. This obviously requires that the therapist be a very patient person. Those who tend to be impatient, needing quick and dramatic results, will not likely find the role of psychotherapist to be a compatible one. The process of therapy is often slow and laborious, requiring that the therapist be able to be satisfied with limited success that comes only after a great deal of painstaking effort.

Capable of Warmth and Caring

Those who find psychotherapy to be a suitable occupation are typically capable of exceptional warmth and caring. The curative impact of these qualities has long been established by researchers such as Carkhuff (1969). Such individuals seem to possess a patient, caring attitude about others, often accompanied by a tolerant, nonjudgmental demeanor which allows them to accept people as they are. Rather than being a rehearsed, artificial caring, this valuing is profoundly genuine and sincere. Although not without prejudice or opinions, such people are able to defer to others in the service of providing comfort, support, or nurturance. As a result, there is a tendency for them to become all things to all people, able to identify with a wide range of individuals, while finding it easy to adapt their own style to the needs and preferences of others (Storr, 1979). They seem to possess a rather fluid sense of identity, or at least the expression of their identity is quite flexible. These qualities suit them well to the therapeutic task, wherein the clinician must relate by identification with the other person, rather than by means of mutual self-affirmation on equal terms. The caring and concern that are then naturally extended to the patient are expressed within a nondemanding atmosphere of acceptance and valuing, the unconditionally positive regard of which Rogers so eloquently speaks (1961). It may be that those who possess this quality are attracted to the profession of psychotherapy because it allows them to express and utilize this ability in a helpful manner. In other words, caring people are naturally attracted to "caring" professions, such as psychotherapy, which allow them to express this characteristic.

Tolerant of Intimacy

Related to this capacity for warmth and caring is a desire for intimacy, contact, and closeness, a quality which motivates many to enter the profession of psychotherapy (Marston, 1984). While there are some potentially dysfunctional aspects to this trait, as discussed later in this chapter, it is commonly found in most therapists and is vital to the therapeutic endeavor. Regardless of theoretical orientation, the effective therapist must be able to sustain and tolerate deep intimacy and closeness with patients, sometimes over a period of months or even years.

Comfortable with Power

It may be that people who enjoy being in a position of power and influence find the role of psychotherapist compatible. As pointed out by Guggenbuhl-Craig (1979), there can be little doubt that therapists are often in a position of great influence and power in the lives of their patients. Many find this rather gratifying, and this is sometimes one of the attractive aspects of a career in psychotherapy for some entering the field (Marston, 1984). In fact, the therapist must learn to be comfortable with the realization that this will usually be true, regardless of theoretical orientation or presenting problem. If this can be accepted with proper detachment, allowing the therapist to avoid the pitfall of feeling omnipotent (Searles, 1979), then the treatment can progress satisfactorily. If, however, the therapist is uncomfortable with this idealization, and either tries to confront, destroy, or exploit it, the treatment process will be hindered (Kohut, 1977). Thus as Storr (1979) points out, it is likely that those who are naturally comfortable being in a position of power and influence are attracted to a career in psychotherapy, and they may be well suited for the power aspects of this position.

Able to Laugh

Finally, those who have a sense of humor and enjoy laughing with others may find the role of therapist to be a comfortable one. There is a certain alternating tragicomic quality to many of life's events, and intimate encounters with other human beings almost always include some dimension of humor. Those who get pleasure from enjoying others, their unique perspectives and sense of the absurd, will find the role of psychotherapist fascinating. There is also a certain healing aspect to humor, when expressed at the right moment in the right manner, which can be shared between the therapist and the patient in a very special way. A person who lacks this sense of humor and enjoyment of life is not likely to be attracted to the intimacy and sharing inherent in the therapeutic role.

Dysfunctional Motivators

The personal characteristics mentioned are motivators for entering the profession of psychotherapy which are functional in that they enhance the person's ablility to provide competent, effective clinical service, while serving to enrich the therapist's own personal life, as well. Unfortunately, some of the motivators for choosing to become a psychotherapist can be dysfunctional, gradually hindering psychotherapeutic effectiveness while undermining personal satisfaction and happiness. Nonetheless, they do at times motivate individuals to enter a career in psychotherapy.

Emotional Distress

Henry et al. (1971, 1973) found that a significant number of psychotherapists chose to enter the profession because of an underlying wish to gain deeper self-understanding. While this makes intuitive sense and seems like a reasonable expectation, this may be combined with a wish to resolve painful personal problems or work through emotional traumas. As Ford (1963) reports, all but one in his in-depth study of 25 psychiatry residents admitted pursuing a career in psychotherapy in order to resolve personal conflicts about life goals and existential issues. Holt & Luborsky (1958) claim that the field of psychotherapy generally attracts people who are in the process of mastering their own personal problems. The desire for "self-healing" may be a powerful motivator for a career in psychotherapy (Goldberg, 1986). Its impact on the therapist's effectiveness has yet to be determined. However, only a moment's reflection is necessary to realize how a constant focus on, or internal pressure from, unresolved personal needs on the part of the therapist may prevent him or her from focusing adequately on those of patients. The needy therapist may unwittingly or even intentionally exploit therapeutic relationships in an attempt to meet his or her own emotional needs, to the detriment of the patient.

On the other hand, the metaphor of the therapist as the shaman, or the "wounded healer," referred to in the introductory section of this chapter, is relevant here. As decribed by Henry (1966), the shamans of primitive societies were commonly described as having a proclivity toward nervous disorders of varying degrees of morbidity. The psychotherapist, our contemporary shaman, is often seen as suffering from emotional distress of varying types and severity (Farber, 1985a). To reserve the role of psychotherapist for those free from any emotional needs or distress would be naive. While there may be some who have entered the profession free of psychopathology of any sort, it seems reasonable to assume that this is often not the case. Although the desire to obtain relief from personal emotional pain may have motivated the career choice of some psychotherapists, it may not be an entirely dysfunctional motivator.

For example, continued attempts to resolve personal issues and conflicts through clinical training and supervision may be largely successful for some individuals, leaving the emerging psychotherapist better able to focus effectively on the needs of patients without internal interference from unresolved needs. As will be discussed more fully in Chapter 2, the very nature of the training required for becoming a psychotherapist promotes introspection, insight, and intrapsychic reorganization. Thus it is likely that some psychotherapists who entered the field to find resolution of and relief from inner conflicts do, indeed, experience varying degrees of growth and "healing." These individuals often become effective therapists because of their own progress and improved functioning, in spite of the potentially dysfunctional aspects of such a motivator.

Those entering graduate training to become a psychotherapist because of their own emotional needs may also achieve a greater degree of wholeness as a result of the didactic psychotherapy in which they may participate as patients during their training. This may be a requirement of the program, or it may be a decision freely made by the student. As pointed out by Greenberg & Staller (1981), it is during the years spent in graduate school that most psychotherapists receive their own personal therapy. As a result of this personal therapy experience, the future psychotherapist may achieve a higher level of functioning, again making him or her more effective as a therapist for others.

Finally, as mentioned earlier, a certain amount of growth and emotional healing takes place within the therapist as a direct result of conducting psychotherapy with others. The insights gained from patients, as well as the satisfactions derived from the intimacy, reportedly promote ongoing change and significant emotional growth in the therapist over the course of a career in psychotherapy.

In the tradition of the shaman, the "wound" of personal distress may itself render the therapist more empathic, sensitive, and effective in treating the psychic pain of others, even if it is unresponsive to the "healing" power of shamanic magic (Goldberg, 1986). Personal experience remains one of life's best teachers, bringing both wisdom and empathy. Thus even if the hope of achieving personal relief, which motivated their entry into the profession, remains unfulfilled, some individuals may be effective psychotherapists. This will be the case, however, only when their own distress is not significant enough to render them unable to attend effectively to the distress of others.

In some cases, the therapist's own pain may serve to motivate entry into the mental health field in the hopes of relieving similar pain in others. There may be a genuine wish to "share" the secrets of success with those in need. This may come out of a deep gratitude for the "healing" that one has received from another therapist/shaman. It may also come from the genuine wish to relieve the pain of others which empathically resonates with the psychic scars that remain within. For those psychotherapists who continue in psychic distress, there may be the wish to share vicariously in the healing of others when personal relief seems unattainable. In such cases, the work of psychotherapy may take on a near messianic quality, as though personal relief will be achieved only when the gods are satisfied with the shaman's self-sacrifice and abnegation.

While one can hope that the motives which prompt the "wounded" to become "healers" are professionally and personally functional rather than dysfunctional, the actual impact of such motives remains to be determined. At best, their shamanic nature leaves them suspect. In cases where the motivating pain is sufficiently resolved through the training and subsequent experiences associated with the role of psychotherapist, the therapist may become a very effective clinician. In such instances, this motivation is quite functional. However, in cases where the motivating personal distress is too severe, or sufficiently unresponsive to the inherent "healing" aspects of a career in psychotherapy, the impact on professional and personal functioning may be negative. This will be examined more fully in Chapters 2, 6, and 7.

Vicarious Coping

Bugental (1964) suggests that some enter the field of psychotherapy as a means of vicariously dealing with the contingencies and realities of life. "Therapists sometimes say that they have found a guide dog—the patient—to go through the mine field of certain threats first in order to reassure themselves that it can be negotiated" (Bugental, 1964, p. 273). In this way, the person anxious about facing life's unknown problems enters the profession to assist others in confronting issues which breed considerable anxiety for the therapist himself or herself. The therapist may become heavily invested in the outcome of a patient's struggles due to the therapist's own needs for resolution which have superceded those of the patient. This can result in a voyeuristic aspect to the relationship which may not always be in the best interest of the patient.

Loneliness and Isolation

Several researchers have suggested that psychotherapists are motivated to this career choice in an attempt to overcome a deep-seated loneliness and social isolation (Goldberg, 1986). Henry et al. (1973) found that over 60% of the several thousand psychotherapists surveyed reported that they had few friends as adolescents and young adults and felt somewhat isolated from others. In an earlier study, he found that therapists tended to come from religious or social backgrounds which increased their sense of apartness and aloneness (Henry, 1966). As Greben (1975) states, such individuals are often people who find it difficult to get close to others and to interact on more than a superficial basis. Similarly, Menninger (1957) has observed that psychotherapists, more than members of other specialities, "suffered overmuch from a sense of loneliness, unlovableness, and rejection" (p. 104). Wheelis (1958) proposes that such individuals decide to enter the profession in the hope of finding the closeness and intimacy that they lack, while remaining somewhat anonymous and invulnerable to hurt. Thus because of the "one-way" nature of the therapeutic relationship, they hope to satisfy their needs for closeness in a safe, controlled, stuctured context that permits them to remain detached. As Bugental (1964) states, "this practice fits the needs of those with a great affect hunger, a great desire of intimacy, and a great fear of affect in intimacy " (p. 273). Unfortunately, this one-way closeness and intimacy has a certain "as if " quality which does not assist the therapist in his or her attempts to relate to others in or outside of work. If anything, the "one-way" quality of therapeutic relationships may serve to exacerbate the therapist's problems with intimacy, self-disclosure, and interpersonal relatedness (Guy & Liaboe, 1986a). As a result, the therapist may find it increasingly difficult to be appropriately vulnerable with both patients and those outside of work. Those entering the profession of psychotherapy because of a need for greater interpersonal intimacy may find that this motivator actually hinders their ability to participate effectively in both professional and personal relationships. This problem will be discussed in more detail in Chapter 3.

Desire for Power

As mentioned earlier, the practice of psychotherapy provides the therapist with a sense of personal power. For those whose power needs are satisfied in other ways, making them comfortable with and somewhat detached from this aspect of the work, an attraction to the power inherent in the role of psychotherapist is a functional motivator for entry into this career. However, the practice of psychotherapy may also be attractive to those who feel frightened and impotent in their own lives, because of the opportunity to exert considerable control and influence over the lives of patients (Bugental, 1964; Hammer, 1972). The patient's idealization of the therapist's power can easily lead to a sense of omniscience and omnipotence on the part of the psychotherapist (Guy & Liaboe, 1986a). The result can be a tendency towards aggression, exploitation, and domination in all interpersonal interactions. This creates a very hazardous situation for the therapist, in terms of both professional and personal relationships (Greben, 1975; Gugenbuhl-Craig, 1979; Searles, 1979).

Related to the desire for power is the wish or need to influence or "convert." It may be that some are attracted to this field because of a strong need to control others. Such individuals will use the role of psychotherapist to influence or convert their patients to their own personal political, religious, or philosophical world view. Rather than respecting the patient's autonomy and right to his or her own opinions, such therapists use therapy as a platform for debate, confrontation, and influence. Because of the power inherent in the role of psychotherapist, those with the need to proselytize may be attracted to this profession.

Need to Love

While it is true that the capacity for caring and warmth can be a functional motivator for a career as a psychotherapist, those who are driven by the need to express tenderness and love may also be attracted to this profession. Bugental (1964) desribes it as "an opportunity to give tenderness, compassion, and love . . . without arousing our own anxieties" (p. 274). For example, he asserts that many males drawn to this profession fear their own emotions, believing that they represent weakness or effeminacy. Thus a career in psychotherapy provides an acceptable outlet for the expression of tenderness for males. While Bugental offered no alternative explanation for females, he does suggest that individuals of both sexes may become psychotherapists because of the mistaken belief that they are able to offer a love and caring which have near magical powers. These people feel that their love and acceptance alone are curative agents which produce profound changes in the recipients. Thus they may feel compelled to enter the field of psychotherapy in order to provide the needed succor for those in emotional pain. This sense of calling can begin to have a messiahlike quality to it which, if it runs its full course, may sabotage both the professional and personal relationships of the psychotherapist. The narcissism and grandiosity that underlie this pattern can foster a self-serving, exploitive posture. Not only can they lead to a neurotic "need to be needed" (Hammer, 1972), but they can also increase the therapist's sense of omnipotence.

Vicarious Rebellion

Finally, some may be attracted to the practice of psychotherapy because it appears to be a relatively safe way to express an underlying sense of rebellion. As Bugental (1964) points out, the prerogatives of the position give the therapist an opportunity to attack authority and tradition. Those whose personal dynamics serve to make such an enterprise appealing, due to unresolved anger over destructive prohibitions and taboos in their own background, may unwittingly act out this rebellion by encouraging patients to disregard societal norms, mores, and conventions. The vicarious enjoyment received by the therapist in such cases may not be in the best interests of the patient. If this pattern is truly outside of the therapist's awareness, such reinforcement may cause it to spill over into his or her personal life as well. In such cases, for example, the therapist may support extremely liberal social or political causes, not because of their individual merits, but as a further expression of his or her "revolt" against societal norms. Those who have a need to act out this rebellion may be attracted to a career in psychotherapy as a further opportunity to express this defiance by encouraging it in others. This, too, may be a dysfunctional motivator for entry into this profession.

While there are undoubtedly other dysfunctional motivations for choosing to be a psychotherapist, those that have been mentioned are most frequently cited by researchers in the field. In each case, they represent a distortion or mutation of a motivator which had the potential to be very professionally and personally functional, but which, in its extreme form, serves to hinder both professional and personal relationships.

Factors Related to Family of Origin

In addition to the personal functional and dysfunctional factors which motivate individuals to pursue a career in psychotherapy, the results of several studies suggest that the family of origin and early family experiences may predispose some toward this vocation. These accounts focus on the early emotional experiences of the future therapist, the characteristics of their parents and their marital relationship, intrafamilial relationships, and the pattern of interactions between the future psychotherapist and other family members.

Early Emotional Experiences

As described earlier, many therapists report that they entered the profession in order to fulfill some of their deeper needs for closeness and intimacy due to a sense of isolation that was prevalent during their childhood (Henry, 1966; McCarley, 1975; Racusin, Abramowitz, & Winter, 1981; Raskin, 1978). For some, this seemed to result from their birth into marginal social, socioeconomic, or religious groups, heightening their sense of "apartness" (Henry, 1966). An example would be someone of Eastern European Jewish heritage growing up in a small midwestern town, who feels somewhat separated from mainstream American society. For others, a sense of isolation resulted from early traumatic events related to family life, such as the death of parents, illness of mother, divorce and remarriage of parents, severe personal illness, and infrequent contact with peers (Farber, 1985a; Hafner & Fakouri, 1984). This led to a recurrent feeling of being "different" from others, a theme frequently reported by psychotherapists recalling their childhood (Henry, 1966). In some cases, the sense of aloneness was the result of feeling rejected by one's family, even at an early age (Menninger, 1957). Similarly, Burton (1970, 1972) states that therapists often recall having felt isolated from other family members due to conflicts and discord. Harris (1976) considers these childhood deprivations to be the "hallmark" of therapists. As a result of unsatisfied early emotional needs related to family life, some are motivated to pursue a career in psychotherapy as a means of providing what is felt to be lacking (Holt & Luborsky, 1958).

Parental Characteristics

Several attempts have been made to create a profile of the parents of those entering the profession of psychotherapist. While they are largely anecdotal and based on self-report, they provide some interesting impressions as to how the resultant parent–child relationships may predispose some individuals to become therapists.

A full range of socioeconomic variables is represented in the parental homes of psychotherapists, according to a survey conducted by Schofield (1964). However, nearly without exception, there is a pattern of upward social mobility among psychotherapists, with the achievement of greater income and higher social class than that of the family of origin (Henry et al., 1971; Racusin et al., 1981). Schofield (1964) speculates that this generalized shift in class identification results in a homogeneity of social values among psychotherapists which are likely to be somewhat different from their parents'.

Mothers are typically described as the central figure in the home. "She is the efficient, organizing one . . . a striving, even competitive person who dominates her husband and home to a high degree" (Ford, 1963, p. 474). Ford goes on to state that, based on his extensive interviews of therapists in training, mothers are often described as either dominantly aggressive, or pseudofeminine and clinging. However, this varying presentation does not change her pivotal controlling role. Henry et al. (1973) reports that the mothers of psychotherapists often exhibit varying degrees of emotional disturbance, ranging from alcoholism to depression and a variety of psychosomatic illnesses. Miller (1981) contends that analysts invariably have mothers who are narcissistic and insecure. The focus of the family is on pleasing her and meeting her emotional needs.

The relationship between the future therapist and the mother described earlier has been suggested as a major factor in determining this career choice. Several have described a special closeness and intimacy which is said to have existed between the mother and child. Sharaf (1960) has suggested that in some cases, particularly with males, the mothers tend to disclose the nature and extent of their marital problems to the child. By making the child the confidant, they force him to process emotional and cognitive issues appropriate to adults. This fosters a psychological-mindedness which makes psychotherapy a likely career choice (Farber, 1985a). According to Ford (1963), the mother is seen by the future therapist as an understanding, caring, giving person who strives to meet the needs of others. This idealization is resistant to change, in spite of possible evidence to the contrary. Ford also reports that many therapists recall having been closest emotionally to their mother, identifying with her as the "underdog" against their father. It is interesting to note, however, that therapists recall having had more conflict with their mother rather than with their father (Henry, 1966). Miller (1981) adds an interesting twist to the mother–child relationship by describing how the narcissistic, insecure mother teaches the child to be keenly attentive to her emotional needs. The child learns to take care of the mother so that she, in turn, will take care of him or her. As Miller describes it, over time this ability is perfected and the child "eventually develops a special sensitivity to unconscious signals manifesting the needs of others" (pp. 8–9). This is later an asset to the practice of psychotherapy and may actually predispose such individuals towards this career.

Fathers of psychotherapists are described by Ford (1963) as generally passive and noninteracting men who contributed little emotional strength to the family or the future therapist. Character types were said to vary from protesting, defensive, and bullying to evident passivity, although they regularly deferred to mother, regardless. In one survey of nearly 400 psychologists, psychiatrists, and social workers, Schofield (1964) found that approximately one-fourth of their fathers had failed to complete the eighth grade, while nearly half had dropped out of high school. While 38% of the psychiatrists' fathers had completed college, this was true for only 15% of psychologists' fathers. Over half of the fathers in each professional sample were in organizational or technological careers. Racusin et al. (1981) reports that all of the fathers in his study of psychotherapists were engaged in nonhuman service, blue collar occupations. None were involved in human service careers, which typically maximize the chance to gratify nurturance needs, according to the authors. This led them to speculate that such individuals were unlikely to provide much emotional nurturance for the family, a somewhat questionable but interesting generalization, to be sure. Little else has been written concerning the fathers of future psychotherapists.

There is also very little written regarding the relationship between the future therapist and his or her father. Fathers seem peripheral in the early development of the psychotherapist, according to therapists' self-report. Ford (1963) states that any contact between the child and father was likely tainted by the alliance against the father which the child shared with the mother. Thus the relationship between them was likely to have been strained and distant. Racusin et al. (1981) also asserts that there was little emotional contact between the father and the future therapist. As a result of this distance between father and the rest of the family, Sharaf (1960) speculates that the passive father provided the male child with a deceptive "oedipal victory" which may have predisposed the career choice of psychotherapy because of the resultant lesson that things are never what they seem, creating an interest in the "intraceptive."

Consistent with the findings of Harris (1976), the previously discussed studies suggest that the parents of future psychotherapists were typically emotionally unresponsive and unable to meet the emotional needs of the child. As a result, this leads to the speculation that the career choice of psychotherapy is the predisposed outcome of this early deprivation, in an effort to provide the closeness and intimacy lacking in the child's relationship with his or her parents.

Parental Marital Characteristics

The parental marriages of psychotherapists are described by Racusin et al. (1981) as being only moderately close, both emotionally and physically. Parents were said to have had only a limited capacity for age-appropriate emotional expression. Poor communication, job-related pressures, and financial strain contributed to the high level of stress found in the marital relationship. However, in the group surveyed, separation or divorce was surprisingly rare.

The future therapist typically played a central role in the marital relationship of his or her parents. As mentioned earlier, Sharaf (1960) found that the mother often confided in the child, particularly in the case of a son, thereby introducing him or her to the affective and psychological dimensions of the marital relationship. Frequently, triangulation occurred whereby the child served as a "buffer" between the parents, helping them to maintain a certain degree of emotional distance by focusing communication on him or her (Racusin et al., 1981). In some cases, the child's role was to provide a substitute for the missing intimacy of the marital relationship by forming a special alliance with each parent. This helped to preserve the status quo. The child was also faced with the task of being the peacemaker, message carrier, and negotiator between the mother and father. In this manner, from a very early age the child was assigned, or assumed, the role of "therapist" for the parental marital relationship. The skills acquired by the child, including intuition, empathy, judgment, and sensitivity, may have served to predispose him or her toward the counseling profession. In addition, the apparent "success" of the future therapist's endeavors to maintain marital harmony, or at least to prevent divorce, may create a self-perception of being a talented "counselor" who is destined similarly to help others. It is interesting to note that in one recent nationwide survey of psychotherapists, nearly half were either a "first born" or "only child," increasing the likelihood of the aforementioned triangulation and caretaking pattern to occur (Guy, Stark, & Poelstra, 1987).

Family Relationships

Several interesting characteristics have been noted regarding the families of psychotherapists. These features include basic demographic information as well as descriptions of the relationships among various family members and the future psychotherapist.

In each of the fourteen psychotherapist families of origin studied by Racusin et al. (1981), there was at least one physically or mentally disabled family member. In every case, the disability had identifiable psychogenic features. These infirmities included heart attacks, high blood pressure, diabetes, asthma, neurosis, character disorders, and various kinds of child abuse. Interestingly, none of the parents and only two of the siblings had ever undergone psychotherapy. Instead, it appears that the future psychotherapist was assigned (or assumed) the role of family therapist.

Both Henry (1966) and Racusin et al. (1981) report that psychotherapists described their primary role in their family of origin as that of "caretaker." They provided parenting, nurturing, and caretaking for those family members who were experiencing varying degrees of physical or emotional disability, whether this involved a parent or sibling. In this manner, they likely learned to be highly sensitive, even intuitive, to the needs of the "identified patient," and they received needed praise and nurturance only after adequately providing these parenting functions. Obviously, this was good training for the eventual role of professional psychotherapist. The role of caretaker included more than the need to provide parenting functions for disabled family members, however. It also involved assuming the role of mediator, negotiator, and family therapist for disputes among various family members (Henry, 1966; Racusin et al., 1981). This required that the child be keenly aware of the family's emotional life, provide advice and consultation to individual family members, and be responsible for resolving arguments and reducing family tensions.

It would seem reasonable to assume that the role of "family therapist" was largely a self-selected one. Perhaps the child began to help others in the hope that they would, in turn, provide love and caring out of gratitude. Furthermore, if future therapists were indeed socially awkward and ineffective during childhood, as Henry et al. (1973) asserts, they might have sought out the role of family caretaker as a means of experiencing some level of closeness and intimacy with family members. Caretaking may have seemed like a small cost to pay for the expected gratitude and attention. However, logical as this scenario seems, research results suggest that the role seems to have been largely an assigned one. In the majority of studies on this topic, therapists reported that they were unofficially assigned the role of "caretaker" by family members due to an early recognition of their ability to satisfy the important emotional needs of family members. As Racusin et. al (1981) explain, "therapists were perhaps defined by their families as affectively or 'therapeutically' oriented, singled out for their effectiveness in dealing with the emotional life, and labeled by other family members as confidants or counselors" (p. 276). Thus in recognition of their empathic skills and caring ability, they were "set apart" to serve the important function of family caretaker.

The impact of this assigned role is difficult to determine. While at first it may appear that this role brings significant gratification and rewards, a closer look suggests that it also brings a sense of alienation and isolation. As Rascusin et al. (1981) suggest, being identified as the caretaker may have resulted in the child being considered as "different" and set apart from the rest. Since the role of caretaker and peacemaker involves moderating emotional conflicts and soothing potential frictions between family members, the future therapist may have been unable to enter into reciprocal, mutually satisfying relationships with other family members (Liaboe & Guy, in press; McCarley, 1975). This is due to the fact that the role of caretaker entails a certain proviso requiring that the child be the "strong one," who sets aside his or her own needs for caring in order to better serve others. There is no opportunity for the child to be "weak" and to seek out, actively and appropriately, caretaking from other family members. This pattern hinders genuine intimacy, further isolating the child from the caring and nurturance that he or she badly needs. Rather than leading to a greater degree of intimacy with other family members, the role of caretaker furthers the alienation of the child.

Future therapists seemed to turn to others for the emotional support and nurturance that they did not receive from their parents. For example, Racusin et al. (1981) reports that they were sometimes closer emotionally with a sibling than with either parent. Interestingly, however, this involved only 25% of those surveyed. The rest found it necessary to seek individuals outside the famliy of origin. This typically involved more distant relatives, such as aunts, uncles, cousins, or grandparents. More often than not, the individuals identified as having provided the sought after nurturance and caring were females rather than males. This suggests that the future therapist was especially seeking a "mothering one" to meet the needs for intimacy and closeness.

Some researchers, like Friedman (1971), suggest that this process of the internalization of the caretaking role was a very important first step towards entry into the profession of psychotherapy. By learning to be sensitive to the needs of others while abstaining from overt attempts to express and meet one's own emotional needs, the child learned to adopt a certain style of relating which may have made the career choice of psychotherapist logical, comfortable, and familiar. Friedman goes further to suggest that the family of origin may even have suggested or encouraged this career choice, perhaps in hopes of guaranteeing that the role of "family counselor" would become a permanent one following the child's departure from home. In this way, the future therapist could be depended on to meet the family's various emotional needs forever.

DISCUSSION

Ultimately it is difficult to determine what motivates individuals to decide to become psychotherapists. For that matter, it is hard to determine what causes people to select any particular job or vocation. As Bolles (1977) points out, career choices are often the result of serendipitous events which seem quite random and happenstance. At best, a career choice is the result of an interaction among personal characteristics, suitable or attractive features of a specific vocational role, and a series of chance events. Each of these three primary variables play a role of varying importance leading to the eventual outcome of a chosen career. This is no less the case for those deciding to become psychotherapists.

For the purposes of discussion, it seems useful to consider four possible combinations of variables related to the career choice of psychotherapeutic practice. These combinations will demonstrate the interaction among the various personal and occupational factors leading to the decision of whether to enter this field.

Not Suited and Not Interested

There is no doubt that there are many individuals who are neither suited nor interested in pursuing a career in psychotherapy. This is often the result of several personal and environmental factors. For some, the nature of the role of psychotherapist is unattractive and unappealing. The negative aspects associated with clinical practice such as isolation, emotional fatigue, troublesome ethical and legal responsibiities, unstable income, limited successes, and so on, may seem serious enough to discourage these individuals from entering the field.

It may also be that a variety of environmental circumstances combined to make such a career option undesirable. For example, perhaps the individual has not encountered a psychotherapist professionally or personally, and lacks an appreciation for the role. He or she may have little information about a career in psychotherapy, and thus, not consider it as a viable option. On the other hand, it could be that previous contacts with psychotherapists were unsatisfactory for a wide variety of reasons. Perhaps, rather than being the result of direct contact, overheard stories concerning psychotherapists may have given a negative impression. For that matter, some aspects of the media's portrayal of psychotherapists might cause some to regard the practice of psychotherapy as a marginal profession. As a result, they might choose not to explore this career option because of their impressions regarding the undesirable nature of psychotherapeutic practice.

It seems reasonable to assume that many choose not to pursue this career because of certain features of their own personality. Some find the tremendous expense and years of required study and training to be sufficiently aversive to eliminate this vocational option. In addition, they may lack the functional personality qualities which often motivate people to become psychotherapists such as empathy, patience, and advanced social skills. Finally, their own interests may be different from those who find the benefits associated with psychotherapeutic practice to be attractive. As a result, such individuals have the intuitive sense to know that they are not suited to a career in psychotherapy.

Individuals in this group have a variety of reactions to psychotherapy and therapists in general. Some seem fascinated with the profession, reading books and seeing "psychological" movies at every opportunity. They may even enter treatment as patients themselves. Yet, though they express their interest, they continue to feel that the role of psychotherapist is alien to their own personality. They cannot imagine undertaking such a career, and may even express wonderment that anyone finds it to be a compatible role. This leads to an excessive idealization of therapists and psychotherapy that is often unrealistic and distorted.

Others in this group appear to have the opposite reaction. Because the role seems so alien or undesirable, for whatever reason, they may devalue psychotherapists and therapy beyond what is warranted. Thus they may consider psychotherapy to be dangerous or "weird." They may accuse therapists of promoting unhealthy dependence, focusing too much on sex, prospering by exploiting the pain of others, and selling friendship. Individuals with such views are unlikely to enter or remain in therapy, and may not enjoy "psychological" books or movies.

Regardless of the nature of the personal reactions of these individuals, whether overly idealizing or devaluing, they find the role of psychotherapist to be quite foreign and undesirable. Such people are not suited to the practice of psychotherapy and not interested in entering the profession.

Suited but Not Interested

Some individuals may possess the characteristics necessary to become effective psychotherapists but lack the interest, motivation, or desire to enter the field. Certainly, the fact that they may be empathic, caring, insightful, introspective, tolerant of ambiguity, warm, and comfortable with conversation and intimacy does not guarantee that they will be interested in becoming psychotherapists. Indeed, such characteristics are important for success in many other careers, particularly those in the "helping professions." Teachers, physicians, counselors, clerics, welfare workers, and other human service providers may evidence the very qualities required for a successful career in psychotherapy. Often, such individuals enter a related vocation with obvious "therapeutic" aspects. Although they may not see themselves as providing psychotherapy, they may be promoting more effective living and relieving psychic distress, nonetheless. These are the "inherently helpful people" of which Rogers (1961) frequently speaks, those who are naturally therapeutic in many of their interpersonal relationships.

Why do such suitable candidates choose not to enter the field? Once again, it may be that certain environmental factors prevent them from such an undertaking. The high cost of graduate education, as well its highly competitive nature, may discourage some from seeking admission. As mentioned earlier, it may be that some have a negative impression of psychotherapists and psychotherapy due to personal experiences or overheard conversations. It may also be that a variety of personal or environmental factors led these individuals toward other careers for reasons totally unrelated to the practice of psychotherapy.

Individuals in this group typically neither overly idealize nor excessively devalue the role of the psychotherapist. They may intuitively know that they would be suitable for such a career. As a result, there is a realistic appreciation for both the benefits and limitations of psychotherapy. Such individuals may occasionally enter treatment and are likely to be successful in this endeavor. Although they are interested in the psychological aspects of human behavior and experience, they are not neurotically driven to read self-help books, nor are they "addicted" to psychologically oriented novels or movies. There is more of an intuitive understanding and less of a fascination.

Perhaps examining the characteristics of those "suited but not interested" serves as a reminder that psychotherapists are not, in the final analysis, particularly special or unique individuals. There are many who could function effectively in such a role, but who choose not to enter this field.

Not Suited but Interested

A recent study by Walfish, Polifka, and Stenmark (1985) found that nearly half of those psychologists in practice for more than 10 years would not choose to become psychotherapists again. It is evident that many who enter the field eventually discover that they are not suited for psychotherapeutic practice. For some, the many related benefits and satisfactions motivated such a vocational choice. Yet these individuals may have lacked the personal characteristics necessary for an effective and successful career as a psychotherapist. In such cases, disillusionment and dissatisfaction begin to set in, eventually motivating a career change or hopeless resignation to a disappointing career in psychotherapy.

There are other motivations for entry into this profession, beyond the benefits associated with the role of psychotherapist. As discussed earlier, a variety of dysfunctional motivators prompt many to pursue this vocational choice as well. The desire to find relief from personal emotional distress, isolation and loneliness, and the desire for power, love, and vicarious living seem to drive some people into this field. Rather than serving to enhance their skill as therapists, such characteristics actually sabotage professional and personal relationships. As a result, such individuals may be destructive as psychotherapists. They may leave the profession due to repeated treatment failures, or because of the negative impact of psychotherapeutic practice on their personal life. This issue will addressed more fully in Chapters 3, 4, 6, and 7.

Some who are not suited but have entered a career in psychotherapy may eventually leave this profession when the original dysfunctional motivations are no longer present. For example, if the needs for intimacy, emotional wholeness, power, and so on, are met through training, supervision, personal therapy, or a meaningful personal relationship, such individuals may no longer "need" to be psychotherapists. Thus they may lose interest and find the negative aspects of this career to be too aversive to warrant their continued participation. This may also be the case for those who enter the field because of being predisposed by early family roles and experiences. If growth and maturity make it no longer necessary to function as the caretaker for those in distress in order to feel valued and needed, then such individuals may find that they do not sufficiently enjoy a career in psychotherapy after all.

Unfortunately, there are psychotherapists who are not suited for the profession, but who remain in clinical pratice. In some cases, they lack the personal characteristics necessary to be "inherently helpful people" or lack the necessary training and experience to provide adequate care. In other cases, they are motivated by dysfunctional factors which cause them to remain in practice due to deep, ongoing personal needs. Finally, some remain due to the financial, social, or intellectual benefits of such a career, in spite of the fact that they remain largely ineffective as therapists. This is obviously an unfortunate occurrence for both patient and therapist. For the patient, it may mean entering treatment with someone who is unhelpful, or even exploitive and destructive. This has given rise to the commonly held belief that the choice of therapist is a perilous undertaking, given the likelihood of encountering one with greater emotional needs than one's own. For the therapist, such a situation leaves him or her vulnerable to eventual signs of significant "distress," such as incompetence, impaired judgment, substance abuse, greater psychopathology, sexual involvement with patients, and even suicide. These concerns will be addressed in a later chapter.

Although not always the case, those who are ill-suited but who choose to become psychotherapists place themselves and their patients at risk of disappointment, failure, and even tragedy. While it may be regrettable when those who are suited to become psychotherapists choose not to, it is frightening when those not suited enter and remain in the field.

Suited and Interested

Fortunately, there are those who are both well-suited for the practice of psychotherapy due to personality characteristics and functional motivators, and sufficiently interested in entering the field, as a result of the benefits of psychotherapeutic practice and a variety of environmental influences. Such individuals typically enjoy long, successful careers as psychotherapists.

As a result of possessing the personality characteristics appropriate for the role of psychotherapist, this group of individuals find such a career to be highly compatible and complimentary with their own inner processing and dynamics. They intuitively experience a "goodness of fit" which allows them to function comfortably and spontaneously in the role of therapist. As discussed in Chapter 2, this process began during graduate training which, while intellectually demanding, was not particularly emotionally trying or traumatic for such individuals. They demonstrated a natural ability often evident to faculty, supervisors, and peers alike. While it is necessary for such individuals to learn "how to think," they rarely need to be taught "how to be." Their intuitive ability to be therapeutic and helpful often causes them to appear more competent than seasoned veterans less suited for this profession.

Because of their natural disposition to be therapeutic, these individuals continue to experience personal growth and fulfillment throughout a long career in psychotherapy. They maintain a certain freshness, vibrancy, and optimism which is apparent to both patients and colleagues. While they are not invulnerable to the hazards associated with the practice of psychotherapy (as will be examined more fully in Chapters 3, 4, and 5), they are much less likely to be negatively impacted by them than those less suited for this profession. There is a sincerity to their claim that they truly enjoy their work, and the evidence suggests that their personal life is enriched by the hours they spend in psychotherapeutic practice. Such psychotherapists are likely to provide high caliber clinical care and supervision to those fortunate enough to enlist their services.

It is interesting to speculate whether these particular individuals feel the sense of calling Burton (1975) speaks of, or whether they simply made a spontaneous decision to become psychotherapists as a result of the interaction between random circumstances and personal characteristics. Although not driven to such a career by personal needs, perhaps such individuals experience some sense of destiny which leads rather than compels them to become psychotherapists. In such a case, it is the "goodness of fit" which motivates and sustains, rather than personal need or former experiences in the family of origin. This leads to an ongoing sense of satisfaction and enjoyment which can only come when one participates in a career for which one is well suited. With this there is also the knowledge that such a career can be left when it ceases to be rewarding.

While it must be admitted that practicing psychotherapists do not fall neatly into these two groups, those well-suited and those ill-suited for the practice of psychotherapy, it will be helpful to keep this dichotomy in mind. As discussed in Chapters 2 through 7, the manner in which individuals experience the impact of training and eventual clinical work on their professional and personal relationships will be, in part, determined by their inherent suitability for this profession. The nature of their personality characteristics, motives and needs, prior experiences, and expectations will largely determine the impact of psychotherapeutic practice on their life and interpersonal functioning.

CHAPTER 2

Training to Become a Psychotherapist

Healers, witch doctors, high priests, wizards, and shamans both choose and are chosen to fulfill their role. There is typically an internal motivation which prompts the individual to answer the "call," fulfill his or her destiny, and obey the wishes of the gods. However, there is often an external selection process at work, as well. The individual must demonstrate that he or she is suited for the role and duties of the position. This is also true for those desiring to become psychotherapists, today's equivalent to the shaman (Bugental, 1964).

In Chapter 1, the process leading to the career choice of psychotherapist was examined, with consideration given to the role of various internal motivations and external circumstances in the decision-making process. However, the personal choice to pursue a career in psychotherapy is only the first step in the long process of evaluation, training, experience, and credentialing necessary for entry into the field. It is obvious that personal choice is not a valid discriminator between those well-suited and those ill-suited for the practice of psychotherapy. Therefore, attempts are made to determine who among those interested will be best equipped to become a psychotherapist.

As Henry (1966) points out, deciding to assume the role of shaman, and receiving society's endorsement for this choice, does not in itself equip the individual for all of the many tasks and duties associated with the role. It is typically necessary for the novitiate to enter a period of training and apprenticeship. During this time, apprentices learn the secrets and mysteries of their trade from the masters. They study both the wisdom of their ancestors and the techniques of current practice. The training consists of both detailed instruction and supervised experience. However, throughout the process, the emphasis on internal awareness is greater than that placed on skill acquisition.

In much the same fashion, those permitted to enter the field of psychotherapy must first complete a rather lengthy training process. Current theories and techniques are taught within the larger context of the teachings and wisdom of the "ancestors" such as Freud, Jung, Horney, and so on. The focus is typically on internal processing and awareness, in addition to the acquisition of skills and knowledge. Following graduation there is a period of supervised work, with a final evaluation prior to licensure or certification which permits the individuals to practice psychotherapy independent of further supervision or instruction.

It must be acknowledged at the outset that the vocational role of psychotherapist is different from that of many other careers. As Raskin (1978) eloquently expressed in his autobiographical article "Becoming," the process leading to a career as a psychotherapist involves one's whole being and impacts one's very personhood. Henry (1966) states that "the career of a mental health professional, at least those in direct therapeutic work, is a commitment to a lifestyle, as well as an investment in a line of work" (p. 54). The emphasis on self-awareness and exploration of inner processes forces the therapist-in-training to confront his or her own vulnerabilities, foibles, and personal pain. As Henry suggests, the training process involves more than a certain degree of socialization and conceptual learning. It also sensitizes the trainee to unresolved inner conflicts, traumas, and hang-ups. While these may never be fully resolved, they must be successfully incorporated or comfortably integrated into the personality fabric of the psychotherapist in order to facilitate rather than sabotage interpersonal relationships and the therapeutic process. In this manner, who a person "is" becomes more important than what he or she "knows." Farber (1985a) states it well when he says that one of the most important changes for the person becoming a psychotherapist is to move from "knowing of" to "knowing about" psychological matters, reflecting an inner awareness and integration that alters one's very perspective on life. This process continues throughout the lifetime of the practicing psychotherapist as a result of ongoing therapeutic encounters . It is not surprising that personality changes often result during a career in psychotherapy, some growth producing and some destructive (Guy & Liaboe, 1986a). Not only are these changes observable in terms of outward behavior, but they may also include altered values and constantly evolving world views (Henry, 1966).

Because assuming the role of psychotherapist involves the total personality of the individual, his or her orientation or world view becomes intricately intertwined with the nature of the work (Kottler, 1986). For example, it has been pointed out that the usage of the phrase "the art and science of psychotherapy" highlights the dual role of the psychotherapist as that of both artist and scientist (Jasnow, 1978). This inherent multiplicity of perspectives creates a tension between "aesthetic" and "scientific" attitudes that influence the therapist throughout his or her career. Those whose personality predisposes them toward the scientific frame of reference are forced to struggle with the artistic, creative aspects of psychotherapeutic practice. On the other hand, those aesthetically inclined often find it difficult to integrate the objective, scientific aspects of the practice of psychotherapy with their natural artisitic predisposition. While this may seem to suggest a somewhat artificial dichotomy regarding an understanding of human behavior and personality, it does nonetheless highlight the conflict that arises for the psychotherapist who must be both scientist and artist while practicing psychotherapy (Barron, 1978). The resolution of this role conflict obviously impacts the world view and personal perspective of the therapist, going beyond simple "knowing" to impact "being." As discussed later in this chapter, the learning involved in the process of this undertaking may alter the very lifestyle and personality of therapist, impacting interpersonal relationships in and outside of work.

The interaction between the psychotherapist's training and lifestyle occurs in other ways as well. Farber (1985a) discussed the role of psychological-mindedness in the development of the psychotherapist. As presented in Chapter 1, psychological-mindedness is defined as "a trait which has at its core the disposition to reflect on the meaning and motivation of behavior, thoughts, and feelings in oneself and others" (p. 170). While it appears that those who are attracted to psychotherapy as a profession are often already psychologically minded as a result of an interaction between genetic endowment and environmental influences, it is intensified and reinforced by the very nature of the training, supervision, and work experience of the developing psychotherapist. As a result, therapists become increasingly psychologically minded during the training required for a career in psychotherapy. This not only affects their work, but also impacts their private life and relationships, as will be discussed in more detail at a later point. For now, it is worth noting that becoming more psychologically minded involves the entire personality and perspective of the individual.

The process of entry into the field of psychotherapy is rather complex and circuitous (Goldberg, 1986). As mentioned, the personal decision to pursue this career is only the first step. This must be followed by admission to graduate training in psychotherapy, successful completion of the academic and fieldwork components of the degree requirements, accrual of supervised experience necessary for credentialing, and successful performance on all exams leading to licensure or certification. Only then will the individual be allowed to function independently as a psychotherapist. At each point in the process there is an interaction between the personal life of the therapist and the training and experience inherent in a career in psychotherapy. This shaping process will be examined in the following section, with special attention given to the interaction between the training process and the life and relationships of the psychotherapist-in-training.

ADMISSION TO GRADUATE TRAINING

Choice of Discipline and Degree

To the uninitiated, it would seem reasonable to assume that the decision to become a psychotherapist is followed by entry into a training program specializing in the practice of psychotherapy. Thus one might expect such an individual to pursue a graduate degree in "psychotherapy." It is indeed confusing to the uninitiated to discover that this is not the case. In fact, while many different degree and specialization programs equip an individual to practice psychotherapy, there is no single program that awards a degree in psychotherapy.

Many roads lead to a career in psychotherapy. The formal training required varies from two to more than eight years, plus the several thousand hours of postgraduate supervised experience necessary to qualify for licensure or registration. While the disciplines of medicine, psychology, social work, and counseling may enable an individual to practice psychotherapy, there is no discipline of "psychotherapy," per se.

Having decided to enter training for a career in psychotherapy, the potential therapist must decide which discipline and degree to pursue. Attempts have been made to identify those personality traits or environmental factors which seem to influence or predispose the choice of one discipline over another. While researchers such as Henry (1966; Henry et al., 1971) and Schofield (1964) have noted that a few demographic variables are loosely related to choice of specialty such as the education level and career of the parents, no definitive pattern could be found. Unfortunately, little is known as to whether or how such variables may have influenced the choice of one discipline over another. More important is the discovery that similarities related to background and life experiences among the various mental health disciplines are far more numerous and striking than the differences. Henry et al. (1971) state that the differences among the various specialties "are insignificant in such issues as relations to parents and siblings, reported sexual histories, and aspects of cognitive development . . . they appear to have had highly similar formative experiences in significant areas of personality development" (p. 182).

It may be more helpful to speculate that personal interests and ability largely determine which field of study will be pursued. For example, for those interested in medicine and the physical sciences, a medical degree leading to the specialization of psychiatry may be the logical choice. In a similar way, those interested in psychological testing, diagnostic assessment, and research may wish to pursue a degree in psychology.

In addition, academic ability, financial resources, and personal motivation also enter into the decision-making process. Yet Henry et al. (1971) note that despite repeated claims that these differing aspects of training are necessary, psychotherapists of various disciplines appear to function in nearly identical roles following graduation. For example, psychologists practicing psychotherapy typically do very little research or testing, and psychiatrists often practice relatively little medicine. On the contrary, experienced psychotherapists eventually "tend to identify as crucial only those parts of their training that are, in principle, common to all groups—that is, the direct, personalized, and clinically relevant experiences that most closely parallel the final end point, the practice of psychotherapy" (pp. 180–181). Henry et al., conclude that although the discipline-specific training programs leading to the practice of psychotherapy are highly organized and complex, they are different in ways which seem largely unrelated to the practice of psychotherapy. Furthermore, the end products, the graduates, are strikingly similar and go on to function in nearly identical roles. A recent study of nearly 6000 psychiatrists, social workers, psychologists, and primary care physicians found striking similarities among the various disciplines in regard to the type of psychiatric patients served, treatments utilized, overall rate of success, and professional roles and responsibilities assumed (Knesper, Pagnucco, & Wheeler, 1985).

While these various programs obviously produce some individuals who decide not to practice psychotherapy and instead function in roles different from those of the other mental health disciplines, those who do function as therapists are much more similar than dissimilar. This is particularly true over the course of a career in psychotherapy during which clinical experience seems to equalize varying ability and skills across disciplines.

The same issues arise regarding the choice of degree and related credentials necessary for the practice of psychotherapy. Obviously, informal counseling or "therapy" may be provided by anyone, at any time, regardless of education or credentials. Whether this occurs among neighbors or family members, or in a more structured self-help or lay counseling program, such assistance is largely outside of the realm of government regulation. However, state governments reserve the right to protect the public welfare and therefore have established the minimum requirements necessary for the state-credentialed practice of psychotherapy (Herbsleb, Sales, & Overcast, 1985). With few exceptions a doctoral degree is necessary for the independent practice of psychotherapy (Perlman, 1985). However, some states allow individuals with lesser degrees to practice independently, such as masters level clinical social workers and various types of counselors. In other locales, those with lesser degrees may be permitted to practice psychotherapy, but only under the direct supervision of a doctoral level psychotherapist.

The individual deciding to enter the field must not only decide which discipline or specialty to pursue, but which degree to obtain. While this may be largely determined by the credentialing regulations of a given state, in some cases the future therapist is faced with many options. For example, in the state of California it is possible to practice psychotherapy—independently for a fee without supervision—with a masters degree in social work, school psychology, or marriage and family counseling, as well as a doctoral degree in psychology or medicine. Thus the individual wishing to become a psychotherapist must decide which discipline, as well as which corresponding degree, to obtain in order to practice psychotherapy.

As mentioned earlier, little is known as to why individuals choose one discipline over another. The same is true for the decision of which degree to obtain. While this is obviously largely governed by credentialing requirements of the given locale, where several options do exist other factors may influence this decision. Unfortunately the lack of available data reduces this discussion to mere speculation. For example, it may be that, regardless of state regulations, the political reality of the work environment makes one degree advantageous over another. Varying policies among third-party payers may also favor one degree or discipline over another. The superior power or prestige associated with one particular degree or specialization in comparison with another may cause some to enter this pathway of training, depending on their own needs and the influence of others. Unique personal needs and beliefs, or the drive for recognition and achievement (or lack of same) may also determine which degree will be obtained. On the other hand, the final decision may be largely the result of financial realities, academic ability, or other practical issues unrelated to personality dynamics.

In summary, little is known as to what factors influence individuals to pursue a particular degree in one discipline or specialization rather than another. While there is obviously an interaction among several variables such as personal interests, abilities, financial resources, motivation, local regulations, and personality dynamics, no definitive pattern has emerged related to the choice of discipline or degree. Many roads lead to the practice of psychotherapy. The actual reasons behind the choice of direction and speed of travel remain a mystery. What is known is that experienced psychotherapists are functionally more alike than not across disciplines and specialities.

Admission to Training

The decision to pursue a particular degree in a specific discipline or specialization is far from the final step to becoming a psychotherapist. In fact, such choices simply prompt the individual to apply for admission into a particular training program. They do not guarantee that the applicant will be accepted, nor do they predict the successful completion of the course of study. In a very real way, admission into an advanced training program in psychotherapy is the first "gate" or "rite of passage" in the journey to becoming a psychotherapist. Thus admissions committees serve as the "gatekeepers" for the profession (Nevid & Gildea, 1984). This is true regardless of the particular discipline or specialty. Those wishing to become psychotherapists will only be able to do so if they are regarded as suitable for training and entry into the profession by members of the admissions committee of the desired training program.

As discussed in Chapter 1, there are those individuals who are both well-suited for the practice of psychotherapy and sufficiently interested in entering the field. Such individuals typically enjoy long, successful careers as psychotherapists. There are also those who are ill-suited for the practice of psychotherapy and yet wish to pursue such a career. In such cases, while some of these individuals may lose interest and change careers without ill effect, others remain psychotherapists, to the detriment of both their patients and themselves. The critical problem is how to tell the difference between the two prior to entry into the field.

In the best of all worlds, only those well-suited for the practice of psychotherapy would be admitted into the appropriate training programs, since this is the first gate or point of entry. Those who were inappropriate for this career would be denied admission and encouraged to pursue another line of work. Admissions committees would serve as gatekeepers by discriminating between these two groups with accuracy and confidence.

A look at the actual situation is rather disheartening. While admissions committees are, for the most part, aware of their responsibility to screen out those interested applicants who are inappropriate for a career in psychotherapy, little is known as to how best to accomplish this task. The first problem is to decide what is to be assessed or evaluated to determine suitability for this profession. Because of the rigorous academic demands of most training programs, whether they be organized graduate programs or training institutes for degreed professionals, suitability is often assessed in terms of academic ability. As a result, objective measures such as undergraduate grade point average and scores on the Graduate Record Exam become major criteria for determining suitability for advanced training (Ingram & Zurawski, 1981). However, it is apparent that academic ability may be unrelated to suitability for a career in psychotherapy. While such criteria may predict academic performance during graduate training, they do not predict competence as a future psychotherapist (Nevid & Gildea, 1984).

In order to better determine suitability for a career in psychotherapy, most programs try to assess another variable, namely that of clinical potential. In this case, an attempt is made to determine whether the individual possesses, or is able to acquire, the skills and characteristics necessary for competent clinical practice. While in theory this sounds good, the reality is disappointing. A review of those traits discussed in Chapter 1 that seem to characterize those well-suited for the practice of psychotherapy (i.e., natural curiosity, ability to listen, comfort with conversation, empathy and understanding, emotional insight, introspection, etc.) reveals motivators and characteristics which are very difficult to inventory and assess. Not only is it difficult to determine their presence or absence, but it is also quite hard to evaluate whether the individual is capable of learning or acquiring those qualities that he or she lacks. At this point, no reliable predictors or means of assessment have been found (Nevid & Gildea, 1984). Nonetheless, several criteria are typically used in an attempt to predict future performance as a psychotherapist. These include the applicant's statement of purpose and autobiography, letters of reference, and behavior and attitudes during personal interviews (Ingram & Zurawski, 1981).

While it is difficult to assess the validity and reliability of the applicant's autobiographical statement of purpose, it does provide data on the individual's self-assessment of his or her strengths, skills, experiences, abilities, weaknesses, and motivations. Careful review of the applicant's comments and observations might provide clues regarding the presence or absence of desirable characteristics and clarify areas where further investigation may be warranted. Unfortunately, there are no known studies which investigate whether the contents of applicants' personal statements are predictive of future performance as a psychotherapist. Therefore, their actual value in assessing clinical promise is undetermined.

Ingram and Zurawski (1981) found that letters of reference constituted the major influence on the admissions committee's ratings of applicants for the clinical psychology program at the University of Kansas. While it is hoped that such letters contain valid and reliable assessments of clinical potential and professional promise, it appears that they often simply summarize a student's academic performance as an undergraduate (Cuca, Sakakeeny, & Johnson, 1976). Another recent study (Baxter, Brock, Hill, & Rozelle, 1981) revealed that letters of recommendation failed to reveal discriminative, consensual, or differentiating patterns of perception, rendering them of little use in assessing clinical potential. Thus although reference letters may occasionally help to discriminate between those well-suited and those inappropriate for the practice of psychotherapy, they are not likely to do so with a high degree of regularity.

Some, like Nevid and Gildea (1981), have speculated that personal admissions interviews are most useful for determining the presence or absence of those qualities found in individuals appropriate for the role of psychotherapist. Their outcome relies on the clinical ability of the interviewers to assess the strengths and weaknesses of interviewees correctly on the basis of a typically brief encounter. While it may be true in some cases that an accurate assessment results, Strickter (1981) suggests that judgments based on admissions interviews are often influenced by intentional distortion by applicants or observer error. In such cases, the resultant decisions may not reliably or validly assess clinical promise or potential. Yet, these limitations notwithstanding, intuition suggests that personal interviews may be more helpful in assessing suitability for the profession than the typical academic performance criteria frequently utilized in admissions decisions.

Obviously, more accurate means must be found for assessing suitability for entry into advanced training in the practice of psychotherapy. In order for admissions committees to screen interested applicants successfully, and thus limit admission to those appropriate for the role of psychotherapist, more research is needed to determine which criteria will best assess and predict a "good fit."

Those Denied Admission

In spite of whatever flaws may exist in present admissions procedures, training programs theoretically do their best to admit only those suited for the practice of psychotherapy. Since there is no way for a training program to keep someone from practicing psychotherapy once they have graduated and met the state's requirements for credentialing, it is assumed that all students admitted to the program are thought to show enough professional promise to deserve an opportunity to pursue training in psychotherapy. In other words, although a social worker may eventually decide to go into public administration rather than the practice of psychotherapy, a psychologist into psychoneurological assessment, and a psychiatrist into brain research, there is no way to determine this at admission. Therefore, it is assumed that all applicants granted admission to a program which leads to credentialing as a psychotherapist (and which includes instruction in psychotherapeutic techniques) appear to be suited for the practice of psychotherapy.

Obviously, most students applying for admission into such programs are rejected. Although this may be largely because of a limited number of available training slots, in response to the economy (i.e., shifts in government funding of graduate programs, financial constraints of a given university causing faculty reductions, etc.) and "supply and demand" factors beyond the scope of this discussion, it is assumed that only those most suited are admitted while those less suited are not. Undoubtedly, this is not always the case. Flawed admissions procedures, along with a variety of other unrelated factors, may sometimes result in the rejection of a well-suited applicant or the acceptance of an individual inappropriate for a career in psychotherapy.

As mentioned, among those rejected for admission are likely to be some who are appropriately suited for the role of psychotherapist. For such individuals, being denied admission may be experienced as a profound disappointment. Not only does it sabotage the applicant's immediate plans for pursuing his or her career goals, but it calls into question the underlying personal sense of calling and suitability that may have actually motivated the application. Such individuals are left to decide for themselves, as well as explain to friends and family, whether the rejection is a valid and reliable assessment of the applicant's suitability for the role of psychotherapist.

If it is decided that the rejection is justified and reflects the applicant's unsuitability, he or she may take one of several courses of action. For example, the applicant may decide to obtain personal psychotherapy in hopes of resolving whatever personal psychopathology may have caused him or her to appear unsuited for this profession. It may be useful to obtain work experience in the mental health field, whereby job-related experience may help equip the person with the necessary skills and attributes. It may also be appropriate to take steps to improve performance on whatever criteria were found to have been deficient such as entrance test scores and undergraduate level grade point average, in order to demonstrate adequate academic ability. These and other steps may be taken in hopes of becoming better suited for advanced training and gaining eventual admission. On the other hand, such individuals may decide instead to pursue other career goals for which they are better suited, which allow them to enjoy some of the benefits of a career in psychotherapy (such as frequent and meaningful interactions with people) without the liabilites for which they are ill-suited. There are many such careers in the "helping professions" which may satisfy these desires. They may also find other ways to work in a "therapeutic" manner, such as by participating in volunteer work in the community.

If, on the other hand, they decide that they are well-suited for a career in psychotherapy in spite of this rejection, such individuals may decide to apply immediately for admission into another program, specialty, discipline, or degree tract for which they may appear better qualified. For example, following rejection by a doctoral program in clinical psychology, the future therapist may obtain admission into a doctoral program in counseling psychology or a masters program in marriage and family counseling. In such cases, they will hopefully find a way to obtain admission to a relevant training program before their motivation, time, or money runs out. In fact, the wise applicant will apply to several programs concurrently, to ensure admission to at least one. Further work experience, better performance on the typical academic measures, more carefully selected references, and better performance in personal interviews may eventually result in admission to advanced training, following one or more initial rejections. It can only be hoped that those suited for a career in psychotherapy will pursue admission to training until it is granted. It is difficult to accept the likelihood that the profession is denied the contributions of numerous talented and well-suited individuals because they fail to obtain admission to the required training programs.

Among those denied admission to advanced training in psychotherapy are those rightfully determined to be unsuited for such a career. In terms of academic ability, it is true that a certain degree of intellectual sophistication is necessary for the successful completion of graduate studies in any one of the various disciplines leading to the profession of psychotherapy. Thus it may well be necessary and appropriate that those unable to demonstrate sufficient academic prowess be denied admission. It is also important that those who evidence that they are unsuited for the practice of psychotherapy and possess little clinical potential be denied the training necessary for becoming a therapist. Thus although this has yet to be conclusively demonstrated, it is assumed that many of those applicants who are rejected are indeed unsuitable for this profession.

Such individuals have the same options as those well-suited who are also denied admission. They are confronted with an obstacle which forces them to reevaluate their desire to become a psychotherapist and the appropriateness of this goal. Those who feel that this rejection is justified may either take steps to make themselves more suitable for this profession, or redirect their plans toward another career. Those who feel that the rejection was a mistake, or due to factors other than their unsuitability, will likely seek to pursue their goals in the same manner as those previously mentioned. If the admission procedures are valid and reliable, they will continue to be denied admission as long as they remain unsuitable, regardless of what steps are taken. However, as will be discussed in Chapter 6, the high rate of impaired practitioners present in the profession suggests that many who are ill-suited for the role of psychotherapist eventually gain admission to training programs. This sobering reality necessitates the existence of several additional hurdles that further attempt to weed out those inappropriate candidates before their final entry into the field.

Those Granted Admission

While most who apply for admission into graduate school or advanced training in the various mental health disciplines leading to the practice of psychotherapy are denied admission, a relative few are accepted for training. For such individuals, the letter of acceptance is a cherished key that unlocks the first door leading to a career as a psychotherapist. This opportunity to begin training serves as the profession's initial affirmation and endorsement of the applicant's personal sense of his or her "goodness of fit." For those already truly suited for the role of psychotherapist, a long and satisfying career is about to begin during which time the individual will more fully develop those traits and skills necessary for successful functioning as a therapist. For those not suited, this marks the beginning of a difficult, intense struggle to achieve compatibility with a role that is both professionally and personally demanding. Some will succeed . . . others will not.

THE TRAINING YEARS

In the classic text *The Seasons of a Man's Life*, Levinson (1978) proposes that the early adult phase of development known as the "novice phase" is characterized by: (1) forming a dream and giving it a place in the life structure, (2) forming mentor relationships, (3) forming an occupation, (4) forming love relationships, marriage, and family (p. 90). It is typically this phase of adult development which coincides with entry into graduate training in the mental health professions. Whether this immediately follows graduation from an undergraduate program or involves a later career change, the transition that occurs during the training years leading to a career in psychotherapy usually involves Levinson's first three stages of the novice phase. This is a time of exhilarating change as well as difficult adjustment. Whereas in the past educational training focused on knowledge acquisition, there is now an emphasis on the development of skills within the larger context of personal awareness and change. In fact, it is no longer what a person knows which is of major concern, but what a person is, and is becoming. The personality of the therapist is the primary instrument of change, regardless of theoretical orientation (Garfield & Bergin, 1978). The unique and intensely personal nature of the training necessary for becoming a psychotherapist has a wide array of associated stressors and hazards which must be successfully overcome before the candidate is ready to enter the field.

Stressors of Graduate Training

The initial phase of training for becoming a psychotherapist occurs within the graduate program of a university or a freestanding, accredited graduate level training program. Goplerud (1980) studied a group of first year graduate students in clinical, social, cognitive, developmental and bio-psychology to evaluate the impact of training on their personal life. He found that graduate students experience severe life stress due to changes in work, finances, living conditions, school, and social relationships associated with the start of graduate training. He found that such stressors tended to promote intense anxiety, depression, sleep disturbance, and a host of physical illnesses during the first six months of school. Goplerud reported that "most of the life changes associated with beginning graduate work cannot be easily prevented" (p. 283). They appear to be the unavoidable result of the environmental changes associated with physical relocation and start of rigorous training.

It would appear that students entering graduate school to become psychotherapists are subject to many of these same stressors, along with many additional ones. These arise largely out of the unique nature and focus of academic programs associated with a degree in psychology, social work, counseling, or the specialty of psychiatry. As will be seen later in this chapter, each is the result of an interaction between particular aspects of the required training and the personality of the individual.

Unspecified Nature of Psychotherapeutic Work

One of the initial stressors which confront the psychotherapist-in-training is the rather undefined, complex, and ephemeral quality of psychotherapeutic endeavors. As Marmor (1953) notes:

> the lack of fixed standards, the necessity of adapting to constantly changing and shifting problems, the complexity of the material, the realistic difficulties involved in achieving success, the constant need to make corrections for subjective blind spots, the disparity between the therapist's human limitations and the expectations of his patients and the public are a constant potential source of anxiety to the psychotherapist. (p. 372)

It is very difficult for the beginning therapist to confront the complexity of the task without becoming overwhelmed or discouraged. For example, Holt (1959) suggests that the general decline in enthusiasm among psychiatry residents is due to their discovery that the practice of psychotherapy is much more difficult than they had anticipated. The wide variety of diagnostic systems, theoretical orientations, and therapeutic techniques can be confusing and disheartening.

It typically takes a long time for the student to develop a sense of mastery and competency. Yet the nature of the training task requires that the student "treat" patients before feeling ready to do so. Farber (1983a) notes that "although achieving an understanding of psychopathology is a necessarily slow and gradual process, the new therapist must immediately deal with the exigencies of treating patients" (p. 101). Thus trainees typically experience a great deal of stress related to their own sense of inadequacy and failure. This is exacerbated by the common practice of assigning the most disturbed, least functional patients to beginning students, furthering their sense of incompetence.

The undefined nature of a cure is an additional source of stress for the student. While the overriding goal may be to alleviate psychic pain and suffering, the concrete features of this accomplishment may be difficult to anticipate. Added to this is the fact that the typical gains made in treatment are often very limited, and the amount of gratification the student therapist derives may be small (Farber,1983a). This lack of clear, concise, measurable gains adds another source of anxiety for the student preoccupied with issues of competency and mastery.

Ford (1963) notes that beginning therapists tend to go through predictable stages of development during initial training, ranging from intense conviction regarding the efficacy of treatment to complete despair over their self-perceived incompetency. Such steps are largely the result of student anxiety regarding the imprecise nature of the psychotherapeutic task.

Psychological-Mindedness

Another initial source of stress for the trainee is described by Farber (1985a) as resulting from the development of psychological-mindedness in beginning psychotherapists. Whatever the amount of psychological-mindedness present at admission to graduate school, it is greatly reinforced and enhanced by the lengthy socialization and training process leading to graduation and professional practice.

This brings an increased focus on early experiences, memories, emotions, and motivations as they relate to the human behavior of both patients and trainees. While this may vary somewhat with the theoretical orientation of the training program and the future therapist, it seems nonetheless true that psychotherapists-in-training typically become more internally focused as a result of academic studies, supervision, personal therapy, and early work experience.

This intense focus on the inner world may be stressful for the trainee. For example, it may reveal or exacerbate underlying personal psychopathology. It may also change how events and relationships are perceived. Immersing oneself in the "psychological world" may cause the student to interpret and analyze nearly all interpersonal interactions, both inside and outside of the psychotherapeutic role. As Farber (1985a) relates, many students

> feel compelled to understand the dynamics of everything going on around them. . . . Relationships with relatives become understood in terms of transferential difficulties, problems with classmates are analyzed in terms of group processes, unfriendly neighbors are seen as manifesting borderline tendencies, and difficulties in accepting supervisory input are attributed to unresolved oedipal issues. It is not just the language that changes; a new way of thinking has taken shape. (p. 173)

This process of constantly thinking psychologically can result in the student losing himself or herself in endless analysis and introspection, curtailing spontaneity and parsimony. This may impact the interpersonal relationships of the trainee is some very unsettling ways. As Farber points out, while it can improve the individual's empathy and sensitivity to the needs of family and friends, it may also create distance when the less psychologically minded member of the relationship feels unable to enter into the psychologically informed tone of the conversation. This can create a gulf between students and their spouses, family, and friends. Students may feel that they are growing away from their loved ones, due to the prevalence and influence of this psychological perspective or worldview. While it may be acceptable to some students for this to occur with family and friends, it is typically very painful when this occurs in relationship to their spouse or significant other. As Ford (1963) notes, the training years are characterized by a great deal of marital conflict and discord, as trainees attempt to incorporate internal changes into their styles of relating.

The stress that results from attempting to keep a balanced perspective on life in the face of mounting pressure to process events and emotions psychologically, continues throughout a career in psychotherapy, as will be discussed at greater length in Chapters 3 and 4. At this point it is important to note that it begins during the training years and is a significant source of stress for the trainee. Learning how to "turn it off" is a major task not easily mastered concurrently with learning how to "turn it on."

Personal Psychopathology

A further source of stress associated with graduate training leading to the practice of psychotherapy is the tendency for students to discover psychopathology within themselves. In some cases this may be the result of the infamous "medical school syndrome," whereby the student comes to believe that he or she has whatever disease is being studied at that particular time. For example, as a result of having taken a course in abnormal psychology, isolated elements of depression or anxiety which may, indeed, be present are feared to foreshadow even more serious psychopathology which has yet to be discovered. This process may be further exacerbated by a tendency for trainees to "overidentify" with patients and their varying distresses, believing themselves to be more like their patients than may truly be the case (Holt & Luborsky, 1958). Farber notes that "beginning therapists may compare their own early development with that of patients and question their own defense mechanisms, and even their own sanity" (Farber, 1983a, p. 100). As Halleck and Woods (1962) note, "perhaps no psychiatrist goes through training without at one time or another worrying about the loss of his sanity" (p. 341). Typically in such cases, students eventually stop "overdiagnosing" themselves, as does the medical student who realizes that he or she is, in fact, quite healthy in spite of a few isolated symptoms.

Unfortunately the stress of graduate study, with the resultant life changes noted, may in fact produce or exacerbate already present psychopathology. In Goplerud's study (1980), 81.8% of the first year psychology graduate students reported periods of intense anxiety, 50% reported depression lasting three or more consecutive days, and 31.8% suffered from severe sleep problems unrelated to studying. Pasnau and Bayley (1971) reported a significant increase in depression among first-year psychiatry residents. Finally, both Halleck and Woods (1962) and Merklin and Little (1967) found that many psychiatry residents experienced moderate to severe anxiety and depression, transitory neurotic symptoms, and psychosomatic disturbances of varying degrees of severity. The onset or discovery of psychopathology during psychotherapeutic training can be extremely unsettling and disturbing for the trainee. It raises the issue of suitability for the role of therapist in the minds of both the student and the faculty. If severe enough, it may lead to a leave of absence or even dismissal. More likely, it may serve to motivate the student to enter personal therapy during the training years in order to find relief and resolve underlying concerns. This will be discussed in more detail later in this chapter. For now, it is worth noting that the discovery of personal emotional psychopathology, whether real or imagined, can be a very serious stressor for the trainee.

Changing Values and Perspectives

The development of psychological-mindedness seems to be related to other changes as well. For example, Henry (1966; Henry et al.,1971) found that psychotherapists-in-training tend to undergo significant shifts in religious beliefs, political views, and personal attitudes. These seem to occur consistently in the "liberal" direction. The reasons for this are unclear. Henry speculates that it is the result of the profound influence of faculty and mentor figures who tend to be more liberal than the parents of the families of origin. Bugental (1964), who notes the same "liberalizing" tendencies among individuals training to become psychotherapists, attributes this to a need to act out against the authority figures of one's youth in an attempt to attain autonomy. Unfortunately, it is not known whether or how this process is different from that of other graduate students. However, it may be reasonable to assume that psychologically oriented training may provide exposure to and increase tolerance for a wide diversity of views and experiences represented by patients. This seems to result in a realignment of personal values and beliefs in a more liberal direction for reasons yet to be determined.

Whatever the cause of changing values and beliefs, it is a growing source of stress for the therapist-in-training. Henry et al. (1971) report that these changes often result in views that are different from those of parents and family members. New attitudes and beliefs may lead to misunderstandings, arguments, strained communication, and alienation. The resultant tension, combined with the distancing associated with becoming more psychologically minded, can lead to a profound sense of isolation and aloneness.

Personality Changes

The sense of alienation described previously is sometimes compounded by the student's difficulty integrating into his or her own sense of self the many internal changes that occur during graduate school. Whether this involves changing values and beliefs, increased psychological-mindedness, changing feelings about significant others, or the onset or resolution of personal psychopathology, the rate and extent of changes occurring during this period are sometimes dramatic. Thus it is not only the reactions of others that are stressful, but the trainee's own discomfort with the internal changes that are typically occurring at a rapid rate.

This time of transition is a difficult one for student therapists to endure. They may find it difficult to understand the accompanying changes themselves, much less to explain them to others. More importantly, while they may have a growing sense of what they are "leaving behind," they may lack even a hint of "where they are heading." This is further compounded by personality changes which sometimes result from the working through of unresolved emotional problems during the course of training. As mentioned in Chapter 1, some student therapists find that the course work, supervision, and clinical experience inherent in the training program promote personality reorganization, resolution of underlying problems or conflicts, and facilitation of growth and maturity within themselves. Obviously, personal psychotherapy which may occur during this period would further increase the likelihood of such changes. This results in a period of rapid and sometimes noticeable change which may be difficult for both the individual trainee, as well as family and friends, to assimilate.

Competition

Although rarely mentioned in the literature, it is widely known that one of the major stressors of graduate training to become a psychotherapist is the competitive aspects of most programs. While this is likely to be true in most advanced academic settings, there are several unique factors inherent in the training of psychotherapists which aggravate the situation beyond a level characteristic of other degree programs.

The most obvious aspect of the competition involves academic performance. Because past academic ability is such a critical factor in an admissions process that selects only a relatively few to enter into training, those who are admitted tend to be excellent students. In fact, the competition to get into a clinical graduate program is fierce, and those who are admitted are typically high academic achievers, often in the top third of their graduating class. They are admitted into training because they learned to compete and achieve in academic settings. It is only natural that such an orientation is often continued during graduate training. While it might be hoped that admission into an advanced training program brings an end to this competition, it may in fact heighten it. Students used to being among the brightest of their peers now find that nearly everyone in a given class is as bright, or even brighter than they are. It is now more difficult to get the highest grade in the class, or even an "A." This forces some trainees to adjust their perceptions of themselves and lower their expectations. It seems to drive others into even more intense effort and competition. Either way, such adjustments may be accompanied by stress and tension. While academic competition is present in many advanced degree programs, it is especially keen among the talented and compulsive students in the field of psychotherapy.

A source of stress more unique to advanced training for becoming a psychotherapist involves clinical ability or psychological prowess. While most students in such programs are familiar with the pressures of academic competition, few are prepared for the competition which may arise among therapists-in-training related to differing levels of psychotherapeutic skill. Those individuals who seem particularly well-suited for a career in psychotherapy may evidence qualities, skills, and abilities not present among those less suited for this role. Furthermore, varying rates of learning, personality changes, and personal growth will cause some students to appear more suited for psychotherapeutic tasks than others. As a result, there may be subtle pressure to compete on more subjective dimensions. Students, as well as faculty and supervisors, may implicitly "rank order" trainees utilizing qualities such as empathy, warmth, caring, genuiness, sensitivity, insight, and maturity to determine which student has the most potential or clinical promise. Such individuals may be given the best teaching assistantships, field placements, internships, letters of reference, and job offers. The tension that results from competing with others on the basis of one's personality characteristics, in addition to acquired skills and knowledge, is stressful for the trainee. It can also engender significant frustration and discouragement, particularly when the subjectivity involved in such comparisons and evaluations is difficult to challenge or correct.

Faculty Relationships

If admissions committees are regarded as the gate keepers of the profession of psychotherapy, then the faculty members of the various graduate programs may be viewed as the caretakers and overseers of the training process. As such, students may find their relationships with various faculty members to be ambivalent and emotionally loaded. This is due to the fact that the faculty serve in the dual roles of both facilitator and evaluator. Thus it is the faculty member's job to both teach and critique the trainee. The same professor who tries to reassure the student concerning his or her abilities and skills must also confront and expose shortcomings, blindspots, and failures.

Goplerud (1980) points out that, while positive, supportive interactions with faculty members greatly reduce the stress of graduate training in psychotherapy, negative, conflictual, and strained interactions with faculty members can be a very significant source of stress, anxiety, and depression for the student. In the trainee's world, the faculty are the authority figures, the parental substitutes who have a great deal of power over the fate of the student. It is they who evaluate academic performance, clinical promise, and therapeutic ability. Whether this involves grading papers, supervising a thesis or dissertation, critiquing a student's clinical work, deciding whether or not to grant a diploma, or some other point of evaluation, the faculty are assigned the task of evaluating the level of skill, ability, and talent of the trainee. This may mobilize a student's feelings regarding past authority figures such as their parents, and these prior relationships may color or contaminate the present relationship with a given faculty member. This sometimes results in a distortion which may cause the student to perceive the professor as either more supportive and nurturant than he or she really is, resulting in eventual disappointment and hurt feelings, or as more critical and rejecting than the professor intends to be, creating feelings of suspicion and fearfulness. In this manner, the underlying personality characteristics and previous experiences of the student will influence the amount of stress and discomfort experienced in such relationships.

Faculty members are given the task of equipping students with the skills necessary for the successful practice of psychotherapy. In addition, most programs recognize that their admissions committees are only partially successful in screening out those who are apparently unsuitable for the profession of psychotherapy. Thus the faculty must attempt some additional discrimination during the training process to eliminate those who have been admitted but who are not sufficiently trainable or remediable.

The most obvious point of evaluation is that of academic ability. Nearly all programs set some type of academic requirements for continuation in the program such as establishing a minimum grade point average necessary for continuation or graduation. Those who fall below this minimum standard are usually put on academic probation or dismissed from the program. Academic suitability may be further evaluated by requiring the successful passage of some type of comprehensive examinations or the successful completion of a thesis or dissertation. However, in most training programs there is an attempt to go beyond mere academic requirements to include requiring a certain level of clinical skill, potential, and even more vague, personal emotional stability for continuation and graduation. This may involve a process which is organized and formal or informal and unofficial. Regardless of how it is conducted, most faculty attempt to screen out those determined by group consensus to be unsuitable for the profession. If it is decided that the problems or shortcomings are remediable, recommendations will be made and interventions provided. When regarded beyond possible remediation, dismissal may be the only alternative. Thus faculty are not only responsible for equipping trainees with the skills necessary for competent clinical practice, but are also assigned the task of screening out those unsuited for the profession.

In view of the important evaluative tasks conducted by faculty members, relationships between therapists-in-training and faculty members are often likely to be somewhat strained, ambivalent, and uncomfortable; sometimes for both parties. Students may find it difficult to confide in a faculty person concerning needs, personal problems, doubts, and fears because of the suspicion that it may later be used against him or her when evaluations are conducted and issues of suitability for clinical practice are considered. Yet there is also the realization that a certain degree of familiarity and intimacy are necessary for training and evaluation purposes, motivating both trainees and faculty to attempt a certain amount of personal interaction. This double bind, the need to be known and yet the fear of the same, may generate significant discomfort and stress for the trainee.

Reducing the Stress of Graduate Training

In view of the rather serious stressors characteristic of graduate training in psychotherapy, it is appropriate to consider suggestions for reducing or eliminating the negative consequences of this period. Several factors seem to help in this regard. For example, Goplerud (1980) found that first year psychology graduate students with preexisting support networks, and those who were able to establish such networks easily during the first few months of school, experienced significantly less stress and tension during this time. Socially isolated students were at significantly greater risk of developing a number of physical and emotional difficulties. Thus the number and quality of social contacts and the presence of a meaningful support network moderated or reduced the impact of the stressors inherent in graduate training to become a psychotherapist. A similar finding was reported by Looney and his colleagues (Looney, Harding, Blotcky, & Barnhart, 1980) who found that emotional support from a spouse or loved one, along with supportive relationships with peers and colleagues, was very helpful in reducing training-related stress of psychiatry residents.

In spite of the conflictual and difficult aspects of student–faculty relationships, Goplerud (1980) found that the more frequently students were able to interact with faculty outside of class time, the less likely they were to experience stress-related health or emotional problems. Faculty were seen as important role models, sources of reassurance and support, and important resources of information and guidance. Ford (1963) also notes that graduate professors serve as an important source of information and support, not only about the profession, but about life. This has led Goplerud to recommend that professors take a more active, initiatory role in contacting and interacting with students. It appears that the benefits of such interactions far outweigh the problems and stresses associated with such relationships.

In addition to the need for social support and helpful relationships, other factors have been identified as helpful in reducing stress related to graduate training in psychotherapy. For example, Looney et al. (1980) found that play and recreation, vacation or time off, reading, creative activities, and exercise greatly improved the overall life enjoyment of students, while helping to reduce self-perceived stress and tension. It seems that maintaining an ongoing active life apart from study, rather than viewing training as life in its entirety, helps sustain a balance necessary for coping with stress in a useful fashion.

The Rewards of Graduate Training

Although the years spent in graduate training to become a psychotherapist are sometimes particularly stressful and difficult for many students, it is also a time of exciting changes and growth. It is challenging and rewarding not only to learn the skills and techniques of psychotherapy, but to focus on self-awareness, growth, and development. As Levison (1978) points out, some of the trainee's most important changes and decisions are made during this period, impacting the course of adult life to follow. While certainly a stressful time for some, it is an exciting and rewarding time for most. As Farber (1983a) explains, the process of training to be a psychotherapist results in several forms of positive growth, both professional and personal.

As mentioned in Chapter 1, on occasion the training process brings personality changes that result in a higher level of overall functioning and greater emotional stability. Holt also reports that trainees develop more mature relationships as a result of the advanced training that they receive while preparing for the practice of psychotherapy. In addition, they tend to become more self-confident, less defensive, and more humble in their interactions with friends and family (Maurice, Klonoff, Miles, & Krell, 1975). As mentioned earlier, there is a tendency for trainees to become less authoritarian and more tolerant of diversity and ambiguity (Henry, 1966). Finally, Perlman (1972) reports that student therapists experience greater self-ideal congruence as a result of the reorganization of the individual's self-concept. While these rapid and often profound changes may engender some stress as they are assimilated into the personality of the student, they also promote more stable, healthy functioning, and good social adjustment.

In addition to these positive personality changes associated with training in psychotherapy, several professionally related changes occur as well. For example, both Holt (1959) and Ford (1963) report that students eventually emerge with a strong, resilient professional commitment to the practice of psychotherapy and their work with patients. While it is one of optimism and confidence, it is informed by realistic expectations and limits. This is an evolving process which may take several years, but one which is necessary for successful clinical practice in the future. In addition to this, Pasnau and Bayley (1971) suggest that the trainee experiences significant gains in substantive knowledge and therapeutic insight which enable them to tolerate periods of self-doubt with a sustaining foundation of confidence based on a realistic sense of competence and ability. These positive gains equip the therapist-in-training with skills and techniques which are combined with the individual's intuition and sensitivity, resulting in a successful socialization process leading to the role of psychotherapist.

Internships and Fieldwork

Virtually every psychotherapeutic training program includes one or more fieldwork experiences which provide students with "on the job" training in the practice of psychotherapy. Such training opportunities allow students to function in a professional role under the direct supervision of a qualified, experienced, licensed psychotherapist who serves as a role model, instructor, and evaluator for the therapist. For some students, fieldwork will take place under the direct auspices of the training program in which they are enrolled, such as at an on-site campus counseling center or clinic. In such cases the supervisors are likely to be faculty members who also serve as classroom instructors. However, for most students, fieldwork training occurs off campus at clinics, hospitals, and counseling centers under the supervision of professionals unrelated to the program of origin. While not always the case, the supervisors are typically members of the same discipline as the student; for example, social workers serving as supervisors for social work students. These fieldwork placements may be located in the local community, or they may be across the country. In some cases, training at a particular site may last for several months, but most arrangements involve a mutual commitment of one to two years. Some trainees will train at three or four sites prior to graduation, while others are assigned to only one or two.

A number of graduate programs assign fieldwork placements to students beginning in their first year of training and continuing throughout the duration of the program. Thus these trainees begin seeing patients at the same time that they are enrolled in academic classes. In other programs, students do not begin practicing psychotherapy until they have completed at least one or two years of classroom instruction. Although fieldwork experience is typically a degree requirement for most graduate programs, it involves features of training which are obviously quite different from that of traditional classroom instruction. Thus it has its own unique rewards and hazards.

The fieldwork or internship experience is an apprenticeship to a greater extent than that of the classroom phase of training and instruction. As mentioned earlier in this chapter, it is reminiscent of the initiation period required of novitiates wishing to become healers, witch doctors, high priests, and shamans. Trainees are expected to observe, imitate, and obey their supervisors in order to master the techniques of "healing." Those who succeed in doing so are allowed to proceed toward graduation and eventual entry into the profession, while those who fail are required to repeat the experience or may be dismissed from the program. As is true of any healer, unless the techniques are successfully mastered, more harm than good will result for those who subject themselves to the therapist's ministrations. Therefore, while this is a time of excitement and rapid learning, it is also a time of serious evaluation and scrutiny.

Transitions and Changes

It must be acknowledged that there is a certain degree of safety in the classroom. Here students are free to consider a variety of ideas, theories, and perspectives, ideally without censure or prejudice. Students are viewed as neophytes, and their mistakes or errors do not typically result in dire consequences. Their "rookie" status elicits a tolerance and patience from the sensitive professor who realizes the difficulty in learning and integrating vast amounts of data and information. There is also a certain amount of empathy for the significant emotional upheavals and personality changes occurring for many students during the early years of training in psychotherapy. While there are certainly many demands placed on them, there is still recognition by both faculty and students that expectations must be realistic and appropriate for this particular stage of training.

This situation undergoes significant changes as the student moves from classroom instruction to fieldwork training. No longer is the trainee an observer of the practice of psychotherapy, simply reading books or listening to lectures on the topic. Now the trainee is a participant, placed in a role of service provider which requires more certainty and initiative. This transition is a difficult one for several reasons.

For some, assignment to a particular fieldwork placement may involve an element of competition. For example, some training sites, particularly the high prestige programs, may require that trainees go through a screening process rather than blindly accepting every student sent by a program with whom there is a training agreement. In such cases, students may be interviewed and have their credentials scrutinized to determine who will be accepted into the specified number of training slots. This may involve direct competition with peers and classmates, often a very uncomfortable process. For others, students may compete with other trainees outside of their program.

This may well be the first time that the student is forced to compete on the basis of clinical skill and professional competency rather than academic ability. While the screening or selection process may include review of academic performance during undergraduate and graduate training, other factors are often more prominent, such as letters of reference, relevant experience, and personal interviews (Burt, 1985; Rickard & Rahaim, 1982). The personal nature of this evaluation process is unsettling for the trainee, who is very aware that desirability will be determined on the basis of who one is as much, or more, than what one knows. While this was true to a lesser degree during the admissions process leading to graduate training in psychotherapy, it is more apparent during the screening process required for many fieldwork placements. Even for those students who are not directly involved in the selection process, such as by way of making application to a particular internship, those simply assigned to a particular practicum or residency are aware that this assignment was usually the result of some type of review process which sought to match the needs of a particular site with the skills, experience, and personality of the student. Comparisons on this basis are often quite stressful for the trainee, who may feel that there is little that can be done to influence or change the outcome of these decisions which seem to be based, at least in part, on rather subjective criteria exempt from student challenge or review. Whether selected or assigned to a particular field placement, the therapist-in-training is faced with the realization that the expectations for personal stability, mastery and competency are higher than was the case during the admissions process and early period of classroom instruction.

It should be noted that the competition described above does not end at the completion of selection or assignment to a particular field placement or internship. On the contrary, interns and trainees report that they continue to experience the same type of competition concerning clinical competency with other fieldwork students at their on-site training programs (Kingsley, 1985). This can increase the stress level of the trainee, who continues to be concerned about how others regard him or her according to the somewhat subjective criteria of clinical skill, professional promise, emotional stability and maturity, and overall competence. Such preoccupations may result in tension, envy, and fierce competition among interns and trainees.

Those students who begin work at a field placement or internship outside of the local area undergo a host of stresses related to relocation. These are similar to those experienced by individuals entering graduate training in another city or state. As described by Lamb (Lamb, Baker, Jennings, & Yarris, 1982) and Solway (1985), such trainees are confronted with the practical stresses associated with moving to a new geographical area as well as the pain accompanying the loss of family and support systems. Even those assigned to local placements may lose contact with faculty and friends previously seen on a regular basis. Either way, there is a loss of some elements of the support system relied on during the beginning phases of training, increasing the need for establishing new relationships with authority figures, peers, and colleagues.

Perhaps the most difficult transition involves the redefinition from student to professional. As reported by Kingsley (1985), who described her own metamorphosis during a year-long predoctoral clinical psychology internship, the trainee is forced to confront that it is no longer appropriate to function in a passive, indecisive, tentative fashion characteristic of a less experienced student. It is now necessary to function somewhat autonomously, with relative confidence, decisiveness, and competency. As Farber (1983a) points out, the student therapist is responsible for the treatment of real patients, many of whom are very disturbed and least promising in their potential for improvement. Nonetheless, it is the expectation of both patients and supervisors that the trainee will exhibit an acceptable level of skill, ability, maturity, and personal stability. Adjustment to these expectations results in significant stress and difficulty for some students.

Doubts concerning clinical competency and personal suitabilty are frequent during this period, as the therapist-in-training moves from "professional adolescence" to "professional adulthood" (Kaslow & Rice, 1985; Kingsley, 1985; Lamb et al., 1982). This is particularly true for those thrust into fieldwork assignments during their first or second year of graduate training. It is a common experience for such beginning therapists to feel like "frauds" or "charlatans" when asked to practice psychotherapy before feeling sufficiently knowledgeable or competent. However, even those who do not begin internships until after their third or fourth year of training often feel unable to provide adequate patient care. The resultant evolutionary process associated with this transition from student to psychotherapist is often characterized by a high degree of stress, discomfort, and inner turmoil. However, most navigate these difficult waters reasonably well. Successful completion of this phase is marked by the emergence of an individual who has attained a noticeable degree of identity as a psychotherapist (Ford, 1963).

The Supervisory Relationship

A central focus of the fieldwork experience centers on the relationship between the therapist-in-training and the supervisor. This relationship has a profound impact on the student's training, self-perceptions, and future practice. Relating successfully with on-site supervisors is an important rite of passage leading to the practice of psychotherapy. As such, it is highly charged with emotion and meaning. The expectations of each party, along with the multiplicity of roles inherent in the relationship, set the stage for problems which must be overcome.

The trainee brings several expectations to the supervisory relationship, some realistic and some rather distorted. Initially, they are usually painfully aware of the limitations and inadequacies of their skills and abilities. In fact, there is often a tendency to underestimate competency initially, as trainees compare themselves with supervisors who seem "bigger than life" (Farber, 1983a). Thus the student therapist approaches the supervisor with a variety of feelings and expectations, depending on his or her own previous life experience. For example, feelings of vulnerabilty and inadequacy may trigger many reactions toward the supervisor, ranging from excessive imitation and idealization to opposition, rejection, and denial (Ford, 1963). Fear of evaluation and criticism may cause the trainee to become withholding, guarded, suspicious, and secretive (Farber, 1985a). If, on the other hand, the trainee has had positive experiences with authority figures, he or she may approach the supervisor with eagerness, openness, and positive expectancy. At any rate, most supervisees recognize that there is much to be learned from the supervisor during the months ahead, in terms of clinical skills and professional propriety. It is also apparent that the supervisor will play an important role in both the present training experience and passage to future practice.

The supervisor, on the other hand, also brings a set of expectations to the relationship. As Marmor (1953) explains, "the supervising therapist, whether he (she) realizes it or not, usually operates under an inner need to demonstrate his (her) superior knowledge or experience, since his (her) sense of usefulness as a supervisor is largely dependent on his ability to point out errors of omission or commission to the student" (p. 374). The pressure to prove his or her worth, by understanding the work of the student on the basis of limited data, may cause the supervisor to feel inadequate. This may lead to defensiveness, guardedness, rigidity, or authoritarianism on the part of the supervisor. In addition, the idealization, dependence, and expectancy of trainees (Farber, 1983a) may be a further burden for the supervisor who feels the need to appear omniscient and to satisfy all the longings and demands of students. The degree of distortion and number of unrealistic expectations of the supervisor will depend, in part, on his or her own comfort with power and authority, which is also likely to be the result of past experiences with authority figures.

The supervisory relationship is characterized by a variety of conflicting roles which further complicate the interaction (Robiner, 1982). For example, the supervisor serves as a teacher and the trainee as a student. The focus of this dimension is on skill acquisition and enhancement. Through the review of tape recordings and process notes, the supervisor instructs the student concerning techniques of diagnosis and treatment. By definition, it is the student's responsibility to seek out instruction and guidance. The nature of the expectations that each party brings to this task will determine the extent to which the teacher–student dimension is successfully incorporated into the supervisory relationship.

A related dimension places the supervisor in the role of journeyman and the student in the role of apprentice. In addition to the training of skills and techniques, it is necessary for the supervisor to serve as a role model of professional propriety and decorum. This includes not only the many facets of functioning as a psychotherapist and mental health professional, but also the adoption of behavior and attitudes unique to one's particular discipline. Thus it is during internship that the trainee learns the differences which exist among counselors, psychiatrists, social workers, and psychologists (Kingsley, 1985). As an apprentice the student learns to act and think like a member of his or her own particular discipline or professional guild. The supervisor, typically of the same discipline, serves as a journeyman by modeling the appropriate characteristics for the apprentice.

Another role fulfilled by the supervisor is that of facilitator and helper. In this regard, the supervisor seeks to support, affirm, and comfort the trainee in a manner not altogether different from that of a parent comforting a child. It is the supervisor who typically reassures the trainee of his or her competence and worth. While this aspect of the relationship may be limited to simple encouragement and support, it may also take on dimensions of diagnostician–patient and therapist–client. In such cases, the supervisor may attempt to highlight the student's personality shortcomings and emotional problems as they relate to clinical work. He or she may also attempt to bring about a "cure" through a therapylike interaction with the trainee.

Finally, the supervisor functions as an evaluator and critic of the trainee's functioning and effectiveness. It is the task of the supervisor to evaluate the student's progress as a therapist-in-training. This evaluation combines with active instruction on an ongoing basis, providing both the student and the supervisor with direction concerning what is yet to be mastered. The impact of this process will be discussed in more detail later in this chapter.

It is apparent that these multiple roles intersect and conflict periodically. It is difficult for both parties to make the shifts necessary for the continually changing dimensions of the supervisory relationship. For example, it is difficult to sort out those times when the most appropriate dimension for interaction is the helper–helpee role, in contrast to the teacher–student, journeyman–apprentice, and evaluator–evaluatee roles. These changing dimensions are further complicated by the obvious inequality of power, status, and expertise inherent in the relationship (Newman, 1981; Robiner, 1982). This may result in the supervisor assuming, and the trainee surrendering, more control and influence than is either necessary or helpful.

While the supervisory relationship is often a source of stress and discomfort for the trainee, as Farber (1983a) points out, it is one of the single most important relationships of the psychotherapist's career. It not only provides training and support, but also significantly influences the trainee's future practice.

Assessing Suitability vs. Unsuitability

One of the dimensions of the supervisory relationship occurring at the internship or fieldwork site involves that of evaluation and assessment of clinical skill and professional functioning. However, this process goes beyond the assessment of clinical ability to include determining suitabilty versus unsuitability for the practice of psychotherapy. It is necessary that this occur because it may be the first real opportunity to examine the student's functioning in a semiautonomous professional role (Kingsley, 1985). No longer is academic ability a major concern or focus. Now full attention is given to the trainee's ability to function in a helpful, stable, consistent fashion in professional relationships with patients who are sometimes rather disturbed and unreasonable. In such situations, those unsuited for the role of psychotherapist may be unable to function in an appropriate and effective manner. It may then become necessary for either the dysfunctional intern or the supervising psychotherapist to terminate the training arrangement, resulting in either reassignment to another fieldwork site, a leave of absence from training, or dismissal from the graduate program of origin.

In one study of predoctoral psychology interns, of 3325 internship positions available during the previous 5 years, 51 interns failed to complete the training experience, with dismissal being considered by internship administrators in an additional 89 cases (Tedesco, 1982). Over half of the 51 terminations that did occur were at the request of the director of training of the internship training program. Reasons given, in rank order of frequency and importance, were emotional instability, personality disorder, lack of knowledge of psychotherapy, lack of knowledge of assessment techniques, unethical behavior, lack of intellectual capacity, and lack of knowledge of consultation techniques. Clearly, this is an important opportunity to screen out those not yet suited for the practice of psychotherapy. While this study is thought to be representative of the rate of impairment among psychotherapists-in-training, other researchers estimate the annual rate of trainee impairment to fall somewhere between 4 to 21% (Boxley, Drew, & Rangel, 1986).

In view of the gravity of the evaluative task occurring during fieldwork, Tyler and Steven (1981) thought it important to review procedures utilized for evaluating clinical performance. Their results indicated that some type of routinely scheduled evaluations of trainee progress were a widespread practice. Although some evaluations were in written form, oral feedback was much more common. In most cases, feedback was given to both the trainee and the graduate training program from which he or she originated. Despite these feedback procedures, few training programs have formal procedures for handling trainee impairment (Boxley et al., 1986). In a thoughtful article on this process of evaluation and screening, Rickard and Miller (1983) stress that it is important for students to have the right of due process, access, and appeal. Furthermore, they suggest that the emphasis be on remediation where possible, rather than solely on dismissal.

While it is a complex task, and one fraught with far-reaching ethical and legal implications, the importance of evaluation and screening during the fieldwork experience is vital. In view of this fact, it is little wonder that the supervisory relationship is loaded with significant emotion and meaning for both the trainee and the supervising psychotherapist.

Reducing the Stress of Internships and Fieldwork

To cope with stress resulting from the loss of support systems, problems inherent in physical relocation, the transition from student to practitioner, and competition among interns and trainees, Solway (1985) suggests that fieldwork sites provide "growth groups," well-planned orientations, and opportunites for meaningful interaction with both outgoing and other incoming interns. By providing an open, structured environment characterized by both honesty and support, trainees will have the best opportunity to cope with the numerous stressors inherent in this experience.

To lessen the stress associated with supervisory relationships, Robiner (1982) and Newman (1981) suggest that the aforementioned issues be openly and honestly discussed as soon as possible by the supervisor and trainee, to allow for mutual input regarding the limits and parameters of the relationship. Working together to formulate the guidelines for the relationship in this manner will facilitate the satisfying of needs and expectations of both parties. It will also hopefully reduce the possibility of misunderstanding and accompanying distress.

Several researchers (Norcross, Stevenson, & Nash, 1986; Rickard & Miller, 1983; Tedesco, 1982) suggest that the stress associated with the evaluation of clinical competence and suitability versus unsuitability can be greatly reduced for all parties by consistent, well-defined, periodic written evaluations conducted at regular intervals. They suggest that these be given to both the student and the school of origin. They also recommend that these procedures follow carefully formulated guidelines that are responsible and fair to the student, field placement site, school of origin, and the larger professional community. These should guarantee the student the right of review and due process when there is a marked difference of opinion. Only in this way will the significant anxiety and distress associated with evaluation be moderated by the realization that this is a necessary process, equitably and reasonably executed.

Finally, in view of Goplerud's (1980) findings concerning the importance of ongoing student–faculty contact for reducing stress and adjustment problems, it would seem important for faculty advisors to maintain close communication with fieldwork students and their supervisors during internship and fieldwork training. Not only will this provide helpful support and encouragement for the students, but it will also allow for a closer monitoring of the quality of the practicum placement and the supervision provided there. Furthermore, such close contact may provide a ready source of advocacy for either the student or the fieldwork supervisor should a problem develop.

The Rewards of Internship–Fieldwork Training

Although this is a period of some anxiety and stress, the on-the-job training received at internships and fieldwork placements results in substantial growth and development in clinical skill, ability, and confidence. As Kingsley (1985) notes, this is the first real opportunity to function in the professional role of psychotherapist. Although some academic training may be continued during this time, the central focus is on learning to function in the role of therapist rather than simply learning about the role. For most students, this is the capstone of the training experience, the chance to finally practice psychotherapy. The personality changes, skill acquisition, and increased sense of competency which accompany this opportunity are extremely gratifying.

While trainees typically appreciate the importance of the academic portion of the training program, most feel that it is during the internship experience that they actually learn how to conduct psychotherapy and function in the role of psychotherapist. The feeling of being "one step away" from entering the profession energizes the trainee during the fieldwork portion of his or her training. As a result, most students avidly anticipate the start of on-site training, and are largely enthusiastic about their overall satisfaction with this portion of their training.

Evaluating the Effectiveness of Training Programs

While not surprising, it is nonetheless disturbing to discover that there has been relatively little research concerning the overall effectiveness of graduate training programs in preparing individuals to become psychotherapists (Aronson, Akamatsu, & Page, 1982). Although there has been ample evidence that well-implemented programs are successful in teaching individuals to become more genuine, caring, and empathic (Aronson et al., 1982; Rogers, 1961; Truax & Carkhuff, 1967), there has been little attempt to determine whether the typical graduate programs are successful in teaching individuals to master the multiplicity of diagnostic, therapeutic, and professional tasks associated with the practice of psychotherapy. While research has provided evidence of some of the factors necessary for therapeutic change (Garfield & Bergin, 1978), no reliable data is available regarding whether or not training programs are effective in equipping their students with the skills and personality characteristics necessary for producing those factors required for therapeutic success. Recent attempts have been made to design adequate measures and assessment techniques for evaluating the effectiveness of clinical training programs (Stevenson, Norcross, King, & Tobin, 1984). Unfortunately, such procedures have yet to be implemented by most graduate training programs in psychotherapy.

It is not only the graduate training programs that lack a standardized, objective means of assessing the effectiveness of their training of psychotherapists. As Drabman (1985) points out, this is true of most internship and fieldwork sites as well. Few, if any, formulate detailed plans for program evaluation to determine how effective they have been in preparing trainees for successful clinical practice. The logistical problems associated with this type of follow-up study are certainly formidable. However, until such data is made available, little will be known about the effectiveness of current fieldwork sites in equipping individuals for the practice of psychotherapy.

It is interesting to note that, while generally avoiding comment on the effectiveness of internships, Drabman does provide a personal opinion regarding the effectiveness of graduate training programs in producing clinical psychologists, based on his experience as an internship director. He notes that students tend to lack sufficient knowledge and experience in the areas of diagnostic assessment, treatment, scientific foundations and history of psychology, human development, psychopharmacology, forensics, epidemiology, and sociology. Even more important, he suggests that the typical intern lacks sufficient clinical experience to function autonomously, both during and following the internship year. Cantor and Moldawsky (1985) express similar views, pointing out that most psychology training programs fail to provide students adequately with instruction concerning the realities of independent clinical practice such as relevant legal and ethical concerns, business management principles, and the importance of ongoing supervision and personal psychotherapy. Unfortunately, comparative data concerning the effectiveness of other disciplines involved in training psychotherapists is unavailable at this time.

Another source of feedback concerning the effectiveness of training programs in psychotherapy is the graduates, who are able to report on how well-equipped they found themselves to be once they entered the profession. Henry et al., (1971) questioned social workers, psychologists, and psychiatrists regarding their opinion of the value of their formal training (including both academic and clinical aspects) in preparing them for a career in psychotherapy. Among social workers, 86% found their training to be helpful, compared to 65% of the clinical psychologists and 72% of the psychiatrists. Regarding academic course work, 65% of the social workers found it to be relevant to their career, compared to 45% of the psychologists and 42% of the psychiatrists. Finally, 81% of the social workers found their clinical experience as a trainee to be helpful for their career as psychotherapists, as compared to 76% of the clinical psychologists and 60% of the psychiatrists. In a more recent survey of clinical psychologists, over 60% indicated satisfaction with the adequacy of their graduate training and 85% felt the same about their internship experience (Norcross & Prochaska, 1982).

Unfortunately, there is no way to be certain that satisfaction with one's training indicates actual clinical competence, overall effectiveness, and suitability for the role of psychotherapist. For example, several studies have suggested that it is the perceived quality of interpersonal relationships with faculty and supervisors that is the main determinant in a graduate's satisfaction with his or her clinical training program and self-perceived competence (Bradley & Olson,1980; Howe & Neimeyer, 1980). Obviously, this does not necessarily reflect the actual clinical competence of the graduate.

Until more careful research is conducted, there will be no way to know whether clinical training programs, both on and off campus, are effective in accomplishing their assigned task. In view of the surprising number of impaired practitioners and the high level of career dissatisfaction among practicing therapists, it seems reasonable to question the adequacy of present training programs in equipping individuals for the practice of psychotherapy and screening out those unsuitable for the role of psychotherapist.

Future Trends

While a more thorough discussion of future trends in training for the practice of psychotherapy will be included in Chapter 8, a brief comment seems warranted at this point. Increased public awareness and the rise of consumerism in health care are bringing about the demystification of the practice of psychotherapy and increased accountability. This is likely to result in even greater public demand for program evaluation to assess the effectiveness of training programs in producing future psychotherapists. As Fox, Kovacs, and Graham (1985) and Peterson (1985) point out, it will take aggressive, ongoing evaluation and progressive, programatic changes for psychotherapy training programs to keep pace with the rapidly shifting roles and responsibilties of tomorrow's psychotherapists.

As mentioned earlier, among the many training issues yet to be resolved is the continued controversy between those who regard the practice of psychotherapy to be a science versus those who consider it to be an art (Jasnow, 1978). A variation on this issue is the ongoing debate regarding whether to train psychotherapists as scientists who both conduct and digest research concerning human behavior, or as professionals whose primary focus is on service delivery (Henry, 1984). While attempts have been made to resolve this conflict by incorporating both emphases into many graduate training programs, the focus is typically in one direction or the other (McConnell, 1984). Conflicting perspectives on psychopathology, treatment, and broader worldview issues further compound the complexity of this debate. Future trends in the training of psychotherapists will likely be influenced by these changing perspectives.

THE TRANSITION TO PRACTICING PROFESSIONAL

The metamorphosis from neophyte graduate student to practicing psychotherapist involves several developmental stages which go beyond academic learning and fieldwork training. The role of psychotherapist becomes a lifestyle, a way of experiencing and processing feelings, behavior, and events which becomes a way of being rather than simply a way of knowing. Toward this end, several additional factors are involved in preparing the individual for the role of psychotherapist. These include receiving personal psychotherapy, choosing a theoretical orientation, deciding on a specialty, and obtaining the necessary state and national credentials for independent practice.

Personal Therapy

Although it is true that some trainees experience little need for personal psychotherapy, it is a widely held belief among psychotherapists that personal therapy is desirable, if not necessary, preparation for conducting psychotherapy (Garfield & Kurtz, 1976; Goldberg, 1986; Guy & Liaboe, 1986b). In one recent study of practicing psychotherapists in which over two-thirds had received treatment at some point, nearly 80% felt that personal therapy was an important prerequisite for competent clinical practice (Norcross & Prochaska, 1982). At this time there is little research data supporting the actual need for personal treatment for future psychotherapists; however, many graduate training programs continue to require (or at least strongly recommend) personal psychotherapy for their students (Greenberg & Staller, 1981). In one study of clinical psychology doctoral programs, 71% required or strongly recommended that students receive some type of personal psychotherapy (Wampler & Strupp, 1976). Several reasons are given for this policy, with the two primary ones being that personal therapy provides a valuable training experience and promotes a higher degree of emotional stability and mental health.

One of the most common reasons given for requiring or recommending psychotherapy for therapists-in-training is that experiencing the role of patient will increase the trainee's awareness of the therapeutic process (Ford, 1963; Wampler & Strupp, 1976). In this manner, the trainee learns what it "feels like" to be a patient, increasing his or her understanding of and empathy for the patient's position in the therapy relationship. As Storr (1979) states, "I think it is valuable for psychotherapists to be exposed to psychotherapy in order to make it easier for them imaginatively to enter into what their patients are experiencing" (p. 181). This personal experience will likely assist the therapist in identifying more accurately with the fears, concerns, and perspectives of future patients. It is hoped that giving the trainee an opportunity to assume the patient role will provide the future therapist with a better appreciation for what is experienced as helpful by patients.

Beyond the opportunity of sampling what it feels like to be a psychotherapy patient, personal therapy provides the trainee with the chance to observe another psychotherapist in action (Wampler & Strupp, 1976). Thus the senior therapist serves as a powerful role model for the trainee who experiences interventions and treatment techniques firsthand. The experienced psychotherapist demonstrates the skill, confidence, and competence desired by the trainee, and helps the student integrate unique personality characteristics into his or her own professional style. The powerful force of experiential learning takes on a new meaning for the trainee who is able to openly and without fear of sanction explore his or her doubts regarding personal competency, the efficacy of psychotherapy, and the meaning of the many personality changes occuring during the training process.

Wampler and Strupp (1976) also suggest that trainees develop a sense of conviction about the validity of the theory and practice of psychotherapy as a result of participating in it themselves. A successful or satisfactory personal therapy experience provides an excellent training opportunity regarding the value and effectiveness of treatment.

The potential training value of a personal therapy experience continues to motivate some future therapists to enter treatment. Norcross & Prochaska (1982) found that nearly one-third of those entering personal therapy did so primarily for training purposes, in the hopes that it would help them to become better psychotherapists.

A far more pertinent reason for encouraging or requiring therapists-in-training to enter personal psychotherapy is due to the fact that many entering the profession have experienced, or continue to experience, moderate to severe emotional disturbance (Ford, 1963). As mentioned in Chapter 1, this may actually have been one of the primary motivators leading to this career choice. In such cases, "the resource of personal psychotherapy cannot be substituted by any other process" (Ford, 1963, p. 480). The working through of unresolved conflicts, the resolution of issues needing closure, and the facilitation of personality growth and maturity will provide a welcome relief for the trainee struggling with sometimes painful and occasionally debilitating problems. Not only will this result in greater personal stability, but it will also improve the ability of the future psychotherapist to be helpful to his or her patients. As Carl Jung (1966) stated, "the patient's treatment begins with the doctor, so to speak. Only if the doctor knows how to cope with himself (herself) and his own problems will he be able to teach the patient to do the same. Only then" (p. 132). Wampler and Strupp (1976) also stress that personal psychotherapy helps to enhance the therapist's ability to conduct treatment by exposing "blind spots" and resolving debilitating "countertransference problems" which might otherwise hinder his or her therapeutic effectiveness. It seems that many psychotherapists recognize the value of a personal therapy experience for dealing with their own conflicts, traumas, and emotional problems and improving the quality of treament to be provided. Norcross and Prochaska (1982) found that over two-thirds of those therapists receiving treatment did so primarily due to a desire to work through personal problems and difficulties.

Personal psychotherapy may also be helpful during the training years to help the student tolerate the pressures, stress, and tensions inherent in the training process leading to the role of psychotherapist. Not only might training related stress exacerbate preexisting psychopathology, but it may precipitate new distress and difficulties as well. In view of the fact that the successful practice of psychotherapy requires that the therapist possess a certain degree of emotional stability (Marmor, 1953), personal therapy begun during the training years is likely to help the student adequately cope with these pressures and concerns. Whether this occurs during internship (Kingsley, 1985), or during the academic portion of graduate school, it may enable the trainee to reduce the potential negative impact of training leading to the practice of psychotherapy.

In addition to the harmful impact of training-related stress, training to become a psychotherapist may precipitate other types of interpersonal problems which might suggest the appropriateness of personal psychotherapy. For example, Marmor (1953) suggests that becoming a psychotherapist often evokes a certain degree of grandiosity in the trainee which may need to be resolved through personal therapy. The power, authority, and influence of the therapist over the lives of patients can have a rather intoxicating effect on the unsuspecting therapist-in-training. In addition, the constant idealization communicated by some clients may enhance the tendency to overvalue one's judgment, opinions, and abilities. While this may be an ongoing problem throughout the clinician's career, as will be addressed in Chapter 4, it is important to note that it sometimes begins during the training years. For those experiencing this problem, a course of personal psychotherapy may be helpful in regaining proper perspective.

In spite of the potential benefits of personal psychotherapy for the trainee, Norcross and Prochaska (1982) found that more than one-third of those therapists surveyed declined to enter treatment at any point in their lives. Guy et al. (1987) found that 36% of the practicing psychotherapists surveyed failed to pursue personal therapy prior to obtaining their graduate degree, while 45% declined to enter treatment after beginning professional practice.

For students, this decision to forgo personal therapy may have been the result of a wide variety of factors. For example, while initiating personal therapy as a student is likely to be well-received by faculty, supervisors, and peers in programs where such action is regarded as normative and desirable, it may be met with suspicion and doubt by individuals associated with a program where this is not required, expected, or encouraged (Kingsley, 1985). Such action may actually lead to verbalized or unspoken questions in the minds of faculty and peers regarding the emotional stability and professional suitability of the trainee who has decided to enter treatment (Wampler & Strupp, 1976). Obviously, this could act to discourage students from seeking the personal therapy that they desire or need.

In addition to fears concerning others' reactions, some students may delay entering personal therapy because of their own belief that such action confirms their unsuitability for practice. This seems to result from the mythical belief that competent clinicians are exempt from the emotional pains and difficulties typically found among the general public. As will be discussed in Chapter 6, this often hinders therapists from confronting the reality of their own needs and vulnerabilities, leaving them at risk of even greater debilitation and distress. It would be ironic if a therapist-in-training failed to receive the benefits of the very services which he or she hopes to provide to others because of this erroneous view.

Regardless of the actual motivation for seeking psychotherapy, it continues to be a widely held belief that a trainee's personal therapy will enhance his or her ability as a psychotherapist by eliminating blind spots and improving empathy and self-awareness, thereby increasing both the quality of future services and present overall functioning (Ford, 1963; Strupp, 1955; Wampler & Strupp, 1976). As such, it can serve an important role in the transition from student to practicing professional. Due to the lack of conclusive data, it cannot be said that personal psychotherapy will result in a higher calibre of service or quality of life for every trainee. However, its potential value warrants serious consideration by all students training to become psychotherapists (Greenberg & Staller, 1981).

Choosing a Theoretical Orientation

Another major aspect of the transition from student to practicing professional is the selection and mastery of a particular theoretical orientation to guide and inform one's view of psychopathology and treatment. This usually represents a familiarity with and a commitment to a certain set of presuppositions regarding human nature and behavior. Specific views on issues such as free will versus determinism, nature versus nurture, the importance of childhood experiences versus later experiences, the uniqueness of each individual versus the universality of human behavior, determining whether motivations are based on physiological needs or higher aspirations, and optimism versus pessimism regarding human nature have been systematized into identifiable, comprehensive theories of personality (Schultz, 1981). Individuals such as Freud, Jung, Adler, Horney, Fromm, Sullivan, Allport, Erickson, Rogers, Maslow, Skinner, Bandura, as well as numerous others, have formulated rather complex theories concerning personality development and the etiology of psychopathology. Out of these theories have emerged uniquely different perspectives on treatment techniques and goals. While typically familiar with several of these views, the emerging psychotherapist usually identifies with one or two particular perspectives, adopting the associated treatment techniques and goals of his or her "favorite." Even for those resisting this decision, or opting to view themselves as "eclectic," there may be a strong tendency to utilize a particular set of techniques for most of the therapy conducted during a career as a psychotherapist. The choice of which personality theory to adopt and which corresponding therapeutic approach to utilize is the result of a very complex process involving many factors and influences. These include factors related to training as well as the individual personality of the psychotherapist. The resolution of this decision process is an important rite of passage in the transition to practicing professional.

How is the choice of theoretical orientation made? On what basis are particular techniques and personality theories chosen by therapists-in-training? Steiner (1978) identified several factors that were important in determining how a theoretical orientation was selected. The most important factor cited by the psychotherapists surveyed was the influence of their own personal psychotherapist and his or her particular theoretical orientation. The second most influential factor was course work and readings in graduate and postgraduate training, followed closely by the influence of the theoretical orientations of instructors in graduate and postgraduate training. The theoretical orientation of superiors and colleagues in clinical settings were noted to be the next most important influence. Finally, the influence of one's assigned clinical supervisor was ranked as least important.

In a related study, Norcross and Prochaska (1983a) reported that psychotherapists do not tend to select a theoretical orientation as a result of inexplicable or accidental circumstances, as is sometimes suspected. On the contrary, this choice appears to be the result of personal, deliberate preferences predicated on clinical experience, personal values and philosophy, graduate and postgraduate training, life experiences, internship experience, and its perceived ability to facilitate self-understanding, in descending order of importance. However, as Halgin (1985) points out, it is interesting to note that many of these factors are often accidentally determined or influenced, thereby making the choice of orientation largely the result of a conscious choice influenced by random events.

It is widely believed that the most influential factors in the selection of a theoretical orientation are the personality dynamics and characteristics of the particular therapist-in-training. As expressed by Barron, "for the psychotherapist, his (or her) methods and techniques are inseparable from his (or her) qualities as a person. Undoubtedly, this is why we find many parochialisms—a selection of doctrines, conceptualizations, and methods of operation that are congruent with the personality of the therapist" (Barron, 1978, p. 310). Szalita (1985) agrees with this opinion, stating "theoretical preferences and styles are very much influenced by the personalities and backgrounds of the practitioners. Every analyst has some idiosyncratic attitude toward the theoretical assumptions which guide him (or her) in practice" (p. 137). Barron suggests that these attitudes are the result of personal perspectives, philosophical presuppositions, worldviews, and values. These factors join together to make one particular theoretical orientation more attractive than another, creating a goodness of fit between the personality of the therapist and the system of thought.

Researchers have attempted to identify those personality factors associated with particular theoretical orientations. When comparing those who identified themselves as psychodynamic with behaviorists, eclectics, and proponents of Rational Emotive Therapy (RET), Walton (1978) found that psychodynamic therapists tended to see themselves as being the most complex, serious, and intuitive. Behaviorists tended to be rather cognitive and low in intuition. The RET therapists perceived themselves to be more humorous and simple than the other groups. They scored high on a rationality factor and low on complexity. Finally, eclectics tended to be low on the rationality factor but moderate on the intuition and complexity factors. It appears that there are differences in how psychotherapists view their own personality makeup which are related to the choice of theoretical orientation. Although this does not establish causality, it is interesting to contemplate the meaning of such relationships. For example, does the more ruminative, introspective personality of some therapists-in-training draw them toward a psychodynamic orientation rather than another more parsimonious viewpoint? Does a tendency to be reductionistic draw others toward a behavioral or cognitive orientation?

Despite finding evidence of a "core" personality found in therapists of various theoretical orientations, Tremblay, Herron, and Schultz (1986) also found personality differences among therapists of several theoretical perspectives. For example, humanistic psychotherapists tended to be more interpersonally flexible, sensitive to their own feelings, prone toward intimate personal relationships, inner-directed, affirming of self-actualizing values, and likely to express feelings in action. Behavioral therapists tended to be more rigid, externally directed, and emotionally overcontrolled. Finally, psychodynamic therapists evidenced a tendency to be outer-directed, emotionally restrained, flexible, and primarily goal-oriented.

Jasnow (1978) speculates that the choice of theoretical orientation is the result of personality characteristics related to the distinction between the psychotherapist as scientist or artist. He suggests that those who consider themselves to be scientists are drawn to theories incorporating the classic model of the physical sciences, such as Freudian psychoanalytic and behavioral formulations. He identifies such individuals as outer-directed. On the other hand, Jasnow suggests that those who tend to be more aesthetic and inner-directed are naturally attracted to humanistic, existential, self-actualizing models of psychotherapy. These long-standing perspectives predispose trainees toward a choice of theoretical orientation which best reflects their own worldview.

Although a number of influences on the choice of theoretical orientation have been noted, the actual nature and timing of the process involved in this decision remain unclear. While psychotherapists report that the decision is typically a deliberate and conscious one made during graduate training, internship, or early postgraduate work, some have suggested that the process may be more circuitous and indirect than might be expected. For example, Halgin (1985) notes that some individuals have chosen an orientation prior to entering graduate training. Whether the result of personal therapy, life experience, or the influence of undergraduate professors, these individuals may actually choose to attend a particular program based on their perceived compatibility with the theoretical orientation of the training faculty. This prior affiliation may also direct a student's choices concerning elective courses and training experiences. Thus they may customize their training experience to fit their own theoretical orientation, which was chosen prior to the start of graduate school.

Those who enter training without having decided on a particular viewpoint are likely to experience growing pressure to make this choice as they progress through their academic and internship training (Halgin, 1985). Eventually, their hesitancy or refusal to select a particular approach may be regarded by peers, faculty, and supervisors as immaturity, inexperience, or lack of expertise. In such cases, this may be to the detriment of the therapist-in-training who is attempting to make the transition to practicing professional. Such impressions may hinder job placement and discourage professional referrals. Both Halgin and Schafer (1979) note that this pressure for closure creates a great deal of stress for the therapist, who may feel forced to rigidly proclaim allegiance to one particular perspective while at the same time attacking, distorting, and devaluing the useful contributions of other orientations.

Some individuals attempt to resolve this issue by identifying themselves as eclectic. Though recent studies have reported that a majority of clinicians do label themselves as eclectic (Norcross & Prochaska, 1982), there continues to be considerable confusion regarding the meaning of this label and widespread disrespect concerning its use. For some, it suggests a permanent state of indecision and lack of commitment to any viewpoint (Halgin, 1985). Such individuals are thought to be unable to make up their minds, and therefore they choose to forestall closure by refusing to identify with any particular perspective. For others, eclecticism suggests a pragmatic blending of diverse techniques and treatment approaches in order to bring about the desired "cure." This blending may be broadly comprehensive, concurrent, or sequential. As Halgin describes it, this blending of orientations usually includes psychodynamic, interpersonal, person-centered, and behavioral components incorporated into the treatment approach according to the needs of each respective patient.

Halgin suggests that this pragmatic blending is a logical attempt to recognize that all orientations have a common goal, that of relief from psychic distress and the promotion of more effective living. It also reflects the growing opinion that the various forms of psychotherapy are more alike than dissimilar, having the same basic core of techniques and goals. This pragmatic blending is best accomplished, notes Halgin, when there is a natural interaction between the unique needs of the patient and the particular abilities of the psychotherapist. This allows the psychotherapist to feel comfortable providing clinical service which reflects his or her own individuality and unique perspectives on life, while recognizing the specific needs and viewpoints of each patient.

Regardless of the potential merits of eclectic positions, there continues to be a tendency for psychotherapists to identify with specific, narrowly defined theoretical orientations. In one recent survey of psychologists practicing psychotherapy (Norcross & Prochaska, 1982), while 31% identified themselves as eclectic, 30% labeled themselves as psychodynamic, 14% as behavioral, 6% as cognitive, 4% as family systems, 3% as Rogerian, 2% as Sullivanian or interpersonal, 2% as humanistic, 2% as existential, and 6% as "other." Furthermore, not only do most psychotherapists tend to identify with a particular theoretical orientation, but they are very satisfied with their orientations and find them to be essential in their work with patients. In this particular study, nearly 90% indicated that they were satisfied with the adequacy and efficacy of their theoretical orientation. In a later study (Norcross & Prochaska, 1983a), psychotherapists reported that, out of 18 different clinical variables, their personal theoretical orientation was the most important single influence on their clinical practice.

In view of the repeated research evidence that there is little or no differential effectiveness among various theoretical orientations (Stiles, Shapiro, & Elliot, 1986), one is left wondering about the meaning of the continuing controversy among the different schools of thought. Perhaps it is the relationship that exists between the personality of the psychotherapist and the choice of orientation which empowers the ongoing debate among practitioners. When one has chosen a particular perspective based on the goodness of fit with one's own personality dynamics, life experience, and the viewpoints of meaningful others, there is likely to be a large investment in this choice. This may lead to a tendency to regard other viewpoints as foreign, erroneous, and threatening. As Kohut (1985) suggests, it may be that there is a great deal of self-esteem and self-definition reflected in the almost universal need among clinicians to defend one's personal theoretical orientation ardently against the questions, challenges, and criticisms of both patients and colleagues.

Once again it becomes apparent that the practice of psychotherapy is more than an occupation; it is a lifestyle. This is particularly true concerning one's theoretical orientation. Rather than simply being a loose collection of techniques and opinions, one's theoretical orientation becomes a worldview which colors one's perceptions and perspective, providing a framework for organizing data and life experience both in and out of the consulting office (Shafer, 1979). As such, the choice of theoretical orientation is a profoundly important decision. Not only does one's personality shape this choice, but the selection of an orientation is likely to shape one's personality as well. There is a dynamic interplay between the two which, on an ongoing basis, results in an interaction affecting both personal and professional functioning. It becomes a way of thinking, interpreting, and understanding events, emotions, and behaviors in both oneself and others. It impacts the therapist's very personality by influencing his or her inner experience. As such, the selection of a theoretical orientation is a very important aspect of the transition to practicing professional. Its significance for shaping the life experience of the practicing psychotherapist must not be underestimated.

Although there is currently no data on the topic, it is interesting to speculate whether or not the choice of theoretical orientation undergoes significant changes during the course of a psychotherapist's career. Given the influence of the therapist's personality and life experience on the selection process, variables which are in constant flux, one would anticipate that the therapist's viewpoint regarding the etiology and resolution of psychopathology is likely to change over time as well. The nature and direction of this evolution remains unclear. One might speculate that perhaps psychotherapists become more similar in techniques and viewpoints over the course of a career in psychotherapy as a result of their recognition of the highly similar goals and techniques shared in common among most theoretical orientations. Yet such convergence may be balanced by the emergence of the unique perspective and style of each psychotherapist which reflects the special individuality of the practitioner. At any rate, it seems likely that the choice and use of a particular theoretical orientation undergoes significant changes over a period of years in clinical practice.

While much remains to be learned regarding the process of adopting a theoretical orientation in the practice of psychotherapy, it is clear that this decision has a significant impact on the life of the psychotherapist. It is a very important factor in the transition from trainee to practicing professional, and it influences the individual's understanding of interpersonal functioning and behavior in virtually all of his or her interactions with others. More importantly, it may well shape one's experience of one's self.

Selecting a Specialization

During the academic and experiential aspects of graduate training in psychotherapy, the trainee may be exposed to a wide variety of theoretical orientations, treatment techniques, and theories concerning the etiology and cure of various forms of psychopathology. Students are also typically assigned a wide array of patients during clerkships, practicum training, fieldwork, and internships. These patients often represent various diagnostic categories, age groups, socioeconomic levels, nationalities, and races. The goal of these training opportunities is to provide the widest possible exposure to the vast spectrum of human experience and behavior in an attempt to equip the future psychotherapist for the diverse challenges of a career in psychotherapy.

While students typically enjoy the opportunity to sample and experience a variety of problems, disorders, and perspectives, they may have an underlying sense of discomfort due to the realization that they will likely emerge from training with a little knowledge about many things, but no particular expertise or specialty in any specific area of practice. Thus one important aspect of the transition from student to practicing professional involves narrowing the range of emphasis to provide more specialized training and experience in more strictly defined areas of expertise. During this process, the emerging clinician begins to select the particular populations with whom he or she feels most comfortable and competent. For example, individuals may decide to specialize in one particular age group, sex, diagnostic problem, or particular form of treatment.

This tendency to specialize is influenced by many variables. Perhaps most obvious is the impact of the particular personality of the therapist. Personal dynamics, life experience, philosophical worldview, and values will likely determine the type of patient with whom the psychotherapist will feel most comfortable.

While therapists are often required to work with a rather wide spectrum of individuals, it is natural to feel most comfortable with those who share similar perspectives on life. It may be that these clients will be experienced as among the most enjoyable and rewarding, perhaps a mutually experienced sense of a compatibility which reduces attrition and leads to a longer, more successful term of treatment. If this is indeed the case, it may motivate the therapist to seek out referral sources who will send similar types of individuals who best fit their own personality. It is also likely that satisfied patients will refer their friends, many of whom share similar perspectives and experiences.

Another obvious factor involved is the nature of the academic and fieldwork experience obtained during graduate training. While these experiences may have been the result of deliberate choices made by the student, such as in the case of the trainee who selects a training program with a particular specialty of interest, in other cases these experiences may be the result of serendipitous events or happenstance. For example, a chance assignment to an admired academic advisor or clinical supervisor with a particular specialty may indeed have a significant impact on the trainee's choice of specialty during later years. In addition, the actual experience received during training in a given specialty will also govern those aspects of practice with which the therapist will feel most competent following graduation. Thus those who received the majority of their fieldwork experience working with depressed female adults under the supervision of a cognitive behaviorist and found this to be enjoyable and compatible with their own personality, may be more likely to specialize in this particular population following graduation, in contrast to working with, say, child schizophrenics.

A final obvious factor is the availability of certain populations for treatment and the amount of freedom permitted the therapist in choosing who to accept into therapy. Regardless of the personal preferences of the novice clinician, the nature of the first source of employment will largely govern the type of clients seen in treatment. While predetermined preferences and selected specialties may influence the choice of employment, financial constraints and the harsh realities of a competitive job market force many to begin jobs which may not provide the luxury of specializing in a given treatment population. However, even in the most inflexible situations, there is likely to be a natural selection process at work which influences the assignment of cases and the success of treatment relationships. Over a period of time, growing seniority and reputation for success with particular types of patients and treatments will usually allow most clinicians a certain amount of freedom in narrowing their focus toward a chosen specialty area. Obviously, those in independent clinical practice eventually have the greatest amount of freedom to determine who they will work with and who will be referred to someone else.

This pervasive tendency to favor certain types of patients, as determined by age, sex, race, diagnosis, and treatment goals, begins during the final phases of training and continues on during the transition from student to practicing psychotherapist. It is another important aspect of assuming the role of an independent professional.

Obtaining Professional Credentials

Most states regulate the practice of psychotherapy in order to protect the safety and well-being of the general public (Herbsleb et al., 1985; Perlman, 1985). Until the psychotherapist has obtained the necessary license or certification, he or she must practice psychotherapy under the direct supervision of another licensed professional. While some states may make exceptions for psychotherapists functioning in certain job settings such as universities or state operated facilities, nearly all states require direct supervision for psychotherapists wishing to offer services by means of a private, independent practice. Thus another important rite of passage from trainee to practicing professional involves obtaining official recognition and certification of clinical competency by qualifying for state sponsored licensure or registration. Until this has been obtained, the clinician is likely to be viewed as a trainee and novice, regardless of his or her particular level of expertise. Whether this involves obtaining a license to practice medicine, followed by board certification to practice psychiatry, or obtaining a license to practice psychology, social work, or various forms of counseling, this certification represents an endorsement by state appointed colleagues and peers that one has achieved an acceptable level of competency and expertise making it permissible to practice psychotherapy without direct supervision.

To qualify for licensure or certification, the candidate must provide sufficient evidence of having successfully completed an acceptable advanced degree program involving the type and amount of course work required by a given jurisdiction. This may be followed by a written and/or oral examination designed to further assess competency, clinical knowledge and skill, maturity, and judgment. While questions remain regarding the effectiveness and legality of such procedures, as noted by Herbsleb et al. (1985), the importance of this certification for governing the practice of psychotherapy is beyond serious debate in most states.

Obtaining official endorsement of one's competency as a therapist and the community recognition that this provides is an important factor in shaping the self-definition and self-esteem of the practicing psychotherapist. It provides a certain amount of evidence of expertise that may help comfort the therapist's secret fears regarding continued feelings of inexperience and incompetency following the completion of graduate training. It symbolizes further affirmation of the profession's trust and endorsement of the clinician's ability to provide helpful service to the general public.

A similar process is at work in the widely experienced need to affiliate with professional organizations and guilds. While membership in such organizations as the National Association of Social Workers, American Psychological Association, or American Psychiatric Association does not imply official endorsement of clinical competency, it does reflect a recognition of the adequacy of the candidate's training and experience. Furthermore, such memberships provide the new therapist with a sense of professional identity and definition as a psychotherapist and a member of a particular discipline within the practice of psychotherapy.

Suited versus Unsuited

Among those who are attracted to the practice of psychotherapy are those who are not well-suited for such an endeavor. Some of these individuals are screened out by admissions committees when they apply to training programs. Others are accepted into training, only to be dismissed at a later point due to their failure to meet acceptable academic or clinical standards as determined by faculty or fieldwork supervisors. However effective these measures may be, they are not the final points of evaluation regarding suitability for the role of psychotherapist. This process is continued at various points during the transition from trainee to practicing professional.

For those unsuitable for clinical practice, the factors involved in this transition process may be difficult ones. For example, they may find that those issues which prompted them to undergo personal psychotherapy remain largely unresolved after months, or even years, of treatment. In such cases, if the problems are serious enough, the personal therapist may attempt to dissuade the candidate from pursuing a career as a psychotherapist. While there is obviously no enforcement behind such recommendations, the opinions of the individual's personal therapist may have a great deal of impact on his or her own views regarding competency and readiness for such a career. Since the personal therapist may serve as a role model and esteemed colleague, in addition to various other capacities and transference roles, strongly expressed concerns may at times be enough to convince an unsuitable candidate to pursue other career options.

Continued confusion regarding the choice of theoretical orientation and specialty following graduation may help to convince some that they are not ultimately suited for the practice of psychotherapy due to their inability to find their own niche and unique area of contribution. While this is not likely to cause the individual to drop out of clinical practice, it may compound already present doubts concerning his or her competency and ability to provide adequate patient care.

These doubts may be further strengthened if the individual has difficulty in finding employment. The screening aspects of the employment process provide additional safeguards for prohibiting some from actually beginning a career as a psychotherapist. Although they may have achieved the necessary academic credits to graduate, and have performed at an acceptable level at their fieldwork assignments, they may not have sufficient expertise to begin functioning in the role of an autonomous professional. As a result, they may not be able to find a job due to perceived lack of experience or unsuitability based on interview impressions. Furthermore, those recently graduated therapists who are hired into clinical positions in hospitals, universities, counseling centers, and clinics may be initially scrutinized by colleagues who recognize that a diploma does not certify competency. As a result, those believed to be unsuitable for practice may not be hired at all, or they may be dismissed following a probationary period of employment. While some recent graduates may go directly into private practice, avoiding this screening process altogether, most do not (Norcross et al., 1985; Tryon, 1983b). Although there is no available data on this subject, it can be assumed that some of those unsuitable for the role of psychotherapist are screened out of the profession by employers.

A further point of evaluation regarding suitability for practice involves certification by the state government regulatory boards. The purpose of the credential reviews, written exams, and oral interviews are to assess clinical competence and suitability for the role of psychotherapist. While there is continued controversy regarding the effectiveness of such procedures (Herbsleb, et. al, 1985), it seems reasonable to assume that some unsuitable candidates are screened out of the profession at this point. For example, they may lack the required type and number of academic course credits or hours of appropriate clinical experience. Furthermore, they may not possess the minimum amount of factual knowledge, as assessed by a written exam. Finally, an oral interview may reveal that they lack the necessary personal maturity, stability, judgment, and expertise to be granted a license to practice independently. For most psychotherapists, this represents the final major hurdle to be crossed during the transition from trainee to practicing clinician. From this point onward, the therapist is able to function in an autonomous fashion, with all the rewards, accountability, and responsibility associated with the role of practicing psychotherapist.

It is naive to assume that only those unsuitable for the practice of psychotherapy are screened out during this transition period. It should be recognized that the ambiguities involved in the screening aspects may occasionally hinder or prevent suitable candidates from entering the profession. In particular, increasing competition for jobs, and the related movement to restrict licensure or certification to fewer individuals by increasing the difficulty of the necessary requirements, may discourage some from eventually becoming psychotherapists. For example, it may be that some candidates possess excellent therapeutic skills, and yet find it difficult to obtain employment or pass a licensure exam. While such cases are likely to be few in number, they are nonetheless regrettable. However, most who are well-suited for the role of psychotherapist will indeed pass through this time of transition with its many hurdles, and go on to practice psychotherapy.

Personal Adjustments

As mentioned earlier, this period of transition entails a reorganization of personal expectations and self-perceptions. No longer is it acceptable to plead ignorance when confronted by the needs of patients or expectations of colleagues. Now there is pressure to possess and demonstrate a level of competence and expertise significantly greater than that of a student. According to Looney et al. (1980), psychotherapists entering into this period of transition are in Levinson's (1978) "settling down" phase, which is characterized by two tasks: (1) establishing one's niche in society and (2) working at advancement and mastery. These tasks are difficult to accomplish, and they are often associated with a significant degree of stress.

Looney et al. note that psychiatrists who had recently completed their residency reported that they experienced a significant amount of distress during this period of transition to practicing professional. For example, 73% experienced moderate to incapacitating anxiety, while 58% experienced depression to a similar degree. In addition, 66% reported experiencing stress regarding the board examinations, 47% cited difficulties with patients, 45% reported stress in marriage, 40% mentioned stress associated with a change in friends, and 39% reported stress about moving. Finally, 28% reported sexual problems, 26% mentioned concerns about health, 24% cited significant sleep disturbances, 23% reported major weight changes, 15% experienced significant health problems, and 14% were in the midst of separation or divorce during this time.

As Farber (1983a) points out, the stress and problems associated with this transition period eventually begin to subside. A number of factors have been reported as being helpful in resolving the distress associated with becoming a practicing psychotherapist. Looney et al. found that these factors included, in descending order of significance, the emotional support of a spouse or loved one, play and recreation, ad hoc consultation with colleagues, relationships with professional peers, vacation or time off, reading, creative activities, hobbies, and exercise. Farber also notes that individuals going through this metamorphosis find strength, support, and encouragement through experiencing overall feelings of personal growth, maturity, and confidence. Finally, Marmor (1953) reiterates the benefits of personal psychotherapy and ongoing supervision in resolving the difficulties associated with assuming the role of psychotherapist.

The many rewards associated with this period of transition make the difficulties encountered worthwhile. At last the trainee fully assumes the role of the practicing professional, providing psychotherapy to patients or clients, and functioning in the role for which he or she has trained for several years. There may be periods of disbelief or wonderment, as the individuals adjusts to the reality that the goal has been obtained, and the journey completed. This brings feelings of relief, anticipation, pride of accomplishment, and increased sense of personal and professional worth. While the individual secretly promises himself or herself "never again," there is the underlying sense that further training, learning, and personal growth lie ahead. At the same time that this transition period marks an ending, it also serves as a beginning: a long career as a psychotherapist now awaits the practitioner.

DISCUSSION

The journey leading to becoming a psychotherapist is a long and arduous one, beginning with the decision to apply for graduate school, continuing through academic and fieldwork training, and culminating in receiving professional certification or licensure. Since research suggests that clinical experience increases overall effectiveness, those entering the process already well-suited for the role of psychotherapist likely emerge even more knowledgeable, skilled, and competent than was the case at the time of admission (Greenberg & Staller, 1981). In addition, those previously unsuited for the practice of psychotherapy may experience sufficient personal growth and change during training to eventually render them more appropriate for the role of therapist. The training process, along with the ongoing screening and evaluation of the suitability of trainees for psychotherapeutic practice, hopefully produces graduates who are now ready to begin a long, successful, satisfying career as psychotherapists.

The Maturing Psychotherapist

Bugental (1964) provides an inspiring description of the psychotherapist who has successfully completed graduate training and is ready to enter the profession. Such an individual is characterized by a maturity which entails traits such as humility, selective participation, encounter, evolving conceptuum, and guilt acceptance.

The humility of the maturing psychotherapist results from the growing recognition of his or her limited knowledge concerning patients' lives. Regardless of the level of ability or insight, the mature therapist recognizes that he or she knows only a limited amount about the life, experience, feelings, and thoughts of the client. This humility creates a deep respect for the patient's perspectives, and the usefulness and value of cooperation, openness, communication, and compromise. Although recognizing the importance of his or her own ability and skill in bringing about therapeutic change, the competent therapist is aware that the patient's opinions, insights, and beliefs are an essential aspect of the process leading to a cure. This results in a genuine humility and respect which permits the client to enter freely and fully into the therapeutic task.

A second characteristic of the mature psychotherapist is knowing when and how to participate in the ongoing growth process of the patient. Competent therapists avoid speaking too much or too soon. They know how to promote autonomy, independence, and self-confidence in their clients by resisting the urge to rescue, dominate, and control unnecessarily. On the other hand, they also avoid talking too little, and they resist any tendency to be withholding, aloof, depriving, or punitive. Experienced psychotherapists know when to be appropriately supportive, confrontive, interpretive, and silent. This ability to modulate participation effectively is an important hallmark of the maturing psychotherapist.

Another notable characteristic of the developing therapist is the ability to encounter patients genuinely. In an authentic fashion, the effective psychotherapist is able to experience intimacy and immediacy with patients, avoiding the tendency to be either too withholding or exhibitionistic. He or she is able to enter into the therapeutic relationship with a spontaneity, immediacy, and openness which energizes each encounter, creating an electric atmosphere of anticipation. In addition, such individuals are able to accept responsibility for their own thoughts, opinions, feelings, and behavior in relationship to the patient. They resist the tendency to be defensive, evasive, or abusive. Regardless of theoretical orientation, the ability to genuinely encounter clients brings a clarity and freshness to the therapeutic encounter which facilitates growth and change.

The growing therapist experiences a dynamic, constantly developing conceptualization regarding himself or herself, the world, the nature of psychopathology and treatment, and the development of the personality. In short, such individuals have the ability to learn and change their minds about previously held beliefs and ideas. In fact, they welcome new advances and feel no need to cling defensively to past theories or views. There is an attitude of openmindedness which accompanies an ability to think critically and clearly. The maturing psychotherapist recognizes that this open-ended perspective allows for the integration of new data and experience in an attempt to attain a greater degree of accuracy and truth. This evolving conceptuum likely results in continued growth and improvement in clinical competence and the quality of service provided to patients during a career in psychotherapy.

Finally, Bugental suggests that the maturing psychotherapist learns to accept the limits of his or her competency, recognizing that there will be unfortunate shortcomings in ability, judgment, and expertise which at times result in treatment errors, ineffective service, or even regrettable harm. While avoiding any tendency to be overly self-critical, the developing therapist holds no false illusions regarding personal limits which are often painfully apparent during their career. The lives of patients will serve as repeated reminders that, although psychotherapy can result in significant changes and growth, there are limits to its effectiveness. More than that, as a therapist grows and improves, he or she must accept the reality that patients seen earlier in a career may not have received the same quality of care as those being seen currently. It is a common experience for the trainee or recent graduate to harbor secret regrets about treatment errors made earlier in the training process. A similar feeling may persist throughout a therapist's career, as increasing skills, knowledge, and clinical ability make previous clinical performance appear unacceptable. It is necessary for the psychotherapist to learn to live with past mistakes and previous shortcomings, while encouraged by their subsequent progress.

It is following the completion of training, during the transformation from trainee to practitioner, that the individual acquires a sense of competence and self-confidence. As Ford states (1963), there is an emergent belief in the efficacy of psychotherapy and a recognition of one's own ability to bring relief and assistance to those in psychic distress. Brenner (1982) calls this a "sense of purposefulness" which motivates and energizes the psychotherapist on an ongoing basis during a career in psychotherapy. Such individuals no longer simply *hope* that they can be helpful; instead, they now *believe* and *know* that they are able to provide competent, effective service. It is because of this that the practicing professional can offer a needed sense of hope and optimism to those in despair. There is good reason to believe that relief is on the way.

The Merging of the Personal and Professional Life

The completion of a therapist's formal training phase reflects the union between a sense of calling and a lifestyle, or way of being. No longer does the candidate experience simply the wish to become a psychotherapist or the hope of someday practicing psychotherapy. Instead, there is the growing sense of having become a therapist. However, while the initial goal has been reached, there may also be a sense of standing on the threshold of an exciting, yet somewhat unknown or perilous undertaking.

Assuming the role of psychotherapist shapes the individual's perspective on life. It is a pervasive experience that influences all the interpersonal relationships and experiences of the individual. There is an ongoing interaction between the personality of the psychotherapist and the practice of psychotherapy. As will be seen, the impact of psychotherapeutic practice on the personal life and relationships of the therapist is surprisingly profound. Furthermore, events and experiences in the personal life of the psychotherapist also have a significant effect on the lives of his or her patients and the overall treatment process. It is this reciprocal relationship which will be the primary focus of the remainder of this book.

CHAPTER 3

Isolation in the Practice of Psychotherapy

Freudenberger and Robbins (1979) provide a candid description of the recently graduated psychotherapist who assumes his or her professional role and begins the clinical practice of psychotherapy. Whether this involves establishing an independent practice, or working as a psychotherapist in a clinic, hospital, or counseling center, there is a typical pattern associated with developing a busy schedule of therapy appointments.

BUILDING A PRACTICE

During the initial weeks and months, the therapist may find that much of the time is spent in nonpsychotherapeutic activities such as attending or presenting workshops, contacting referral sources, establishing professional liaisons, reading, organizing the business aspects of the practice, completing necessary paper work, and various other housekeeping chores. In short, the therapist may find it necessary to wait for patients to present themselves for treatment. Regardless of the setting, this tends to take some time, and a caseload of clients often grows rather slowly. Whether individuals are referred to the therapist for treatment by other staff members within a clinic or hospital, or as a result of referrals from people in the community, few beginning psychotherapists are deluged by patients during the first weeks or months of work. Not only is it necessary to wait for client referrals, but some of those who appear for an initial evaluation will not return for further sessions or may quit after only one or two appointments. As a result, the process of building up a stable, full caseload of patients is usually a slow one.

Psychotherapists tend to experience a variety of reactions to this situation. For some, the waiting gives rise to considerable anxiety. This may be due to several reasons. For example, if the individual's income depends on client fees, questions immediately arise as to whether the practice of psychotherapy will indeed provide adequate financial resources to support a comfortable lifestyle, not to mention the need to repay typically large student loans! In a very real way, if clients don't present for treatment, the practitioner will need to find other sources of income. Even for those who are paid by a salary not directly related to collected fees, the waiting may promote feelings of being unneeded and expendable. Fears of dismissal, with the resultant loss of income, can become quite troubling to the new therapist who feels useless while waiting for patient referrals.

There may also be increasing anxiety related to lingering doubts regarding competency and clinical ability. While these are present in most new therapists, they are sometimes compounded by an initial lack of patient referrals. Such a situation may cause the psychotherapist to wonder whether colleagues and other referral sources doubt his or her ability. In addition, the frequent premature terminations which typically occur increase the therapist's self-doubts and insecurities. Client attrition is a difficult thing to accept calmly when one has many appointment openings and few referrals. While an initial lack of referrals and a rather high "drop out" rate may indeed reflect a lack of expertise on the part of the beginning psychotherapist, this is rarely true to the extent feared by the typical clinician during the difficult months encountered while building a solid practice. Since many psychotherapists tend to feel that the size of one's caseload reflects skill and ability (with that, in turn, being directly related to public reputation and status in the local community), a meager list of appointments compounds the new psychotherapist's doubts regarding his or her competency and suitability for professional practice.

While the gradual process of developing a full schedule of appointments causes anxiety in some therapists, others may experience a secret relief. Because of their doubts regarding competency and skill level, the free time resulting from a lack of patients allows them to read and study in an attempt to fortify areas of perceived inexperience or lack of knowledge. Furthermore, extra time is available for building relationships with peers, colleagues, and other professionals in the community. This provides an important source of support for the beginning practitioner. Finally, relief may result from being permitted to avoid dealing with patients and their needs. Those feeling inadequate and inexperienced may welcome the opportunity to postpone the inevitable anxiety which results from facing a wide array of new patients and presenting problems.

Farber (1983a) describes another reaction, that of depression, which may also arise during this time when the therapist realizes that the practice of psychotherapy is far more difficult than was anticipated. It is sobering to learn that highly motivated, intelligent, verbal, and insightful individuals rarely flock to the newly opened office of the psychotherapist, particularly in the case of those starting an independent practice. Instead, the precious few clients who initially present for treatment may be ambivalent, suspicious, unappreciative, resistant, and hostile. Rather than affirming the therapist's competency and expertise, working with such individuals (several of whom may quit prematurely) tends to increase the beginning psychotherapist's doubts and insecurities. As a result, therapists may experience some degree of discouragement in the face of a slowly building practice.

Establishing a Lasting Pattern

In spite of the difficulties and anxieties encountered, most individuals are eventually successful in building up a busy clinical practice. As Freudenberger and Robbins (1979) point out, there is a geometrical progression in the number of referrals received, with satisfied referral sources and clients tending to refer yet more individuals, and so forth. As a result, in a relatively short period of time the practitioner has established a certain status, reputation, and prestige among colleagues and the surrounding community. Appointment slots are filled, a waiting list is begun, and the practicing psychotherapist becomes busier than was ever imagined possible. Although at times he or she may wistfully recall those early months of boredom and lack of referrals, there is an underlying sense of satisfaction at the apparent success. As Freudenberger and Robbins describe, "the hectic pace seems worth it. The financial reward, the status, and the sheer business of it all literally buoys up the therapist's sense of self-esteem" (p. 281).

A pattern of practice has now been established which will typically remain intact during an entire career in psychotherapy. While the employment setting may change, the pace and nature of the individual's psychotherapeutic practice will remain much the same. The resultant lifestyle, with it's various associated benefits and liabilities, will profoundly impact the personal experience of the therapist. The role of psychotherapist is nearly all-encompassing, and its impact on the emotions, thoughts, and behavior of the individual is profound. Even more, it affects relationships with family and friends to a very great extent. Perhaps the most significant factor which impacts the life of the psychotherapist is that of isolation.

Isolation: Number One Hazard

It may be surprising to learn that isolation has been repeatedly identified as one of the greatest sources of stress and displeasure among psychotherapists in professional practice (Bermak, 1977; Deutsch, 1984; Goldberg, 1986; Hellman, Morrison, & Abramowitz, 1986; Kottler, 1986; Tryon, 1983a). In view of the intimacy that is implied by the psychotherapeutic relationship, this may seem paradoxical. In fact, the expectation of experiencing closeness and attachment with patients is sometimes a strong motivator for entering a career in psychotherapy (Wheelis, 1958). However, recent research has left little doubt that psychotherapists, almost without exception, find the practice of psychotherapy to be a very isolating experience. This isolation is due to a variety of factors.

PHYSICAL ISOLATION

Inherent in the practice of psychotherapy is a physical isolation of a magnitude which few anticipate. To begin with, patients are typically seen within the confines of an office. While not always the case, few consultation offices are very large or spacious, whether they are in a privately leased office building or a larger hospital or clinic. Instead, most therapy sessions take place in a rather small but comfortable room. With the possible exception of group therapy, the therapy session, itself, is usually approximately 50 minutes long. During this time there are likely to be no telephone calls, no knocks at the door, nor any other of the usual interruptions of life. Finally, although some therapy sessions are held with couples, families, and groups, most typically involve only one patient and the therapist. In a very real sense, once the session has begun, both individuals are enclosed in a type of cocoon which surrounds them for a specified period of time. Only after the end of the session will either individual emerge to encounter the outside world. As some have joked, only an act of God or nuclear war could interrupt a therapy session in progress.

At first glance, this isolation appears to be attractive. Few situations provide this degree of control over and insulation from the distractions and unpredictable interruptions of everyday life. As Greben (1975) points out, the guarantee of being "left alone" with a patient, protected from outside interference, seems ideal for the task of psychotherapy. The privacy and isolation of the therapy hour seem to create the optimum environment for accomplishing the desired goals of treatment (Kottler, 1986). This temporary insulation from the chaos of family and job-related stresses provides a unique opportunity to pause, reflect, and listen to one's feelings and thoughts. Both the patient and the therapist value the chance to confer about the client's concerns, free from outside distractions and interruptions.

While beneficial to the practice of psychotherapy, this physical isolation can eventually become a source of discomfort for the therapist. Busy clinical practices often require that psychotherapists schedule appointments in rapid succession, omitting breaks or free time. Hour after hour the therapist remains in his or her office, meeting with clients to discuss their issues of concern. This results in a pronounced sense of physical isolation which separates the psychotherapist from the events and interactions of everyday life in several ways.

Isolation from Colleagues

Perhaps the most obvious aspect of the isolation inherent in psychotherapeutic practice is the lack of interaction with peers. As Farber (1983a) notes, during internship and fieldwork training the student enjoyed many opportunities for staff interaction and discussion with colleagues. This occurred in supervision sessions, in-service training meetings, and informally in the hallways between appointments. However, once the new psychotherapist begins working, the increased tempo and busy appointment schedule often eliminates these opportunities for visiting and interacting. Adjusting to the seclusion associated with conducting therapy sessions hour after hour can be quite difficult, as the therapist sits alone in an office for much of the day, isolated from colleagues and peers (Marmor, 1953).

For those who work in group practices, hospitals, or clinics, the isolation from colleagues may be interrupted once or twice per day, for committee meetings or in-service workshops. This brings welcomed opportunities to relax, discuss current events, and share personal interests. Unfortunately, concerns regarding productivity and cost accounting render such important times few and far between. There is little chance to consult with peers regarding either professional or personal matters. In some cases, it is even difficult to arrange to meet colleagues for lunch, due to varying appointment schedules. As a result, some individuals may go for several hours (or even days) without having an opportunity to visit with other staff members, creating a profound sense of physical isolation.

For those in private independent practice, the isolation may be even more oppressive. Both Tryon (1983a) and Bermak (1977) found that this was the number one complaint among private practitioners. Once again, busy appointment schedules precluded opportunities to meet colleagues for lunch or dinner. Furthermore, the lack of adequate breaks during the day made even social telephone contact nearly impossible. The very nature of the work prevents others from "dropping by to say hello." When sessions are scheduled back to back, there is no opportunity for interaction, consultation, or even casual conversation with others during the entire course of an often lengthy work day.

Isolation from the Outside World

Due to the secluded and uninterrupted nature of the practice of psychotherapy, in a very real sense the therapist is physically isolated from the outside world and daily events. He or she remains in an artifically lighted, climate controlled environment which is often unaffected by physical changes in the outside surroundings. If the therapist is unfortunate enough to be in an office with no windows, he or she may even be isolated from the passing of time and the changing of the seasons. Some individuals work 10 to 14 hours per day in order to provide a wide variety of available appointment times to suit the work schedules of clients who may work any one of three different eight hour shifts. Therapists with especially large caseloads may begin and end their days in darkness, particularly during the winter months.

Not only is the therapist isolated from the surrounding environment, he or she is largely insulated from daily local, national, and world events. This is true for several reasons. Most obvious is the fact that they are unable to listen to the radio or television during the typical work day. If their schedule does not include breaks, they may go an entire day without hearing news broadcasts. Furthermore, there is usually little time to read the local newspaper during a day full of appointments. The lack of interaction with colleagues and peers inherent in clinical practice furthers this sense of isolation. Finally, emotionally distraught clients who typically pay high fees for their therapy sessions are unlikely sources of information concerning current news events. While other careers may be similar in this regard, relatively few isolate individuals to the extent of that experienced by the psychotherapist.

While at first glance this may not seem like a significant point, consider how isolated the practicing psychotherapist feels during times of world crisis when situations radically change within a matter of hours (e.g., terrorist bombings, riots, military confrontations, etc.). In such cases, the therapist may find himself or herself unwittingly questioning clients for news updates on the world situation. Even significant local or national events, such as assassinations, airplane disasters, and so on, may occur without the therapist's awareness. It is a strange feeling to emerge from a day of back-to-back appointments to learn of some dramatic change in national or world events.

A related aspect of this isolation is the fact that the practicing psychotherapists spend most of their time separated from "normal" people. This notion must obviously be considered with caution in order to avoid disrespectful and distorting stereotypes. Yet, as Chessick (1978) points out, the very nature of the psychotherapist's work results in a general isolation from emotionally "healthy" individuals during the typical work day. Patients presenting for psychotherapy are often in distress, and they are not likely to "be at their best." Instead, they may be tense, anxious, depressed, confused, or distraught. Since practicing therapists are likely to spend most of their day interacting with such individuals, there is a very real way in which they experience an isolation from those less troubled or distressed among the general public. This isolation may give the therapist the sense that everyone in the surrounding community is characterized by the same symptoms, emotions, beliefs, and behaviors as those presenting for treatment.

The serious distorting aspects of this phenomenon are obvious: if a clinician spends an entire workday, week after week, conducting psychotherapy with seriously disturbed child molesters, there can be a tendency to assume that they characterize the general population. Such an outcome makes hiring a babysitter a very difficult experience, indeed! In other words, failing to recognize that the typical caseload of clients is not necessarily representative of the larger society leaves the practicing clinician vulnerable to all sorts of distortions, fears, and false impressions. This type of isolation can leave the psychotherapist wondering whether he or she is the only "normal" person left on the planet.

Isolation from Family and Friends

On a more personal level, the practicing psychotherapist may feel isolated from the lives of family and friends during a workday. The fact that the therapist can rarely be reached directly by telephone makes him or her virtually unavailable except in the most serious of emergencies. Few therapists would welcome a call interrupting a therapy session to learn of a minor accident, illness, or problem (e.g., keys locked in the car, questions from the household plumber, etc.). While the subject of many jokes, it remains true that it is nearly impossible to reach a psychotherapist directly by telephone during the day. As a result, he or she is nearly completely isolated from the daily events and concerns of family and friends. There is little opportunity for a family member or friend to call or stop by to "say hello." It is clear to everyone involved that the practicing psychotherapist is unavailable during the workday except for those with a scheduled psychotherapy appointment.

Environmental Deprivation

Greben (1975) describes the unique isolation which results from spending hour after hour with clients, focusing on emotions and thoughts in a very intense manner. Not only does this isolate the therapist from colleagues, family, friends, and daily events, but it also restricts the wide range of possible human behaviors. As Greben puts it:

> The analyst's task is not simple. It is intellectually and emotionally complex. But, his (her) environment is also constant and hence not sufficiently stimulating. So he suffers from a uniquely different kind of environmental deprivation: that which comes from the repeated exercise of a most complex, and at the same time, limited task. (p. 430)

A common complaint among therapists is that, although each person presents uniquely different perspectives and histories, over years of practice there is a tendency for patients to sound more and more alike, with increasingly similar complaints and stories. More to the point, the therapist begins to function in a similar fashion with all patients, behaving in a highly prescribed and narrowly defined manner. This results in a tedium and boredom that can be very troubling. Few therapists find it possible to escape the sense that human behaviors and experiences are more alike than not, leaving the clinicians with an occasional feeling of "not this again" as they encounter a new patient who expresses very familiar complaints.

The environmental deprivation which results from discussing familiar problems in stereotypical ways can be disabling. There is little opportunity to function in an innovative manner. Basically, the practice of psychotherapy involves listening, talking, and little else. Hour after hour of such highly similar activity can produce a sense of boredom and isolation which can have a significant impact on the inner experience and satisfaction of the psychotherapist.

Physical Inactivity and Fatigue

A related aspect of the physical isolation associated with the practice of psychotherapy is the physical inactivity involved in conducting therapy sessions. As Will (1979) notes, "some therapists meet with one patient after another eight or more hours each day. From such a program there comes simple physical fatigue resulting from the near immobilization in a chair and the imprisonment in a room" (p. 564). Farber (1983a) also notes that practicing psychotherapists spend most of their time sitting in a chair, immobile and inactive. This sedentary aspect of clinical practice combined with the emotional intensity of psychotherapeutic interactions can leave the therapist feeling drained and tired. Bermak (1977) reports that several of the therapists surveyed found this physical inactivity and enforced passivity to be stressful and uncomfortable. Bellack (1981) goes so far as to suggest that the seemingly endless sitting, physical inactivity, and excessive affective and motor control are likely to result in frequent incidents of low back pain, excessive weight gain, hypertension, and coronaries.

While several occupations are also characterized by varying amounts of physical inactivity, few require that the individual stay riveted to a chair for 50 minutes at a time, without the opportunity to stand up, stretch, or walk around. If the therapist fails to appreciate the need for regular, extended breaks to allow for sufficient physical activity, his or her only exercise is likely to be an occasional brief stroll to the water cooler and restroom between appointments. Day after day of such a sedentary pattern creates a physical fatigue which can negatively impact both the professional and personal functioning of the individual.

The Isolation of Confidentiality

There is an old joke wherein God punishes the minister who plays golf on the sabbath by giving him a hole-in-one, the punishment being that he cannot tell anyone what he has accomplished. In some ways, the nature of psychotherapeutic practice is very similar. Due to the strict constraints of patient confidentiality, there is little opportunity to share the details of one's work appropriately with family, friends, or the general public. As a result, the notoriety of certain patients, dramatic treatment results, concerns regarding the adequacy of patient care, and other issues related to clinical practice must remain the secret of the psychotherapist (Goldberg, 1986). While it is permissible to share with others in general terms, it is not possible to disclose the very details that make the work meaningful, exciting, or worrisome. As Storr (1979) points out, in this way the work of the therapist is similar to that of a government spy: there is so much to tell, none of which can actually be disclosed to family and friends.

It is a lonely experience to work hour after hour, for years on end, in an occupation which must remain largely confidential (Freudenberger & Robbins, 1979; Kottler, 1986). There is a profound physical sense of isolation, not to mention the associated emotional isolation, in recognizing that the intense encounters and interactions which characterize the work of the therapist must remain secret. It is difficult to describe to one's family and friends what it means to be a psychotherapist, while limiting the disclosure of information. The sense of mystery which results isolates the psychotherapist from the support of family and friends in ways which will be discussed in more detail in a later chapter.

Other Isolating Aspects of Practice

When not conducting psychotherapy, the therapist is often engaged in equally isolating activities such as report writing, testing and diagnostic assessment, record keeping, account billing and posting, maintaining professional records and process notes, and so on. Remaining within the confines of the consulting office while working in this manner adds to the physical isolation associated with the role of psychotherapist. Even answering telephone messages can leave the therapist feeling cut off from the outside world, alone in the office with little or no opportunity to interact face-to-face with others, with the exception of patients.

Another physically isolating aspect of practice involves the frequent need to wait. Psychotherapists are often in a seemingly passive position. They must wait for referrals to present for treatment. Once this is accomplished, they must then wait for them to appear for their scheduled sessions. Few individuals are as tied to a clock as the psychotherapist, who typically schedules appointments very close together. The need to begin and end on time becomes important for a smoothly running practice. Any deviation from the structure that this provides is unsettling and disruptive to everyone. Thus the need to "wait" for clients to appear, many of whom find it difficult to fit into the therapist's rather rigid regimen and are sometimes late for their appointments, leaves the psychotherapist feeling isolated and alone. Few scenes are as pitiful as that of the therapist who absent-mindedly pages through a magazine while waiting for a missing client, entertaining fantasies about the patient's possible premature termination, acting out, or devaluing of the relationship. This experience of aloneness can be intense, as the therapist feels the need to remain in the office until it is clear that the client is not going to appear. Even after having established this fact, the psychotherapist may have only a few minutes before the next appointment is due to appear, making it necessary for him or her to remain. The isolation associated with waiting becomes a common experience for the therapist.

Summary

It may be surprising for some to confront the physically isolating aspects associated with the practice of psychotherapy. At first the sense of aloneness may come as a welcome relief following the frantic years of graduate school and clinical training. However, as the pace begins to pick up, there is no longer any free time during which to be completely alone. Instead, there is an increasingly busy schedule of appointments and activities which fill each working hour. Yet, the sense of isolation and loneliness often remains, in spite of the many patient encounters and clinical duties. The difference is that it now lingers in a more covert fashion, with few realizing the full impact of this physical isolation on their inner experience. After all, who expects to feel physically isolated when so many hours are spent in the company of others? Yet, the physical isolation associated with the practice of psychotherapy remains, varying in intensity but continuing to affect the practicing clinician at both conscious and unconscious levels.

Although many complain of the impact of this physical isolation on their own functioning and satisfaction, most agree that the emotional or psychic isolation inherent in psychotherapeutic practice is far more serious and problematic. This aspect of professional practice not only affects the therapist, but also has a potentially significant impact on his or her relationships with family and friends.

PSYCHIC ISOLATION

As the psychotherapist shuts the office door to begin a session, he or she also shuts away a portion of himself or herself, setting aside personal concerns, feelings, and preoccupations as much as possible. As Freudenberger and Robbins (1979) describe it:

> By the very nature of analytic (psychotherapeutic) work, the therapist stands alone, separate and autonomous. The normal amount of social give and take that is commonly associated with most work situations is quite limited and often absent. The therapist attends to the "as-if" relationship between himself (herself) and the patient, as well as responding in a limited sense to the "real" relationship. In most other work environments there is some opportunity for sharing and even some acting out without dire consequences. Relatedness for the analyst (therapist) is specifically limited to aiding the therapeutic process. To be sure, there is interpersonal contact, but it is a skewed one. There is intensity but at the same time there are limitations on the extent of mutuality. Under these controlled conditions, analytic work can be exciting and challenging, but also very lonely. (p. 288)

As described, the therapeutic encounter creates a profound sense of emotional isolation in the psychotherapist. The focus of the therapy relationship, by definition, is on the feelings, thoughts, concerns, and behaviors of the client. Patients are encouraged to openly self-disclose while the therapist only minimally self-discloses. As Greben (1975) notes, "two people are engaged in exploring the hidden, most intimate thoughts and feelings of one of them" (p. 429). Although over a course of treatment the therapist will intentionally or inadvertently reveal a bit about his or her values, interests, and views, there will always be a certain reluctance to participate fully in the relationship as a peer. Again, the very definition of the encounter mandates that the personal needs and concerns of the therapist be set aside during the therapy session. This therapeutic "abstinence" impacts the inner experience of the clinician in several ways.

Withholding Personal Information

The most obvious aspect of this abstinence is the typical therapist's tendency to be somewhat withholding concerning data about his or her private life. Although there is a certain amount of variation among psychotherapists related to individual theoretical orientation, most hesitate to take valuable therapy time to share personal information with patients. While some find it acceptable to disclose marital status, political views, religious affiliation, and other factual data, others decline to share more than a minimum of information about themselves. However, regardless of personal style or theoretical orientation, few psychotherapists volunteer such information unless they are specifically asked. Furthermore, it is rare indeed for the therapist to consider it appropriate to share more intimate information such as financial status, social relationships, and family events.

Clients are typically aware of the therapist's desire to withhold personal information. For some, this is a constant source of frustration and disappointment. For others, there is the recognition that this is necessary in order to keep the focus of the encounter on the concerns and needs of the client. For the therapist, there is the realization that he or she is largely unknown to patients whose feelings, thoughts, and behaviors have become very familiar. While the clinician knows a great deal about clients' lives, there is a way in which he or she remains a stranger. This brings with it a certain sense of emotional isolation and aloneness. It is not unusual for the therapist to be aware of a passing fantasy or wish to disclose a recent personal event or experience in detail to a client. Unfortunately, the prohibition of abstinence often means that such personally gratifying storytelling cannot occur during the therapy session.

Therapists report that the need to withhold personal information is one of several major sources of stress associated with the practice of psychotherapy (Hellman et al., 1986). Not only must psychotherapists restrain the natural impulse to self-disclose, but they must quickly determine the most helpful response in answer to clients' often probing questions about their personal life and experiences. Rarely do therapists feel completely free to share whatever comes to mind concerning personal data and information.

Setting Aside Personal Concerns

A related source of psychic isolation is the requirement that the therapist set aside personal needs and concerns for the duration of the therapy hour. In order for the focus to remain on the needs of the client who presents for treatment out of a need to receive some type of help or assistance, it is necessary that the psychotherapist refrain from sharing personal concerns in the hopes of receiving help, assurance, or understanding from the patient. Most would agree that the therapist who gives in to the urge to share information with a client concerning personal marital discord, financial problems, or psychic distress is behaving in a most unprofessional fashion. As Greben (1975) points out, the therapist is not free to share such personal needs with clients. It is necessary that these be set aside; when this cannot be successfully accomplished, it may be necessary to discontinue psychotherapeutic work, at least temporarily.

Out of a desire to provide the opportunity for clients to work through their problems and conflicts, most psychotherapists attempt to lock away their own needs and preoccupations, keeping them outside of the patient's awareness (Chessick, 1978). This furthers the sense of emotional isolation in the therapist who learns to forestall personal concerns for hours on end, as he or she focuses exclusively on the needs of patients. This can result in an intense loneliness in the clinician who senses that patients may be only too willing to provide the nurture, support, and love that the therapist needs. Unfortunately, this is unlikely to be in patients' best interests, and the urge to inappropriately self-disclose is typically resisted by the competent therapist.

Deutsch (1984) reports that this aspect of psychic isolation is a significant source of distress inherent in the practice of psychotherapy. She notes that several of the therapists surveyed mentioned that it is especially difficult to keep personal needs from intruding when clients bring up issues that happen to be particularly sensitive areas in the therapist's own life.

Emotional Control

The experience of psychic isolation is furthered by an emotional withholding or control on the part of the therapist. To a certain extent it is necessary that psychotherapists modulate or control their emotional responses to issues and events within the therapy hour. In an attempt to provide a stable, somewhat neutral and safe environment for the client, psychotherapists typically restrain emotional reactivity. While the amount of this restraint may vary according to the preferred theoretical orientation of the therapist, most psychotherapists are aware of the need to monitor and control emotional expression for the benefit of the client and the treatment. For example, most would regard it as inappropriate to express intense emotion when the client brings up a topic that is of great personal importance to the therapist while being of little interest or relevance to the patient. Furthermore, most therapists attempt to partially restrain their emotions when discussing issues about which clients feel quite strongly. For example, there may be little value in expressing the same or greater amount of rage concerning the repeated failings of a client's parents.

This tendency to suppress emotional expression may develop into an "emotional tightness," as the therapist attempts to keep the focus on the patient's feelings and inner experience while minimizing or denying his or her own (Malcolm, 1980). As a result, the clinician may feel increasingly isolated from others, as he or she restrains emotional expression during hour after hour of psychotherapy. Even more serious is the possibility that the therapist will become isolated from his or her own feelings, as a by-product of this constant suppression and restraint (Freudenberger & Robbins, 1979).

Several studies (Bermak, 1977; Deutsch,1984; Hellman et al., 1986) report that psychotherapists find emotional restraint to be quite difficult and stressful. Among the factors mentioned as problematic were the need to keep personal feelings from interfering with work, controlling emotional reactivity and expression, and suppressing feelings thought to be detrimental to treatment.

One-Way Intimacy

As mentioned in Chapter 1, Wheelis (1958) points out that many are drawn to a career in psychotherapy due to a hunger for closeness, intimacy, and meaningful attachment. At the same time, these individuals are often frightened and uncomfortable with self-disclosure and personal vulnerability. As a result, the role of psychotherapist initially seems ideal in that it provides a "safe" intimacy whereby the client takes most of the risks. It is the client who must share the most intimate of secret feelings, thoughts, fantasies, hopes, and fears while the therapist frequently keeps such notions to himself or herself. This "one-way" intimacy allows the psychotherapist to experience intimacy with several individuals without taking personal risks or exposing his or her own vulnerabilities.

While initially such a situation seems ideal for the psychotherapist who finds self-disclosure uncomfortable or even frightening, it eventually becomes clear that this aspect of psychotherapeutic practice actually compounds the isolation and loneliness of the therapist. Rather than satisfying the inner hunger for closeness and attachment, the therapist soon realizes that he or she is unable to fully meet such needs within the therapeutic relationship. If anything, the one-way intimacy merely tantalizes the therapist with a taste of intimacy that is insufficient to satisfy the personal loneliness which comes with the detachment, isolation, and aloofness which may have been characteristic of his or her interpersonal style even prior to beginning a career in psychotherapy. As Greben (1975) notes, although the therapist may be able to reduce this isolation to some extent by means of his or her psychotherapeutic relationships, the "incest barrier" which prevents true mutuality and reciprocated intimacy makes it inappropriate, if not impossible, for this isolation to be fully overcome. As a result, for some psychotherapists the hunger for intimacy and the fear of closeness remains unabated, if not exacerbated.

Maintaining the Interpretive Stance

Regardless of theoretical orientation, the primary role of the psychotherapist is to provide understanding and clarification regarding patients' distress and psychic pain in order to facilitate a cure or relief through the use of a variety of therapeutic techniques. While the therapist enters into the world of the patient, it is in the role of "participant observer." This occurs out of necessity, in recognition of the fact that the contact between therapist and client will be relatively restricted, minimal and brief. Few psychotherapists are able to enter into the life of the client fully. For example, contact is typically limited to one or two hours out of an entire week. Both parties recognize that there will be ways in which the therapist must remain an observer in the life of the patient, participating in a meaningful yet limited fashion. This stance permits the therapist to remain somewhat more objective and removed, providing him or her with a different perspective on the client's life and problems which will hopefully facilitate efforts to be helpful and effective in promoting therapeutic change and bringing relief.

In an attempt to provide clarification and understanding, psychotherapists offer interpretations, observations, and descriptions of what they observe in the behavior, thoughts, and feelings of their clients. These formulations are typically consistent with the therapist's particular theoretical orientation and constitute an organized, coherent perspective on reality which influences how various events and experiences are to be understood. Farber (1983a) suggests that this worldview becomes internalized and forms the basis of the interpretive stance maintained during the therapy hour.

An unfortunate result of functioning in the role of participant observer is the tendency for some therapists to lose the ability to respond in a spontaneous, genuine fashion to the remarks and experiences of their clients. As Freudenberger and Robbins (1979) note, this may lead to a somewhat artificial interaction wherein the psychotherapist ceases to be a real person and merely concentrates on providing certain "functions" for the client. He or she may even grow out of touch with inner needs, feelings, and beliefs as a result of focusing intensely on clarifying those of the patients. This results in an intense emotional isolation for the clinician who at times experiences this interpretive stance as smothering and restictive. It interferes with emotional expressiveness and spontaneity by creating a sense of detachment and distance (Farber, 1985a).

Idealization and Omnipotence

In a seminal article Marmor (1953) vividly describes the emotionally isolating impact of patient idealization and the therapist's growing sense of omnipotence and grandiosity. This hazard is a serious one which further separates the psychotherapist from others.

Farber (1983a) agrees with Marmor concerning the dangers associated with feelings of superiority among practicing psychotherapists. He offers several reasons why problems often result. For example, the therapist is sometimes cast into the position of "savior" by patients who feel that all other alternatives have been exhausted. This frequently leads to a strong tendency to idealize the therapist as the rescuer and "good parent." Receiving constant adoration and idealization can distort the therapist's perceptions concerning his or her ability and importance. This is further compounded by the lack of communication which occurs among psychotherapists. As Marmor points out, it is easy to overestimate the virtue of one's own particular approach and ability in contrast to those of colleagues as a result of apparent therapeutic success and a lack of knowledge about the success rate of other colleagues. The tendency for the general public to idealize, romanticize, or respect the role of psychotherapist may further a growing sense of omnipotence and grandiosity, particularly when this idealization is distorted to the point of attributing near magical omniscient powers to the therapist. Finally, Farber suggests that feelings of omnipotence may arise as a defense against the therapist's underlying anxiety regarding difficulties associated with clinical practice.

In addition to hindering effective treatment in several important ways, feelings of superiority and omnipotence serve to compound the therapist's own sense of emotional isolation (Goldberg, 1986). There may be a tendency to become more secretive and withholding with patients than is either necessary or appropriate in the hopes of disguising true limitations, humanness, and vulnerability (Marmor, 1953). Patient idealization can be experienced as a significant burden by the therapist who feels hesitant to destroy a patient's expectations and idealized beliefs. Maintaining the illusion of omnipotence, or attempting to protect the idealized images which clients frequently need to hold about their therapists, requires a certain amount of self-denial, withholding, and even subterfuge. This can lead to a sense of aloneness which is extremely burdensome if left unresolved.

Devaluation and Attack

While some patients regard the psychotherapist with great respect and admiration, others actively seek to criticize, attack, devalue, and challenge the professional competency, individual personality, values, and beliefs of the therapist. This may occur in a variety of ways, some of which are subtle and others which are painfully apparent and blatant. These reactions serve to further compound the isolation and loneliness of the clinician.

Some clients experience the therapist in much the same manner as they experienced their parents. While this may have been characterized by the aforementioned idealization and respect, it may also have involved a fear of criticism, humiliation, and rejection. In response to feelings such as these, clients may seek to prove the therapist wrong and inadequate in order to feel safer and more competent themselves. These individuals will aggressively disagree with nearly every observation, interpretation, and recommendation of the therapist. They may also covertly sabotage treatment-related progress and success. The therapist is left feeling discouraged, inadequate, and exposed. The devaluation which results causes the therapist to feel very alone in his or her efforts to help the client. In reality, this is an accurate perception since the client has failed to join with the psychotherapist in bringing about a cure, leaving the clinician to labor alone on the patient's behalf.

Feelings of isolation and loneliness may be reinforced by the tendency of some clients to reject the values, beliefs, and perspectives of the therapist due to their own unique points of reference. Rather than being the result of a wish to embarrass and neutralize the therapist, such rejection comes from a sincere disagreement with the views of the therapist. Will (1979) says it well when he states:

> Our feelings of isolation and loneliness may be reinforced by the challenges made by our patients to some of our beliefs and values. We say that the human relationship is of vital importance to our existence and is never neutral in its influence, but it is an agent of good as well as evil. We believe this and seek for its confirmation in our living. We want the patient to say "yes" to our value system, to affirm it, and thus to help do away with whatever ambivalent feelings we may have about it. In spite of all we do, he (she) may say "no." In time, we may quietly perhaps, without recognition of what we do, come to say "no" also. (p. 572)

The feelings engendered by such an experience may further the sense of aloneness of the practicing therapist who is constantly forced to reevaluate his or her worldview and value system.

Goals of Treatment

In order for treatment to occur in a relationship characterized by a healthy warmth, caring, and concern, the therapist must learn to be attentive, respectful, and genuinely interested in the patient's wellbeing and progress. At the same time, therapists must remain detached enough to permit an objective perspective on patient concerns and problems. This requires that the clinician strike a balance between an objective detachment and a caring and concern arising out of personal involvement. As a result, the psychotherapist is caught between the opposing forces of growing intimacy and the need for a certain amount of restraint. The inner conflict that therapists experience is compounded by the very goals of therapy: patient individuation, increasing autonomy and separation, and eventual termination (Will, 1979). In an ongoing way, the practicing therapist participates in time-limited relationships involving a seemingly never ending stream of "hellos" followed by inevitable and sometimes painful "goodbyes." This cycle leaves the therapist experiencing repeated feelings of loss, loneliness, abandonment, and isolation.

From the very start of the therapeutic relationship, it is clear to both parties that it is likely to be time-limited, at least in its present form. Yet, in spite of this knowledge, there is often a natural pull towards intimacy and attachment. For the patient, depending on personal need and the theoretical orientation utilized in the treatment, deep attachment and its eventual resolution may constitute a curative dimension of the therapy experience. Most therapists allow their patients to become attached or dependent for a limited time if this is helpful in reaching long-term objectives. This attachment eventually matures, leaving the client feeling autonomous and individuated from the psychotherapist, and able to "go it alone." While there is often sadness at the time of termination, the client realizes that he or she no longer has the same need for ongoing contact with the therapist as was once the case. The satisfaction and relief associated with the termination of a successful treatment relationship usually outweighs the client's regrets concerning its ending. It is necessary that clients be allowed to proceed towards complete autonomy and self-sufficiency.

For the therapist, the experience is often different. Will (1979) puts it well when he states:

> The life of the therapist is one of arrivals and departures. He (she) is in a sense a prostitute for the lives of others, a sparring partner, but not a contestant in the "main event." He cannot keep emotion out of it all since he is participant as well as observer. . . . The therapist is concerned with problems of attachment, dependency, transferences, tantalizing and frustrating movements of approach and withdrawal, and finally, separations. Repeatedly he becomes attached to other human beings—patients. He finds them dependent on him, struggles with his own dependencies on them, must endure their shifting transfigurations of himself. He must effect farewells. These repeated attachments and losses accent the essential loneliness of our lives. (p. 571)

As a result of these experiences, therapists may at times be ambivalent concerning a client's movement towards individuation and separation. Therapists do become attached to the individuals with whom they work. Appropriate or not, they often develop a deep sense of caring, concern, and connection with certain patients. The repeated experience of saying goodbye to such individuals (when it is in their best interest, regardless of the therapist's personal needs) can be a difficult experience which compounds the psychic isolation of the psychotherapist. It may be that psychotherapists learn to resist attachment to a certain degree in order to protect themselves from the hurt and pain associated with the client's eventual departure. Therapists recognize that the attachment which clients form is based, at least in part, on temporarily felt needs which will hopefully be resolved during the course of treatment. They are also typically aware that their own needs for intimacy and attachment should be met outside of the therapeutic encounter. Thus goals of patient individuation, separation, autonomy, and termination must take precedence over the wish or need of the therapist to prolong such attachments. Yet, while certainly desirable, this is at times difficult for some therapists to accomplish. The feeling of isolation which results from the reoccurring pattern of attachments followed by terminations is likely to be intense at times, particularly for the therapist who lacks a sufficient number of intimate relationships outside of work (Chessick, 1978).

Both Bermak (1977) and Deutsch (1984) found that psychotherapists experience patient terminations as stressful and sad, especially when they occur after a treatment relationship of several years. In addition, several spoke of the sense of abandonment that is experienced when a client terminates treatment "prematurely," that is, before the psychotherapist has had the chance "to disengage" adequately from the relationship. Such experiences can be very wrenching for the therapist who is caught off guard by such an abrupt departure.

Saying goodbye is typically a difficult human experience. The repeated goodbyes associated with the practice of psychotherapy increase the loneliness and isolation of the therapist who recognizes that the intimacy in which he or she has participated has an illusory quality which at times seems inseparable from the real components of the relationship. Regardless of the feelings which may exist between the therapist and patient, however, eventually the relationship typically comes to an end.

Professional Competition

In view of the ever increasing number of practicing psychotherapists, along with continuing reductions in third-party reimbursement payments for psychotherapy, there is a growing amount of competition for patient referrals. This increases the need for the practicing clinician to appear competent, capable, mature, and well-balanced in order to gain the respect and professional status necessary to guarantee a stream of ongoing referrals. As a result, psychotherapists may tend to become more secretive about physcial or mental impairment, treatment failures, and personal limitations (Guy & Souder, in press). This increases the sense of isolation and loneliness of the therapist who is hesitant to self-disclose with anyone due to the fear of jeopardizing future referrals and professional status.

In addition to economic concerns, there is sometimes a desire to gain a high level of prominence and prestige among colleagues by presenting a public persona of professional success and infallibility. This precludes any meaningful sharing of personal needs, problems, and concerns. Instead, there is an investment in maintaining a facade of total well-being which leaves the psychotherapist alone with personal issues and pain. The desire to be highly esteemed by one's colleagues can become a source of personal isolation for the therapist who feels unable or unwilling to admit to being merely human, with many of the same needs and shortcomings found among the general public.

Sadly, it must be admitted that the mythology of therapist infallibility and mental/emotional wholeness and perfection is perpetuated even among therapists who know better. The recurring notion that the competent therapist must be free of personal problems and difficulties causes them to be secretive even with colleagues, out of a fear of censure or criticism. The isolation and loneliness resulting from this process furthers the separation of the therapist from peers and associates.

Public Perceptions

The experience of psychic isolation and loneliness is further compounded by public perceptions concerning the role of psychotherapist and the practice of psychotherapy. It is not only the patient who harbors impressions and opinions regarding the role of the therapist. On the contrary, most individuals have a variety of beliefs, attitudes, and stereotypes concerning those who enter this profession and the nature of psychotherapy in general. These perspectives can further the sense of isolation experienced by the psychotherapist both in and out of the office.

In the minds of some people, psychotherapists are members of a "marginal" profession who make their livelihood by capitalizing on the problems of others, encouraging a self-serving dependency in their patients, and occupying themselves with bizarre thoughts of sex and aggression (Will, 1979). They are regarded as bearers of bad news, someone to consult as a last resort, and perhaps a person with near extrasensory powers who can see through the defenses of others against their will (Guy & Liaboe, 1986a). They seem to sell friendship and caring in a manner not unlike that of a prostitute, providing concern and assistance in exchange for an exorbitant fee. Such a view of psychotherapists characterizes them as wierd at best and evil at worst.

Individuals who regard therapists in this manner may find it difficult to approach them in friendship. They are also likely to be uncomfortable interacting informally with therapists in social situations. Suspicion and fear may even cause them to avoid both conversation and eye contact with therapists at parties or gatherings. On discovering the occupation of a practicing clinician, such individuals are likely either to terminate the conversation or become guarded and somewhat hostile.

Reactions such as these further the sense of emotional isolation and loneliness of the therapist who finds it difficult to make contact with individuals who regard his or her profession in such a negative manner. On sensing this suspicion and hostility, the therapist may find it difficult to relax in a genuine and spontaneous manner. There is a natural tendency to recoil from such animosity, thereby deepening the clinician's sense of separation and loneliness.

There is another reaction to the role of psychotherapist which increases isolation and loneliness. This is the tendency of some individuals to idealize and admire the therapist unrealistically. In such cases the clinician is regarded as a type of saint who silently carries the burdens of the world's psychic pain on his or her shoulders. The therapist is assumed to have no personal problems, shortcomings, or worries. Instead, such individuals view them as invulnerable paragons of mental health who solve all of the dilemmas and problems of everyday life with little effort or difficulty. Not only is the role of practicing professional admired and exhalted, but the very person of the therapist is idealized as being special and gifted.

Individuals who tend to value overly the role and person of the psychotherapist increase the sense of isolation which he or she experiences. By seeking advice, offering dreams for interpretation, and sharing symptoms for diagnosis at parties and informal gatherings, these individuals make it very difficult for the therapist to step outside of the professional role in order to interact in a spontaneous and real manner. There is little opportunity for the psychotherapist to feel the freedom to be vulnerable, needy, and basically human in such interactions. As a result, the therapist feels increasingly isolated and separate from those with whom he or she wishes to interact in an atmosphere of mutuality and intimacy.

It is not only internal factors inherent in the practice of psychotherapy which promote loneliness and isolation. As can be seen, the reactions of the general public to the role of the therapist compounds this sense of separation as well. Unrealistically positive or unduly negative public perceptions hinder the psychotherapist from interacting with others in a spontaneous and open manner. The impact of this process on relationships with family and friends, in particular, will be addressed in the next chapter.

THERAPIST REACTIONS TO ISOLATION

There are several ways in which the isolation of the therapist may impact their life and functioning both inside and outside of the office. While these issues will be discussed in more detail in Chapter 4, it is appropriate that some initial observations be made at this point.

Impact on Professional Relationships

The more practiced a therapist becomes in setting aside personal problems, withholding factual data about his or her own private life, suppressing emotions, maintaining one-way intimacy, remaining in an interpretive mode, and keeping somewhat detached and aloof from clients, the greater is their personal sense of isolation and aloneness. This increasing isolation may have varying effects on treatment relationships with clients.

For some therapists there may be a tendency to carry the detachment and restraint too far, beyond that which is necessary and appropriate for successful treatment. This can occur in several ways. For example, Marmor (1953) notes that some therapists create a sense of mystery resulting from a need to create or maintain a sense of superiority and omnipotence over the client. By keeping patients "at arms length," these therapists foster unrealistic expectations and fantasies on the part of clients, gratifying their own personal needs for admiration to the eventual detriment of the therapy relationship. Their resistance to being known arises more out of the wish to hide personal limitations, foibles, and problems in order to maintain subtle grandiosity than in response to the needs of patients. The isolation that results only serves to increase the fantasies of infallibility and superiority, which in turn increases the need for concealment and mystery.

Wheelis (1958) notes that some therapists find it necessary to create more distance than is therapeutically indicated due to their own fears regarding intimacy, vulnerability, and closeness. Thus the therapeutic requirement for maintaining some distance and objectivity provides the opportunity to remain far more hidden than is necessary. In a circular fashion, the better the therapist is at creating personal distance and detachment in the face of intimacy, the more isolated he or she becomes. Such therapists may resist clients' attempts to know them on a more intimate level. They often refuse to answer personal questions, share their own opinions or viewpoints, or become more "real" with clients. By rigidly focusing on "mirroring" patients and directing attention solely to their interests and feelings, they are able to maintain nearly complete anonymity. While this may enhance treatment in some cases, depending on theoretical orientation and the needs of individual patients, it is rarely necessary to the extent that some therapists may carry it due to their own fears of encounter.

A further complication arising from this isolation is the tendency for therapists to exhibit an intense fear of personal emotionality and the expression of personal feelings. Kernberg (1965) notes that some therapists seem to develop a "phobic attitude" regarding experiencing feelings and sharing emotions with patients far beyond that which is required for the successful practice of psychotherapy. It is difficult to determine whether this is the result of considering clients to be more fragile than they truly are, or because of a need to remain detached and aloof from them. What is clear is that some therapists consciously resist sharing feelings which might be quite beneficial to clients and the treatment process. Once again, clients are denied the opportunity to encounter the therapist in a more genuine and intimate fashion, creating an air of artificiality in an otherwise meaningful relationship. Even more worrisome is the observation of Freudenberger and Robbins (1979) who suggest that psychotherapists sometimes become alienated from their own feelings and reactions as a result of the restraint and excessive control associated with the practice of therapy.

Farber (1983a, 1985a, 1985b) notes that the isolation created by maintaining an interpretive stance becomes self-perpetuating and difficult to set aside. As a result, the therapist may respond interpretively in the treatment session at times when it might be far more appropriate to respond to the manifest content of a patient's remarks at a deeper, feeling level. Becoming too psychologically minded in treatment may cause the therapist to overly interpret the feelings, remarks, and behaviors of patients. Not only does this prevent a more "human" response from the therapist, but it furthers the distance between psychotherapist and patient by causing both to intellectualize rather than experience together the meaning of the patient's material. If left unchecked, this can be detrimental to treatment. The therapist becomes a type of vending machine, spewing forth interpretations and observations devoid of genuine feeling and concern. The safety of the interpretive stance can prevent the therapist from risking true intimacy with patients, furthering the isolation of both.

In contrast to those who respond to the smothering effects of isolation by becoming more isolated and withdrawn, some psychotherapists appear to react instead with unrestrained expressions of caring, emotionality, and personal self-disclosures (Freudenberger & Robbins, 1979). Rather than withholding information and restraining the expression of emotion, such individuals freely share all sorts of private thoughts and feelings with clients with little regard for the impact of such behavior on the treatment relationship. In short, these therapists give priority to their own needs to overcome feelings of isolation by sacrificing the appropriate need for clients to be the central focus of the therapy relationship. They cross the "incest barrier" of which Greben (1975) speaks in the hope that clients will satisfy their longings for attachment and intimacy. It is as though the isolation inherent in the practice of psychotherapy drives them to ever increasing attempts to reach out to patients for the solace, caring, and support that they lack. As Greben points out, relying on clients to help overcome the isolation associated with psychotherapeutic practice hinders treatment and sabotages chances for meaningful success.

Freudenberger and Robbins (1979) suggest that some therapists respond to the stifling effects of psychic and physical isolation by resorting to showy "innovative techniques" in an attempt to mask an inner lack of fulfillment and increasing loneliness by drawing public attention to themselves and their work. This may include public presentations and advertising of questionable ethics, as well as exaggerated claims of dramatic success and competence. If such a pattern is not restrained, it may lead to patient exploitation and questionable clinical practice.

Impact on Personal Relationships

The effects of isolation on clinical practice and professional relationships can be very troublesome if left unchecked. However, it is the impact of isolation on the personal life and relationships of the psychotherapist which typically goes unnoticed until the negative effects are serious enough to be apparent to everyone involved.

Perhaps the most serious result of physical and emotional isolation is the psychotherapist's increasing inability to overcome these restraints in his or her own private life. In other words, the very factors associated with the role of psychotherapist which promote a sense of loneliness and separation in professional relationships carry over into personal interactions as well. This is often due to the fact that the practicing psychotherapist finds it difficult to set aside the professional role outside of the office. For example, Farber (1983b) notes that as many as 72% of those therapists surveyed reported that they at least occasionally acted "therapeutically" towards others outside of the office. He notes that some individuals find it very difficult to stop being a therapist when they are in social situations.

One of the aspects of the role of psychotherapist that seems particularly difficult to set aside is the interpretive stance which restricts the therapist to the role of observer, rather than participant, in human interactions. There is a tendency to become overly psychologically minded, approaching all interpersonal interactions therapeutically and interpretively, seeking to "understand" rather than to freely enter into the interaction with true mutuality (Farber, 1985a). In this way, a lack of genuine relatedness resulting from prolonged hours of participation in professional "as if" relationships carries over into personal relationships outside of the office. The therapist finds it increasingly difficult to break out of the therapeutic stance, and as a result, all relationships begin to take on the same "as if" quality (Goldberg, 1986; Guy & Liaboe, 1986a).

The tendency to approach all human interactions with the desire to elucidate underlying motives, understand the meaning of others' feelings and beliefs, and influence their opinions and behaviors locks the therapist into a detached, controlled, and emotionally neutral stance which furthers the sense of isolation and aloneness (Farber, 1985a; Greben, 1975; Henry et al., 1973). This brings an aloofness and rigidity which prevents the individual from entering into interpersonal relationships in a more spontaneous and vulnerable fashion. There is a tendency to mirror others' feelings and thoughts rather than disclosing personal processes in a manner which would promote true intimacy. As a result, the psychotherapist becomes a master at encouraging others to share intimately with him or her, while remaining distant and secretive. Those who are truly adept at this skill are able to conduct themselves in such a way that the other individuals do not actually realize how hidden and invulnerable the therapist remains during conversations which seem mutually intimate but, in truth, are not.

Maintaining an interpretive stance reduces all human interactions and behavior to a series of signs and symptoms (Will, 1979). Everyone falls into the category of "patient," and a subtle feeling of superiority develops in the therapist who sees himself or herself as "expert." This makes it difficult to enter into interpersonal encounters with a sense of mutuality and equality. As Marmor (1953) notes, grandiosity compounds the therapist's tendency to withdraw and isolate himself or herself from others. A belief develops whereby there is little reason to interact with individuals who have failed to master the level of insight and maturity supposedly reached by the therapist.

Associated with this process of withdrawal may be a tendency to become more secretive and withholding. While this can be the result of a wish to protect feelings of superiority, it may be due to other reasons, as well. For example, the most obvious hindrance may be a therapist's life-long discomfort with self-disclosure, a problem which partially motivated the career choice of psychotherapy for some individuals, and which may have become more serious due to his or her mastery of one-way intimacy. In such cases, the therapist becomes even more uncomfortable stepping out from behind the wall of secrecy, even when there is a genuine desire to do so. The risks associated with allowing oneself to be truly known are significant compared to the relative safety and control inherent in the role of psychotherapist.

Even more unsettling is the suggestion that some psychotherapists resist self-disclosure because they simply have nothing to say. That is, they have focused so vigorously on being neutral in the face of the intense needs, concerns, feelings, and attitudes of others that they have lost their own personal identity (Freudenberger & Robbins, 1979). As a result of attempting to be "all things to all people," such individuals have sufficiently neutralized their own sense of self so as to be unable to truly know how they think or feel about a given issue. It has been suggested that these psychotherapists have become so proficient at operating in the interpretive mode that they seem to have lost themselves. Storr (1979) describes it well when he says:

> There comes a point at which a certain kind of therapist may almost disappear as a definable individual. . . . (they become) people who are simply there for others rather than existing in their own right. When psychotherapy is practiced every day and all day, there is a danger of the therapist becoming a non-person; a prostitute parent whose children are not only illegitimate, but more imaginary than real. (p. 182)

Such individuals become unable to self-disclose in a meaningful way, preferring merely to mirror back the perceptions and feelings of others, regardless of the social context.

Public perceptions concerning the role of psychotherapist may further compound this tendency to resist self-disclosure. It is difficult for an "expert" in human behavior to admit to having emotional problems, concerns regarding professional competency, and marital and family conflicts. There may be a fear of jeopardizing future referrals should word get out that he or she has not completely mastered life's many problems. Therapists may fear rejection should they disappoint those who have unrealistically idealized them and the quality of their lives. In addition, there may be a desire to avoid confirming the negative stereotypes of those holding the role of psychotherapist in disrepute. Regardless of which type of public perception is encountered, these factors combine to make it diffcult for the psychotherapist to resist the urge to remain mysterious and unknown in any interpersonal encounter.

The constant need to monitor, suppress, and control emotions and their expression may also carry over into relationships outside of work. Practiced proficiency in such restraint may make it hard to "turn it off," particularly if there is intense "phobic fear" of emotional expression. For such individuals, the free and spontaneous expression of emotions is replaced by a detached, intellectualized excessive control which has an emptiness and blandness associated with it (Farber, 1985a; Henry et al., 1973). They may be aware of how they feel but are fearful or unable to express these emotions. More disturbing is Freudenberger and Robbins's (1979) observation that some psychotherapists have actually lost the ability to be aware of their own emotions. As a result of repeatedly focusing externally on the emotions of others, they have become alienated from their own inner processes.

Finally, the practice of detachment which many therapists develop in order to protect themselves from the repeated cycles of attachment followed by termination and abandonment may impede their ability to develop meaningful relationships with family and friends. This self-protective distance allows therapists to tolerate the loss of clients who eventually become independent of them and leave treatment. In order to minimize the cumulative effects of these terminations, psychotherapists tend to remain somewhat aloof, maintaining a certain degree of invulnerability. It may be that this same tendency is expressed in relationships outside of work for therapists who begin to experience all relationships as transitory and impermanent. In such cases the therapist may be unable to risk the vulnerability necessary for intimate encounter and unrestrained attachment. Rather than entering fully into relationships, he or she may remain detached and uncommitted due to a continuing sense of the transient nature of interpersonal relationships, an unfortunate carryover from time-limited professional relationships. If this feeling of ephemerality is left unchallenged, the individual may become unable to resist preparing for the eventual departure of all individuals in his or her life. Waiting for inevitable abandonment further isolates the therapist from others. Carried to its extreme, this pattern can actually become a self-fulfilling prophecy, as others who sense the detachment and restraint respond by pulling away, enacting the very abandonment feared by the therapist to begin with.

REDUCING ISOLATION

It has been noted that a certain degree of physical and psychic isolation is inherent in the practice of psychotherapy. For example, little can be done to alter the need for uninterrupted therapy sessions, confidentiality, and therapist abstinence. However, this isolation appears to breed further isolation, often greater than that which may be necessary and appropriate for conducting effective psychotherapy. As previously described, this impacts both the professional and personal relationships of the therapist, resulting in a loneliness and separation which can be quite profound. Several steps must be taken to reduce this isolation to its minimum and mollify its negative impact on the life and relationships of the therapist.

Professional Activities and Relationships

In order to reduce the isolation associated with psychotherapeutic practice, it may be necessary to diversify and incorporate other professional activities into the work week. For example, pursuing teaching, supervision, research, writing, or consultation opportunities provides intellectual and emotional stimulation, interpersonal interactions, and a variety of creative endeavors which help to reduce the feelings of isolation and aloneness resulting from long hours spent conducting therapy (Farber, 1983a; Freudenberger & Robbins, 1979; Guy & Liaboe, 1986a). Therapists, by the nature of their training and experience, possess a wide array of skills and expertise which qualify them for positions such as these. Furthermore, the ability to wedge these activities in between therapy appointments allows them to pursue such opportunities, particularly in the case of those in independent clinical practice. Since most of these roles do not require the same degree of restraint and abstinence characteristic of the role of psychotherapist, they help to reduce the isolation and loneliness by allowing a freer interchange and mutuality between the therapist and others. They also get the therapist out of the professional office and into the surrounding community.

In addition to pursuing professional activities related to the practice of psychotherapy, some individuals may find it helpful to develop a second career outside of the mental health field. For example, it may be possible to combine the practice of psychotherapy with part-time work in real estate, insurance, investment management, career counseling, or music. Involvements such as these provide balance and refreshment and can be incorporated into the weekly schedule around therapy appointments, depending on the work setting. A second career in a totally different field is likely to reduce isolation, provide diversity, and allow the psychotherapist to additional pursue interests as well.

In order to combat isolation from other professionals, several researchers have suggested that therapists obtain regular ongoing supervision and consultation from respected colleagues who are able to support, encourage, and direct therapists concerning professional practice (Farber, 1983a; Freudenberger & Robbins, 1979; Marmor, 1953). In some cases, this might best be accomplished through a structured, scheduled, fee-for-service arrangement with a specific colleague. For others, informal and irregular contacts with a variety of individuals might be more appropriate. In either case, the opportunity to interact with other psychotherapists regarding both professional and personal issues is a powerful antidote to the feelings of isolation associated with clinical practice. Unfortunately, few seem to be able or willing to engage in such encounters. For example, in a recent study of psychologists practicing psychotherapy, over 60% of the 153 respondents reported that they do not receive any type of clinical supervision, either formal or informal (Wahl, 1986). These individuals practice in relative isolation, without the support and guidance that could be provided through such contacts.

It has been suggested that the pursuit of additional training, either inside or outside of one's speciality, provides opportunities for dialogue and meaningful contact with other professionals, improving competency and also reducing separation and isolation (Farber & Heifetz, 1981; McCarley, 1975). Periodic continuing education brings new input, stimulation, and interpersonal encounters to the life of the therapist, energizing and enriching him or her. Where opportunities are limited, such as in rural areas, Freudenberger and Robbins (1979) suggest that therapists form local discussion groups to provide case conference seminars, mutual supervision, and informal interchanges. If the psychotherapist practices in complete isolation, with few or no other therapists nearby, these groups could be made up of other human service professionals, such as physicians, lawyers, teachers, and so on. In fact, Farber (1983a) and Marmor (1953) suggest that interdisciplinary contacts such as these are very helpful, regardless of the opportunities for contact with members of one's discipline. It is important for therapists to take steps such as these in order to provide regular contacts with others, thereby combating their sense of aloneness.

Some have found that it is helpful to join local, regional, and national mental health organizations in an attempt to develop a network of contacts with other therapists. Whether this involves organizations within one's own discipline, such as the American Psychiatric Association, or interdisciplinary groups, such as the American Academy of Psychotherapists, such memberships provide opportunities for interaction and support which counter feelings of alienation and isolation.

It may be necessary for the practicing psychotherapist to reconsider whether it is wise to work in a solo independent practice. Some will experience no special problems related to the isolation inherent in such a situation. They do not seem troubled by working alone with patients in a small office throughout an entire day. For others, the lack of contacts with colleagues may become too alienating. In such cases, it may be beneficial to affiliate with a group practice, hospital, clinic, or counseling center. This provides more opportunities for informal interaction and periodic contacts with other professionals. As Freudenberger and Robbins (1979) note, this type of arrangement also permits the sharing of clinical responbilities, making it easier to take extended vacations and sabbaticals.

Personal Life and Relationships

The therapist who is alert to the potential impact of isolation inherent in the practice of psychotherapy on his or her personal life and relationships is better able to minimize its negative effects. Marmor (1953) notes the importance of therapist self-awareness and self-assessment in this regard, and he suggests that the individual must constantly be "on guard" throughout a career in psychotherapy. In addition, it may be beneficial to alert family members and friends to the potential hazards of this isolation, in order to enlist their help in monitoring and correcting increased emotional distance or withdrawal (Guy & Liaboe, 1986a). Giving others permission to confront and expose tendencies towards aloofness, detachment, and isolation could be very helpful in providing external validation for the therapist's ongoing self-assessment. Furthermore, their assistance may be necessary in helping the therapist resist the self-perpetuating effects of isolation.

Personal psychotherapy has been suggested as a further resource for those battling the debilitating effects of isolation on personal relationships (Chessick, 1978; Freudenberger & Robbins, 1979; Marmor, 1953). Its benefits in this regard are self-evident. By providing an opportunity to confront underlying fears of intimacy and attachment, and the possible negative impact resulting from mastering the one-way intimacy inherent in psychotherapeutic practice, one or more courses of personal treatment during a career in therapy could greatly assist the therapist in his or her attempts to develop and enjoy personal relationships with family and friends. Unfortunately, as will be discussed in more detail in Chapters 6 and 7, many practicing psychotherapists seem unable or unwilling to avail themselves of the benefits of the very services which they provide for others (Guy & Liaboe, 1986b). It should also be noted that personal therapy does not, in and of itself, provide mutual, reciprocal intimacy. Instead, it is still one-way intimacy with the therapist now experiencing the role of patient, separated from his or her personal therapist by many of the same factors previously noted. If the practicing psychotherapist is able to be vulnerable only with his or her own personal therapist, there is still likely to be a continuing sense of isolation and aloneness in personal relationships. Personal therapy simply facilitates individual attempts at building meaningful relationships in one's personal life. What is learned and experienced in treatment must still be generalized to outside relationships.

Pursuing hobbies and interests outside of the field of psychotherapy may also reduce feelings of isolation and loneliness by providing opportunities to develop relationships uncontaminated by factors related to the role of psychotherapist (Farber, 1983a). For example, joining a local health club, interest group, social or civic organization, or enrolling in an adult education class at a local community college allows the therapist to step outside the role of mental health professional in order to relate with others as a "normal" person. This can serve as a useful counterbalance to the controlled, circumscribed role of psychotherapist.

Marmor (1953) suggests that it is very helpful to develop friendships with people outside of the profession. This reduces the isolation of those who feel cut off and separated from "normal" people due to the nature of their clinical practice. It gives the therapist a more balanced, well-rounded perspective on human behavior and concerns as well as providing a feeling of connection with others outside of the mental health world. Relationships with individuals who are relatively uninterested or unimpressed with the practice of psychotherapy can serve as an important balance in the life of the therapist. These relationships reduce the therapist's isolation, serving as a reminder that life outside of the consultation office may at times be quite different from life within its four walls.

Extended vacations and sabbaticals not only serve to refresh and replenish the practicing clinician, but they also enable the therapist to participate more fully in the pleasures of life and experience the diversity which it has to offer. This serves as an important corrective for the tendency of some therapists to become mere observers and analyzers of life, eventually losing their ability to experience passion and enthusiasm (Farber, 1985a). As Freudenberger and Robbins (1979) note, some therapists become so preoccupied with work and the "inner world" of the psyche that they end up experiencing less of life's diversity and stimulation than do their patients. Paradoxically, they "live" less and less, while encouraging their patients to experience more of life. Providing time to participate fully in the many recreational activities and opportunities of life reduces the alienation and depletion that some experience as a result of practicing therapy.

Minimizing the potential negative impact of isolation on the personal life and relationships of the psychotherapist is a critically important endeavor. A more detailed analysis of this problem, and suggestions for coping with this and other hazards associated with the practice of psychotherapy, will be provided in Chapter 4.

DISCUSSION

As Bugental (1964) notes, shamans or healers have always been marginal members of society, acknowledged as a necessary "evil" but isolated and shunned, nonetheless. The mixture of fear and respect, abhorrence and intrigue, and attraction and repulsion which many feel towards such individuals leaves them separated from the larger group, unable to fully participate in the normal activities of the majority, while delegated to meeting the needs of the suffering minority. For the most part, the healer works alone, fighting enemies which cannot being seen, utilizing cures and forces which can be experienced only internally. He or she typically lives at the edge of the village, and the isolation is both physical and emotional. The shaman has few friends. The role is lived twenty-four hours a day, throughout an entire lifetime.

In a similar fashion, the practicing psychotherapist experiences an isolation which is both physical and psychic, impacting both professional and personal relationships. Idealized by some and unfairly criticized by others, the psychotherapist fulfills an important but often poorly understood role in our society. The work of the therapist involves both the real and unreal, the seen and unseen. There is a certain bizarreness to it all which isolates the practitioner from the common, everyday world that most people experience. For the therapist, things are never as simple and clear as they may seem to others. There are underlying meanings and motivations for every thought, feeling, and behavior.

Will (1979) describes this phenomenon in the following manner:

> A therapist may experience himself (herself) as a prisoner held in a room filled with the phantasmagoria of his and others' lives. If he works long hours, vacations only by going to conventions, searching for companionship, some learning, and now "points" for continuing education, he may, without recognizing the fact, begin to lead a vicarious existence through the dreams and actualities of those who come to him for help. Dream and "reality" tend often to merge, one into the other. (pp. 571–572)

This isolation and separation from the mainstream of life can create an "as if" existence which traps the psychotherapist, separating him or her from others, leaving the individual locked inside a world of "near" reality.

It is ironic indeed that the practice of psychotherapy should produce greater ability for intimacy on the part of patients while increasing the isolation and loneliness of some therapists. Since the focus of treatment is often on helping the client develop a greater capacity for vulnerability, openness, risk, attachment, and closeness, one is left wondering whether the price need be that of greater isolation and aloneness for the therapist. While a certain amount of isolation seems inevitable, some therapists report that the practice of psychotherapy actually exacerbates a pattern of detachment in their personal life and relationships, negatively impacting all of their interactions. It is important that practicing therapists take active steps to reduce or eliminate the hazards associated with this isolation.

Isolation is only one of several aspects related to the practice of psychotherapy which impact the therapist's personal relationships with family and friends. Chapter 4 will focus on ways in which the work of the psychotherapist influences his or her interpersonal functioning and the quality of these relationships.

CHAPTER 4

The Impact of Psychotherapeutic Practice on Personal Relationships

Most would agree that the interpersonal relationship between the psychotherapist and the patient is both the subject and mode of psychotherapy (Henry et al., 1973). This relationship is often intense, emotionally significant, and important for both individuals. Although a substantial body of literature has emerged regarding the impact of this interaction on the patient, surprisingly little is known about its effect on the therapist (Guy & Liaboe, 1986a). For example, the preponderance of recent research has demonstrated that psychotherapy often has a helpful, positive impact on the life and interpersonal functioning of the patient (Garfield & Bergin, 1978). While not always successful, it usually helps to reduce emotional distress and improve the client's relationship skills. Very little is known, however, about the impact of conducting literally tens of thousands of hours of psychotherapy on the personal life and relationships of the therapist. A number of therapist personality changes have been associated with long-term psychotherapeutic practice. As a result of these influences, it seems reasonable to assume that conducting psychotherapy has a noticeable effect on the therapist's relationships with family and friends.

It has already been established that the work of psychotherapists involves nearly every facet of their being. As OttoWill (1979) notes, "the personality of the therapist will inevitably be involved and exposed in such an undertaking: there is no way whereby one can keep oneself as a person, detached from the therapeutic process, nor should there be" (p. 563). Since their personality is the "tool" used to conduct this clinical work, who a psychotherapist "is" undergoes constant challenge, review, and transformation. One would certainly hope that the resultant changes are largely positive, improving the therapist's satisfaction with life and relationships. Regrettably, as noted in the case of isolation, it may also be that certain changes have the potential to hinder interpersonal functioning in and outside of work. The limited research conducted in this area suggests that there are both positive and negative effects associated with the practice of psychotherapy. These warrant the careful attention of therapists in order to more maximize fully potential benefits while reducing possible hazards.

FAMILY RELATIONSHIPS

It is with family members that most people are able to be themselves truly, where facade and pretense become both inappropriate and unnecessary. This is no less true for practicing psychotherapists. Although there may be a need for considerable restraint and self-control when working with clients, most psychotherapists want to be genuine, spontaneous, and vulnerable with their own family members. They also wish to be loving, considerate, patient, and caring towards their spouse, children, siblings, and parents. In short, most individuals hope that family relationships will be characterized by mutual intimacy, fulfillment, and satisfaction. As a result, therapists who spend countless hours assisting others in their quest for family harmony hope to achieve the same success in their own relationships.

In the best of all worlds, career related activities promote an individual's mental health and social adjustment, enhancing the overall quality of life both in and outside of work. For psychotherapists, one would hope that the hours spent facilitating others in their attempts to initiate and maintain meaningful relationships result in positive benefits for the therapist, as well. At the very least, it is essential that the practice of psychotherapy not have a deleterious effect on the clinician's personal life and interpersonal functioning.

Recent research suggests that psychotherapeutic practice has the potential to have both a positive and a negative impact on family life and relationships. Due to the nature of the role and work of the psychotherapist, it cannot help but effect his or her interpersonal interactions with spouse, children, extended family, and friends in a variety of significant ways. While the impact of psychotherapeutic practice on these relationships may vary with each individual, influenced by such factors as gender and marital status, there is a surprising similarity in its effects.

Relating with Spouse or Significant Other

As with other individuals, most psychotherapists marry (Guy, Stark, & Poelstra, 1987; Wahl, 1986). They experience the same need for intimacy and attachment and the same desire for a lasting, fulfilling marriage relationship. Given the fact that most psychotherapists have received training and experience in marital therapy, and spend much of their professional time attempting to improve the marriages of their patients, it seems reasonable to expect that they will be more successful than most in their own marriages. In fact, several studies have reported that psychotherapeutic practice has a positive impact on a therapist's ability to experience meaningful intimacy with a spouse or significant other.

Positive Consequences for Marital Relationship

Farber (1983b) found that psychotherapists reported experiencing important personal growth as a result of clinical practice. For example, they noted that working with psychotherapy patients caused them to become more psychologically minded, self-aware, and self-assured. Furthermore, increases in assertiveness, self-reliance, introspection, self-reflection, sensitivity, and self-disclosure were reported to be the result of psychotherapeutic practice. Finally, these psychotherapists suggested that clinical practice helped them to become more open, thoughtful, confident, and patient. Burton (1975) notes similar patterns of emotional and intellectual growth resulting from interactions with patients over several years of clinical practice. In a more recently published article, Farber (1985a) suggests that the type of personal growth reported to be associated with the practice of psychotherapy greatly enhances interpersonal relationships, "adding depth, subtlety, nuance, and irony to the understanding and appreciation of others" (p. 174).

Changes such as those noted above are very likely to impact positively the most meaningful interpersonal relationships of psychotherapists. In particular, they should improve the therapist's ability to relate to his or her spouse. In a provocative article by a professional mental health couple (Cray & Cray, 1977), it is suggested that this is indeed the case. They report that psychotherapeutic practice causes the therapist to become more tolerant, accepting, understanding, and patient in relationship to his or her spouse. As a result, he or she is better able to experience meaningful intimacy and fulfillment. Improvement in self-esteem and self-awareness help enrich one's ability to enter into a love relationship with spontaneity, vulnerability, and openness. Put simply, experiencing the growth associated with the practice of psychotherapy makes one a better person, and thereby, a better spouse.

A recent survey of practicing psychotherapists found that over 75% indicated that they believed that therapeutic practice had a positive impact on their marriage (Guy, Stark, & Poelstra, 1987). While this perception may be distorted by self-report bias, it is interesting to note that most of those questioned believed that their work increased the satisfaction that they obtained from their marital relationship.

In view of the positive changes and benefits associated with clinical practice, and their likely helpful impact on the therapist's marriage, it seems reasonable to assume that psychotherapists are more successful in their marital relationships than others. Unfortunately, this does not appear to be the case. Several studies have found that psychotherapists experience marital discord and failure at a rate equal to or greater than that of the general population (Ford, 1963; Looney et al., 1980; Schofield, 1964). For example, in a recent survey, Norcross and Prochaska (1986a, 1986b) found that nearly one-third of the respondents reported that marital problems and divorce were a major source of distress. In another study, Wahl (1986) found that nearly 40% of those therapists surveyed had been divorced at least once.

While disappointing, the fact that psychotherapists experience marital discord and divorce at a rate approaching that of the general population is not completely surprising. Therapists are people with the usual host of everyday problems. Yet it is ironic that the ability to help others with marital problems does not render one less vulnerable to such difficulties in one's own marriage. Furthermore, in view of the reported benefits of clinical practice, it seems reasonable to expect that these should help to compensate for, or overcome, the typical sources of marital discord. Yet this does not appear to be so.

What is more troubling, however, is the suggestion that psychotherapists experience marital discord and failure partially as a result of the impact of psychotherapeutic practice on their interpersonal functioning. In other words, some have claimed that rather than improving the therapist's ability to initiate and maintain a meaningful marital relationship, several factors associated with psychotherapeutic practice actually hinder and sabotage healthy marital adjustment. In view of the seriousness of this assertion, careful consideration of the potentially negative impact of clinical practice as it relates to marital adjustment is warranted.

Negative Consequences for Marital Relationship

As noted in Chapter 3, a number of factors associated with the practice of psychotherapy have been reported to have a negative impact on the life and relationships of the therapist. Some are associated with the isolation inherent in clinical practice. Others are the result of the interaction between the nature of the work and the individual personality of the therapist. While it is unfortunate when these affect social relationships, it is particularly tragic when they negatively impact the marriage of the therapist.

Psychotherapists report that their work is often extremely demanding, emotionally draining, and personally depleting (Burton, 1975; Tryon, 1983a). After spending a long day with emotionally troubled and distressed clients, many therapists feel exhausted and "used up" when they leave the office for home (Farber, 1983b; Kottler, 1986). For some, there may be the wish to turn to their spouse for support, encouragement, nurturance, and understanding. Rather than feeling equipped to enter into a mutually supportive interaction, these individuals experience the need to be unilaterally replenished by their spouse (Bermak, 1977). For others, there may be a desire to be left alone to watch television, read a book, or stare at the wall. There is a strong tendency to withdraw into a cocoon of isolation in order to replenish personal resources (Henry et al., 1973). Regardless of the pattern, few arrive home ready and willing to meet the emotional needs of the spouse (Farber, 1983a).

This pattern can impact the marital relationship in several ways. For example, it may be difficult for therapists to listen to the personal concerns, problems, and needs of their spouse. There can be a profound sense of emotional depletion which leaves little in reserve for providing support and understanding (Hellman et al., 1986). As Bermak (1977) notes, this empty feeling reduces the therapist's desire to be interested and concerned with the burdens of his or her spouse. This often results in a decrease in the therapist's ability to be empathic. Cray and Cray (1977) describe it as follows:

> When the psychiatrist (psychotherapist) does get home to his (her) family, the very skilled listener is no longer in a mood to listen. He would like to talk for a change. He has been suppressing his talking all day. Moreover, the problems of his family seem

very trite compared to the problems he has been focusing on. His sensitivity is dulled. (p. 33)

Emotional depletion and an associated decrease in the desire to listen empathically reduces the psychotherapist's ability to encounter his or her spouse in an intimate, genuine fashion. Instead, it causes the therapist to be emotionally unavailable to the spouse. The interpersonal distance that can result does little to promote healthy marital adjustment.

A related factor associated with the practice of psychotherapy which has the potential to negatively impact marital adjustment is the tendency for therapists to become increasingly withdrawn and isolated. As discussed in Chapter 3, the isolation inherent in the role of psychotherapist hinders interpersonal functioning in both professional and personal relationships. This is particularly relevant in regards to marital adjustment.

In a very interesting study conducted among university graduate students, Layne (1978) reports that even relatively brief training in clinical psychology caused students to become more preoccupied with their own thoughts, feelings, and problems, as well as significantly more introverted and withdrawn. Farber (1983a, 1985a) suggests that this tendency accelerates during a prolonged period of training and experience as a psychotherapist. The practiced pattern of withholding personal information, setting aside personal needs and concerns, emotional control, and one-way intimacy associated with clinical practice can cause the therapist to be distant and withdrawn from others, including his or her spouse. Henry (1966) notes that this tendency seems to reduce the therapist's investment and interest in marital and family relationships, decreasing his or her motivation to withstand the pull towards withdrawal and isolation. Even when there is a desire to resist these patterns, Wheelis (1958) suggests that it is extremely difficult for those who have become skilled at remaining invulnerable and anonymous to risk self-disclosure.

As Cray and Cray (1977) note, this can have a significant negative impact on marital intimacy, creating a chasm between husband and wife, a veritable breeding ground for misunderstanding and discontent. In such a situation it may become increasingly difficult for the therapist to set aside the tendency towards anonymity in order to encounter his or her spouse in an open, spontaneous fashion. Instead, the pull towards withdrawal and isolation may paralyze the relationship, hindering deeper intimacy and eroding that which is already present.

Farber (1985a) has suggested that the tendency to become increasingly psychologically minded as a result of therapeutic practice also has the potential to have a detrimental effect on marital adjustment. Due to the impact of clinical training and experience, the psychotherapist sometimes loses the ability to "turn off" an interpretive, analytic orientation (Farber, 1983b). There may be a growing tendency to regard all behavior, thoughts, and feelings with scrutiny and suspicion. This is not only true for therapeutic interactions, but it becomes the norm for all encounters, including those with one's spouse (Greben, 1975). No longer are things thought to be what they seem. Instead, there is a constant, almost obsessional need to look for hidden meanings and motives, underlying causes, and unconscious processes.

This pattern can negatively impact the marital relationship in several ways. For example, if the therapist's spouse is unable to enter into this interpretive perspective, the therapist may begin to experience increasingly greater alienation from him or her as the motivation to "explain" things decreases (Farber, 1985a). Furthermore, the tendency to constantly interpret a spouse's behavior reduces mutuality, increases defensiveness, and renders intimate interaction emotionless and highly intellectualized. For example, the "objectivity" inherent in the interpretive stance can become a weapon to express hostility. Thus, as Cray and Cray (1977) point out, when "a member of the family expresses rage, and the psychotherapist replies: 'Having expressed that, do you feel better?'" (p. 140), the tendency to remain interpretive prevents meaningful encounter and intimacy.

Many psychotherapists report an inability to set aside this interpretive, therapeutic role when interacting with spouse, family, and friends (Deutsch, 1984; Farber, 1983b; Hellman et al., 1986). As Farber (1985a) points out, the increasing ability to observe and understand human behavior accurately is an intoxicating experience which is not easily set aside. Unfortunately, if it is not surrendered when relating to one's spouse, it limits emotional closeness and mutuality. In addition, it reduces spontaneity and true self-disclosure (Farber, 1983b). Therapists who are unable to set aside the role of psychotherapist sometimes seem to lose their sense of self. They become so split off from their feelings and personal opinions that they lose the ability to regain contact with their own, unique experience (Freudenberger & Robbins, 1979). They become observers rather than participants, even in their own marriages. Rather than sharing personal feelings and needs, they merely "mirror" those of their spouse, remaining detached, interpretive, and uninvolved. The marital relationship takes on the same "as if" quality as therapeutic encounters (Guy & Liaboe, 1986a). As Storr (1979) points out, such individuals become nonpersons, incapable of meaningful self-disclosure, out of touch with their inner process, alienated from themselves as well as their significant others.

Cray and Cray (1977) note that this lack of spontaneity and self-awareness can have a paralyzing effect on marital decision making and goal setting, causing the therapist to be unable to know or disclose what he or she really wants. This is frustrating for both parties and leaves the therapist feeling further alienated and cut off from his or her spouse. While knowing and disclosing personal opinions and feelings is not always necessary in therapeutic interactions, it is essential for the development and maintenance of marital intimacy.

Another by-product of inappropriately remaining in an interpretive, analytic stance with a spouse or significant other is the tendency to be intrusive and controlling. The ability to uncover motives and expose hidden meanings may, at times, have an invasive quality to it. On such occasions it may seem as though the therapist psychologically rapes his or her spouse, exploring and unveiling sensitive material without permission. Not only does this leave the spouse little place to "hide," but it also gives a decided advantage to the therapist who is skillfully able to remain invulnerable and well-defended against similar intrusions by the spouse. There may also be a resultant tendency for the therapist to use this ability to control or dominate the spouse. Feelings are simply explained away, behaviors are interpreted rather than responded to, and concerns are analyzed and devalued rather than taken seriously. In the worst of cases, the therapist may even actively attempt to manipulate the spouse, capitalizing on recently discovered weaknesses and exposing well-known vulnerabilities in order to influence and control. The spouse may eventually learn to defend successfully against and distance themselves from their intrusive therapist mates. Unfortunately, this pattern can hinder intimate mutuality, leading to marital alienation and disharmony.

Marmor's (1953) concerns regarding the dangers of the growing sense of omnipotence and grandiosity sometimes associated with psychotherapeutic practice are especially pertinent in regards to the marital relationship of the therapist. The constant idealization and admiration of patients at times creates a sense of omniscience and superiority in the mind of the therapist (Goldberg, 1986). Such individuals begin to believe mistakenly that their insights, opinions, and viewpoints are nearly inerrant and inspired (Greben, 1975). All other individuals, including one's spouse, are experienced as less informed "patients" who lack the expertise and insights possessed by the therapist (Will, 1979). This can produce a grandiosity and arrogance which becomes inappropriate and troublesome in the marital relationship. Not only is it offensive to the spouse, but it obviously reduces the mutuality and equality necessary for healthy intimacy.

One of the unfortunate side effects of this grandiosity is a tendency for the therapist to become authoritarian and dogmatic in the marital relationship. As Marmor (1953) points out, the therapist is used to being "obeyed" by his or her patients. Therapists typically exercise a great deal of authority and influence over the lives of their patients. Their advice is valued, and their opinions are given serious consideration and weight. This can create a sense of superiority and the expectation that others will regard the therapist's views with similar reverence. It may be disappointing and annoying to discover that personal opinions and expectations are not received by one's spouse with the same degree of respect and regard (Cray & Cray, 1977). In fact, at times they are not even solicited! Hurt feelings, misunderstanding, and anger can result when the therapist faces the reality that the individual he or she most values in life does not consider him or her to be particularly superior or "special."

Another feature of this grandiosity is the expectation that one's marriage must be perfect and ideal. This can occur for several reasons. First, therapy relationships, particularly when there is a great deal of admiration and idealization, are often conflict-free and pleasant. The "as if" quality often precludes the typical disputes, petty arguments, and irritations of everyday life. If the marital relationship is compared to such idealized relationships, its conflicts and annoyances may cause it to appear deficient in comparison (Burton, 1975). Furthermore, psychotherapists may feel better about themselves as they consider their own behavior and attitudes in therapeutic interactions as compared to those evident in the marital relationship. It is difficult to accept one's shortcomings, selfishness, conceit, impatience, and insensitivity, qualities often much more apparent at home than at the office (Raskin, 1978). It may also be troubling to discover that perceived problems and deficiencies in the marriage or one's spouse do not seem to respond to "interventions" and interpretations with the same degree of success as occurs in therapy relationships. Spouses may not want "help" from their therapist mate, and even when they do, they may not evidence the same degree of progress and improvement as favorite patients. Finally, when there is either internal or external pressure to appear to the community as the ideal married couple, limitations and problems become sources of embarrassment and shame (Bermak, 1977). Feelings of superiority and grandiosity may unrealistically increase the expectation that one's marriage must be perfect and free of problems, making it hard to accept the flawed, mortal nature of most marital relationships (Cray & Cray, 1977). Such tendencies can put considerable pressure on the marriage, creating burdensome discontent and disillusionment. This may also at least partially explain why many psychotherapists are reluctant to enter personal marital therapy when difficulties do arise (Wahl, 1986). For example, in one recent survey, fewer than 15% of the practicing therapists questioned had received marital therapy at anytime (Guy, Stark, & Poelstra, 1987).

The absorbing nature of psychotherapeutic endeavors can begin to take the place of the private life of the therapist in terms of investment and energy. There is sometimes a tendency for psychotherapists to live vicariously through the lives of their clients (Bugental, 1964; Burton, 1975; Goldberg, 1986). Guggenbuhl-Craig (1979) provides a provocative description of this process:

> The analyst may be completely absorbed in the work with his (her) patients, which at first glance would seem a very good thing. His own private life takes a back seat to the problems and difficulties of his patients. But a point may be reached where the patients might actually live for the analyst, so to speak, where they are expected to fill the gap left by the analyst's own loss of contact with warm, dynamic life. The analyst no longer has his own friends; his patient's friendships and enmities are as his own. The analyst's sex life may be stunted; his patients' sexual problems provide a substitute. (p. 56)

Not only is this hazardous for the treatment relationship, but such vicarious living can have a significantly detrimental impact on the marriage as well. There may be a tendency to divest emotional energy and withdraw from one's spouse, seeking to obtain needed gratification from "safer," more strictly defined therapeutic relationships. It may seem easier to live through the experiences of patients rather than taking the risks involved in genuine encounter and intimacy with a spouse. Obviously, this does little to promote healthy marital adjustment.

In addition, there are several more practical considerations which may also affect one's marriage. The first of these is the need for the therapist's work to remain largely confidential (Freudenberger & Robbins, 1979). As mentioned in Chapter 3, the strict constraints of professional ethics and legal restrictions regarding patient confidentiality limit the therapist's ability to share the details of clinical practice with his or her spouse. Specifics concerning the notoriety of certain patients, dramatic treatment results, concerns regarding the adequacy of patient care, uncertainty regarding dangerousness, and so on, cannot typically be disclosed. It is a lonely experience for the therapist, who feels constrained and restricted from sharing "secrets" with his or her spouse. Much like a government worker with access to state secrets, the psychotherapist is often forced to refrain from sharing the very details that make clinical practice both exciting and worrisome (Storr, 1979). This practice prevents the spouse from sharing in the most meaningful aspects of the work, especially when the need to speak in generalities lessens the likelihood of the therapist receiving needed support, empathy, and comfo

Those who work in the "helping" professions are well acquainted with the problems associated with attempting to prioritize time and energy in order to divide up limited resources between work and family. This is no less true for the psychotherapist. As Cray and Cray (1977) point out, there are many occasions when the needs of patients—particularly those in crisis—take priority over family needs and concerns. This can be very hard on the marriage relationship. The need to return telephone calls after work hours, late night contacts with patients in distress, constantly changing appointment schedules, and the frequent need to work evenings may be a source of marital tension and conflict. Because of the legal, ethical, and moral obligations of clinical practice, the needs of a husband or wife may sometimes take a back seat to those of clients. This gives poignant meaning to jokes about the need to make an appointment in order to get the attention of the therapist mate. However vigorously the therapist tries to establish personal boundaries in order to protect the integrity of the marriage, there are likely to be moments when the needs of clients intrude on the marital relationship. Furthermore, the odd work schedules, with rigidly adhered to appointments which patients may feel freer to change than therapists, often leave the spouse alone to handle routine concerns and family emergencies.

A related factor is the time pressure and the demands of a busy practice. Therapists report that this is a major source of stress and difficulty (Tryon, 1983a). In addition to the financial incentives involved, it is often difficult to turn down referrals from friends, present or former clients, and valued referral sources, causing the therapist to schedule more appointments than desirable. As Freudenberger and Robbins (1979) note, clinical practices tend to increase in size exponentially, achieving a frenzied pace which begins to feel out of control. Obviously, this can have a detrimental impact on the marital relationship as well. In spite of the continued belief in the myth that quality of time is more important than quantity of time, most eventually discover that there can be no quality without quantity. In short, marital intimacy cannot be maintained when the therapist mate is too busy to spend sufficient time with his or her spouse. In the face of a lack of external restrictions and structure, some therapists eventually find themselves scheduling appointments at all hours between 6:00 A.M. and 11:00 P.M. It is simply impossible for a marriage to survive such a lifestyle, at least in any meaningful, recognizable form.

While there is some variation, depending on the place of employment, many therapists tend to earn an income based on "commission" rather than a salary. In other words, they are paid by client fees, earning money only when conducting psychotherapy with patients who faithfully pay for this service. Even in the case of those earning a salary, many have a part-time private practice in addition. A number of problems can result. Although there is significant earning potential when a therapist's income is directly related to the effort that he or she puts into the practice, there is obvious pressure to limit the amount of time taken for rest and relaxation. Hellman et al. (1986) report that psychotherapists tend to take insufficient vacation time. There is obvious financial incentive to forgo time off from work. Not only is there a loss of income when the therapist takes a vacation or a day off, but there may also be fears of patient attrition, the disappointment of referral sources, and even the loss of clinical acuity. The longer the time off, the greater these fears can be. While this clearly has a detrimental impact on the well-being of the therapist, it can also have a negative effect on the marital relationship. Couples need time to play together, to relax and enjoy each other's company. Without time for recreation, a marital relationship takes on the flavor of a business endeavor with a focus solely on practical concerns rather than a balance which includes mutual pleasure and enjoyment. Furthermore, this resistance to taking time off sometimes renders the therapist unavailable for dealing with the needs of the spouse, such as during times of illness or distress.

A related concern involves the economic uncertainties associated with a career in psychotherapy. Monthly income can vary significantly, depending on the number of sessions conducted, fees collected, the speed of insurance company reimbursements, and varying expenses. Dramatic fluctuations are not uncommon, an unsettling experience for all but the most seasoned veterans. This is reported to be a major source of stress for most clinicians (Tryon, 1983a). Personal financial planning and goal setting become a difficult and uncertain endeavor in such cases. This is worrisome not only for the therapist, but for the spouse as well. It is very challenging to live within a budget which must constantly adjust for uncontrollable fluctuations in income. The therapist may find that his or her spouse becomes concerned about the financial instability of clinical practice during times of low collections or few referrals. In the worst of cases, this concern may give rise to not so subtle pressure to earn more money, develop a greater number of referrals, and prolong terminations with dependable clients. The marital tensions and stress which may be caused by this kind of financial insecurity can have a markedly detrimental effect on the marriage. Resentments, misunderstandings, and anxiety often result when income is subject to the degree of swings typical of some psychotherapy practices.

The ongoing need to cultivate referrals can become a burden on the marriage as well. This results from several factors. For example, those in private clinical practice receive many of their referrals from friends and acquaintances. This may make some therapists self-conscious and hesitant to disclose personal problems or needs in a genuine manner. In particular, there may be a wish to present one's marriage as an ideal model of harmony and bliss. In other words, it is difficult to disagree or argue in public, even when that would be appropriate, if there is a fear of jeapordizing future referrals. Those with whom the couple feels that they can "let their hair down" become fewer in number.

There are other ways in which the need to generate referrals and community goodwill can have an impact on the marriage relationship. For example, it may influence decisions regarding which social clubs, house of worship, or community organizations are to be joined. It may also necessitate more and different types of social entertaining than the couple might otherwise find comfortable. The type and number of friendships to be cultivated may be influenced by the need for developing dependable referral sources. While some spouses may find such concerns to be reasonable, and may even enjoy participating in building propitious social contacts, others may come to resent the need to "market" themself and their therapist mate. They may also grow tired of the stress and anxiety that result from such a calculated approach.

It is not only those in private clinical practice who report that their social life, as a couple, is impacted by a career in psychotherapy. Therapists tend to develop friendships primarily with other psychotherapists. Thus, social gatherings become times for professional exchange and "shop talk." While perhaps stimulating and interesting for the clinician, frequent parties of this type can easily become tiresome and boring for the spouse, who largely feels excluded by the nature of the conversation. It is possible for a couple's social life to be characterized by get-togethers with other therapists and their spouses, weekend professional workshops attended by the therapist while the spouse finds other ways to entertain himself or herself, and referral-generating parties. It is not uncommon for spouses of psychotherapists to begin to feel that their own careers and personal interests have little impact on the couple's social life. This can easily give rise to resentment, bitterness, and dissatisfaction if left unresolved.

It will be noted that there has been no distinction made between male and female psychotherapists in regards to the impact of psychotherapeutic practice on their marital relationship. This has been intentional in recognition of the fact that, as Freudenberger and Robbins (1979) note, the marital problems associated with clinical practice are far more similar than dissimilar for both sexes. Changing roles and societal values, along with a dramatic increase in the number of female therapists entering the field, have resulted in strikingly similar consequences for the marital relationships of both male and female therapists. However, it is interesting to note that one study of marital satisfaction among practicing therapists found that females were significantly less satisfied with their marriages than males (Wahl, 1986). Several attributed this to the perceived need to "mother" their patients, children, and spouse, a task which they found burdensome and overwhelming. Several reported that their spouses were not supportive or appreciative of the demanding nature of their career, and left them feeling dissatisfied with their marriage. While this may be true of career women as a group, it is interesting to note that this may be one gender-related hazard for the marital relationships of female psychotherapists.

The Spouse of the Psychotherapist

In view of the potential positive and negative consequences of psychotherapeutic practice on marital adjustment, it seems reasonable to wonder what it is like to be married to a therapist. As can be surmised by the preceding description, there are several decided advantages and disadvantages associated with marrying a therapist. The reaction of a spouse to these varies with the type and degree of its impact on the marital relationship.

Benefits

The spouse of a psychotherapist enjoys several advantages not afforded to others. For example, even though they may not conduct therapy, most spouses learn a great deal about psychopathology, treatment, and diagnosis through conversations with their therapist mate. Some find this to be fascinating and exciting, opening up a new world of unconscious processes, hidden meanings, and underlying motivations. Some spouses are so intrigued that they read many of their mate's books and journals, and they may even elect to attend a professional workshop with him or her. While some are happy to pursue other career interests, others actually decide to enter the mental health profession as a result of this introduction.

Depending on how strictly the therapist withholds information about patients, many spouses are able to enjoy vicariously the clinical work of their therapist mate. While usually lacking specific details and identifying information, spouses often become familiar with clients and their lives as a result of informal conversations at home. They may even derive pleasure from their mate's vicarious enjoyment of the events, growth, and progress of therapy patients. Although there are obvious limits to this experience, those who are given the opportunity to enter into the world of their therapist mate through late night conversations sometimes find it fascinating. The endless variety, intellectual stimulation, and personal enrichment enjoyed by the therapist can be a shared experience for those who make the effort to do so while respecting patient confidentiality.

The financial rewards associated with a career in therapy are obviously a shared advantage, regardless of whether the spouse is also employed. The prestige and community recognition afforded psychotherapists can be of benefit to spouses as well. While such considerations must not be overvalued, it is clear that some spouses are very proud of the occupation of their therapist mate, and they experience personal satisfaction because of it.

Although a career in psychotherapy can result in a life which is too busy, pressured, and frantic, some therapists set rigid boundaries on their schedule, deciding in advance which days they will work and how many hours of therapy they are willing to conduct. In such cases the flexibility and freedom to schedule appointments when desired is a decided advantage for the marital couple. For example, it may become possible for the therapist to take Fridays off regularly, permitting three day weekends and short vacations. Some therapists in private practice refuse to work more than four days a week, increasing the amount of time spent together as a couple if the spouse can arrange to be free on the same days.

It may also be possible for the therapist to pattern his or her appointment schedule around that of the spouse, maximizing the amount of time available for family recreation or household projects. As mentioned in Chapter 1, few vocations provide the potential flexibility afforded to the psychotherapist, particularly in the case of the private practitioner. This can be significantly benefitial for marital harmony, since it allows for the possibility of quantity as well as quality time together as a couple.

Perhaps most importantly, the emotional and personal growth which many psychotherapists experience as a result of clinical training and therapeutic endeavors often serve as a catalyst for the same in the life of their spouse. This can occur directly, such as when a spouse makes the decision to enter personal psychotherapy in order to better understand the therapist's career, resolve personal problems, and keep up with the clinician's emotional growth so as not to be "left behind." It may also occur indirectly, as a result of conversations with the therapist mate, personal reading, and the influence of a new circle of friends. Certainly, the changes and development of the therapist mate serves as a powerful motivator for personal growth and emotional maturity. While it is obvious that many spouses may be in little need of such growth, most would agree that their personal growth was challenged by the personality changes and career interests of their therapist mate.

Liabilities

Although the benefits associated with being married to a psychotherapist are encouraging, there are also several liabilities which need to be addressed. Some are rather minor and can be handled with little effort. Others are more serious and they can undermine the integrity of the marital relationship if left unattended.

Some spouses have a great deal of difficulty understanding and accepting the emotional depletion of their therapist mate. They may feel hurt and resentful when there seems to be little motivation to listen supportively and empathically after a long day of conducting therapy. It is understandably difficult for the spouse to accept the realization that patients often get more caring, sympathy, understanding, and support than they do (Cray & Cray, 1977). First, this seems grossly unfair. Second, it may be difficult to regard as inevitable. Since the therapist spends much of the day sitting and listening, it may be hard to accept that such endeavors result in a fatigue that justifies occasional rudeness and neglect (Bermak, 1977). Furthermore, this rationale implies that empathy and caring exist in a limited quantity, as in a finite energy supply. It is interesting to note Farber's (1983b) report that over 40% of those psychotherapists surveyed rejected this notion. It is likely that at least as many spouses would concur. Realistic or not, most spouses expect to receive as much, if not more, empathy and emotional support as do their mate's patients. When this does not occur, it is likely to have a serious negative impact on the spouse and overall marital adjustment.

The emotional withdrawal and isolation sometimes exhibited by psychotherapists in regards to their personal life and relationships can have an unsettling impact on the spouse. In a very real way, the more practiced the therapist becomes at one-way intimacy and anonymity, the more of a stranger he or she becomes to the spouse. Furthermore, the loss of self-awareness which is sometimes associated with clinical practice may leave the therapist mate unable to experience and express feelings, opinions, and beliefs. The decrease in intimacy and genuine encounter which often follows leaves the spouse feeling alone and abandoned. Resultant fears and insecurities are intensified if the therapist seems to invest more energy in and experience greater enthusiasm for his or her clinical work and relationships, a not altogether uncommon experience (Henry et al., 1973). The tendency for some therapists to live vicariously through the lives of patients, and to compare treatment relationships erroneously with the marriage, further undermines the integrity and strength of the partnership. These concerns become particularly troubling when spouses sense the erotic quality of some therapeutic relationships. Repeated explanations concerning transference phenomena are little comfort to a spouse who recognizes that the attraction is more often mutual than not. Unless the tendency to withdraw and isolate is resisted by the therapist, it can erode the very intimacy which was the foundation for the marriage in the first place. Memories of past intimacy may become devoid of meaning under the strain of increasing alienation. No one is able to live with a stranger forever.

Few spouses willingly endure unrestrained psychological-mindedness, constant interpretations, and unceasing analysis on the part of their therapist mate. While initially it may be entertaining to listen to him or her diagnose neighbors and relatives, the inappropriateness and arrogance of this eventually becomes clear. If it continues, annoyance and boredom result. Over time, the controlling, authoritarian, and grandiose features of remaining in an interpretive mode also become apparent. It can be difficult to live with someone who views himself or herself as an "expert" on human behavior and everyone else as a "patient." Interpretations are given, invited or not, and the feelings, behavior, and needs of others are simply regarded as symptoms in need of diagnosis. Fortunately, most spouses will confront their mates with the manipulative, intrusive, and superior aspects of this attitude. Hopefully, with help the therapist will learn that true mutuality can only be achieved when such tendencies are overcome.

The need for the therapist to respect patient confidentiality sometimes results in the spouse feeling left out of some very important aspects of the life and work of the therapist mate. Regardless of attempts to share information and experiences, the limits of confidentiality inevitably result in the exclusion of the spouse to a certain degree. Furthermore, because of the intensity and emotionally laden quality of psychotherapeutic work, a simple recounting of the facts afterwards fails to communicate the depth and meaning of the experience. Thus it is often difficult for the spouse to share fully in the excitement, stimulation, and concerns associated with the practice of psychotherapy. While this occurs to some extent in most marriages, it can be especially noticeable in this situation due to the tendency for clinical work to become rather engrossing and absorbing. It is difficult for the therapist to "leave the work at the office," and a spouse may feel the impact of a difficult therapy session on their interaction later that day without understanding the source of the stress. Even when it is clear to both individuals that patient concerns are occupying the therapist's thoughts, the spouse may fail to appreciate and to comprehend fully its impact on the marital relationship. Furthermore, the spouse is often unable to offer specific help or suggestions in such situations. Due to the nature of psychotherapeutic work, it cannot be fully a shared experience.

A related problem involves the moodiness and emotional lability of some therapists, a phenomenon occasionally associated with psychotherapeutic practice (Rippere & Williams, 1985). Some spouses may find this to be rather unsettling, leaving them to wonder whether the therapist's anger or depression, for example, is due to a marital conflict or a difficult therapy session. Most find it necessary to keep from hastily personalizing these mood swings, recognizing that they may be the result of therapeutic encounters. The psychological warfare in which a therapist engages will occasionally result in emotional wounds which impact the marriage and spouse in unseen, but nonetheless significant ways. It is necessary for both individuals to recognize this, to allow both to identify correctly the source of trouble and distress. This will reduce the likelihood of projection and misunderstanding.

It is not unusual for the spouse of a psychotherapist to grow resentful about the need for patient concerns to occasionally take priority over those of the family (Cray & Cray, 1977). Late night phone calls, emergency sessions, and busy schedules are often significant intrusions on the home and marriage. While the fact that the therapist's livelihood is directly related to the amount and quality of service rendered, making such interruptions necessary, hurt and anger grow if the spouse senses that the therapist may actually be more invested in the lives of his or her patients than in the marriage relationship. A tendency for "going beyond the call of duty" stops being a cause for admiration and begins to be a source of resentment if the spouse feels neglected by the therapist mate. While it is sometimes necessary and appropriate for patient needs to take priority over those of the spouse and family, this had best be the rare exception rather than the rule. In order to ensure the well-being of the marriage relationship, it is necessary that the therapist schedule regular and sufficient days off, vacations, and time for recreation. Once scheduled, the sanctity of such commitments must be guarded. Few spouses will be satisfied to remain on the bottom of the priority list, to be given attention and time only when nothing more important has come up.

As mentioned earlier in this chapter, the tendency for the couple's social life to become centered around the therapist's work can serve as a source of dissatisfaction for the nontherapist spouse. If the couple is typically invited to parties and social gatherings which are attended primarily by other psychotherapists, the spouse may frequently feel excluded by the topics of conversation and the "inside jokes" in which he or she cannot share. This problem may be furthered by the tendency for psychotherapists to isolate themselves from those outside of the profession, making them less willing to socialize with friends and acquaintances of the nontherapist spouse. This can obviously become a source of contention and misunderstanding. Unless there is a concerted effort to balance out the number and types of social contacts, the spouse may feel increasingly less satisfied with their outside involvements, leading to greater alienation and withdrawal.

A related concern is the rather unique occurrence of accidentally meeting a former patient of the therapist mate in a social situation. As Cray and Cray (1977) point out, this is not an altogether uncommon experience. The highly personal nature of therapeutic relationships as well as the constraints of confidentiality and discretion make such encounters uncomfortable for everyone involved. If the therapist is present, the spouse can hopefully rely on him or her to carry the conversation and prompt the appropriate response. However, if this is not the case, the individual is left to decide what and how much to say. Perhaps one of the most uncomfortable aspects of this situation is when the spouse senses that the former patient has shared an especially meaningful relationship with the therapist mate. This may be particularly unsettling when the therapeutic relationship involved someone of the opposite sex from the therapist. Feelings of jealousy, suspicion, and competition may arise, increasing the awkwardness of encounters with such individuals. Most spouses, although curious, prefer not to knowingly meet former patients of their therapist mate for these reasons. Because this cannot be avoided completely, however, most will face the problems and embarrassment which result regardless of their hopes to the contrary.

Schwartz (1986) points out another problem associated with being married to a psychotherapist. In an article entitled, "Know When to Drop the Shop Talk," she describes the misunderstandings that arise when the spouse fails to find the career of the therapist mate to be particularly interesting or exciting. In other words, it is highly likely that some spouses will be frankly bored with the field of psychotherapy, show little interest in patient concerns, and remain largely uninformed about the details of their mate's career. They simply do not share in the fascination and excitement of the therapist who finds conducting therapy to be an absorbing, engrossing task. This can be a real blow to therapists who wish to discuss theories of personality, innovations in treatment techniques, and diagnostic problems with their spouse. Admittedly, the practice of psychotherapy is a highly specialized, technical endeavor which may be of little interest to some spouses. Unfortunately, subtle grandiosity and overinvestment on the part of some therapists may cause them to regard such a spouse to be superficial, shallow, and narrow-minded. If the therapist persists in the expectation that the spouse experience the same job-related highs and lows, the spouse may begin to feel intruded on, attacked, and devalued. Boundaries must be respectfully established which allow the spouse to focus on individual interests and separate concerns free of criticism and pressure. While difficult, it is important that the therapist realize that the emotional intensity experienced when conducting psychotherapy can be a highly idiosyncratic experience that does not need to be shared by the spouse. Although many couples struggle with similar issues of individuation, psychotherapists seem to have a particularly difficult time tolerating a spouse's apathy and disinterest in a career which he or she may find very rewarding and exciting.

Perhaps one of the most disturbing aspects of being married to a psychotherapist is dealing with the profound personality changes which often occur during the training years and a career in psychotherapy. As Farber (1983a) notes, the change in values, opinions, and interests, along with sometimes rather dramatic personality reorganization, can create a chasm between a husband and wife which occasionally leads to the break-up of a previously stable relationship. Regardless off how adaptive and caring, the spouse may find it difficult to adjust to the changing personality of the therapist mate. In fact, such changes may leave little in common for providing the necessary foundation of intimacy. Unless they are successful in maintaining communication and closeness in the face of these significant transformations, there may be a tendency to "grow apart" over the years. In addition to this risk, some spouses may find the resultant pressure on themselves to change and "grow" to be rather intrusive and offensive. It may be that some are uninterested or unwilling to work through the unresolved conflicts, unconscious motivations, and hidden problems so relentlessly elucidated by the therapist mate. They may feel that personal or marital therapy is unnecessary or undesirable. Resentment and anger may result if the therapist mate continues to pressure the spouse towards unwanted self-exploration, actualization, and awareness. Once again, appropriate boundaries need to be respectfully established to allow for individual differences. Yet the need for such autonomy must be balanced against the potential for alienation and estrangement which may result if mutual and compatible growth and change fail to occur.

Husband and Wife Psychotherapists

There appears to be a growing trend for therapists to marry other psychotherapists (Guy, Souder, Baker, & Guy, in press). For example, in a recent survey of practicing psychotherapists, 15% reported being currently married to another psychotherapist, while an additional 5% indicated that their previous spouse had been a therapist (Guy, Stark, & Poelstra, 1987). The reasons for this are unclear. Perhaps psychotherapists tend to postpone marriage until after the completion of their training, increasing the likelihood of meeting other eligible therapists while attending graduate school. Or, perhaps the tendency for some psychotherapists to socialize exclusively with other therapists eventually restricts their choice of potential mates. It also appears that some of these relationships involve second or third marriages, by which time these therapists may prefer to share their life with another person who truly understands and supports their work. Whatever the reasons, this interesting phenomenon brings with it several unique additional benefits and liabilities to the marital relationship. As can be imagined, the problems encountered when one spouse is a practicing psychotherapist are multiplied when this is true of both.

A host of practical concerns are affected by shared careers in psychotherapy. For example, the couple must decide whether or not to practice together, work for the same employer, or seek entirely separate jobs. Professional specialities and areas of concentration must also be negotiated. Household and family issues such as child care, scheduling, and division of labor must be addressed in light of similar career needs and demands. Most importantly, the marital relationship is uniquely impacted by the shared vocation. Many of the liabilities previously mentioned such as emotional depletion, social withdrawal, inappropriate psychological-mindedness, and so on, are markedly increased when both spouses are therapists. Furthermore, many of the practical concerns regarding time pressures, patient demands, financial insecurity, unusual work schedules, and public perceptions are magnified by shared careers in psychotherapy.

Despite the potential pitfalls, the trend for therapists to marry other therapists appears to be growing. This may be due to some of the many benefits that therapist couples report. For example, attending professional workshops and conferences together can be a great source of pleasure. It may also be enjoyable to share books, journals, and ideas together. Finally, the mutual supervision, consultation, and therapy which may occur as a result of this situation can be very meaningful to both individuals (Guy et al., 1987). There seems to be a special degree of empathy and support which grows out of the mutuality of shared experience that is unique to therapist couples.

Summary

It is apparent that being a psychotherapist is a mixed blessing in regards to marital adjustment. Some aspects of a career in psychotherapy are beneficial to the marriage relationship. Others have the potential to undermine the strength and integrity of marital intimacy. Perhaps it is best to recognize that it would be presumptuous, indeed hazardous, to overlook these considerations. This is certainly not meant to imply that psychotherapists should forgo marriage. To the contrary, it is the spouse who often helps the therapist keep perspective and balance (Cray & Cray, 1977; Guggenbuhl-Craig, 1979). Nor is it necessary to avoid marrying a psychotherapist in order to elude the potential liabilities. Most spouses seem to find that the benefits outweigh the hazards. However, the impact of psychotherapeutic practice on the marital relationship is significant enough to warrant ongoing evaluation and reflection by both spouses in order to enhance the positive efffects and minimize or eliminate the negative ones.

Relating with Children

As in the case of spouses of psychotherapists, children of therapists are often significantly impacted by the nature of the professional relationships and experiences associated with this career. While in some cases children experience unique benefits, there may be several liabilities which result as well. Although these considerations may be irrelevant to psychotherapists who are unmarried or childless, they are very important for those with children of their own (Freudenberger & Robbins, 1979).

Changing role expectations, employment patterns, and values have significantly reduced gender-related differences concerning the impact of a career on one's children (Salholz, 1986). Consequently, individual differences among couples require that each carefully consider the implications of a clinical practice on the resultant quality of parenting and child rearing regardless of whether the therapist is male or female.

Benefits

Children benefit from many of the same positive impacts of clinical practice on the marital relationship. For example, the growth that many psychotherapists report experiencing in the area of self-esteem, self-awareness, self-assurance, self-disclosure, introspection, and sensitivity is likely to make the therapist a more effective parent. Furthermore, a tendency to become more open, thoughtful, confident, and patient as a result of a career in psychotherapy cannot help but improve the therapist's parenting skills. A mother or father who is intellectually and emotionally stimulated by his or her work is likely to be more nurturing, involved, and interested in his or her children. Increased empathy skills related to the practice of psychotherapy also presumably improve the therapists' ability to understand and support their children. While there is as yet no known research which directly supports these suppositions, they make intuitive and logical sense. Furthermore, it seems that psychotherapists believe this to be true of themselves. For example, 71% of those surveyed in one study indicated that they felt that their clinical practice had a positive impact on relationships with their children (Guy, Stark, & Poelstra, 1987). The skills which are necessary for conducting effective psychotherapy are extremely similar to those required for good parenting. The ability to listen, understand, support, nurture, confront, clarify, and so on, is necessary for both undertakings. At the very least, it seems apparent that an effective therapist has the potential to be an excellent parent.

Not only does a career in psychotherapy enhance the therapist's parenting skills, but it may improve the family environment in several other ways. For example, the advanced education required for becoming a psychotherapist may motivate the parent to provide stimulating educational and cultural opportunities which naturally arise from a life personally enriched by the education, training, and experience related to conducting therapy with so many diverse and stimulating individuals. Furthermore, the advanced verbal skills required for becoming a skilled therapist are likely to be incorporated into family life and interactions. It also seems plausible that the rich emotional life of the psychotherapist, with its constant emphasis on self-awareness, sensitivity, and caring, would have a noticeable modeling effect on the children. Of course, this assumes that they witness these qualities in the therapist parent, a somewhat questionable assumption for numerous reasons. At any rate, it might be that some home environments are characterized by many of the same qualities that psychotherapists attempt to provide for patients, such as accurate empathy, genuineness, and positive regard. If this is true, certainly the children will benefit from being raised in such an environment (Rogers, 1980). Finally, if the therapist parent carefully and thoughtfully structures his or her schedule, they may be able to be more available to their children. For example, the ability to regularly take three day weekends, or certain afternoons off, could provide special opportunities for sharing in the children's world. This could have a meaningful impact on the overall family environment.

As the children of a therapist grow older, they may come to appreciate many of the aspects of their parent's career. They may find psychology to be fascinating and they may enjoy talking over issues related to diagnosis and treatment of psychopathology. It is not unusual for at least one child to eventually pursue a career in mental health. For example, Guy, Stark, and Poelstra (1987) found that 6% of those therapists surveyed had a child who was also a practicing therapist. Children may also share in the community status afforded the psychotherapist and experience pride in their parent's career. Professional parents, and the status and income that are sometimes associated with such careers, may be highly regarded by peers and teachers, a decided advantage for some children.

Liabilities

Unfortunately, children of psychotherapists experience some of the same hazards and liabilities as do spouses. However, they may be impacted in rather unique ways related to their particular age and level of maturity. For this reason, the potential negative impact of psychotherapeutic practice on one's children must be given careful evaluation in order to minimize any potentially negative effects.

Perhaps one of the most unfortunate hazards associated with a career in psychotherapy is the therapist parent's occasional emotional withdrawal, preoccupation, and exhaustion (Cray & Cray, 1977). A day full of difficult therapy sessions may leave the therapist unable or unwilling to attend to the needs of his or her children. As a result, the therapist may ignore, avoid, or even abuse children who have a need for more patience, nurturance, and guidance than they provide. If this becomes a chronic occurrence, it can have an obviously detrimental impact on the emotional well-being of the entire family. Children may begin to feel unwanted or unloved. They may misunderstand the actual reasons for the therapist's inability to listen and to attend to their needs, attributing this to their own misbehavior or lack of worth. They may sense that the therapist parent is more invested in the lives of patients than in their own, leaving them resentful, jealous, or hurt. The resultant feelings of rejection and anger can be intense. Few children have the capacity to understand and accept the emotional depletion of their therapist parent. There can be little doubt that children need as much or more attention, love, and intimacy than the therapist's most disturbed patients. Yet their inability or unwillingness to verbalize their needs may cause the therapist to overlook and neglect them, a most unfortunate occurrence.

In addition to the negative impact of emotional depletion and withdrawal, the tendency for some psychotherapists to remain unknown and obscure to their children is also troublesome. The detrimental impact of maintaining one-way intimacy on the therapist's ability to self-disclose, share opinions and feelings, and familiarize children with his or her personal values creates an anonymity that leads to alienation and estrangement. In a very real way the therapist parent can remain a stranger who is both unfamiliar with his or her children, and seemingly quite foreign to them. The lack of true intimacy which results denies the children the nurturance and care that they need. They can begin to feel that patients know their parent better than they do, giving rise to feelings of jealousy and competition. This may be especially difficult for children of therapists who specialize in the treatment of children, who may come to realize that their parent spends more time with young clients, often in "play," than with themselves. This can give rise to the poignant wish expressed by one child of a psychotherapist, who when asked what he wanted to do when he grew up, answered "I want to be a patient" (Cray & Cray, 1977, p. 338). Once again, the child may misunderstand the parent's reason for remaining distant, aloof, withdrawn, and annonymous, attributing it to a lack of love, concern, and investment due to their own shortcomings and lack of worth.

A related concern is the therapist's difficulty with setting aside the acquired ability to remain somewhat neutral and nonjudgmental with clients. When this approach is used at home, it is easy to imagine how inappropriate and detrimental it can become. The more indecisive a therapist becomes, the less able he or she is to provide the guidance and direction children require. As Cray and Cray point out, "It can be quite vexing when a family wants a decision. 'Should I go to school tomorrow with the head cold?' the child asks. 'What do you think you should do?' replies the psychotherapist parent" (p. 339). Obviously, therapeutic neutrality is not always a useful style when at home with children. It can sabotage attempts to respond to their needs in a stage-appropriate, developmentally specific manner. Furthermore, it can leave children with the feeling that their parents simply do not care about their concerns and needs. Neutrality can easily be mistaken for apathy and disinterest by a child.

The occupational hazard of remaining overly interpretive and psychologically minded with one's children can have a serious impact on their emotional life if care is not taken to limit these tendencies. If the therapist parent tends to analyze inappropriately the child's behaviors, feelings, and thoughts, they may unwittingly impede their emotional development. Kohut (1977) mentions that he has had the occasion to analyze many adults who, as children of psychotherapists, had been negatively impacted by their parents' tendency to overanalyze and interpret their behaviors. He states that the "pathogenic effect of the parental behavior lay in the fact that the parents' participation in their children's life, their claim—often correctly made—that they knew more about what their children were thinking, wishing, feeling than the children themselves, tended to interfere with the consolidation of the self of these children" (pp. 146–147). The therapist parents unwittingly overburdened their children with insights, explanations, and analyses which were neither appropriate nor helpful. By intruding on them in this way, they prevented the children from developing their own self-awareness at a developmentally appropriate pace. It is almost as though the parent became the "observing ego," leaving the child unable to explore fully his or her own feelings or inner processes. The child perhaps began to believe that the parent "knows better" concerning their motives and needs, retarding the development of personal emotional insight and maturity. Not only did this prevent them from gaining a deeper understanding of themselves, but as Kohut points out, these "children became secretive and walled themselves off from being penetrated by the parental insights" (p. 147). Rather than creating greater intimacy, the tendency to intrude on the children with frequent interpretations and analyses resulted in greater distance and alienation, as the children attempted to ward the emotional assaults of the therapist parent.

At this point, it is interesting to note the results of a recent survey of practicing psychotherapists who were asked to consider the validity of the stereotype that psychotherapists' children are "crazier" than the average child (Farber, 1983b). Those agreeing with this stereotype (51.1%) offered several explanations: "that therapists raise their children therapeutically either by being too interpretive or by paying excessive attention to feelings; that therapists with problems tend to have children with problems; and that therapists' children act-out to get attention from otherwise phlegmatic parents" (p. 179). If true, such tendencies appear to hinder the normal emotional development of these children. On the other hand, the 48.9% who rejected this stereotype claimed that such popular beliefs stem from a need to deflate the mystique of the therapist by criticizing his or her parenting skills. Rather than being more disturbed, this group felt that the children of psychotherapists are simply more emotionally expressive than other children.

The tendency for some psychotherapists to become grandiose and arrogant can have a detrimental impact on their children, as well. The constant idealization of patients and the authority and control that some therapists possess over their lives can create a sense of omnipotence and superiority which carries over into family interactions. As Cray and Cray (1977) note, some therapists are used to being listened to and even obeyed by their clients. As a result, they begin to sometimes overvalue their opinions and abilities. This can lead to a rather authoritarian, dominant, and controlling style of relating which influences their interactions with their children. It is indeed a shock for such individuals to discover that their children are often uninterested in their insights, and unimpressed with their viewpoints. Furthermore, such an outlook makes the occasional disobedience and disrespect typical of children harder to cope with and accept. Even for those therapists who have a realistic view of their abilities and wisdom, the devaluation and disregard sometimes expressed by children (especially adolescents) can be a source of hurt, anger, and misunderstanding. If not monitored, this pattern can lead to either excessive punitiveness or under-involvement, as the therapist decides whether to "conquer" or "retreat" from the children and parental responsiblities. For example, Freudenberger and Robbins (1979) note that some therapists tend to compensate for their perceived failures as a parent by investing themselves all the more in "parenting" their patients, an endeavor at which they seem to be more effective than with their own family.

Children may come to feel that their behavior and responsiveness to parental direction (or lack thereof) is unfairly compared with that of the parent's clients. They may grow to resent the idealization that the therapist receives from patients and the grandiosity which they sense results. It can indeed be difficult to be the child of an "expert" in human behavior. Arguments and disagreements take on a new meaning when the child realizes that the therapist parent believes that their profession has equipped them to be an authority on all matters related to emotions, thoughts, and behavior. Deep frustration and anger can result from the inability of the therapist parent to admit mistakes and acknowledge the views of his or her children. As important as it may be for childen to be allowed to idealize their parents (Kohut, 1977), it is also essential that they be permitted to see the limitations and shortcomings that are associated with being human. A parent's ability to admit errors and weaknesses in a stage-appropriate manner can have a very positive impact on the child's own self-acceptance and development. Thus the tendency towards grandiosity and superiority must be curtailed as much as possible.

A related concern is the tendency for some therapists to be unable to accept and admit the shortcomings and failures of their own children. It is as though their sense of superiority and omnipotence must extend to the children as well. They, too, must be perfect and well-adjusted. As Bermak (1977) suggests, the families of psychotherapists are often "seen as living examples by society of the nature of their practice and proof of their skill as therapists" (p. 143). Thus the personal and professional reputation of the therapist seemingly depends on the behavior of their children. If left unresolved, this attitude will result in a great deal of pressure being placed on the children to fit into a mold which may not be in their best interests. Instead of encouraging the children to express themselves in a spontaneous, genuine manner, there may be coercion for them to behave and interact in a highly prescribed, overcontrolled way which stunts the development of their own personality or causes them to rebel against such constraints in an extreme fashion. The expectation that one's children must be living examples of mental health and maturity is not likely to be helpful to their personality development.

The need for confidentiality and limited disclosure of work-related information can surround the therapist parent's occupation in a shroud of mystery. Storr (1979) describes it well when he notes:

> Professional discretion means that the therapist is virtually unable to discuss his (her) work with his family, who often have very little idea of what his work entails. . . . If the most important thing which has happened to one during the day is that a particular patient has shown a sudden improvement, or that another has broken off treatment, being unable to talk about this "in front of the children" may increase a parent's remoteness and make the children feel excluded. (p. 183)

Much like the children of government workers, politicians, or spies, they are left largely in the dark concerning the occupation of their parent. This makes it difficult for them to enter into discussions with their peers concerning what it is that their parent does for a living. More important, it denies them the opportunity to feel a part of this important aspect of their parent's world. Unfortunately, this is as it should be. Not only is this necessary to safeguard a patient's confidentiality, but it is unlikely to be appropriate to introduce children to the rather bizarre world of psychopathology and mental illness, at least at too young an age. Those lacking the necessary maturity are simply not ready to hear about the traumas of child abuse, suicide, and psychosis, to name a few. Consequently, for the sake of all those involved, the children are left out of the clinical world in which the parent works. The realization that their parent is preoccupied with unknown events and people may leave them feeling somewhat alienated from him or her. Unfortunately, this seems to be largely unavoidable.

The time constraints associated with the practice of psychotherapy may occasionally place children near the bottom of the priority list. The needs of patients, particularly in the case of those in crisis, take precedence over those of the family (Cray & Cray, 1977). The parents rigidly adhered to professional schedule, which often includes evening and sometimes even weekend appointments, may render them unavailable for the special events, concerts, school programs, ball games, and teacher conferences of the children. Furthermore, a child's sickness or accident may be experienced as an annoying inconvenience to be grudgingly scheduled around rather than an opportunity for providing needed nurturance and support. Children may soon get the feeling that the therapist parent is uninterested and unavailable, a tragic outcome for the skilled "helper" and his or her family.

The financial instability associated with private practice has the potential to impact the children in several ways. Perhaps most basically, they learn that time with the therapist is a commodity to be purchased. The aforementioned tendency for some therapists to give patient appointments priority over the needs of their children may cause guilt and frustration in the offspring, who are told that the parent must prioritize their time in this manner in order to provide for the financial needs of the family. After all, how can a child feel that they have permission to be resentful and angry about being neglected when the parent attributes this regrettable occurrence to his or her role as provider? Furthermore, it may be unsettling for the children to sense anxiety and concern in the therapist parent during times of low referrals and high client attrition. The income swings typical of clinical practice dependent on client fees can be marked, and children may be aware of the stress that results while not being fully equipped emotionally to see it in a broader perspective.

If the therapist's social life begins to revolve around entertaining referral sources, attending professional conferences, and participation in career-related meetings, the children may be left out of such activities. Instead of accompanying their parents, they may be left at home. Children are not typically welcomed at such gatherings, and this can become a chronic pattern if not monitored closely. While the professional feels confident attending such events in the company of his or her spouse, there may be a secret relief resulting from the need to leave the children behind. This can be particularly true for those therapists who feel that the behavior of their children is a bad reflection on their clinical skill. Since children may be able to contribute little to the therapist's marketability (and may even be a liability in some circumstances) they may not have the opportunity to participate in the social life of their parents.

This discussion largely assumes that the children are living in the home with the psychotherapist parent, an assumption that may not be justified given the present rate of divorce among mental health professionals. Those children whose parents have divorced may face some additional negative consequences beyond those already discussed. For example, they must deal with the dissonance which results from reconciling the fact that the parent has been unsuccessful in his or her own marriage while serving as an expert for other couples in marital distress. While a certain cynicism can result from such a realization, there may also be bitterness due to the possible belief that the therapist parent simply did not care enough to utilize his or her expertise to bring about a successful reconciliation with the estranged spouse. If the therapist becomes the noncustodial parent, the children may need to deal with feelings of abandonment and jealousy concerning the time he or she invests in clinical practice rather than in family activities. Career-related time constants may leave little opportunity for the children to see the noncustodial therapist parent. The resultant feelings of rejection, hurt, and alienation may cause these children to reject overtures for reconciliation from the therapist parent. While experiencing divorce is difficult for most children, those with one or both parents employed as therapists may experience some unique additional concerns, as well.

Summary

In the face of a dearth of research in this area, it must be recognized that most of the factors considered in this area are largely the result of conjecture and supposition. However, it does seem reasonable to conclude that having one or both parents employed as a psychotherapist is a mixed blessing. On the one hand, there can be several benefits associated with the personality and behavior of the therapist parent which are directly related to changes which occur during a career in psychotherapy. On the other hand, the role and obligations of the psychotherapist have the potential to impact the children in several negative ways as well. While some children grow up experiencing the advantages that having such a parent affords, causing them to idealize and desire to emulate the therapist parent, others have the opposite reaction. For example, Cray and Cray (1977) quote one child who shouted angrily at his psychotherapist father, "When I grow up, I'll never be a doctor" (p. 338). It appears that a number of personality and environmental variables combine to determine the type and extent of the impact of a career in psychotherapy on the therapist's children.

In view of the seriousness of the potential liabilities associated with clinical practice, some therapists may actually elect not to have any children. While this seems extreme (or perhaps a rationalization), it may be that some therapists will decide that it would be best for everyone if they were not to have children. This would allow them to concentrate solely on the needs of their patients and spouse. Unfortunately, there is no known published data to clarify whether psychotherapists have fewer children than the norm.

For those who decide to have children, suggestions will be given at the end of this chapter on how to minimize the potential negative impact of becoming a psychotherapist on the family and children. While increased awareness is certainly necessary, more aggressive interventions may be appropriate.

Relating with Extended Family

The preceding discussions have been addressed primarily to therapists with a spouse and children. Since most therapists do eventually marry, it seemed appropriate to begin at this point. In addition, those who live, instead, with a "significant other" will also confront many of these same issues. However, the impact of clinical practice can also be felt in the life and relationships of single therapists. This is particularly true regarding the relationships which exist with extended family such as parents and siblings. Regardless of marital status, most individuals maintain some type of relationship with extended family members during the course of a lifetime in clinical practice. For some individuals a career in psychotherapy has a positive impact on these relationships, bringing about growth and desirable change. For others, being a therapist seems only to complicate matters, bringing with it liabilities which weaken already tenuous family ties.

Positive Impact on Family of Origin Relationships

As has been demonstrated, many of the benefits associated with a career in psychotherapy have the potential to positively impact the nuclear family of the therapist. As can be easily surmised, many of these same benefits also apply to a therapist's extended family. The increase in sensitivity, patience, confidence, self-awareness, and self-disclosure which some therapists report experiencing as a result of their practice is likely to have a positive impact on relationships with members of their family of origin. Furthermore, an increased ability to initiate and maintain meaningful intimacy cannot help but benefit relationships with other family members. Most therapists indicate that their work seems to have a positive impact on these relationships (Guy, Stark, & Poelstra, 1987).

In addition to those positive factors summarized previously, there appear to be several benefits associated with a career in psychotherapy which uniquely impact relationships with members of the family of origin. For example, it has been noted by several authors that psychotherapists are typically highly motivated to resolve lingering conflicts, disagreements, and problems with their parents and siblings (Anonymous, 1978; Burton, 1975; Colon, 1973; Fine, 1980; Freudenberger & Robbins, 1979; Friedman, 1971; Henry, 1966). Because conducting psychotherapy involves encounters with patients whose own family problems may parallel those of the therapist, there is often a continued reworking of earlier issues and conflicts which compel the therapist to attempt to resolve them with the family members concerned. In other words, it is difficult to avoid and deny problems with family relationships when the therapist is faced with constant reminders by way of ongoing material discussed with clients. This can be an important positive benefit for relationships with parents and siblings, since the motivation to pursue and confront remaining problems and disputes may result in their successful resolution, improved family intimacy, and more effective communication. The therapist may bring about dramatic reconciliation in an estranged extended family, either through direct interventions or as a result of his or her indirect prompting.

Another benefit to the family of origin is the availability of the therapist for informal consultation and advice on issues related to the mental health and emotional well-being of the extended family. As mentioned in Chapter 1, many who enter the field of psychotherapy were acting in a therapeutic role long before entering formal training. As a result, they were often the emotional caretaker for the extended family prior to assuming the role of therapist (Farber, 1985a). This pattern may continue, with the therapist remaining in this role permanently. Following graduation and entry into the profession, family members often enjoy the benefits of having an "expert" in the family to turn to for advice, support, and appropriate referrals (McCarley, 1975). Having access to someone with expertise in the area of mental health and personality development may be regarded as a privilege by those relatives who encounter stresses and difficulties associated with changing developmental needs over the course of a lifetime. The knowledge and training possessed by the therapist may also be of significant benefit to the family during times of crisis and need. Even when it is obvious that the therapist cannot directly assist or intervene, he or she may serve as a valuable entry point and source of referral in order to facilitate bringing help and relief to those in distress.

Once again, the extended family may take pride in the education, training, and accomplishments of the psychotherapist. Whatever prestige and community status are assigned to the mental health professional may be shared by a parent who feels especially pleased to refer friends and acquaintances to "my daughter, the psychotherapist."

Negative Impact on Family of Origin Relationships

As with the benefits associated with clinical practice, many of the liabilities which negatively impact the nuclear family of the therapist may also affect the extended family. The tendencies toward emotional depletion, withdrawal, psychological-mindedness, loss of self-identity, grandiosity, authoritarianism, secrecy, and emotional preoccupation are likely to have a detrimental impact on relationships with siblings, parents, and more distant relatives as well. Those factors which hinder intimacy within the nuclear family may nearly eliminate it in extended family relationships.

In addition to these considerations, there are several occupational hazards which may uniquely affect family relationships in negative ways. For example, while the tendency for therapists to attempt to resolve families issues and disputes can result in growth and positive change within the family system, its destabilizing effect may create havoc as well. Some family members may experience the therapist's attempts at reconciliation as intrusive, assaultive, obnoxious, and inappropriate. They may be uninterested in dredging up old sources of hurt and conflict, and actively resist attempts toward resolution. It is easy for some individuals (such as parents of the psychotherapist) to mistakenly, if not understandably, feel accused and attacked by the therapist who seems to be indicting them for their personal shortcomings or failures. Rather than resolving conflict, the overeager therapist may find that attempts to reopen past disputes result in greater hurt, anger, and misunderstanding than existed before. Interpretations can begin to sound like accusations, and interventions may be experienced as patronizing directives by siblings and relatives who question the therapist's motives and intentions. In such situations, it is easy to imagine that the extended family may wish that the therapist had pursued a different occupational goal unrelated to mental health. If left to continue, communication may deteriorate altogether as family members withdraw from the therapist due to fears of continued intrusion, confrontation, and criticism. Clearly, unless it is done with great sensitivity, respect, and patience, attempts by psychotherapists to initiate the resolution of long-standing family disputes will likely be met with resistance and even open hostility. In such cases, the therapist, too, may wish that he or she had pursued another vocation, since the training and experience associated with being a psychotherapist make it very difficult to overlook and ignore whatever psychopathology may exist in one's own family system.

A related liability is the inner pressure which the psychotherapist may feel to confront psychopathology within individual family members. While he or she may be able to resist addressing family system pathology, it may be very difficult to decide whether and when it is appropriate to confront directly a family member regarding individual emotional needs. For example, a therapist who notes an increasing number of depressive symptoms in a parent or sibling may not feel that it is appropriate to comment. However, if the symptomology becomes serious enough, the therapist may feel compelled to address this concern openly, even when he or she has not been given explicit permission to do so. The dilemma that this creates for the therapist who attempts to set boundaries and avoid "dual role" conflicts can be very distressing. While individual privacy must be respected, it is difficult to determine when one must speak out regardless of the reactions that such interventions may elicit. Again, this can lead to serious misunderstanding, anger, and hurt feelings. All involved may wish that the psychotherapist would mind his or her own business. Even the therapist may wish, once again, that such distress could be ignored. Unfortunately (or perhaps fortunately), those trained to diagnose and treat mental illness often find it increasingly hard to overlook it when it occurs in serious forms within the family. The burden to confront openly the situation and make an appropriate referral may fall on the therapist. Again, such situations can be very troublesome and are a potential liability for both therapist and the extended family.

As can be seen, the work of the psychotherapist may not always promote positive changes in relationship to the family system or individual family members. In addition to the aforementioned problems, it may be that regularly conducting therapy with patients who complain about family injustices and oversights unrealistically exacerbates the therapist's feelings toward his or her own parents or siblings. Listening to clients express anger or hurt regarding unresolved family conflicts or traumatic memories may irritate or increase the therapist's own negative feelings about his or her family of origin. As a result, distortions or exaggerations can occur which may be detrimental to the therapist's relationships with parents and siblings. On the other hand, the therapist may decide to mistakenly overlook personal family issues which seem minor in comparison to those which are disclosed by his or her patients. Furthermore, there may be an attempt to rationalize poor conflict resolution by distorting clinical theory to support his or her own viewpoint. The training and experience received by the psychotherapist will not necessarily promote healthy family relationships since it basically depends on how the therapist chooses to utilize his or her expertise.

While it is helpful to have an "expert" in the family, some therapists report resenting the implication that they are expected to meet all of the emotional needs of the extended family (McCarley, 1975). While they may have willingly and gladly fulfilled this function prior to entering training, they may now find such expectations to be unrealistic and burdensome (Farber, 1985a). Psychotherapists who are reasonably successful in setting boundaries typically resist serving as the "answer man or woman" regarding mental health issues. Instead, they wish to relate to extended family members in a normal, nonclinical manner. Rather than entertaining family gatherings with stories about patients, they prefer to talk about other things such as sports, politics, religion, and the like. However, the tendency for others to either highly idealize or overly criticize psychotherapists may render this wish impossible. Instead, therapists often find themselves bombarded with questions about a particular person's symptoms, another's medication, an innovative treatment regimen recently begun by an acquaintance, and a neighbor's psychiatric hospitalization. Whether met with overly positive or negative reactions, the therapist finds that the assigned role of the family expert becomes a very restrictive and tiring one which limits spontaneity and true encounter. In such situations, it may be the therapist rather than the family member who withdraws and isolates from the extended family in order to avoid being burdened with the needs, questions, and complaints of relatives. Unless boundaries are clearly drawn and respected, this tendency may further undermine intimacy and communication within the family.

Although the need for these precautions seems reasonable, some family members may misunderstand the actual motivation of the therapist who seems to be withholding valuable input. They may accuse him or her of being uncaring, stingy, or insensitive. It may appear to them that the therapist only cares for those who are willing to pay his or her professional fee. As a result, while the therapist feels exploited by such requests, relatives feel rejected and hurt by his or her refusal to respond in a professional, helpful manner. Again, it is necessary for all involved to understand fully the need for the therapist to be able to step out of the professional role when with relatives. On the other hand, the therapist may have somewhat of an ethical and moral obligation as a professional to function in a helpful manner when appropriate, even if only to provide a referral to another therapist.

Some therapists have found that the public's image concerning the lucrativeness of a career in psychotherapy (a questionable assumption at best) can be a liability regarding relationships with extended family. Because of the surprisingly common misperception that psychotherapists earn a large income, it is not entirely unusual for some parents, siblings, or more distant relatives to approach the therapist for loans and financial support (McCarley, 1975). For example, McCarley reports that several psychotherapists who participated in a therapist support group complained of family members frequently requesting financial assistance. It appeared to them that this was viewed as a natural extension of the caretaker role that they played in the family. The imposition and intrusion that such requests represent may offend and anger the therapist. If the therapist is unwilling (or unable) to support members of the extended family, those requesting financial assistance may react with hurt, anger, and disbelief at being sent away "empty handed." After all, someone in the "helping professions" seems like an appropriate person to approach for assistance. Consequently, once again misunderstanding and alienation may result on both sides if this issue is not carefully and openly discussed.

Summary

Due to the impact of a career in psychotherapy on the personality of the therapist, it is not uncommon for parents, siblings, and more distant relatives to be affected by his or her vocation as well. In some cases the impact will be quite direct and apparent, while in others it will be more indirect and subtle. Regardless, the family of origin, in particular, is likely to experience the impact of this career choice on the family system. Again, the results may be a mixed bag of assets and liabilities.

Family relationships are the ultimate testing ground for the personality of the psychotherapist. It is here that he or she must confront personal shortcomings and failures. Although therapists may be perceived as experts in human relationships, few feel accordingly when relating with family members. It is difficult for the therapist to accept that, despite extensive training and experience, many of the same relationship problems remain. Furthermore, while many of the positive changes which occur in the emotional life of the therapist impact relationships with family members in helpful ways, it appears that some occupational hazards can have a detrimental effect as well.

As the old adage states, "A prophet is never a prophet in his (her) own hometown," making it all the more difficult for everyone involved to accept the shortcomings of the therapist while acknowledging his or her expertise in helping others. Rather than the subject of scorn, however, it must be admitted with gratitude that psychotherapists are able to effectively assist others with relationship problems even while experiencing many of their own.

SOCIAL RELATIONSHIPS

Having examined the impact of psychotherapeutic practice on relationships with one's spouse, children, and extended family, it is time to turn attention to its effect on relationships with friends. By now it should be apparent that the personal assets and liabilities of being a psychotherapist noticeably affect interactions with nearly everyone with whom the therapist experiences an intimate relationship.

Thus it is not surprising to find that therapists report that their work also impacts their social relationships.

Positive Impact on Friendships

Cogan (1977) surveyed practicing psychotherapists regarding their perceptions of the effect of therapeutic practice on friendships and social relationships. He found that a majority reported that the training and experience associated with becoming a therapist improved the depth, intensity, and openness of their friendships. These individuals expressed the belief that they were becoming better able to participate meaningfully in relationships with friends outside of therapy because of their work as therapists. Guy, Stark, and Poelstra (1987) found a similar pattern in their study of psychotherapists, with 74% of those surveyed reporting that clinical practice positively impacted on relationships with friends.

A number of factors may contribute to this outcome. For example, Farber (1983b) found that "many therapists (56.4% surveyed) felt that as a result of their work they now had a greater appreciation of human diversity and a greater understanding of the universal difficulties and vulnerabilities of people; some (14.5%) felt, too, that as a result of their practice, their faith in people had been raised" (p. 180). These therapists reported experiencing a greater appreciation for others, with an increased ability to be accepting and tolerant of diversity. It would seem reasonable to conclude that these changes result in an increased ability to develop friendships with others, resulting in a mature and tolerant attitude.

In a later article, Farber (1985a) notes that the development of psychological-mindedness also improves the quality of the therapist's social skills and interactions, "greatly enhancing interpersonal relationships, adding depth, subtlety, nuance, and irony to the understanding and appreciation of others" (p. 174). Thus the understanding and insight which are associated with the ability to think analytically result in a greater acceptance and appreciation for the thoughts and feelings of others, increasing the therapist's ability to approach others in friendship.

Many of the benefits and assets associated with clinical practice are also likely to impact the friendships of therapists in several positive ways. For example, the increase in self-awareness, self-assurance, self-disclosure, assertiveness, sensitivity, tolerance, and caring reported by psychotherapists to be a result of their practice of psychotherapy presumably will make them better able to build meaningful and lasting friendships. Such improvements and personality changes are apt to enhance the quality of social interactions, making them better friends while causing them to be more accepting of and satisfied with others.

Friends of therapists may experience some additional benefits not directly related to the personality of the therapist. For example, they may find that the therapist is willing to give informal advice regarding everyday problems, childrearing, dealing with aged parents, and the like. The availability of such a resource can become important during times of crisis. Furthermore, the therapist friend is able to make appropriate, thoughtful referrals when the concerns are serious enough to warrant professional attention. Friends may also find that the psychotherapist is willing to share interesting clinical caveats, psychological concepts, treatment and diagnostic techniques, and general information which make for interesting and stimulating discussion. Finally, some individuals may be very proud of the work and accomplishments of their therapist friend, and they may share in some of the community prestige afforded to him or her by virtue of their association and friendship.

Negative Impact on Friendships

For many of the same reasons mentioned in regard to spouse and family, the practice of psychotherapy may not always be conducive to successful friendships and social relationships. As Freudenberger and Robbins (1979) note, the training and experience associated with being a therapist sometimes decreases the pleasure and comfort of social encounters for a variety of reasons.

The emotional depletion and exhaustion resulting from conducting therapy sometimes leaves little in reserve for friends and acquaintances (Burton, 1975). Following a long day of professional appointments, a therapist may feel unable or unwilling to be supportive and empathic toward friends who approach with personal needs or concerns, either in person or by telephone. Since it is sometimes hard to extend such caring towards one's spouse and children with regularity, it may be all the more difficult to do so towards others outside of the family. Therapists may feel intruded on when friends approach with personal problems and they may resent their expectations and requests.

When emotional depletion causes the therapist to ignore either implicit or explicit requests for support or assistance, friends may feel hurt, rejected, and even abandoned. They may interpret this to mean that the therapist is uncaring or overly self-involved. It is hard to accept that the therapist invests himself or herself in the needs of paying clients while distancing from friends in distress. On the other hand, even if they accept and understand his or her inability to provide help or encouragement, the friendship may be strained due to their resultant hesitation to impose or intrude on the therapist's privacy. Rather than "pester" the psychotherapist, they may call infrequently and hesitate to initiate social contacts. Misunderstandings such as these can create a gulf between the therapist and his or her friends, hindering meaningful friendship.

The isolation inherent in the role of the psychotherapist in both its physical and psychological forms hinders attempts to initiate and maintain friendships. Tendencies towards one-way intimacy, anonymity, and overcontrol reduce therapists' ability to be spontaneous, genuine, and vulnerable with friends. This may result in a tendency to withdraw and avoid social encounters. Lacking both the emotional energy and motivation for spending time with friends, the absence of intimacy which results when the therapist remains aloof and invulnerable may rob social encounters of meaning and importance for all concerned (Freudenberger & Robbins, 1979). As a result, the psychotherapist may find friends to be boring and superficial compared to his or her patients, while the friends may find the therapist to be increasingly aloof and unavailable. If this pattern continues, there remains little reason to maintain the friendship.

It may also be that as a result of spending hundreds or thousands of hours with individuals who struggle with a variety of emotional or behavioral problems, the therapist's view of humanity becomes sufficiently distorted to make it increasingly hard to trust others enough to even initiate friendships. In other words, if the world begins to seem populated by suspicious, needy, troubled, or impulsive individuals, such as those comprising the majority of a therapist's caseload, he or she may feel hesitant to approach anyone for friendship. This may increase social withdrawal and isolation to unhealthy proportions.

Psychotherapists who find it hard to set aside the therapeutic role, and consequently remain interpretive and analytic with friends, find that this can hinder intimacy and satisfying friendship. Becoming too psychologically minded may result in the therapist behaving in an intrusive, controlling, authoritarian, and superior manner which often hurts and offends friends and acquaintances. Such tendencies sabotage interpersonal relationships, decreasing the mutuality and equality necessary for satisfying closeness. Friends may grow to resent uninvited interpretations and "interventions" or become bored with the grandiose, superior attitude of the therapist who seems compelled to act like an authority on living. In either case, the therapist will likely be avoided as friends grow weary of dealing with this relentless clinical style. As mentioned previously, many psychotherapists report that they find it very difficult to resist being interpretive and "therapeutic" with friends and acquaintances (Deutsch, 1984; Farber, 1983b; Hellman et al., 1986). Thus the potential negative impact of this pattern requires serious consideration on the part of practicing therapists who are likely to fall into a similar pattern if corrective measures are not taken.

This increasing lack of spontaneity and the loss of self-identity may have a detrimental impact on the ability to relate to friends as well as family. If all the therapist is able to do is mirror others, friends will begin to realize that, while they risk self-disclosure and vulnerability, the therapist remains a stranger who is invulnerable and detached. As a result, it is very difficult for friends to feel that they really "know" the therapist at a meaningful, personal level. While most therapists are excellent conversationalists and particularly talented at putting others at ease, an inability to express oneself in a spontaneous, self-revealing fashion creates a gap between therapist and friends.

The tendency for some therapists to live vicariously through the lives of their clients may reduce their motivation and perceived need for friends and social encounters outside of work (Bugental, 1964; Burton, 1975). The safe intimacy experienced in the therapy relationship may become preferrable to that experienced with nonpatients. Furthermore, since conversations with patients are typically emotionally charged and significant, the therapist may compare such encounters with social interactions which seem superficial and mundane in comparison. After spending all day struggling with issues such as suicide, divorce, incest, and existential angst, conversations with friends regarding sports, finances, and the price of radial tires pale in comparison. Actually, the mistake is made in making the comparison to begin with. Psychotherapists who fail to recognize the important differences between relationships with patients and those with friends may mistakenly prefer the highly prescribed professional encounters over the more uncertain ones outside of the office.

As was true with family relationships, the need for confidentiality restricts the amount of information that a therapist can disclose to friends about patients and clinical responsibilities. While it is possible to talk in general terms, a therapist may feel the need to be even more careful discussing his or her work with friends than with family, since the risk of violating patient confidentiality increases once the information has left the home. As a result, most friends of therapists will know few details about the work and the patients encountered. The sense of mystery that results can add to the aforementioned tendency toward distance and aloofness. Even when the therapist feels free to discuss his or her work, its complex, highly specialized nature may make it very difficult to describe what the work actually entails (Farber, 1983a). If, after a detailed explanation about the nature of psychotherapy, the friend replies by saying in astonishment, "People pay you for that?," the therapist begins to realize that it is very difficult to describe its importance to others.

The need for the therapist to place patient concerns above those of friends can negatively impact these relationships. For example, a therapist may have to cancel a social engagement if a patient in crisis needs an emergency session or psychiatric hospitalization. The frequent need to schedule some appointments in the evening may prevent the therapist from participating in social activities with friends. A hectic, rigidly followed appointment schedule may make it nearly impossible for friends to reach the therapist by telephone during a work day, for either casual conversation or at a time of need. As a result of these factors, friends may feel quite low on the therapist's priority list. The busier the therapist becomes, the greater may be the tendency to resist calling or visiting with him or her, due to the belief that career concerns have depleted the emotional resources of the psychotherapist. In such cases, friends may decide that it would be more caring to leave him or her alone, an unfortunate but understandable conclusion.

While it may seem advantageous to have a psychotherapist for a friend during a time of emotional crisis, expectations for receiving support, caring, and guidance may not always be met. Due to the emotional depletion, withdrawal, and hectic lifestyle of some therapists, they may be unable or unwilling to be very helpful to friends in need. Furthermore, as in the case of the extended family, the therapist may resent the assumptions of friends who expect free advice, ongoing support, and frequent help. Such expectations can result in the therapist feeling "used" and exploited by friends who seem to take advantage of the situation. From the other perspective, friends may find it very difficult to understand the therapist's hesitancy to get involved and assist during a time of need. Expecting help from a therapist friend who willingly attends to the needs of paying clients may not seem like an imposition to friends in distress, and misunderstanding can result if this issue is not fully discussed and mutually agreed on boundaries established.

As discussed in detail in Chapter 3, public perceptions regarding the role of psychotherapist can further hinder friendships and social encounters. In the case of friends who have an overly idealized image of the psychotherapist, the therapist may feel uncomfortable acknowledging personal concerns, problems, and failures, fearing rejection if they become disappointed with the therapist's mere mortality. Friends with this impression will also find it difficult to be themselves, since it is hard to be comfortable admitting personal limitations when in the presence of perfection. On the other hand, friends who seem suspicious or critical of the therapist's profession may cause him or her to feel defensive and uncomfortable, making it difficult to be vulnerable and open about needs, disappointments, and failures out of a fear of attack or ridicule. Such individuals may also resist being open with the therapist, since, for example, they may be fearful of being "analyzed" or manipulated. In either case, the fact that the friend is a therapist seems to loom large in the minds of both parties, making it nearly impossible for either to feel and behave like normal, everyday people. Unless friends can set aside their stereotypes of the psychotherapist (regardless of whether they are positive or negative), chances for comfortable, meaningful friendship will be greatly reduced.

The inner pressure that the therapist may feel regarding the need to generate referrals may impact relationships with friends. As mentioned previously, the need to market one's clinical ability sometimes influences which parties are attended and clubs joined. While few therapists are likely to choose their friends on this basis, they may feel the temptation to encourage friends to refer their acquaintances for therapy, creating a potential for exploitation and misunderstanding. Furthermore, therapists may hesitate to disclose personal needs and problems to friends in order to keep from jeopardizing future referrals. After all, who will refer an acquaintance to a therapist friend who has yet to master life's assorted problems? Regarding personal friends as good sources of referrals can lead to these, and similar, distorted beliefs and behaviors. Such tendencies will certainly contaminate personal friendships if left unrestrained.

Summary

In view of the potential hazards associated with the practice of psychotherapy, one is left to wonder to what extent they combine to impair a therapist's ability to initiate and maintain meaningful friendships. While recent research findings do not provide conclusive data concerning this question, some trends are emerging which suggest that these factors do seem to have an impact.

Farber (1983b) reports that the therapists he surveyed indicated that their career in psychotherapy had a noticeable impact on their social relationships. He notes that "according to 64.9%, people tend to be more self-disclosing and even expect advice or dream analysis" when they learn that the person they are talking to is a psychotherapist (p. 180). On the other hand, "many therapists (52.6%) also felt that some people are threatened by their presence and become less self-disclosing" (p. 180). Either reaction may hinder mutual self-disclosure and reciprocal intimacy. It is difficult for therapists to set aside their clinical persona and behave in a spontaneous manner in the face of such reactions. In regards to therapists' social patterns, Farber notes that although some (30.6%) reported that being a therapist had no particular impact on their own social behavior, a greater number (40.8%) indicated that they tended to socialize less as a result of their work. Several reported that they found it increasingly difficult to relate in a genuine, spontaneous, and comfortable manner with friends.

Cogan (1977) found a similar pattern among the therapists he surveyed. Although most reported that being a psychotherapist improved the depth and quality of their friendships by helping them to be more open and sensitive, there was a dramatic decrease in the number and intensity of friendships among those in practice for 10 years or more. Thus while therapists reported enjoying friends more, in reality they spent increasingly less time with friends, and they noted that the relationships had become less intense.

Freudenberger and Robbins (1979) suggest that the social life of psychotherapists often begin to merge with their professional life. An increasing amount of time is spent in the company of other therapists, while less and less time is spent with friends outside of the profession. Psychotherapists tend to cluster into cliques and exclusive groups which rarely include nontherapists. Parties and social gatherings become opportunities for discussing difficult patients, new treatment techniques, the latest diagnostic buzzwords, and the shocking ethical violations of a formerly esteemed colleague. As a result, there is a peculiar blending of work and play, an intertwining of social and professional concerns which allow the therapist to remain largely in the clinical mode, comfortable behind the well-practiced persona. The pattern of one-way intimacy perfected by many therapists creates a rather bizarre situation at such gatherings, as each psychotherapist diligently mirrors the other and no one actually reveals a thing! As noted in Chapter 3, these patterns increase the psychic and physical isolation that the therapist experiences in regard to the everyday world, allowing for the development of gross distortions and a sense of superiority and detachment. Most of all, it can lead to a deep loneliness, dissatisfaction, disillusionment, and eventual burnout.

As was the case when considering the impact of psychotherapeutic practice on family relationships, its impact on friendships and social relationships has the potential to be both positive and negative. It would appear, once again, that it is up to the psychotherapist, and those with whom he or she relates, to strive to maximize the benefits while minimizing or eliminating the liabilities. If left unattended, the work of the therapist has the potential to undermine the foundation for intimacy in nearly every important personal relationship.

RECOMMENDATIONS

In view of the potential for psychotherapeutic practice to either enhance or sabotage intimate relationships with family and friends, it is necessary for therapists to be alert and prepared for its impact on their private life and personal relationships. Perhaps this self-awareness is the most important step in confronting these issues. Truly, "forewarned is forearmed". Unless psychotherapists take frequent inventory of the impact of their clinical practice on their emotional well-being and interpersonal functioning, they are likely to be affected in ways outside of both their awareness and control. In light of this self-awareness, the concerned psychotherapist may wish to take one or more practical steps to ensure a balanced, healthy lifestyle which will increase the potential for meaningful social relationships. While some of these recommendations were given in Chapter 3, they bear repeating here.

Intimacy with a Significant Other

Most importantly, psychotherapists need to place their own private life and relationships at the top of the priority list. Unless they live a full, satisfying life of their own, they will have little of substance to offer their clients (Freudenberger & Robbins, 1979). In order to combat the debilitating effects of psychotherapeutic practice, the therapist must invest time and energy in developing "non-sublimated forms of intimacy with friends and lovers" (Bermak, 1977, p. 144). Chessick (1978) agrees with this assertion by noting that psychotherapists need mature love relationships in their personal life in order to replenish their "anguished souls". The meaning and fulfillment received from such relationships then empowers the therapist to effectively function in the vacuous world of loneliness, isolation, and distress inherent in conducting psychotherapy with often severely disturbed individuals. Guggenbuhl-Craig (1979) notes that investing energy in developing love relationships outside of work provides a corrective balance to the many distortions resulting from the surreal world of clinical practice.

While it is not necessary for a psychotherapist to be married to enjoy psychic balance, it seems important for the therapist to have one or more sufficiently intimate relationships in order to provide the support, empathy, and reality testing needed for resisting the depletion and isolation associated with the practice of psychotherapy. As Gugenbuhl-Craig (1979) puts it:

> What the analyst (psychotherapist) needs is symetrical relationships, relationships with partners who are up to his (her) mark, friends who dare to attack him, to point out not only his virtues but his ridiculous sides. This kind of stimulation may be found with friends of the same sex; it can also take place within a marriage - the depths of the shadow must be plumbed in love. People not schooled in analysis develop largely through intensive interpersonal relationships. The analyst has no choice but to do the same. (p. 135)

It will be extremely difficult for a therapist to resist the potential negative impact of clinical work on social relationships without the help of a significant other, an intimate soul mate who will confront tendencies towards isolation, withdrawal, grandiosity, authoritarianism, and superiority. In a world in which everyone begins to seem like a patient, the psychotherapist desperately needs someone who will be an accurate mirror, a cattle prod, and a nurturing breast.

In order to provide the type of intimate relationship, whether with a spouse or friend, several steps must be taken to initiate and maintain this level of closeness. First, time must be given to cultivating the relationship. This requires mutual commitment to make the association a top priority. Schedules and obligations must be adapted to allow for both quantity and quality time together. The potential hazards of the profession must be openly and periodically discussed in order to enlist the partner's help in combating emotional withdrawal, isolation, decreasing empathy, inappropriate psychological-mindedness, superiority, vicarious living, and overcommitment. Explicit permission and invitation must be extended to the partner to ensure honest confrontation when such patterns are noticed. The therapist will need help in resisting a tendency to unnecessarily withhold information and create a sense of mystery about his or her work. Even more importantly, psychotherapists need at least one person who will confront their inclination to become over-extended and too busy with clinical obligations to allow for sufficient relaxation and communion with the significant other.

If the therapist is to maintain this level of closeness with at least one person, whether or not this is a spouse, this relationship must be regarded as a top priority. If the concerns cited above are legitimate, this must be done for the therapist to function effectively in both professional and personal spheres. Nothing appears to be more important for overall emotional health than the maintenance of this crucial relationship (Looney, et. al., 1980).

Relating with Family

While the therapist needs at least one intensely intimate relationship to combat the debilitating side-effects of clinical work as they impact his or her personal relationships, most individuals need more than this relationship alone. As Cray & Cray (1977) suggest, the psychotherapist needs a family to provide a balance and corrective to the distorting influence of his or her career role. This is not to suggest that the therapist must be either married or have children. Rather, it reflects the realization that therapists need relatives, from both the nuclear and extended family who will openly address those issues and concerns. Relatives, such as parents or siblings, often have the unique ability and freedom to be honest with their perceptions, perhaps because their personal investment and caring is greater than that of friends. Or, maybe blood relatives feel an implicit permission to give feedback, since they have a sense of perspective and history with the therapist which permits them to more open about their concerns. Family members can be important allies for the therapist attempting to minimize the impact of the hazards associated with practicing psychotherapy.

Since most psychotherapists do marry, it is usually the spouse and children of the therapist who function in this capacity. As Marjorie Cray (Cray & Cray, 1977) notes:

> The family provides many advantages, which can certainly help the emotional well-being of the psychiatrist (psychotherapist). We are reality. If the psychiatrist is getting this distorted view of self-importance, his (her) children can take him down a beg.

When he gets the distorted impression that everyone is going to Europe, his family, the necessity of educating his children, will quickly bring him back to reality. (p. 338)

The spouse is often the significant other, the individual who is most intimately acquainted with the therapist's shortcomings and limitations. Thus, it is he or she who may serve as the primary source of feedback, support, and understanding. However, if the therapist has children, they are likely to be an important source of help as well. Guggenbuhl-Craig (1979) points out that children are often able to be extremely honest and insightful concerning an increase in emotional deple- tion, isolation, withdrawal, decreasing investment, and so on. They are typically very sensitive to flucutations in intimacy and emotional investment, and they may sense the impact of clinical practice in ways that are outside of the therapist's im- mediate awareness.

> Children, in their free and open development, can also penetrate to the analyst's (psychotherapist's) shadow and drag it out into the light. The tragedy of childless therapist's is not that their natural need for descendants remains unfulfilled, but that they miss the challenge which children offer. (Guggenbuhl-Craig, 1979, p. 136)

While children can be an important source of help to the therapist, they can also be a burdern and source of inconvenience. It will be necessary for the therapist to decide with his or her spouse how to equitably assign the many responsibilities associated with parenthood. Beyond the everyday duties, children get sick, emergencies do arise, and time must be given to coping with the many needs of the children as they occur. However, the benefits which they bring to the therapist's personal well-being, and the overall quality of the therapist's treat- ment ability, more than surpass the inconveniences which may result.

As mentioned above, if family members are to serve as partners in the therapist's attempts to resist the negative impact associated with the practice of therapy, it will be necessary for these relationships to have sufficient priority in the therapist's life. Time must be spent in open dialogue, mutual sharing, and meaningful self-disclosure in order to confront tendencies toward withdrawal, and so on. The psychotherapist will need the family's help in order to keep the noted occupational hazards from sabotaging family relationships. While it may seem banal, the most important precaution that a therapist can take, apart from in- creased self-awareness, is to solict and listen to the feedback of family members regarding personality changes that they perceive in the therapist over a period of months and years. The accuracy and honesty of family members can greatly as- sist the therapist in reducing the negative impact of his or her clinical work.

Relating with Friends

The need for psychotherapists to have friends is one which is widely recognized. Guggenbuhl-Craig (1979) states, "friendship intensely lived, and intensely suf- fered, saves many a therapist from inextricable entanglement in his (her) own dark and destructive side. Hatred and love flow back and forth between friends;

love circles around the positive potential, and hatred around the negative" (p. 136). Friends are sometimes able to provide the honest, pointed feedback described above as necessary, assisting the therapist in resisting the debilitating effects of his or her work on interpersonal functioning. They can help to replenish depleted emotional reserves, provide empathy and understanding, and give support and nurturance when needed.

It is not only important that the therapist have friends, but that the circle of friends include individuals outside of the profession (Guy & Liaboe, 1986a). Storr (1979) suggests that this is one of the more significant ways that therapists can battle the hazards of being in clinical practice. He states, "I think it very important that therapists have as normal a social life as possible, in which they meet as friends people in entirely different walks of life who pursue entirely different vocations" (p. 184). By expanding one's social life beyond professional acquaintances, a more balanced perspective on human behavior and experience is promoted. Friends who are neither idealistic nor critical of the therapist's profession, but simply unaffected by it, will be an excellent balance to tendencies towards grandiosity, authoritarianism, superiority, and dominance. They may also confront more aggressively the therapist's wish to remain interpretive and anonymous, pointing out the inappropriateness of this pattern. Friends outside the profession will introduce the therapist to activities and interests far from the professional workshops, seminars, retreats, and conferences which often dominate the free time of therapists whose only friends are other psychotherapists. Finally, the priorities which non-therapist friends model for the psychotherapist may be of great help in maintaining the proper perspective on life. While patient concerns regarding self-esteem, narcissistic wounds, and depression are certainly important, they are no more so than issues such as neighborhood crime, poverty, political corruption, nuclear threat, and a child's hurt feelings. Friends have a way of bringing this type of balance to a therapist's life.

Other Considerations

There are a number of additional steps that may need to be taken in order for the practicing psychotherapist to minimize or to eliminate the potential negative impact of work on interpersonal relationships. Most of these focus on creating a balanced, well-rounded lifestyle which increases personal adjustment and overall life satisfaction. For example, as recommended previously, the practicing psychotherapist may find it necessary to diversify professional activities to include supervision, teaching, consultation, research, or writing in order to reduce the isolation associated with conducting psychotherapy (Farber, 1983a; Freudenberger & Robbins, 1979; Guy & Liaboe, 1986a). It may also be helpful to develop a second career outside of the mental health field in order to provide variety, stimulation and exposure to different types of people.

Pursuing personal psychotherapy, supervision, or formal consultation may provide additional support, understanding, and guidance (Freudenberger & Robbins, 1979; Goldberg, 1986). The pursuit of further training, either inside or outside of one's specialty, provides fresh input and new social encounters (McCarley, 1975). Regular interdisciplinary interactions are another way to enrich one's professional life. Joining regional, state, and national professional organizations may be a further way to expand one's horizons and meet other professionals. Finally, taking regular vacations, sabbaticals, and days off enable the therapist to participate more fully in the pleasures and excitement of life (Farber, 1985a).

DISCUSSION

The importance of maintaining meaningful interpersonal relationships cannot be overstated. Psychotherapists need as much, if not more love, understanding, nurturance, support, confrontation, and guidance as any other person. Without these sources of personal emotional nourishment, the therapist may experience loneliness, depression, and ultimately, despair (Chessick, 1978). This can result in a growing sense of dissatisfaction and disillusionment with life, rendering it meaningless and void of purpose. As discussed, some aspects associated with conducting psychotherapy have the potential to hinder interpersonal effectiveness and sabotage meaningful relationships. Their impact on the ability to experience intimacy with family and friends can be quite profound, in some cases. Unless psychotherapists, and their loved ones, are alerted to these hazards and strive to reduce their effects, they may find that it becomes increasingly difficult to relate in sufficiently satisfying ways. When this occurs, the psychotherapist has lost one of the primary joys of living, that associated with experiencing interpersonal intimacy. Regardless of how wealthy or successful, without meaningful personal relationships the therapist may find little fulfillment and pleasure.

A psychotherapist who lacks sufficient love relationships in his or her private life will have little to offer patients. Regardless of the level of expertise and clinical talent possessed by the therapist, therapeutic encounters will have a certain hollowness to them which most clients will sense. Since the experiential component is as critical as the instructional aspects of the therapy relationship, patients may become aware of the therapist's despondency and emotional pain. In some cases, such therapists will turn to their patients to satisfy their needs for intimacy and love, to the detriment of the patient and the treatment relationship. In other cases, the therapist will simply go through the motions of conducting therapy, attempting to encourage growth and development in a rather unconvincing manner. It is difficult for such therapists to encourage patients to optimistically embrace the potential of life if they have not found meaning and satisfaction in their own personal relationships. Thus, not only will the personal life of the therapist suffer in such cases, but treatment relationships will be negatively impacted as well.

In this chapter, attention has been focused on the varying impact of conducting psychotherapy, with its potential benefits and liabilities for personal relationships with family and friends. While greater stress has been placed on the need to directly confront the hazards of the profession in order to eliminate or reduce their detrimental effects on interpersonal functioning, it warrants repeating that the practice of psychotherapy also has the potential to enhance the nature and quality of relationships with family and friends due to the emotional growth and personality changes which it often promotes. These potential benefits usually outweigh the liabilities for most therapists. As a result, many therapists report that their personal life and relationships are enriched by the practice of therapy, improving their ability to experience interpersonal intimacy and increasing their satisfaction with life, in general. While it is important to be on guard against the eroding effects of the hazards of the profession, it is encouraging to remember that the assets outweigh the liabities for most individuals.

In Chapter 5, attention will be turned towards the impact of significant developmental events in the life of the psychotherapist. Major changes such as marriage, pregnancy, parenting, family crisis, divorce, illness and disability, death of a loved one, and aging and retirement affect not only the therapist's personal life, but treatment relationships and the ability to conduct psychotherapy as well. The discussion will focus on the interaction between the personal and professional concerns of the psychotherapist, as these events are experienced by both therapist and patient.

CHAPTER 5

Significant Events in the Life of the Psychotherapist

Daniel Levinson, author of *The Seasons in a Man's Life* (1978), recently summarized his conceptualization of adult development by dividing the life cycle into several distinct eras (Levinson,1986). These eras include: the Early Adult Transition; ages 17 to 22; the Entry Life Structure for Early Adulthood, ages 22 to 28; the Age 30 Transition, ages 28 to 30; the Culminating Life Structure of Early Adulthood, ages 33 to 40; the Mid-life Transition, ages 40 to 45; the Entry Life Structure for Middle Adulthood, ages 45 to 50; the Age 50 Transition, ages 50 to 55; the Culminating Life Structure for Middle Adulthood, ages 55 to 60; and the Late Adult Transition, ages 60 to 65. Each era has its own distinct goals, conflicts, and developmental issues which must be confronted. As Looney et al. (1980) point out, Levinson's model has particular relevance for the psychotherapist whose personal and professional life are impacted as he or she passes through each of these eras. In addition to the developmental issues and concerns common to most individuals, therapists seem to experience several others which are uniquely related to the role of psychotherapist and the practice of psychotherapy.

Regardless of psychotherapists' attempts to remain stable, neutral, and anonymous in therapy relationships, their life and work are often significantly impacted by the major life events associated with passing through each developmental era. Marriage, pregnancy, parenthood, moving to a new location, death of a loved one, personal illness or accident, aging, retirement, and eventual death may profoundly affect the psychotherapist, impacting both private inner life and professional encounters. Guy, Stark, and Poelstra (1987) found that 75% of the psychotherapists surveyed nationwide reported that they had experienced one or more such potentially distressing episodes during the past three years. The interacting relationship between the personality of the psychotherapist and the practice of psychotherapy creates several issues concerning the impact of these significant life events on patients and the therapist's ability to conduct psychotherapy effectively.

This chapter will focus on the impact of several significant events in the life of the psychotherapist, their potential effects on therapy patients and the practice of psychotherapy, and ways in which being a therapist influences how these events are experienced in the personal life of the clinician.

THE PROBLEM OF THERAPIST SELF-DISCLOSURE

Before considering these significant life events, it is necessary to address first the issue of self-disclosure as it relates to the practice of psychotherapy. In most treatment relationships, the therapist seems to be a reasonably stable, steady figure who appears capable of handling life's many trials with little difficulty (Bellak, 1981). Yet, regardless of the therapist's wish to provide a treatment relationship which allows the focus to remain unerringly on the client, unaffected by events and circumstances in their own life, it is often impossible to create such a sterile, unchanging enviroment. The impact of many of life's significant events is often powerful enough to influence the therapy relationship in ways obvious to both patient and therapist. For example, it may be both difficult and unhelpful to avoid discussing the therapist's change in marital status, pregnancy, recent illness, and the like. As a result, these issues must be addressed at some level in the treatment relationship. Yet, when and how this is to be done is often unclear.

As Flaherty (1979) notes, there is a wide divergence of opinion regarding the issue of therapist self-disclosure, varying from permitting an extreme amount to almost none at all, depending on the theoretical orientation and the personality of the psychotherapist. This diversity of viewpoints is reflected in the literature, with some writers warning against the hazards of self-disclosure while others suggest its usefulness. As a result, there are no uniform standards to guide the therapist who must decide when and what to share with a client regarding significant events in his or her own personal life as they may relate to the therapy relationship.

Some theorists suggest that therapist self-disclosure is almost always detrimental to the treatment relationship. For example, Freud (1912) recommended that psychoanalysts remain opaque to their patients. He states that, like a mirror, they should only reflect back what is given to them, revealing very little about their own thoughts, feelings, and experiences. Weiner (1972) also suggests that therapist self-exposure is typically inappropriate for the therapy relationship because it can disturb a weak therapeutic alliance, add fuel to a "negative transference" in which the patient may already be experiencing the therapist as self-centered and weak, and draw attention away from the needs and concerns of the patient. However, despite his negative view of therapist self-disclosure, Weiner admits that a limited amount may be helpful in establishing a real relationship between the therapist and an adolescent or adult borderline patient. However, such exceptions are rare, and disclosure must be done carefully and in limited amounts to ensure that it is in the best interest of the patient rather than in the service of the therapist's own personal needs.

While nonpsychoanalytic therapists may find these concerns to be outmoded or exaggerated, it is interesting to note the results of a recent study in which it was found that the greater the use of therapist's self-disclosure, the lower the patients' impressions and evaluations of the therapist's empathy, competence, and trustworthiness (Curtis, 1981). Curtis summarized his findings by saying:

> The results raise doubt regarding the predictability of therapists' self-disclosure as a psychotherapeutic technique and suggest that, at least with respect to the type of self-disclosure used in this study (e.g., "I sometimes feel depressed too"), therapists who utilize self-disclosing techniques may risk adversely affecting essential impressions on which a therapeutic alliance is established. (p. 127)

It would appear that there may be some empirical justification for concern regarding the impact of self-disclosure on the therapy relationship.

In contrast to these warnings, other leaders in the field have noted important benefits of self-disclosure for many treatment relationships. For example, A. Freud (1954), Gitelson (1952), and Greenson (1967) suggest that a certain amount of self-disclosure on the part of the therapist allows the client to discover him or her as a real person, and facilitates the establishment of the "real" relationship, a necessary component for successful treatment. In this view, the limited sharing of personal interests and concerns can strengthen the "working alliance" between the therapist and the patient, providing an opportunity for deeper intimacy and more meaningful encounter.

While there is disagreement among theorists concerning the appropriateness of voluntary therapist self-disclosure, few would suggest that complete anonymity is possible. Both Fromm-Reichmann (1960) and Weiner (1972) note that inadvertent disclosures often result from intercurrent events in the life of the psychotherapist such as marriage, parenthood, illness, and others. Despite attempts to keep such occurrences from impacting the practice of psychotherapy, their effects will sometimes be noticed by patients who will (perhaps correctly) wish to discuss them openly with the therapist. For those who already regard voluntary self-disclosure to be useful, such situations will present little cause for alarm. However, for therapists who prefer to remain anonymous and opaque, they may be troubled when confronted with situations that require some degree of self-revelation. Regardless of views concerning voluntary self-disclosure, both groups are confronted with the need to decide when, what, and how to share these intercurrent events and their possible impact on the treatment relationship.

While there are no definitive guidelines for determining what amount of sharing is appropriate, several authors have discussed factors to be considered. Fromm-Reichman (1960) states that

> it is, of course, possible for a significant occurrence, such as a death, marriage, childbirth, or divorce, to take place in the life of a psychiatrist (psychotherapist) while a patient is under treatment. It may then be advisable for the psychiatrist to interrupt treatment for a sufficiently long period of time to take care of his (her) preoccupation with his own affairs. As treatment is resumed, he may unassumingly comment on his reasons for the interruption and add that he is now ready for work. He should bear in

mind that the patient may wish to express condolences, congratulations, or merely make a comment, and so he should not fail to give him an opportunity to do so . . . the frank admission that the psychiatrist is human and not infallible shows far more respect and consideration for the patient than evasion would. It may also contribute to the process of maturing, which is part of the goal of the psychotherapeutic process. (p. 212)

Bellak (1981) echoes Fromm-Reichmann's call for a sensible, reasonable approach to the issue of therapist self-disclosure.

In all intercurrent conditions of the therapist, one main rule must be observed, namely that one should attempt to maintain as much therapeutic neutrality as is possible without, however, creating artificial situations or deceptions or failing to respond and interact with the patient in a reasonable and human way where it is indicated. (pp. 227–228)

He points out that to do otherwise is to risk confusing the patient's reality testing and wounding his or her dignity. Rather than attempting to be a "stone mask," Bellak encourages therapists to self-disclose about life events when it seems reasonable and helpful to do so.

While Fromm-Reichman and Bellak describe the attitude which they feel best facilitates helpful therapist self-disclosure, others have attempted to provide more concrete suggestions for determining when and how to reveal personal information to a patient. For example, Flaherty (1979) suggests that psychotherapists should consider three sets of factors when deciding about the appropriateness of self-disclosure, particularly when it cannot helpfully be avoided. First, therapist-related factors such as their personality style, dynamics, background and training, and the degree of comfort with disclosure should be considered. Those for whom disclosure is congruent and comfortable will be better able to incorporate it into the treatment in a useful fashion. Second, patient-related variables such as diagnosis, dynamics, degree of reality testing, and his or her interest in learning about the therapist's life warrant careful consideration. For example, Flaherty notes that patients who are more disturbed (e.g., borderlines or schizophrenics) may need to know the therapist in a more personal way in order to form an attachment. Finally, patient–therapist interaction factors must be evaluated. These include the type of therapy, the specific relationship or transference at the time of the occurrence, and any precedents established by previous disclosures. For example, if failure to disclose an important event in the life of the therapist is likely to be regarded as a breach in the alliance, it may be necessary to be more open with this particular patient than with another for whom this would not be the case.

Glazer (1981) proposes a similar set of criteria to use when considering whether and how to self-disclose information about significant life events. He suggests that a therapist whose personality lends itself to comfortable self-revelation should regard it more permissible to do so than those for whom it is difficult. He also notes that the situation in which the therapist works may influence what is to be disclosed. For example, if the consulting office is in the home, it may be both foolish and unwise to refrain from announcing the impending birth of a child or its recent arrival. The psychic structure of the patient should also be considered, with more developmentally primitive patients requiring a greater amount of disclosure than those more advanced. Furthermore, Glazer mentions that the nature of the therapeutic alliance, the type of transference that predominates, and the specific issues being focused on at the time of the occurrence should all be evaluated before the disclosure is made. Finally, it is important for the therapist to recognize that different degrees of self-disclosure will be appropriate, depending on the needs of individual patients at that particular time.

While there will likely always be a difference in viewpoints concerning the appropriateness, timing, and extent of therapist self-disclosure, most experienced therapists readily admit that it is an issue that they are forced to confront on a regular basis. This is not simply because of the patient's need to know the therapist as a real person. It also results from the therapist's need to be a real person and to interact with another human being in a reciprocating manner, particularly during a time of personal need. As will be discussed in more detail later in this chapter, therapists sometimes feel an inner compulsion to share with clients about the impact of a significant event on their life, often motivated by an unconscious (or even conscious) wish to receive nurturance, empathy, and support. While this may be understandable, it is typically not in the best interests of the patient or the therapy relationship. Yet, as will be seen, this impulse often adds further confusion to the issue of determining when and what to reveal.

Having briefly considered the thorny issue of therapist self-disclosure, the discussion can now turn to the impact of significant events in the life of the therapist as they relate to the practice of psychotherapy. As each one is considered, the issue of therapist self-disclosure will again be addressed as it relates to the unique aspects of the specific event. It will become apparent that the practice of psychotherapy both influences and is influenced by the impact of each event on the personal and professional life of the therapist.

EARLY ADULTHOOD

Levinson (1986) divides the era of Early Adulthood into three subphases: Entry Life Structure for Early Adulthood, ages 22 to 28; Age 30 Transition, ages 28 to 33; and Culminating Life Structure for Early Adulthood, ages 33 to 40. Levinson notes that this era entails the greatest amount of energy, abundance, and stress. In addition to reaching their biological peak during this time, individuals in this period form and pursue youthful aspirations, establish their niche in society, raise a family, and eventually reach a more "senior" position in the adult world. While this can be a time of considerable satisfaction regarding love, sexuality, family life, occupational advancement, creativity, and the realization of life goals, it is also typically a time of great stress and conflict. As Levinson notes:

> Early adulthood is the era in which we are most buffeted by our own passions and ambitions from within and the demands of family, community, and society from without.

Under reasonably favorable conditions, the rewards of living in this era are enormous, but the costs often equal or even exceed the benefits. (p. 5)

For the therapist, this period roughly corresponds with the novice phase of professional development, during which time the individual has received training and supervision in the practice of psychotherapy and has subsequently entered the profession as a practicing therapist. As discussed in Chapter 2, this is often a time of many career-related concerns and stresses such as those resulting from undergoing personal therapy, choosing a theoretical orientation, selecting a specialization, and obtaining the necessary professional credentials. As Farber (1983a) notes, this is also the time when fears regarding competency and the probability of future success are the most debilitating. While no longer beginners, psychotherapists in this phase of professional development lack the experience, confidence, and expertise necessary to enjoy their work fully without fears and self-doubts about the efficacy of treatment, the adequacy of their clinical ability, and the guarantee of continued financial success.

Personal and professional concerns associated with this period interact in ways which can be very distressing to the psychotherapist. For example, Looney et al., (1980) notes that psychiatrists in this age range reported experiencing moderate to significant levels of stress concerning Board examinations (66%), difficulties with patients (47%), stress in marriage (45%), stress about a change in friends (40%), stress about moving (39%), sexual problems (28%), concerns about health (26%), significant sleep disturbances (24%), major weight changes (23%), significant physical illness (15%), and separation or divorce (14%). The professional world impacts the personal life (and vice versa) during this era to create distress noticeable not only to the therapist, but to some perceptive clients as well.

The major life events that tend to occur during this era include marriage, pregnancy, parenthood, and relocation. The impact of these events on the personal life and the professional work of the psychotherapist will be considered.

Marriage

In Chapter 4, consideration was given to the impact of a career in psychotherapy on marital satisfaction. Both positive and negative effects were noted, resulting in several important benefits and liabilities for the spouse and the marriage relationship. At this point, however, it is necessary to shift the focus in order to consider the impact of a change in therapist marital status on the practice of psychotherapy as it relates to both practitioners and their patients.

Depending on the theoretical orientation utilized, marital status of the psychotherapist may be an important variable in the therapy relationship. For example, at the beginning of treatment, a client may wish to know whether or not the therapist is married, due to a belief that this will influence his or her ability to understand and empathize with the problems of the patient in this regard. For example, if a patient who is married discerns that the therapist is not, he or she may doubt the therapist's ability to understand and assist with marital disputes and conflicts. On the other hand, if the therapist is married, an unmarried client may wonder whether he or she can fully understand the problems, conflicts, and feelings associated with being single. Finally, even if both individuals are of the same marital status, this can be threatening to a client who may fear that his or her relationship is being compared with that of the therapist. Thus each match-up has its own unique issues associated with it.

For the therapist, marital status can be a mixed bag as well. Unmarried therapists may have greater freedom to pursue career interests, training, and work without fear of the possible impact on a spouse or family. There may also be a greater degree of flexibility in scheduling for both routine clinical duties and crisis management. Finally, after a long day of conducting therapy, the unmarried therapist who lives alone may be freer to withdraw in order to replenish depleted emotional resources and "center" himself or herself. On the other hand, a spouse serves as an important source of empathy, support, nurturance, and reality testing. He or she is also typically an important ally in the battle against the potentially debilitating effects of therapeutic practice on the personal life and relationships of the therapist. Again, there are varying benefits and problems associated with the marital status of the psychotherapist, whatever it may be.

Change in Marital Status

Perhaps the central issue of concern is not the particular marital status of either the patient or the therapist, but a change in the marital status of the psychotherapist during the course of psychotherapy with a particular patient. Several factors seem to support this point. For example, if the marital status of the therapist is an important issue to the patient, it is most likely to arise very early in the treatment relationship. The client may directly and persistently question the therapist regarding this issue until either an answer is given or the need for such information is eliminated. In the former case, many therapists eventually disclose their marital status during the early phase of treatment if this seems helpful in forming an alliance with the patient. (In fact, nonverbal cues such as a wedding ring or a picture of a spouse in the office may make such inquiries unnecessary.) Even when a therapist refuses to disclose his or her marital status, a client may acquire this information from mutual acquaintances, the initial referral source, newspaper announcements, or overheard conversations in the waiting room. While certainly not always the case, most patients discover the marital status of their therapist early in the treatment relationship.

Having learned of the marital status of the therapist, the patient typically begins to form certain notions regarding the lifestyle, relationships, and activities of the psychotherapist. More important, he or she combines these fantasies and assumptions with known facts, forming the basis for relating to the therapist in the treatment relationship. Thus marital status is one of several important factors which influence how clients regard their therapist and how they expect the therapist to relate to their world. Any change in this area can have an unsettling effect on the treatment relationship and the patient's feelings toward the therapist.

A change in marital status from single to married may become an important treatment issue for both the patient and the therapist. As Bellak (1981) points out, while the clinician may initially assume that it is not necessary to disclose this fact to patients, as with many other aspects of his or her private life, clients may inadvertently learn of this event regardless of such intentions. For example, the sudden appearance of an engagement or wedding ring is an obvious cue, forcing the therapist to decide whether or not to wear rings while conducting therapy. Since the decision to refrain from doing so has a lasting impact, requiring that the rings not be worn for the entire duration of the treatment relationship, most therapists elect to wear their rings and avoid the inconvenience and deception associated with leaving them at home. Thus most clients will learn of the marriage in this fashion, if not sooner. Others may learn of the change in marital status from the variety of sources discussed previously. If a honeymoon is taken which interferes with regularly scheduled sessions, it may become necessary to disclose the event at this point. Regardless of how and when the disclosure occurs, in most cases a therapy patient will learn of an impending or very recent wedding of the therapist.

The Problem of Self-Disclosure

Given the likelihood of patients learning about the marriage of the therapist, it is necessary for him or her to determine if, when, and how to provide this information to them. Obviously, some therapists prefer to wait and see whether clients discover this occurrence on their own. If they do learn about the marriage from other sources, the therapist accepts its inevitability and then actively helps the patient examine the feelings, thoughts, and behaviors which result from this discovery. If the patient does not discover this information on their own, however, these psychotherapists continue treatment without making mention of it, believing that it is irrelevant to the concerns and issues of the client. Due to the likelihood of patients learning about the change in marital status, it is rare that the therapist escapes the need to make some type of disclosure regarding this event.

Both Bellak (1981) and Flaherty (1979) suggest that there may be times when it will be necessary for the therapist to voluntarily disclose an impending marriage to particular therapy patients. For example, Bellak states:

> If the patient has had good reason to become aware of the therapist's changed status, it would be reasonable for the therapist to make a simple declaration of fact. While we do not share our private lives with our patients voluntarily or unnecessarily, it is erroneous to stay protected behind analytic anonymity (possibly because to do otherwise might be uncomfortable for the analyst). This would create an inordinately artificial situation or further confound the patient, impairing reality testing and judgment. (p. 230)

He notes further that even when the patient does not question or comment about this issue, if the therapist has reason to believe that the patient has learned, or may eventually learn, of the marriage, he or she should consider bringing it up voluntarily in order to avoid deception, confront and explore the patient's possible denial, and protect the dignity and integrity of the therapy relationsihp. Flaherty (1979) echos Bellak's views, but goes a step further to suggest that it may be appropriate to disclose the event even when the patient may not learn of it, in order to protect the therapeutic alliance. If the patient is likely to feel deceived, inordinately hurt, or unnecessarily rejected on the eventual discovery of this information, regardless of how unlikely their learning of it may be, the therapist should consider voluntarily disclosing this event. Furthermore, if refraining from doing so creates feelings of guilt in the therapist concerning the deception, or fear of eventual discovery which are serious enough to impact the treatment relationship, it may be best to consider discussing this openly with the client.

Whether the result of inadvertent discovery by the patient or voluntary disclosure by the therapist, the problem of what and how to disclose about the marriage remains a separate issue to be confronted by the psychotherapist. Bellak (1981) recommends that the therapist make a simple declaration of the facts without going into needless detail. He then suggests that the therapist pay special attention to any changes in affect, behavior, dream content, or therapeutic material which may result. These should be carefully examined to determine the meaning of this event in relationship to the patient's inner experience as well as the external therapy relationship. Flaherty (1979) also found that a brief disclosure of the basic facts surrounding the event were sufficient to satisfy most patients and allow the therapeutic work to continue undisturbed. Fromm-Reichmann (1960) adds that it is often helpful to reassure the patient regarding the therapist's ability to set aside personal concerns regarding this event in order to concentrate adequately on the needs of the patient. In this regard, she relates the following story:

> I recall the example of a psychiatrist who was engaged to be married. Several of her young women patients who happened to hear about the engagement expressed skepticism as to the psychiatrist's ability to concentrate on her work with them. She replied that, had she doubted her ability to do so, she would temporarliy have discontinued seeing patients. Following this, psychotherapeutic work was resumed as usual. (p. 212)

Patient Reactions

Having learned of the impending or recent marriage of the psychotherapist is likely to evoke a variety of reactions. Flaherty (1979) reports that several of his patients expressed seemingly sincere happiness and excitement when they learned of his marriage. For most this revelation appeared to enhance their ability to work on genetic issues related to the marriage of their parents as well as their own feelings and experiences regarding intimacy. It also seemed to increase the trust and openness of the therapy relationship. For a few others, it seemed to increase feelings of jealousy, competition, depression, identification, and guilt regarding sexual attraction to the therapist. However, while uncomfortable, these were not reported to have been detrimental to the overall treatment relationship. In fact,

Flaherty maintains that working through such reactions actually precipitated important progress and growth.

Bellak (1981) suggests that patients may experience a wide range of feelings in reaction to learning of the therapist's marriage, many of them less positive than those reported by Flaherty. These include feelings of jealousy, competition, rivalry, oedipal strivings, and resentment. Fromm-Reichman (1960) notes that some patients will become very concerned about the impact on the emotional energy and investment of the therapist, fearing that the marriage will reduce the therapist's ability to provide the caring, support, and empathy formerly conveyed. Other reactions may result as well. These include an increase in feelings of sibling rivalry, fear of abandonment, sexual attraction for the therapist, personal inadequacy and undesirableness, and rejection. Some clients may even worry about whether the typical arguments and conflicts associated with the early months of marriage will detract from the therapist's ability to concentrate on the patient's concerns!

As a result of learning of this event, patients may need to reorganize their perceptions and fantasies concerning the therapist. They may begin to relate differently, due to their changing expectations and beliefs concerning the impact of the marriage on the life and personality of the therapist. While some may anticipate a more negative outcome, the benefits of marriage discussed in Chapter 4 may well positively impact treatment relationships in ways which become apparent to both patients and the therapist.

Therapist Reactions

Since an impending marriage is typically a joyous time for most individuals, it is natural that the therapist should wish to share his or her excitement with others, particularly those with whom he or she enjoys an intimate relationship. As a result, the therapist may feel a surprising inner compulsion to discuss this event with patients. In most cases, training and experience will cause the therapist to evaluate the appropriateness of this disclosure in light of the needs and issues of each client. However, even the most disciplined psychotherapist will be aware of the difficulty of consistently placing the client's needs above personal ones, particularly in the case of significant events in the life of the therapist.

Some therapists will feel a strong impulse to reveal the impending marriage to patients for several reasons. These may include a desire to share one's good fortune with others, include patients in the meaningful events of his or her life, model successful living, and demonstrate his or her humanness and vulnerability. While this voluntary self-disclosure may be motivated by a sincere desire to enhance the treatment relationship, there can also be an underlying bravado and pride which may influence the clinician's judgment regarding the usefulness of such a disclosure. Others may wish to reveal this event because of a belief that it is simply in the best interests of the therapy relationship.

Obviously, there are a number of reasons which may cause a therapist to avoid sharing this information with clients. Some may feel that it will unnecessarily burden clients, negatively impact the therapy relationship, or create problems unrelated to their reasons for seeking treatment. If there is a strong desire to disclose this information, the need for abstinence may give rise to feelings of resentment or anger in the therapist who must deny his or her need to share about this event due to the needs of the patient. On the other hand, some therapists may readily decide to withhold this information due to their own feelings and needs such as embarrassment, guilt, fear of patient reactions, defensiveness, or an excessive need for privacy. If these personal feelings are strong enough, they may take precedence over the needs of patients, causing them to refrain from sharing the news of this event when it would have been more beneficial to the treatment relationship to have done so.

A wish to focus on the new spouse and the marriage relationship may result in some changes in how the therapist engages in professional work. As mentioned in Chapter 4, the need to protect the integrity of the marital relationship may require that the therapist work fewer hours, set firmer and more restrictive boundaries on professional activities and responsibilities, and put more energy and emotion into the marriage. This may cause the therapist to pull back from clients somewhat and reduce his or her emotional intensity and investment. This will be especially true if the therapist was relying on patients to meet personal needs for intimacy and closeness. However, for most, the advent of marriage often provides a helpful balance and source of feedback which ultimately benefits treatment relationships.

Summary

Since few therapists will be able to keep patients from learning about their marital status at the outset of treatment, or a change in status from single to married, it is necessary for them to consider carefully the issues previously outlined. Decisions must be made concerning whether, when, how, and what is to be disclosed to therapy patients should the therapist marry during the course of treatment. Obviously, these decisions will need to take into account patient, therapist, and treatment relationship variables. Therapists who attempt to provide a stable, unchanging presence will need to confront openly and thoughtfully the impact of this significant life event on patients who may have come to regard them as parent, sibling, lover, or friend. A change in marital status can percipitate a wide variety of changes in both the therapist and the patient which must be carefully addressed. A new spouse may well become an unseen presence in the therapy relationship, influencing how both parties perceive the other. The myriad of transference and countertransference reactions which may result will need to be worked through in order for treatment to progress unhindered.

Pregnancy

The impact of pregnancy on the therapist, patient, and the treatment relationship can be significant. This is true for both female and male psychotherapists and patients. Many of the issues concerning self-disclosure are pertinent to this event as well. Regardless of the therapist's desire to remain anonymous and oblique, pregnancy in the life of the clinician will often affect treatment relationships in numerous ways.

Patient Reactions

For the female therapist, pregnancy serves as an unmistakable nonverbal communication which partially destroys whatever anonymity has existed previously (Paluszny & Poznanski, 1971). As Bellak (1981) points out, "the pregnancy of the female therapist makes it clear to patients that there is a man in the therapist's life" (p. 230). It becomes apparent that the therapist has a separate, private, and personal life apart from work which includes sexual activity and family ties (Ashway, 1984). Patients react to this event in a variety of ways. Some may respond with genuinely warm and tender feelings, role modeling, identification with the baby, infantile feelings and wishes, symbiotic desires, a reviving of childhood memories, new attempts to "test" the therapist, increased dependency needs, denial and resistance, ambivalence about sexuality, and hostile fantasies about the death of the therapist during childbirth (Guy, Guy, & Liaboe, 1986). There may also be an increase in maternal transference reactions, sexual identity issues, preoccupation with maternal loss and deprivation, hostile fantasies about the unborn child, and envy of the therapist as a sexual, fertile person and mother (Nadelson, Notman, Arons, & Feldman, 1974). Defense mechanisms such as isolation of affect, denial, and reaction formation may be utilized, along with acting out, premature termination, or self-destructive behavior (Ashway, 1984). Clients who are painfully aware of their dependency on the therapist at this time may become either more or less dependent in reponse to learning of the therapist's pregnancy (Naparstek, 1976). Some reactions seem to parallel each trimester. Initial fears of separation and termination, along with resolution of parental conflicts, are followed by a middle phase of increased concerns about sexuality, parenthood, and sibling rivalry. The final phase brings renewed concerns about separation and termination (Balsam & Balsam, 1974; Underwood & Underwood, 1976).

In addition to these general reactions, some authors have suggested that particular patient groups experience reactions unique to their individual needs and characteristics. For example, Lax (1969) found that female patients were more excited by the pregnancy, prone to undergo intense "transference storms," and likely to experience feelings of sibling rivalry, separation anxiety, hostility, and envy than were males. In contrast, male clients tended to deny the reality of the impending pregnancy longer and utilize isolation and withdrawal as defenses against whatever feelings were being generated by it. Ashway (1984) reports that child and adolescent clients reacted in ways directly related to their own emotional development and level of maturity. Cole (1980) and Paluszny and Poznanski (1971) found a similar pattern among adults, noting that patient reactions could be differentiated according to their underlying character structure and stage of development. Some patients responded by attempting to solve personal conflicts through reliving them in the therapy relationship, others responded with greatly intensified defensive reactions, and a third group used the new emergent material related to the pregnancy to confront current life issues more effectively. Finally, Breen (1977) reports that individual therapy patients tended to focus on issues of sharing and deprivation, while group therapy patients focused on sexuality and sexual identity in response to the pregnancy of female psychotherapists.

It is interesting that some male psychotherapists assume that their patients will have little or no reaction to an impending birth in the therapist's family. This is often because they mistakenly assume that patients will not learn of this event (Guy, Guy, & Liaboe, 1986). Actually, there are a variety of sources from which a client may learn of the pregnancy of the therapist's spouse such as mutual friends or acquaintances, overheard conversations among colleagues, or direct questioning of the therapist. Furthermore, since many males now elect to participate actively in the pre- and postnatal care of the infant as well as the actual delivery and birth, the male therapist will likely have to explain the reason for his absences, a sudden cancellation, or the need for an extended vacation following the birth. Since it is important to speak truthfully about such issues, the male therapist may find it necessary to reveal the pregnancy, partially destroying anonymity in a way similar to that experienced by a pregnant female therapist. Even if he elects not to do so, the inadvertent discovery of this information by patients may require that this issue be addressed in treatment. As a result, the male psychotherapist may be surprised to find his patients reacting in ways very similar to those encountered by pregnant female therapists, with many of the same conflicts, issues, emotions, and behaviors. If a patient learns of this event, which Guy et al. (1986) found to occur with surprising frequency, he or she may have intense reactions which profoundly impact the therapy relationship. Unfortunately, the lack of research on this topic hinders attempts to discriminate between those patient reactions which are similar to those encountered by female therapists and those which are unique to male therapists.

Therapist Rections

Deutsch (1944) maintains that pregnancy creates significant disturbances in the psychic balance of all women, characterized by reactivated early conflicts, intense introversion, time-limited regression, ambivalence, and identification with the fetus. Hormonal fluctuations, fatigue, and a growing sense of physical vulnerability may result in noticeable emotional changes (Nadelson et al., 1974). It is easy to appreciate how these factors combine to impact the work of the pregnant female therapist. Some report experiencing a growing sense of helplessness, guilt over leaving patients, generalized anxiety, fears and fantasies of harm to self and/or the baby during pregnancy and delivery, withdrawal of energy and decreased investment in work with patients, mood swings, narcissistic preoccupation, and boredom (Baum & Herring, 1975). Even the kicking fetus may be experienced as a growing distraction, intrusion, or reminder of role changes yet to come (Ashway, 1984). Naparstek (1976) suggests that there may be a tendency to want special attention and treatment, growing fear of physical attack, resentment concerning personal exposure, and increasing self-absorption and withdrawal. Guy et al., (1986) note that

> logistical considerations, such as when and how to announce the pregnancy, as well as the issues surrounding either termination, with its implicit abandonment, or separation, with the determination of dates for leaving and returning to work, intrude into the ongoing therapeutic process in ways resented by both patient and therapist. Thus the female therapist finds herself experiencing physical and emotional consequences common to all women as well as those additional ones unique to her profession. (p. 299)

It is likely that the anger, guilt, confusion and fear which result will have an impact on her practice of psychotherapy.

While many negative effects have been suggested regarding the impact of the pregnancy on the female therapist, it may be that there are some positive consequences as well. For example, pregnancy and impending motherhood may generate a nurturing, caring response in the therapist, making her better able to feel and express support and tenderness towards clients. It may also be that the pregnancy forces the female therapist to confront and work through unresolved issues concerning her family of origin, sexual identity, and other family related issues, to the benefit of her own patients and their work together. It is curious that such a significant life event is almost universally portrayed in the literature as having a markedly negative impact on the life and work of the female psychotherapist.

It would seem reasonable to consider the impact of the pregnancy on the male therapist as well. Whether or not patients learn of this event, the prospect of parenthood, particularly in the case of a first child, is likely to stir up a variety of reactions ranging from the reactivation of oedipal and developmental conflicts to new concerns about suitability as a father and provider. The male therapist may find himself becoming increasingly self-absorbed, less emotionally available to his patients, preoccupied with concerns regarding the mother and baby's health and safety, anxious about the unpredictable day and time of the impending birth, and emotionally labile in the face of the many changes which may result. The added financial responsibility of a growing family may increase anxiety regarding professional competency, fluctuating patient referrals, and inevitable premature terminations. The male therapist may be surprised by the variety and intensity of his reactions to patient material related to family life, domestic conflict, parenthood, pregnancy, abortion, and sexuality as a result of the impending birth. In some cases the male therapist may even experience some changes in his sleep, appetite, and general physical well-being, related to the physical changes occurring in his pregnant spouse, which could also have an impact on his functioning as a therapist.

As in the case of the female therapist, it may be that pregnancy and parenthood will have a positive impact on the therapist's ability to express caring, tenderness, and nurturance. Unfortunately, this is only speculation since there is no known research on this topic. Certainly, impending fatherhood has the potential to motivate the resolution of intrapsychic issues to the benefit of the therapist and his present and future patients.

Summary and Suggestions

Since many therapists will share in the experience of pregnancy and childbirth, most male and female therapists will need to confront its impact on their practice of psychotherapy at some point. This will be particularly true of the first pregnancy, with its many unknowns, challenges, and role changes. A number of steps can be taken to prepare for this significant life event.

First, following the discovery of conception, the therapist is well advised to acknowledge and confront its likely impact on the therapy practice (Guy et al., 1986). It is best to anticipate the issues and problems which may result rather than to minimize or deny their potential to disrupt treatment. This allows for adequate and thoughtful preparation. For example, it will be necessary to examine one's caseload to determine when and how this issue should be addressed. While all female therapists will be forced to deal with patient reactions, many male therapists will find it necessary as well. The individual needs of each client should be evaluated, with careful consideration given to the possible meaning of the pregnancy to the patient, the theoretical orientation employed, the nature of the therapeutic relationship, and the personal issues of the patient.

Both male and female therapists may find it useful to further inform themselves regarding this issue by reading articles and books on the subject and by discussing it with colleagues. It may also be helpful to pursue personal psychotherapy, supervision, or occasional consultation at this time in order to confront and work through reemerging unresolved-intrapsychic issues and receive support, nurturance, reality testing, and guidance from others. Not only will such measures improve patient care, but they will likely reassure the therapist during a time of personal transition and vulnerability.

Parenthood

While the issues associated with pregnancy, obviously apply to the impact of parenthood on the treatment relationship, some additional comments seem warranted. Parenthood is an important developmental stage encountered by most psychotherapists (Wahl, 1986). Its profound impact on the personal life of the therapist cannot help but have an effect on his or her practice of psychotherapy at one time or another. As a result, it has implications for clinical practice worthy of careful consideration.

Patient Reactions

It is not unusual for patients to inquire about whether the psychotherapist has children of his or her own at the initiation of the treatment relationship. As in the case of marital status, patients often use such data to determine whether the therapist will be able to understand the uniqueness of their own situation. They are often insistent regarding the disclosure of such basic information about the therapist's life. If the clinician decides to withhold these facts from clients, they will often find other ways to obtain the information, such as those mentioned previously. As a result, most therapists tend to answer these inquiries truthfully and openly, in addition to exploring their meaning for the patient.

As in the case of pregnancy, patients have a wide variety of reactions to learning about the therapist's family (Bellak, 1981). Many of these will be the same as those noted previously regarding childbirth. For example, some will experience very positive fantasies about the therapist as parent. They may respect the responsibility and maturity that parenthood requires. The fact that the therapist has children of his or her own may give a certain credibility to suggestions made to patients regarding family problems. Those with fond memories of parents and family interactions will possibly attribute to the therapist many of the positive qualities found in their own parents.

Of course, some patients will experience very different reactions to this disclosure. Feelings of envy, rejection, rivalry, resentment, hostility, oedipal strivings, and depression, as well as fears of abandonment, may emerge in response (Bellak, 1981). Such reactions are especially common at times when the needs of the children must take precedence over those of the client, as may occur at times of illness, accident, or special events (e.g., concerts, graduation, awards banquets, family vacations, etc.). There may also be reemerging developmental conflicts (with renewed ambivalence regarding dependency, separation, and individuation) which will impact the therapy relationship. Finally, for those with unresolved negative feelings toward their own parents, learning of the parenthood of the therapist may evoke similar feelings in the treatment relationship, as the patient mistakenly attributes many of the same negative qualities to the psychotherapist.

Therapist Reactions

As mentioned in Chapter 4, the practice of psychotherapy may have both a positive and negative impact on the therapist's family, and specifically, the children. More pertinent to this discussion, the presence of children in the life of the therapist can bring several benefits and liabilities to his or her clinical practice.

It may be true that parenthood brings a maturity and sense of perspective that enriches the life of the therapist. For example, Guggenbuhl-Craig (1979) suggests that having children satisfies a natural need for descendants. It may be that this allows the therapist to experience feelings and events somewhat differently from those who do not have children of their own. Obviously, such generalizations must be made with care. More importantly, Guggenbuhl-Craig maintains that children play an important role in helping the therapist achieve balance and emotional health in his or her life. Their sensitivity, guileless candor, and spontaneity allow them to penetrate the therapist's defenses, expose distortions, and confront unhealthy withdrawal and isolation. Cray and Cray (1977) echo such comments, noting that children serve as a source of reality testing and perspective for the therapist who benefits from their love, support, understanding, and honesty. Participating in their growth and development may sensitize the therapist to similar developmental issues and conflicts in the lives of patients, increasing empathy and helpfulness. If these assumptions are correct, therapists with children may at times be aware of the positive impact that parenthood has on their practice. In addition, they may find the idealization and positive transferences which some patients experience as a result of their learning about the therapist's family to be beneficial to treatment relationships.

However, the parenthood may occasionally have a detrimental impact on the work of the psychotherapist. As mentioned in Chapter 4, the conflicting priorities associated with balancing the needs of children with those of patients can be a source of considerable stress for the therapist. Despite changing societal values and roles, this may be an especially difficult task for the female therapist who finds it hard to negotiate the role conflicts which arise relating to the duties of therapist, wife, and mother. As Freudenberger and Robbins (1979) note:

> How readily can you (female therapist) respond to "the lost child" within a patient when your own child is sick in bed, possibly in the next room? Ideally, one's mate may well relieve some of these pressures. Sadly, however, the male in our society seems far more content with the role of achiever and provider that with the role of mutual participant in family troubles and triumphs or of helper to the mother-therapist. (p. 282)

As cited previously, Wahl (1986) found that many female therapists reported being unsatisfied with their family life due to the pressures of combining the responsibilities of motherhood with those of clinical practice. Regardless of how the division of labor is negotiated between spouses, both male and female therapists are likely to feel stress resulting from the conflicting demands of therapist and parent, especially since both roles deplete similar emotional resources.

In addition to the inner conflicts associated with parenthood, some therapists will find it difficult to deal with the potentially negative reactions that some patients experience on learning of the existence of the therapist's family. As a result of the envy, rivalry, and anger wich some are likely to express, the therapist may react with defensiveness, righteous indignation, anger, or guilt. In addition, the negative qualities mistakenly attributed to the therapist as a result of painful childhood memories may feel burdensome and frustrating to the clinician who is striving to provide a safe, helpful environment for the patient.

Summary and Suggestions

It is likely that most psychotherapists will experience the impact of parenthood on their clinical practice at various times. Furthermore, it would appear that some clients will also become either directly or indirectly aware of this impact. As a result, therapists should expect to address this issue in a manner which is both realistic and appropriate to the needs of all involved. Bellak (1981) suggests that such an approach facilitates trust, promotes patients' reality testing, and protects their dignity.

Freudenberger and Robbins (1979) recommend that the issue of parenthood be given careful consideration:

Young parents who are also professionals need a very thorough ongoing personal inventory to assess their capacity to integrate complex roles and pressures. Both members of a working marriage may well have to talk through very carefully the extent of their professional commitments and the space allowed for parenting needs. Therapists with children can be very forthright with their patients as to their priorities in terms of schedules. Children do get sick, personal emergencies do arise, and time can and should be afforded to deal with these pressures. The very responsible analyst (psychotherapist) may be constantly tempted to take precious time and energy away from a young and growing family to meet patient responsibilities. These issues are of equal importance to fathers and mothers. (pp. 290–291)

Such "no nonsense" advice is refreshing in its blunt acknowledgment of the necessary ordering of priorities which must occur to ensure the well-being of therapist, family, and patients.

In view of the interrelationship between the therapist's personal and professional life, it is not surprising that parenthood is often an issue of importance for the treatment relationship. Careful consideration must be given to addressing the needs of all parties in the most appropriate and helpful manner possible. Given the complexity of the issues involved, it may be best to evaluate these concerns prior to their becoming an urgent issue.

Relocation

As a result of career advancement, attempts to find the most suitable and advantageous employment and living environment possible, and the unavoidable exigencies of life, it may become necessary for the psychotherapist to move to a new nearby office, or even to another city or state during the course of a career in psychotherapy. While this can occur at any point, it is most likely to happen during the early adulthood phase of life. Such an important life event has a significant impact on both the therapist and his or her patients which warrants brief consideration.

Several factors may make it necessary for a therapist to relocate to a different nearby office. In some cases, this may be the result of completing a time-limited internship, residency, or fieldwork placement. When this occurs, the therapist may elect to remain in the area and continue work with his or her patients. The relocation may also be the result of a change in employment, such as would occur if the therapist assumes a position at a new nearby clinic, hospital, or university, or if he or she decides to enter private practice in the immediate area. Finally, an expired lease or the desire for different quarters may necessitate that the therapist relocate the office to another location within easy driving distance.

The decision to move to another city or state, requiring the termination of ongoing therapy relationships, is a very serious one with implications that are typically dreaded by most therapists. In some cases, the departure is necessitated by the completion of a training program located in an area where the therapist does not wish to permanently reside. In others, it may be that an opportunity for career advancement or desired occupational transition motivates the therapist to make the move. Finally, the wish to relocate to a more desirable locale may bring about the decision to move to a new city. The latter reason may become particularly pertinent during the middle and late adulthood phases of life when more subjective, aesthetic qualities take precedence.

Patient Reactions

If the relocation is to a new nearby office, allowing for the continuation of treatment, patient reactions will likely be noticeable but hopefully not seriously disruptive. As Bellak (1981) explains:

> When an analyst (psychotherapist) moves, even within a relatively small perimeter, the patient experiences a variety of changes: a different kind of a trip, a different kind of a neighborhood, and above all, a different office. The lack of familiarity often produces some anxiety. Critique of the new office often represents transference feelings. Last, though not least, patients are very acute observers because their perception is sensitized by their transference feelings and they will find many faults which may not be comfortable to the analyst or therapist to hear about. Very frequently, the change in the location will produce dreams which reveal a patient's unconscious reactions to the change. (p. 229)

While such reactions will likely be tempered by the theoretical orientation employed, the personality structure of the patient, and the nature of the therapeutic relationship, it is important to consider the impact of relocation on various clients. Thoughtful evaluation will facilitate the discussion and working through of issues which may emerge as a result. Feelings of anxiety, insecurity, or annoyance which may arise must be discussed in an open, nondefensive manner to reduce the disruptive impact of a change which is typically the result of the therapist's unilateral decision. Since it is indeed rare for therapists to make such a decision in serious consultation with their clients, care must be taken to work through their feelings of vulnerability and dependency. It may be a bit jarring for patients to discover that the therapist is not as stable and unchanging as they believed.

If the therapist decides to relocate to another city or state, the impact on therapy clients may be much more significant. In most cases, the forced termination is likely to be experienced as premature, even when the treatment relationship was begun with a full disclosure of the eventual need to terminate due to the impending departure of the therapist. As a result, patients may experience feelings of rejection, abandonment, betrayal, anger, depression, anxiety, dread, and grief. Few will welcome such news with relief and excitement. Past issues concerning separation and individuation may reemerge at this point, along with other unresolved issues regarding past goodbyes and terminated relationships. While some clients may benefit from working through these feelings and concerns with the departing therapist, most will find the experience to be painful and difficult, depending on the meaning and impact of the termination on their emotional well-being.

Therapist Reactions

If the therapist is simply going to relocate to a new office in the immediate area, he or she may be surprised by the variety and intensity of patient reactions. Feelings of defensiveness, resentment, guilt, and regret may emerge in response to patient complaints. In the midst of all the chaos that such a move entails, some therapists will find it difficult to patiently cope with the seemingly petty concerns and comments of clients who resent the intrusion that this represents on their life and routine. Those who anticipate the possibility of such a response may actually postpone or decline a relocation out of a wish to avoid the resultant problems.

Therapists who must prematurely terminate their work with patients due to a decision to move will typically (and perhaps appropriately) experience feelings of guilt, regret, remorse, sorrow, and depression. Not only will these feelings result from recognition of the realistic impact of this event on the well-being of their patients, but the feelings may be exacerbated by a reawakening of their own unresolved issues concerning separation, individuation, and termination related to their past. In addition, therapists may resent the sense of obligation and responsibility which causes them to feel so accountable to patients, and this can lead to anger and defensiveness. Avoidance and denial are typical, particularly among inexperienced therapists who wish to minimize the impact of this event on their clients. It is difficult for many therapists to acknowledge that this is primarily a unilateral decision which they have rather selfishly made, even though this may be perfectly appropriate, necessary, and understandable. While the impact may be regrettable, few therapists are able or willing to place patient needs in this regard above their own, nor perhaps should they be. Regardless of the theoretical orientation employed, departure to a new, distant locale results in severed relationships with past and present clients and is likely to be a very difficult and stressful experience for most therapists.

Summary and Suggestions

The therapist who relocates to a nearby office may find it necessary to warn clients of this impending move several weeks or even months in advance in order to lessen the unnecessarily disruptive aspects of this change. Informing patients about the move in a direct, forthright manner will likely increase feelings of trust, security, and openness. While a few therapists will err by disclosing such information too soon, many may mistakenly postpone revealing the anticipated move until it has become absolutely necessary to do so. It would seem best to deal openly with this issue at the earliest appropriate time. Following this disclosure (as well as during and after the move), the therapist will need to observe any change in patient behavior, emotions, or comments which may be related to this relocation. This will facilitate their discussion and resolution.

Regarding forced termination due to therapist relocation, Bellak (1981) recommends:

> If the analyst (psychotherapist) actually changes his location to another city or another state, extensive preparation of the patient is necessary. If possible, the patient should

be told at least months in advance, and a termination date set. The patient must be helped to make realistic alternative arrangements. Separation problems must be worked through, and an adequate summary prepared for use by another therapist, should the patient choose to continue with someone else. (p. 229)

In order to avoid deceit, it may be appropriate to disclose the need for the termination as soon as it is discovered by the therapist. In other words, rather than waiting for the "right moment," a rationale which may permit the acting out of therapist denial or avoidance, it may be best for the therapist to share this information with patients as soon as possible. This would suggest that those participating in time-limited training programs may need to mention this fact to patients during the intake process, in order to protect their right to choose whether to enter into a treatment relationship which may end with a premature termination.

This may be an excellent time for the therapist to receive personal therapy, supervision, or consultation to work through feelings and reactions which may hinder his or her helpfulness. Since personal unresolved issues may surface, as well as realistic questions regarding the need to determine what is ethical and appropriate, therapists are advised to consider discussing these issues with a trusted colleague. Since most treatment relationships are formed on the assumption that the therapist will continue to meet with the patient until a mutually agreed on termination point is reached (Guy & Souder, in press), it will be disruptive for the therapist to announce his or her departure to another city or state. Both parties will find this to be a difficult intrusion on the therapy alliance which deserves to be carefully explored and thoughtfully discussed. A move in the life of the therapist has the potential to impact profoundly the treatment relationship, and the role of psychotherapist is likely to impact his or her personal experience of such relocations as well.

MIDDLE ADULTHOOD

As the therapist moves through the Early Adulthood era, many of the aforementioned life events will be encountered, and the conflicts which they entail will be confronted by the therapist and his or her family, and resolved with varying degrees of success. In many cases, these significant life events will not only affect the therapist's personal life, but will impact his or her patients and professional practice as well. The many changes and transitions associated with this era present a formidable challenge to everyone involved, requiring a certain amount of sensitivity, good judgment, and courage to bring about a successful resolution of the resultant problems. Yet, as Levinson (1978,1986) notes, this is also a period of potentially great rewards and satisfactions in both the personal and professional life of the therapist. While some scars may remain, most individuals emerge with a greater maturity, inner strength, and sense of purpose.

Between the Early and Middle Adulthood eras is the tumultuous Mid-Life Transition, ages 40 to 45, better known as the period of "mid-life crisis." According to Levinson, the individual in this phase begins a new step towards individuation, bringing about sometimes profound changes in life-goals, values, and behavior. There is often a reprioritizing of objectives and a renewed search for meaning in relationships and vocation. Hopefully, individuals in this phase will become more "compassionate, reflexive, judicious, less tyrannized by inner conflicts and external demands, and more genuinely loving of themselves and others" (Levinsion, 1986, p. 5). Without such changes, life may become increasingly meaningless, trivial, and stagnant.

The period of Mid-Life Transition is an important one for psychotherapists, a sort of watershed which marks the termination of a career in psychotherapy for some and a time of transition in specialty or technique for others. Farber (1983a) notes that it is during this period that some psychotherapists reconsider their reasons for entering the profession. Perhaps a career in psychotherapy has turned out to be more difficult than they imagined, motivating them to leave the profession. "Therapists must continually deal with the widest range of human emotions and are often themselves the target of irrational expressions of love, hate, envy, or need" (Farber, 1983a, p. 103). This may eventually take a toll on the confidence and satisfaction of the therapist. After several years of conducting therapy, some become disillusioned with the limited success, frequent failures, and lack of visible changes which may result (Bugental, 1964; Farber, 1983a; Fine, 1980). Despair and discouragement may increase over time (Chessick, 1978; Fine, 1980). As will be discussed in Chapter 7, many factors may contribute to increasing burnout and job dissatisfaction, motivating a career change during this period. The type of resolution achieved will determine the professional activites engaged in during the Middle Adulthood era. While some will continue to practice psychotherapy in the same manner and setting characteristic of the Early Adulthood phase, others may change to a different specialty, treatment population, or employment setting, or they may leave the field altogether.

Levinson (1986) divides the Middle Adulthood era into three subphases: Entry Life Structure for Middlehood, ages 45 to 50; Age 50 Transition, ages 50 to 55; and Culminating Life Structure for Middle Adulthood, ages 55 to 60. He notes that

> during this era our biological capacities are below those of early adulthood but are normally still sufficient for an energetic, personally satisfying and socially valuable life. Unless our lives are hampered in some special way, most of us during our 40s and 50s become "senior members" of our own particular worlds, however grand or modest they may be. We are responsible not only for our own work and perhaps the work of others, but also for the development of the current generation of young adults who will soon enter the dominant generation. (p. 6)

For the practicing therapist, several concerns are typically confronted during this era. In addition to resolving the issues of the Mid-Life Transition phase such as those concerning the efficacy of psychotherapy, the level of personal competency possessed, and the degree of pleasure and fulfillment derived, there is a need to cope with the stress and responsibilities associated with being regarded as a "senior clinician." For example, both Farber (1983a) and Fine (1980) suggest that the mid-life therapist often experiences the cumulative effects of the isolation and withdrawal discussed in Chapter 3. At this point, there is little opportunity for receiving peer support, supervision, or encouragement. This lack of feedback can increase the therapist's anxiety about his or her ability to evaluate treatment progress appropriately, modify techniques, or set termination dates. Instead of receiving solace, reassurance, or advice from colleagues, therapists in this era of life must provide this for others. In addition, mid-life therapists sometimes become more acutely aware of the impact of their work on relationships with family and friends. As mentioned in Chapter 4, the effects of clinical practice can have a profound effect on these interactions which often becomes apparent to therapists by this point. Hopefully, the Mid-Life Transition has brought about a reconciling of the assets and liabilities, enabling the therapist to maximize the benefits associated with this career while reducing or eliminating the hazards. Finally, as Marmor (1968) notes, the middle aged therapist begins to sense the impact of aging on health and productivity, and he or she recognizes that many personal goals may not be achieved.

A number of significant life events may occur during this period which will have serious implications for the professional activities of the psychotherapist. In addition to those of the Early Adulthood era such as marriage, pregnancy, parenthood, and moving to a new location (any of which may also occur during the Middle Adulthood phase), many therapists are likely to experience divorce, the departure of their children, personal illness or accident, or the loss of a loved one. Each of these events may have a significant impact on the therapist and his or her practice of psychotherapy. In some cases, the impact on patients will be minimal and out of their direct awareness. In others, patients may be very aware of the event and experience its effects on the treatment relationship directly. Each of these events will be considered as they relate to the life and work of the psychotherapist.

Divorce

As noted in Chapter 4, most psychotherapists marry at some point during their career. While there are certainly exceptions among those who elect to participate in alternative lifestyles and relationships, most therapists follow a more traditional path and choose to live with a spouse. Unfortunately, therapists appear to be no more successful in their marital relationships than others, despite the training and experience they've often received in marital and family therapy. Several studies have found that therapists experience marital discord and failure at a rate equal to, or greater than, that of the general population (Ford, 1963; Looney, et. al., 1980; Schofield, 1964). Consistent with the findings of Levinson concerning the general population (1978), it appears that the greatest degree of marital dissatisfaction and discord tends to occur during the Mid-Life Transition and Middle Adulthood phases (Wahl, 1986). Consequently, it is possible that the mid-life therapist will be forced to confront the impact of divorce on his or her practice of psychotherapy.

The Problem of Self-Disclosure

At first glance, psychotherapists experiencing divorce may expect that such a typically painful and wrenching personal event will remain private and outside of patients' awareness if they so choose. The belief that knowledge of this occurrence will be detrimental to the patient and the treatment relationship will motivate some to elect to withhold this information. While this may include a decision not to mention a previous divorce, these concerns are likely be especially pertinent when one is occurring during the ongoing work with a particular patient. As in the case of other significant events, a psychotherapist's divorce may have little to do with the focus and nature of the treatment relationship, making it unnecessary or even inappropriate to burden the patient with such details. Furthermore, the personal pain or humiliation sometimes associated with a divorce may cause the therapist to be unable or unwilling to discuss this with all but a few close friends and family, at least without the passing of time. Thus the therapist may elect to withhold this information from patients out of his or her need for privacy. Fear of negative patient reactions may also motivate a certain amount of secrecy and concealment.

It is interesting to note that, while several authors encourage the open self-disclosure of other life events such as marriage and parenthood, most implicitly or explicitly discourage voluntary self-disclosure regarding divorce. Such an expectation is certainly understandable, given the potential feelings of both therapist and patient regarding this issue. However, one cannot help but wonder whether this is also the result of a desire to protect the omnipotent image of the psychotherapist as someone who is invulnerable to personal problems or failures (Marmor, 1953).

Despite the likely intention of most therapists to keep this event from their patients—particularly when in the midst of a divorce—it is not unusual for some to discover it anyway (Bellak, 1981). In addition to learning from overheard conversations among colleagues or staff, they may learn of its occurrence from mutual friends or acquaintances. They may also notice changes in the therapist's life such as a move to a new office or location, altered appearance, the absence of a formerly worn wedding ring, a return to a maiden name, or the perception of tension or upset in the therapist's demeanor. Even more subtle, they may note the therapist's sudden hesitation to refer to his or her spouse, or they may sense a reaction in the therapist when they discuss the patient's marital or relationship concerns. Such impressions may motivate a few patients to ask very directly concerning the personal life of the therapist, and it may become necessary to confirm their suspicions regarding this event. To fail to do so may confuse the patient's reality testing and insult the integrity of the relationship.

Bellak suggests that this issue be addressed directly if it appears necessary or unavoidable that the divorce be disclosed to the patient. In such cases a simple and forthright statement of the facts are likely to be sufficient to allow the treatment to continue uninterrupted after patient reactions and concerns have been sufficiently worked through.

Patient Reactions

Upon learning of the therapist's impending or recent divorce, patients may experience a number of feelings and reactions. For example, they may reexperience the pain and conflict associated with the divorce of their own parents. Such an event may stir up a host of memories and unresolved conflicts regarding the impact of this event on their emotional development. Furthermore, this knowledge may cause them to see suddenly the psychotherapist in a different light, "as an available male or female figure, or generally speaking, as a sexual figure and at times as a failure, as a person with poor control of impulses" (Bellak, 1981, p. 231). This may elicit feelings of attraction, sympathy, support, or caring toward the therapist. It may also evoke disappointment over the "plain humanity and fallibility of the therapist" (p. 231), increasing concerns about the clinician's competency and stability. On the other hand, some clients may feel reassured about the therapist's ability to understand and accept their own failures and shortcomings, and there may be an increase in comfort and trust as a result.

Concerns and reactions such as these will need to be discussed openly and completely. The astute therapist will be sensitive to changes in the patient's feelings, comments, or behavior which may result from this revelation, and time will be spent working through their relationship to past experiences as well as the present treatment alliance. Little will be gained by a defensive style of denial, avoidance, or minimization, regardless of the theoretical orientation employed. While it is obviously not appropriate to burden the client with personal problems and needs, it might be a violation of mutual trust and respect to deceive or mislead the inquiring patient about the impact of this event on the personal life and professional ability of the therapist.

Therapist Reactions

As mentioned, it seems reasonable to assume that most therapists will not voluntarily disclose the occurrence of a recent or impending divorce to current clients. This is because of an assortment of both personal and patient needs which may suggest that such a voluntary revelation would be unhelpful, perhaps painful. If this has been the decision, the therapist may experience some anxiety about the possible inadvertent discovery of this event by one or more patients. There may also be guilt about keeping such information from patients who would likely have strong reactions, either positive or negative. There may also be renewed doubts concerning personal and professional competency associated with the sense of failure that often accompanies a divorce. While our society no longer stigmatizes divorced individuals, the mental health professional who specializes in helping others achieve lasting, successful, and meaningful intimacy may experience considerable embarrassment and humiliation at his or her own failure to do so with a spouse.

If confronted by a patient who has learned or suspects about the divorce, the therapist may feel defensive, suspicious, apologetic, fearful, or vulnerable to their reactions and feelings. The tendency to be either evasive and provide an inappropriately vague reply to pointed questions, or to go into unnecessary detail in order to solicit support or sympathy, can be detrimental to the treatment relationship. If the therapist is unable to gain a balanced, realistic stance, it may become necessary to temporarily discontinue professional activities until some resolution and restoration has occurred. It may also be helpful to pursue personal therapy or supervision during this difficult time in order to ensure that needs for support, nurturance, guidance, and reality testing are met outside of treatment relationships.

Summary

Optimally, the therapist will emerge from this significant event with more insight into his or her own personal relationship needs. Not only will this be growth-producing in their personal life, but there may be a newfound empathy, understanding, and caring for those undergoing a similar experience. Rather than serving as lasting evidence of the therapist's own interpersonal inadequacies, a divorce may become a source of valuable learning which enriches his or her practice of psychotherapy. In addition, while knowledge of this event may be troubling for some patients, it may be usefully incorporated into therapeutic work with others.

The Departure of Children

Middle Adult therapists with children of their own will likely face their entry into the Early Adulthood era during this period. As a result, they will be confronted with a host of personal changes and transitions related to the children's departure from the home and entry into a career, marriage, and parenthood. As Levinson (1978) notes, these role changes and transitions can have a significant impact on the individual's self-perceptions and sense of purpose. While there may be little resultant impact on the therapist's work, a few comments about this possibility seem warranted.

In Chapter 3, the process of patient termination was noted to be a source of feelings of loneliness and isolation for the therapist. The pattern of increasing individuation, autonomy, separation, and termination characteristic of therapy relationships closely parallels that encountered in parent–child relationships. Thus the mid-life therapist may find that the sense of abandonment resulting from the frequent departures of patients with whom intimacy has been shared is strangely similar to that experienced in relationship to his or her children's growth and departure from the home.

As a result, there may be a compounding of feelings of obsolescence, uselessness, abandonment, loneliness, and isolation as the therapist struggles to allow his or her children to individuate and separate, in the midst of continual and repeated terminations with patients. Fine (1980) suggests that there is a resultant increase in feelings of despair and depletion as the therapist is "left behind" by those in whom he or she has invested such caring and guidance. The interactive effects of the departure of children and patients may have a profound impact on the therapist's self-esteem and sense of worth.

Should this indeed be the case, the therapist may find it difficult to time and conduct terminations appropriately in treatment relationships. There may be a tendency to rely on patients to feel worthwhile and valued, and a desire to prolong those relationships that are particularly satisfying and pleasurable. It may even be that the therapist will begin to relate to certain patients in a parental fashion, due in part to a refusal to surrender this role as one's own children mature and leave the home. On the other hand, it may be increasingly difficult for the therapist to form attachments with patients who will eventually depart, due to a fear of experiencing the rejection and hurt associated with previous patient terminations or the departure of one's own children. If there is a negative cumulative effect resulting from the individuation of one's children and that of therapy patients, clients may become aware of the therapist's inordinate need for assurance and support. The clinician's desire to be valued, respected, and liked may become a burden on the treatment relationship, sabotaging its potential effectiveness for the patient.

As with other life events, while there are potential liabilities, there may be benefits as well. For example, the similarity between these two experiences may actually bring about growth and positive change in the life and work of the psychotherapist. Perhaps experiencing the healthy individuation and separation of children and their eventual successful departure from the home and entry into Early Adulthood will better enable the therapist to encourage and support the growth and increasing autonomy of his or her therapy patients. Rather than being left with feelings of uselessness, the fully integrated therapist learns to recognize and accept his or her role in fostering the growth and development of others, a task appropriate to a parent, therapist, and "senior" participant in the Middle Adulthood era. Entering personal psychotherapy or supervision during this period of transition could be helpful in assisting the therapist–parent with the role changes and personal redefinitions associated with the departure of children from the home.

While such scenarios are admittedly speculative and highly tentative, these possible patterns are worthy of consideration and reflection. They are presented as further examples of ways in which the personal and professional life and relationships of the therapist interact interdependently.

Illness and Disability

The very nature of the psychotherapy relationship, with its emphasis on consistency, commitment, and predictability, may create in both the therapist and client the expectation that the psychotherapist is almost invulnerable to illness or accident (Guy & Souder, in press). Both parties typically assume that the treatment relationship will continue uninterrupted to the point of a mutually agreed on termination. While this assumption may seem necessary for the establishment of the therapeutic alliance, it is unrealistic. As Henry, Sims, and Spray (1973) discovered, disruptions due to illness or accident are no less common among psychotherapists than among the general population. In fact, since the majority of therapists practice psychotherapy most extensively during the Middle Adulthood era, a time when illness and disability are more likely to occur than during the earlier life phases, therapists may be likely to experience such events at some point in their careers (Halpert, 1982). For example, Guy, Stark, and Poelstra (1987) found that nearly 20% of those psychotherapists surveyed reported experiencing serious personal illness or accident during the past three years. As can easily be imagined, illness or accident in the life of the psychotherapist can have a profound impact on treatment relationships and patients.

The Problem of Self-Disclosure

Personal injury or physical illness may unexpectedly force a therapist to cancel or reschedule therapy sessions from time to time. While it may be possible to evade the questions of patients or withhold information about the cause of the absence, in many cases it will be necessary to make a full disclosure. This will be particularly true in the case of more severe disability, if it becomes necessary to temporarily or permanently discontinue professional practice. Even when work can be resumed, there may be external physical evidence of illness or injury which is observable to clients, such as a bone cast, eye patch, or loss of weight. Therefore, the issue of how much information is to be disclosed, and by whom, is of primary importance.

Both Abend (1982) and Dewald (1982) suggest that clients should be told only the absolute minimum amount of information necessary regarding personal illness or accident of the therapist, and nothing at all when possible. Those who choose to inform clients about the reason for the interruption of treatment may be succumbing to their own needs for comfort, care, and sympathy rather than protecting the client from needless anxiety and burden. Not only is this likely to be detrimental to the well-being of the client, but it may impede treatment as well. For example, detailed information about the therapist's illness or accident may prevent patients from fully exploring their own affective response to the disruption of treatment due to guilt or anxiety resulting from their own anger at the therapist's absence.

From the other perspective, some have suggested that it is preferable to make a complete, voluntary disclosure about such events. Silver (1982) maintains that some clients have an uncanny ability to discover such occurrences by means of overheard conversations among colleagues, the disclosures of mutual acquaintances, or an ability to sense the impact of this event on the demeanor of the therapist, prompting direct questioning regarding his or her physical well-being. Therefore, it may be important for the therapist to inform clients about the basic facts, as they are known, in an open and forthright manner. This ensures accuracy and allows for meaningful exploration of client reactions. This also dignifies their realistic concerns for the therapist's well-being. To fail to address this issue in a truthful manner may inadvertently facilitate patients' denial as well as that of the therapist (Dewald, 1982). When and what is to be disclosed must be an individually based decision that takes into account the particular needs of each client and the nature of the therapeutic relationship (Silver, 1982).

The problem of self-disclosure in regard to this issue is certainly a very complex one. The therapist's natural desire for sympathy and understanding at this time is typically restrained by self-imposed restrictions and injunctions against therapist self-disclosure. Yet some therapy relationships are characterized by a level of warmth and caring which naturally elicits in the therapist a desire to share concerns and needs freely regarding the disability, especially when the therapist knows that the client will readily respond with the desired nurturance and support. This makes it difficult to determine what is truly permissible to share with patients, and what is better left unsaid. While theoretical considerations and clinical judgment may prompt the therapist to decide that it is in the best interest of the client to refrain from self-disclosure, this can result in a certain artificiality in the relationship which creates a sense of deprivation, loneliness, and isolation in the therapist (Greben, 1975). Furthermore, what seems to be in the best interest of the client may actually be more the result of feelings of omnipotence and superiority, an inability to admit personal vulnerability and weakness, or denial and avoidance on the part of the therapist (Greben, 1975; Searles, 1979). As Guy and Souder (in press) note:

> Maintaining the facade of omnipotence in the face of such obvious vulnerability and suffering may not only serve to increase the stress experienced by the therapist, but may be a serious disservice to the client, as well. Denying a client the right to correctly assess the seriousness of the therapist's misfortune, and prohibiting the spontaneous human show of caring and support, may only serve to increase the suffering of both parties. (p. 11)

On the other hand, the therapist's need for sympathy and nurturance may compel him or her to self-disclose when it would be far more helpful to abstain. It is difficult for the psychotherapist to correctly make these determinations at a time of such personal need and vulnerability.

Ideally, if disclosure is deemed to be appropriate, it is best that the client be informed of this information by the therapist during the therapy hour (Abend, 1982; Dewald, 1982). However, if this is not possible due to sudden or severe disability, it may be necessary to have a secretary or colleague make the initial contact by telephone, during which time only a minimum of information is given. A more complete explanation can be best provided by a colleague by means of a letter or a face to face interview (Lindner, 1984). In the case of complete disability or death, an experienced colleague will need to contact clients promptly, initially by telephone, in order to schedule one or more sessions to provide adequacy and continuity of care (Cottle, 1980; Halpert, 1982). Hopefully, this will be accomplished before they learn from another, impersonal source such as a newspaper account.

Practical Considerations

Upon learning the full extent of the disability, the therapist must decide how long a leave of absence will be required before work can be resumed. In the case of a brief illness, this may be a matter of days. However, in the case of more serious impairment, it may involve a period of weeks or months. It may be necessary to refer patients to a colleague for interim care. For brief sabbaticals, this could be arranged informally on an "as needed" basis, giving clients the freedom to call a specifically identified colleague without fear of jeopardizing or insulting the primary therapeutic relationship (Lindner, 1984). Obviously, in the case of extended or prolonged absence it will likely be most appropriate to reassign or refer clients to another therapist permanently (Dewald, 1982; Silver, 1982). Research findings suggest that both clients and therapists typically prefer to endure the forced interruption of treatment without terminating the therapy relationship and making a referral to another therapist. This is usually done with the goal of resuming sessions as soon as possible. However well-intended this plan may be, it may not always be in the client's best interests. Patients may find it difficult to wait for the therapist's return, and yet fail to seek other treatment due to feelings of loyalty or guilt. Therapists, on the other hand, may feel obligated to return to work prematurely before they are able to adequately focus on patient concerns due to their own understandable preoccupation with personal needs (Halpert, 1982).

Deciding when and how to return to work after an absence due to illness or accident involves the careful consideration of several factors. Even after patients' needs for continuity of care have been adequately met, a therapist faces a variety of issues which often make it difficult to determine the optimal time for returning to work (Guy & Souder, in press). On the one hand, family, friends, and physicians may encourage the therapist to prolong the leave of absence to ensure adequate recovery. This gives him or her the permission to enjoy the break from work-related responsibilities and stresses. On the other hand, mounting financial pressures, fear of losing clients and referral sources, need for reassurance of competency, and the emotional satisfactions derived from the work may motivate the therapist to resume work prematurely (Silver, 1982). It is not surprising to find that therapists typically return to work before all visible signs of physical disability are gone (Abend, 1982; Cottle, 1980; Frank, 1975). Unfortunately, the impact of this pattern on therapeutic practice remains undetermined.

A number of additional practical concerns confront the psychotherapist who has been disabled due to illness or accident. Even when the decision has been made to postpone resuming therapeutic sessions, there are still likely to be phone messages to answer, bills to be paid, correspondence to be written, and various other housekeeping chores to be completed (Dewald, 1982). If the therapist is unable to handle these duties, it may be necessary to pay a colleague to do so. Decisions regarding whether and how to attempt the collection of unpaid accounts, as well as mounting financial pressures due to a loss of income and referrals, must be given careful attention. Finally, receiving gifts, letters, phone calls, and visits from well-meaning patients present particularly unique challenges to the therapist's desire to respond in a sensitive, appropriate manner at a time when the personal need for privacy and rest is the greatest.

Patient Reactions

Patient reactions to a therapist's illness or accident will be highly idiosyncratic, depending on the type and length of treatment (i.e., psychoanalysis vs. behavior modification), nature of the patient's problems and past experiences with illness and death, and the personality of the therapist. While some aspects of the patient's reactions will undoubtably be influenced (and perhaps distorted) by prior traumas and experiences, there may a "reality" component as well. The feelings, thoughts, memories, and behavior changes which result will need to be carefully discussed and analyzed in the treatment relationship.

It appears that anger is the most common reaction to therapist disability (Dewald, 1982; Frank, 1975; Lindner, 1984; Silver, 1982). The inconvenience and "betrayal" of trust that the interruption represents to the client can give rise to considerable rage. According to Cottle (1980), there may be related feelings of anger and resentment over the vulnerability and weakness of the therapist who is now seen as "damaged" and impotent. These feelings are likely to be followed by guilt and remorse, as the client feels shame over his or her self-preoccupation at a time of personal need in the life of the therapist. There may also be guilt at being a "survivor" while the therapist appears to be the "victim" of life (Cottle, 1980; Halpert, 1982). Some clients may feel renewed concerns about adequacy of care or possible future abandonment. Finally, some patients choose to ignore the issue, deny its impact, and avoid discussion of it completely (Halpert, 1982).

Therapist Reactions

The most common reaction of therapists to their debilitating illness or accident is that of denial and avoidance. As with most human beings, they typically resist confronting the reality of their own vulnerability and mortality (Cohen, 1983; Halpert, 1982; Lindner, 1984). Added to this, factors inherent in the practice of psychotherapy make it increasingly difficult for the therapist to confront the reality and full impact of a disability due to accident or illness. For example, the physical and psychic isolation associated with clinical practice may leave a therapist unable or unwilling to discuss concerns about personal disability with other colleagues (Cohen, 1983). There may be a fear of the evaluation or criticism of other professionals who may take exception to the manner in which this issue was handled by the therapist, increasing secrecy and isolation (Guy & Souder, In press). Fear of jeopardizing future referrals and uncertainty regarding whether and when to resume work may also keep the disabled psychotherapist from discussing these concerns with others. Finally, perhaps the subtle grandiosity and omnipotence which results from years of patient idealization prevents the therapist from facing the reality of his or her personal vulnerabilty and weakness (Searles, 1979). The therapist may find it especially hard to accept that he or she will be unable to keep the implied promise to "always be there" for the client. As a result of these factors, therapists often find it difficult to confront the facts concerning the impact of a personal illness or accident on their clinical practice and the lives of their patients. The tendency toward denial and avoidance can hinder initial attempts at assessing the severity of the impact and formulating an appropriate plan of action in response.

Dewald (1982) reports that psychotherapists debilitated by illness or accident seem to experience a typical pattern of the initial denial mentioned previously, followed by increased self-absorption, and then an eagerness to return to work. This is accompanied by increased fears regarding professional competency and personal adequacy which may prompt subtle attempts to receive appreciation and gratification from patients on return to clinical duties. There may be renewed feelings of guilt regarding having abandoned patients during their time of need. On the other hand, therapists may experience envy of the health and vitality of some patients during this time of weakness and vulnerabiltiy. This is a particulary difficult experience for therapists who typically feel strong, competent, and in control.

Several authors have mentioned that therapists often feel a strong impulse to self-disclose far more information than is necessary for the resumption of treatment, perhaps out of a desire to receive nurturance, reassurance, and support from patients (Abend, 1982; Dewald, 1982; Silver, 1982). Yet, it may also be an attempt to avoid client anger or resentment subtly due to their untimely disruption of treatment (Guy & Souder, in press). At any rate, it is difficult for the therapist to balance the various needs of all involved during a time of such personal distress and uncertainty.

Finally, in response to the sincere expressions of patient care and concern during and following the therapist's recovery, some have reported experiencing deeper feelings of care and appreciation for their patients (Lindner, 1984; Silver, 1982). This profound gratitude apparently strengthened their commitment to therapeutic practice, facilitating their successful return to work.

Summary and Suggestions

Given the numerous and complex issues associated with the impact of therapist disability due to accident or illness on the practice of therapy, it seems important for therapists to give this issue thoughtful consideration prior to its occurrence. As Guy and Souder (in press) note:

> Few therapists will find it easy to carefully consider the therapeutic appropriateness of various decisions if these are left to be decided at a time when the therapist injury, disability, and basic survival become the predominant concern. Since illness and injury are often unexpected and quite sudden, it seems efficacious to formulate a course of action in advance.

Several practical steps can be taken prior to this occurrence in order to facilitate coping with its potentially disruptive impact on therapy patients. For example, it is important for the professional to keep his or her records up to date and accurate, with clear presentation of client phone numbers and addresses along with a designation of the current status of treatment (active vs. terminated, diagnosis, progress notes, etc.). It may even be appropriate to contract with a colleague formally to enlist his or her services as a "guardian" of these records and accounts should an actual emergency arise (Cohen, 1983). Advance negotiations concerning expectations for case referrals or transfers, the location of records and keys, and the reimbursement for such services will guarantee adequate and continued patient care at a time of personal crisis. While such steps are particularly important for those in private clinical practice, it seems equally necessary for clinics and hospitals to establish similar procedures in writing to address these issues in order to facilitate effective follow-up care if the need should arise. It is interesting to note that in a recent nationwide survey of psychotherapists, nearly half of those surveyed indicated that they had made no prior arrangements for patient care or the handling of records in the event of their sudden disability or death (Guy, Stark, & Poelstra, 1987). While making such advance plans may seem sensible, many practitioners apparently fail to do so.

There are obviously a number of complex and confusing ethical issues associated with these procedures. In fact, there is heated debate about whether records should be kept at all, much less turned over to a colleague. The patient's right to confidentiality must be carefully weighed against his or her need for adequate and timely care in the event of the sudden illness, accident, or death of the therapist (Bellak,1981). Advance discussion with patients concerning their personal preferences, obtaining the necessary "release of information," and agreeing together on a plan to either destroy or transfer records should the need arise will provide a clear and sound course of action for the therapist or his or her associates (Cohen, 1983). Of course, the therapeutic impact of raising this issue with each client must be considered in advance on an individual basis. In some cases, despite the potential for later confusion, it may be best to forgo such a discussion due to the patient's current mental status. Finally, it might be useful for the therapist to draw up a "will" that includes detailed instructions for the colleague enlisted for follow-up patient care concerning the deciphering of records, handling of client information, collection and payment of bills, and liquidation of assets in the event of severe disability or death.

On a more personal level, it may be helpful for therapists to give advance consideration to the feelings, needs, and expectations that are likely to arise in response to their potential disability due to accident or illness. This will assist them in confronting the many issues concerning patient care prior to encountering crisis, allowing for thoughtful reflection and analysis of personal and professional needs. Bellak (1981) recommends that the ill or injured therapist seek out personal supervision and/or psychotherapy in order to receive needed support, nurturance, guidance, and reality testing during and after the time of incapacitation. This, of course, assumes that he or she is physically able to do so.

Given the serious financial ramifications of extended disability, it would seem highly expedient for the practicing therapist to obtain professional disability insurance. Coverage is available to all clinicians through local, regional, and national professional organizations. For very little cost, disability insurance provides guaranteed income and payments for office overhead expenses during extended illness or recovery from an accident. All psychotherapists, including both full-time and part-time practitioners, should obtain this coverage if they have not already done so.

The impact of therapist disability due to illness or accident has received far too little attention in the profession of psychotherapy (Bellak, 1981). It is critically important that these issues be carefully considered by practicing therapists in order to ensure adequate patient care. Furthermore, advance attention to these concerns will also likely have a positive impact on the psychotherapist's personal life and relationships, bringing a sense of balance and perspective at a time of personal crisis.

Note that the this discussion has focused solely on therapist physical illness or accident. Issues concerning psychotherapist mental illness, emotional impairment, burnout, and death will be addressed in later sections.

Death of a Loved One

One of the most difficult events likely to occur during the Middle and Late Adulthood eras is the death of a loved one. Guy, Stark, and Poelstra (1987) found that approximately 20% of the therapists surveyed had experienced such a loss during the previous three years. Whether this was expected or sudden, the loss of a friend or family member can have a significant impact on the personal life and professional work of the therapist. Despite the training and experience received in regard to helping patients with similar issues related to grief and loss, the therapist suffers many of the same consequences of this event in his or her own life. Thus consideration should be given to evaluating its effect on the therapist's ability to practice.

The Problem of Self-Disclosure

As with the other significant life events, deciding whether, what, and when to tell patients about the loss of a loved one is a complex issue requiring individualistic consideration. It would seem unwise to adopt a uniform policy which does not take into account variables such as the theoretical orientation employed, diagnosis and mental status of the patient, past and current therapeutic concerns, and the specifics of the occurrence (Givelber & Simon, 1981). As with therapist illness and disability, it is important to strike a balance between unnecessarily burdening and frightening the patient and denying his or her correct assessment of the impact of this event and resultant wish to express appropriate condolences. Achieving this balance is extremely difficult. As Givelber and Simon note:

> To include the patient in some measure of one's experience of loss may repeat a childhood trauma; either the stress trauma of an acute illness or depressive episodes in the parent, or the "chronic strain" caused by a depressive or inadequate parent who habitually turns to the child for parental help. Yet, excluding the patient from some discussion of a loss when the patient is aware that something has occurred does not necessarily help the patient. Such exclusion may mimic an earlier disturbed family interaction. The patient may once again perceive a confusing change of mood in an important figure on whom he or she depends and feel forbidden to ask about it. (p. 144)

Despite the potential pitfalls associated with self-disclosure, it may be in everyone's best interest for the therapist to reveal voluntarily his or her recent loss in order to give patients permission to discuss freely their fantasies and reactions to perceived changes in the therapist, the partial truths that may have been inadvertently learned from independent sources, and their thoughts and feelings in response to this disclosure (Fromm-Reichmann, 1960; Givelber & Simon, 1981). This seems like a useful course of action since the impact of this event on the therapy relationship will likely be noticeable to most patients. In addition to a change in the therapist's demeanor, cancelled sessions or an extended absence resulting from an out-of-town funeral or the need to provide support to distant family members, may necessitate some sort of explanation to patients. Regardless of whether the disclosure will contribute to their eventual growth or temporary fragmentation, it may need to be made to ensure the integrity of the relationship. It will then be necessary for the therapist to note carefully the resultant impact on patient thoughts, feelings, and behaviors in order to work through issues that may arise in response. As with other similar events, it will be important that the therapist share only as much information about the loss as is necessary to continue the therapeutic work. This must not be used as an opportunity to exploit patients in order to meet personal need.

Patient Reactions

Givelber and Simon (1981) describe a number of patient reactions to the discovery of their therapist's loss. Some seemed to relive past losses and traumas, recalling memories and feelings which were then profitably resolved in the therapy relationship. Others experienced a mixture of anger and resentment regarding the therapist's past or present preoccupation with personal concerns as a result of the death. Several patients felt paralyzed by their inability to offer comfort or "say the right thing," increasing their anxiety and feelings of inadequacy. There was also a tendency for some patients to attempt to deny, avoid, and ignore the event and its impact on the treatment, prompting their refusal to discuss it beyond a few cursory acknowledgments.

In addition to these reactions, patients may experience intense guilt at their preoccupation with their own problems and needs at a time of personal crisis in the life of the therapist. At a more primitive level, they may even feel guilt due to the belief that their desire to have the therapist all to themselves resulted in this death. Preoccupations with overall adequacy of care, availability of the therapist, and fears concerning whether the therapist will recover sufficiently to attend once again to the patient's needs are likely to be prominent at this time. Finally, there may be a sincere wish to comfort, support, and protect the psychotherapist following this loss. At times such as this, the commonality of human experience often awakens sincere empathy and concern in clients who wish to give to the therapist some portion of the nurturance and encouragement that they have received during the course of treatment.

Therapist Reactions

As with other individuals, psychotherapists are prone to deny or minimize the impact of this event on their life and work (Givelber & Simon, 1981; Granet & Kalman, 1982; Lewis, 1982). This may cause some to overlook its effects on their ability to practice therapy. As a result, there is often a return to work before the acute impact of the loss has been adequately dealt with. Premature resumption of clinical work may also be due to internal expectations. As Givelber and Simon state, "the therapist often feels that no matter how devastating the personal loss, he or she should be able to manage grief within a set period of time, usually a far shorter time than one would think adequate for one's patients" (p. 142). Feelings of loneliness, low self-esteem, fear of lost income and referrals, and a desire for comfort may also cause the therapist to return to work prematurely. There may be a tendency for the psychotherapist to use their practice to compensate for the loss of the loved one, perhaps by utilizing particular patients to "replace" the individual who has died.

Whether or not the therapist resumes work at an appropriate point, he or she may be confronted with renewed feelings of depression, sadness, mourning, and inadequacy when meeting once again with patients. Furthermore, there may be a tendency to avoid discussing certain issues with clients due to a fear of reawakening feelings of sorrow and grief which might cause the therapist to"break down" in the presence of the patient. There may also be anger regarding a patient's seemingly inadequate or uncaring response to this event, or on the other hand, guilt over receiving their caring and support.

Granet and Kalman (1982) report that some therapists experience anniversary reactions associated with the loss of a loved one. These are sometimes experienced in response to patient material which reminds the therapist of his or her loss. They may also occur independently of the content of patient remarks, resulting from a more traditional reaction to the annual anniversary of a death in the therapist's past. Regardless, such phenomena may precipitate renewed depression, sorrow, grief, anger, or loneliness which the therapist may mistakenly attribute to his or her work with particular therapy patients. It is important that therapists recognize the potential for this to occur, monitor the ongoing impact of the loss on their inner processing and therapeutic work, and seek consultation and/or supervision during times when anniversary reactions are likely or already occurring.

On a more positive note, the therapist may find that undergoing personal loss increases empathy and sensitivity for similar experiences in the lives of patients (Givelber & Simon, 1981; Lewis, 1982). Not only will it heighten the ability to identify with the pain of patients, it will also provide a perspective on life that is helpful in assisting them with recovery. Lewis suggests that this event may impact the manner in which therapists regard termination of treatment, making them more sensitive and aware of the many issues regarding loss and abandonment which both they and patients are liable to experience.

Summary

While admittedly somewhat morbid, it seems wise for the practicing psychotherapist to acknowledge the eventual reality of encountering the loss of a loved one and its impact on personal and professional life and relationships. While Givelber and Simon (1981) wisely point out that it will be impossible for the therapist to anticipate all of his or her reactions to this event (much less those of patients), thereby making it futile to "plan ahead" for this eventuality, it is nonetheless important that consideration be given to some of the aforementioned issues. As in the case of therapist disability due to personal illness or accident, the death of a loved one may have a debilitating effect on the therapist's ability to decide rationally how to handle the needs of patients in a sensitive and appropriate manner. While there may certainly be reason to hope that the therapist will respond with good judgment, it would be a serious mistake to assume that this will be easy.

LATE ADULTHOOD

According to Levinson (1986), the era of Middle Adulthood is followed by the Late Adult Transition, ages 60 to 65; Late Adulthood, ages 65 to 80; and a less defined era of Late Late Adulthood, ages 80 and beyond. For purposes of this discussion, Late Adulthood and Late Late Adulthood will be considered together in this section. Various marker events bring about the transition from Middle to Late Adulthood such as illness or retirement. During this time of transition, the individual becomes increasingly aware of the physical and mental effects of aging and the need to confront the reality of his or her mortality. Personal illness as well as the disability or death of friends serve as reminders of the limited amount of time left for fulfilling any remaining fantasies or goals.

The critical developmental task to be overcome during Late Adulthood is the integration of youth and age in order to achieve the appropriate balance between vitality and maturity (Levinson, 1978). Positions of leadership and authority must gradually be given up to members of the Middle Adulthood era. The role of "grandparent" and "retiree," not to mention that of "senior citizen," must be assumed with willingness and dignity. Work activities become increasingly focused on creativity and self-expression rather than achievement for the sake of advancement. There must be a new balance between involvement with society and the self. As Levinson notes, "A man (woman) in this era is experiencing more fully the process of dying and he should have the possibility of choosing more freely his mode of living" (1978, p. 36). The emergence of wisdom, peace, integrity, and tranquility allows the individual to become more "centered" in himself or herself, thereby allowing a greater contribution to be made to the well-being of society. A strong altruistic attitude emerges which increases the older adult's concern for the well-being of future generations.

During the period of Late Late Adulthood, there is a narrowing of focus centering on physical infirmities, the loss of friends, and the imminency of death. Severe disability may rob life of its meaning. Mental deterioration may distort its reality. However, for some, social development and activity continues. Regardless of varying levels of health and happiness, the reality that death lies ahead must be openly confronted during this era. This increases involvement with the inner life. As Levinson so aptly describes:

> He (she) is reaching his ultimate involvement with the self. What matters most now is his final sense of what life is about, his "view from the bridge" at the end of the life cycle. In the end he has only the self—and the crucial internal figures it has brought into being. He must come finally to terms with the self—knowing it and loving it reasonably well, and being ready to give it up. (1978, p. 39)

This process may result in a more "spiritual" perspective on life, as the older adult gains a broader perspective on human existence.

For the psychotherapist, the issues associated with Late and Late Late Adulthood (which will be combined from this point onward under the rubric of Late Adulthood) represent a unique interaction between personal and professional concerns. For some, there is difficulty reconciling the personal costs of conducting psychotherapy with the rather limited success achieved. There is the need to accept that the therapist has helped relatively few individuals during his or her career (Bugental, 1964; Farber, 1983a). More than that, there is recognition of the fact that a career in psychotherapy in and of itself has failed to create a lasting, meaningful existence for the therapist (Wheelis, 1958). This may result in feelings of despair, depletion, and futility (Fine, 1980). On the other hand, there may be an emerging sense of resolution, dignity, and acceptance regarding the value, however limited, of a life of clinical work. Rather than experiencing despair, the therapist in Late Adulthood may feel satisfied and fulfilled at having had an impact on the lives of so many individuals. The older adult therapist often enjoys seeing the fruits of his or her labor, as former patients go on to live happy, productive lives, renewing contact from time to time, and referring family and friends for treatment. There may be a sense of privilege at having shared in their lives as well as gratitude for the personal growth that has occurred in the therapist as a result of these contacts.

Several life events become particularly significant in the life and work of the psychotherapist during this era. In addition to those mentioned during Middle Adulthood (i.e., divorce, departure of children, illness and accident, and death of a loved one, any of which may occur during this period as well), the psychotherapist will confront aging and retirement, possible terminal illness, and death. Each of these events has the potential to impact the practice of psychotherapy and the lives of patients significantly.

Aging and Retirement

As the profession of psychotherapy has matured, so have its practitioners. One survey of psychotherapists revealed that 26% of those in active clinical practice were between the ages of 50 and 60, while nearly 10% were over 60 years of age (Henry, Sims, & Spray, 1971). More recently it was reported that the mean age of psychologists belonging to the Clinical and Psychotherapy divisions of the American Psychological Association was 46 and 47 respectively, with an age range of 24 to 80 (Prochaska & Norcross, 1983a). As the baby boomers grow older, the mean and modal age of practicing psychotherapists will continue to advance. Furthermore, it may become increasingly acceptable to continue clinical work beyond the standard age for retirement. Even now it is not entirely unsual to encounter a practicing psychotherapist who continues to work with clients beyond his or her seventieth birthday. In fact, some have been known to maintain limited practices into their nineties.

With increasing age comes the need for determining its impact on the clinician's work and the practice of therapy. Currently there are no generally accepted definitions of competency, nor are there acceptable means of detecting, sanctioning, or remedying incompetency within the profession (Clairborn, 1982; Laliotis & Grayson, 1985). This is especially true of age-related impairment. As a result the therapist is left alone to evaluate the impact of advanced age on his or her clinical competency, and to determine when it may be best to retire.

For most individuals, the transition from gainful employment to retirement is a major milestone viewed with varying degrees of ambivalence (Van Hoose & Worth, 1982). Additional factors associated with the practice of psychotherapy may further complicate this transition. For example, those in private practice enjoy a relative independence that exempts them from the administrative policies or procedures of hospitals, clinics, or universities regarding competency-related evaluations and eventual retirement. Once the therapist has obtained licensure or certification to permit private independent practice, there are typically no other points of mandatory evaluation regarding clinical practice. Thus the therapist is free to work as long as he or she desires, regardless of decreasing competency (unless this results in legal action or professional censure). Even for those working in institutional settings with mandatory evaluations and retirement, most also have part-time private practices that they are free to continue beyond the age of 65 or 70 (Norcross, Nash, & Prochaska, 1985; Tryon, 1983b). Furthermore, they can begin private practice following forced retirement if they so choose. Ultimately, this leaves the therapist alone to decide whether it is best to discontinue professional work due to age-related impairment. In the absence of well-defined criteria, the practitioner must make this decision loaded with significant personal meaning without the benefit of structure or guidance.

Since the psychotherapist's personal and professional identity are inseparable, the decision to discontinue work can be a very complicated one (Will, 1979). The high social value and personal satisfaction associated with a career in psychotherapy may make it difficult to surrender this source of personal worth

(Gaitz, 1977). A reduction or cessation of work may result in the loss of an important social role, creating feelings of uselessness and despair in the therapist whose very identity is encompassed by this career role (Halloran, 1985). Avoidance and denial concerning issues of mortality, feelings of commitment and responsibility for the care of patients, and a sense of omnipotence resulting from patient idealization may further hinder the therapist's attempts to address this issue openly and directly. Any or all of these issues can make it difficult for the therapist to determine objectively when and if it is necessary to discontinue the practice of therapy due to age-related impairment.

The Problem of Self-disclosure

The physical and psychic isolation associated with clinical practice may make it difficult for the aging psychotherapist to discuss his or her concerns with other colleagues. Furthermore, fear of criticism, ridicule, and the loss of referrals may prevent the therapist from approaching other professionals with issues and concerns regarding the impact of aging and retirement. Thus the therapist is left largely alone to ponder the problems related to self-assessment and self-imposed retirement.

Obviously it is difficult for the therapist to approach clients for feedback regarding possible declining competency related to advancing age. Yet in one study the majority of psychotherapists surveyed indicated that they regarded client feedback to be a primary source of data in determining whether or not they had become impaired, second only to their own self-assessment (Guy, Stark, & Poelstra, 1987). This is unfortunate because clients may not be reliable sources of such information. For example, they may not be in a position to assess the therapist's clinical ability objectively, nor are they likely to be completely truthful if age-related impairment has been noted. If the therapist succumbs to sharing concerns regarding his or her competency with patients and/or questioning them regarding their own views on this issue, clients may respond with reassurance, support, encouragement, and concern, regardless of whether this is appropriate. It is not likely to be helpful for the therapist to burden patients with personal insecurities, conflicts, and fears regarding advancing age. On the other hand, to avoid carefully discussion of this issue may facilitate denial on the part of both parties, leaving the client alone with his or her fantasies, fears, and opinions about the aging clinician. While it may be most appropriate to wait for these concerns to appear in the comments, emotions, and behavior of clients, addressing them fully when they arise, it may become necessary for the therapist to bring up the issue voluntarily in order to promote a full discussion of patient concerns and views. Obviously, this is to be done for the benefit of the patient rather than to reassure or assist the therapist.

Patient Reactions

Patient reactions mentioned earlier regarding therapist illness or accident are pertinent here. Many of the same fantasies and concerns will arise in response to the advancing age of the therapist which do not warrant repeating at this point. However, there may be some unique additional ones as well. For example, patients who have had intermittent contact with the therapist over many years may be saddened or disturbed by the apparent deterioration of health and/or mind. This may evoke memories of aged parents or grandparents as well as feelings concerning their own advancing age. Preoccupation concerning the health of the therapist, with fears about his or her eventual death, may bring concerns about adequacy of care and possible abandonment. There may also be anger at the therapist's inability to remain invulnerable to the impact of aging, particularly when this brings illness or disability.

Those who have recently begun work with the aged therapist may be unaware of any deterioration or loss of vitality during recent years. However, many of the aforementioned concerns may arise as well. Depending on their own views of aging and past experience with older adults, there may be either an overly idealized view of the aged therapist as wise, omniscient, and omnipotent, or a devaluing view of him or her as "out of touch," naive, sickly, and obsolescent. There may be a desire to protect and comfort the psychotherapist (causing the patient to avoid confrontation or disagreement), or there may be a need to discredit, criticize, and devalue the clinician's views.

If the psychotherapist fails to bring up this issue in treatment, or avoids a full discussion of it when it was raised by the patient, it can become a mutually agreed upon "secret" that leaves the client alone with the fears, fantasies, and concerns which it evokes. If the therapist unduly postpones his or her retirement, concerns about adequacy of care, health of the therapist, and possible death may increase. There may also be mixed feelings of anger and guilt regarding the patient's reactions to the therapist's advancing age. The inability for these issues to be openly discussed with the therapist may undermine trust, confidence, and ultimately the treatment alliance.

On the other hand, should the therapist raise the issue of his or her advancing age, the client may be flooded with concerns about the well-being of the clinician, the future of the therapy relationship, eventual termination, and possible abandonment. If the therapist should announce the decision to retire, this may evoke a number of reactions, such as anxiety, fear, guilt, regret, and depression. Feelings of rejection and abandonment are likely, as well as anger and disbelief.

For some patients, the advancing age of the therapist and the prospect of his or her retirement will present little difficulty, depending on diagnosis, type of treatment, and status of the therapy. They may actually join in the therapist's realistic resolution by recognizing the dignity and satisfaction that can be part of the aging process.

Therapist Reactions

The effects of aging on the overall functioning of the psychotherapist are highly variable and idiosyncratic, with some individuals experiencing little or no age-related decrements while others suffer severe debilitation (as in the case of

Alzheimer's or dementia). Despite this variation, advancing age is likely to impact therapeutic practice in several common ways.

The later adult years bring a natural decline in physical health and vitality (Kimmel, 1974; Van Hoose & Worth, 1982). In addition to changes in physical appearance, there is typically a decrease in visual and auditory acuity and a slowing of sensimotor processes. There is often a decline in physical energy and endurance. Finally, there may be an increase in chronic disease and disability. Although the practice of therapy does not require a great deal of physical strength and endurance, a certain amount of stamina and energy is required to enable the therapist to interact with clients for extended periods of time with little or no breaks. A decrease in physical vitality may limit the therapist's ability to maintain prolonged intensity during the course of therapy (Eissler, 1977). Furthermore, preoccupation with an increasing number of physical discomforts or symptoms may further limit the therapist's attending ability. Increased illness, frequent absences, and the specter of death or disability may be unwelcomed and unsettling intrusions in the therapist's life and work.

For most individuals, advancing age brings a slowing in response time related to retarded functioning of the central nervous system which may affect perception, attention span, and short-term memory (Kimmel, 1974). There may also be increasing difficulty maintaining prolonged concentration, a diminishing of effective vocabulary, a persistent and insistent repetition of thought patterns, and a decrease in overall motivation (Charness, 1985; Van Hoose & Worth, 1982). While intellectual skills involving logical reasoning and verbal ability remain fairly stable, tasks requiring speed and accuracy become more difficult. The desire and energy to learn often decreases, even when the ability to do so remains constant. These changes may make it difficult for the aging therapist to maintain prolonged concentration, impair memory functioning, and decrease motivation for work (Eissler, 1977). The ability to understand the patient deeply, attend to the material presented, and maintain and communicate accurate empathy may be affected by declining mental acuity.

A number of emotional changes may also affect the practice of psychotherapy. Individuals in this era of life are forced to assess and evaluate the meaning of life. Aging individuals typically become more introspective, self-focused, and internally oriented (Levinson, 1978). There is a need for a sense of satisfaction and fulfillment as the individual undergoing a "life review" takes inventory of past accomplishments and experiences in an effort to achieve dignity rather than despair (Erikson, 1968; Kimmel, 1974). Depression results if the individual arrives at a negative appraisal of his or her life and worth, increasing fears of age-related declines which are likely to hinder future attempts to reach the desired personal or vocational goals (Kolb & Brodie, 1982). Psychotherapists may find that an increased self-focus, internal orientation, and narcissism hinders their ability to attend to and empathize with therapy patients effectively (Eissler, 1977). While the transition to integrity will help some therapists experience and express positive regard for their clients (Rogers, 1980), those falling into despair may find it increasingly hard to care for the needs of demanding patients. In addition, the potential for job-related depletion and disillusionment may deny the therapist the integrity that he or she desires. Fears of displacement and rejection may prevent them from discussing this issue openly and realistically with patients. Finally, the lack of dialogue, evaluation, structure, or guidelines in the field of psychotherapy regarding age-related impairment and the possible need for retirement leaves the clinician alone to face the anxiety, depression, or stress which may result from this issue.

The loss of identity, sense of worth, and personal power associated with the cessation or reduction of clinical work may make it difficult for the therapist to confront the need for such a decision. In addition, the loss of friends and family may make it painful to terminate with therapy patients. As a result, the aging psychotherapist may postpone announcing his or her retirement and prolong clinical practice beyond an appropriate point. It is interesting to note that nearly half of those therapists surveyed in a recent study indicated that they planned to continue clinical practice beyond the age of 70, with 15% stating that they expected to conduct psychotherapy until their death (Guy, Stark, & Poelstra, 1987). Not only may this reflect unrealistic optimism regarding the absence of age-related or illness-related disability during later life, but it may also indicate the hesitancy of many practitioners to surrender willingly their role as psychotherapist through retirement. A mixture of personal and patient needs seem to combine to cloud good judgment regarding the need for and timing of this event. Economic necessity alone is not likely to explain this pattern fully.

Following retirement, therapists may feel abandoned by colleagues, patients, and associates. Whereas before retirement they may have been actively sought out for supervision and consultation, retired therapists may find that no one is interested in their viewpoints any longer, and their skills, expertise, and knowledge are likely to be regarded as increasingly suspect by younger professionals. The rare exception would be those who have achieved particular notoriety and prominence in the field. Such individuals may feel professionally useful and productive right up until their death.

Summary and Suggestions

Since the practicing psychotherapist currently has the sole responsibility for determining if it is in the public's best interest to discontinue clinical work (at least in regards to private practice), it is important that this event be anticipated and its arrival adequately prepared for. To begin with, the practicing therapist must confront his or her own mortality and advancing age with as much objectivity and integrity as possible. Educating oneself concerning the likely physical, mental, emotional, and social effects of aging is a crucial first step. This will sharpen self-assessment skills concerning likely decrements and deficiencies that may impact clinical work and reassure the therapist regarding the appropriateness of the decision to either continue or discontinue practicing at any given point.

As the therapist notes changes associated with advancing age that negatively impact clinical competency, several steps may be helpful. For example, compiling more detailed session notes or tape recording sessions may compensate for memory failure, allowing an opportunity for review prior to the next session. Correcting visual or auditory problems by means of corrective lenses or a hearing aid will sharpen observation and perception. Ongoing consultation with colleagues, along with regular continuing education, will provide valuable input and feedback. Reentry into personal psychotherapy may help the aging therapist resolve concerns regarding the issue of integrity versus despair. Periodic consideration should be given to limiting the number of clients and appointments in order to be consistent with current levels of stamina and motivation. Diversification of clinical duties to include teaching, supervision, and writing may be helpful as well. Scheduling frequent breaks during the day or clustering appointments during the time of day when energy levels are typically the highest will help the therapist stay alert. Developing outside hobbies or interests will broaden the therapist's personal horizons and provide a sense of purpose and meaning apart from work-related activities. Taking steps to prepare for possible illness disability, or eventual death will also guarantee adequate patient care.

It would likely be helpful for the aging therapist to overcome personal fears and hesitations and openly discuss his or her advancing age with other colleagues and professionals. This will facilitate obtaining guidance, feedback, and reassurance from others regarding the decisions and problems associated with the effects of aging on clinical practice. In addition, it may also be useful to address this issue openly with current and future patients in order to encourage them to discuss freely their own feelings and views. Rather than hindering the work of the psychotherapist, such dialogues are likely to increase insight, good judgment, and personal resolve.

Finally, there is a need for the psychotherapeutic profession to take a proactive stance regarding the issue of age-related impairment. Perhaps periodic evaluations of clinical competency at times of licensure renewal, along with aggressive attempts to establish therapist support networks for education and feedback will assist aging psychotherapists with the decisions that must be made regarding potential retirement. Most important, further research on this issue is needed to counteract harmful stereotypes and ignorance regarding the impact of aging on the delivery of clinical services.

Terminal Illness

Although the previous discussion of therapist disability due to illness and death presents the problems encountered by both therapist and patient in such situations, a few comments will be made here about the special circumstances surrounding the terminal illness of a therapist. Due to the increase in the incidence of certain terminal illnesses in the general population, such as in the case of cancer, AIDS, and similar infirmities, it is possible that the therapist will fall victim to a fatal illness or disease during his or her career in psychotherapy. Obviously, such an event will have a profound impact on the clinical work of the therapist and the lives of his or her patients.

The Problems of Self-Disclosure

Unlike the previously discussed events in the life of the therapist, the discovery of terminal illness makes full disclosure to patients mandatory rather than optional. Bellak (1981) suggests that this be done in a straightforward manner as soon as the facts are known. There is little to be gained by postponing the announcement, since both the therapist and patient are likely to sense the impact of the illness and knowledge of impending death on the therapist's demeanor. Patients' questions should be answered truthfully and completely. Decisions will need to be made together regarding a termination date, and arrangements should be made with another therapist for patients who wish to continue treatment. The termination process will need to address the meaning and impact of the impending death on the patient, and time will need to be given for grieving and saying an adequate "goodbye." However, this process should not be unnecessarily prolonged, and provisions should be made in case of sudden deterioration or death. It will also be necessary to schedule sessions with realistic consideration given to the failing strength and physical health of the therapist. In some cases it will be necessary for the termination phase to be somewhat abbreviated due to the rapidly deteriorating condition of the therapist.

Despite a natural tendency to minimize and deny the seriousness of this event, it will be important for the therapist to discuss this openly with patients, allowing them to express appropriate grief, sympathy, and condolences without restraint. While admittedly painful for both parties, it may well be necessary for terminating the treatment relationship in the most helpful manner possible.

Patient Reactions

Little needs to be said about the reactions of patients, since many are self-evident or have been summarized previously. Upon learning the news of the therapist's illness and impending death, patients are likely to go through the typical stages associated with facing the death of a significant loved one, namely denial, sadness, anger, guilt and self-reproach, anxiety, loneliness, fatigue, helplessness, shock, numbness, and yearning (Worden, 1982). There may be a tendency to talk incessantly about the illness while avoiding the need to work through its impact sufficiently to allow for a referral to another therapist. In this way, the patient may try to hold on to the therapist (i.e., "If I need you, perhaps you won't die"). On the other hand, the client may avoid talking about the news and its impact altogether. In such cases, there may be a premature termination by the patient so as not to be left behind. There may also be increased acting out as an expression of rage at being abandoned. Finally, some patients will experience normal, uncomplicated bereavement, much of which may need to be worked through with the help of a subsequent therapist.

Clients may wish to know of the therapist's status following termination. They may telephone, send flowers and gifts, and wish to visit them in the hospital. Decisions regarding how to handle such issues will need to be made on an individual basis, taking into account the needs of both therapist and patient. If possible, a client's wish to attend the funeral should not be discouraged. Instead, clients should be given permission, if not the suggestion, to attend the funeral in order to facilitate the mourning process.

Therapist Reactions

As can well be appreciated, the discovery of terminal illness will profoundly impact the therapist's ability to work. Not only will there be increasing physical limitations, but the appropriate self-absorption that results will make it difficult to conduct therapy. The many problems associated with informing clients and referral sources, facilitating the permanent referral of current patients, selling or closing a private practice, and discontinuing clinical work present a gargantuan challenge for the therapist at a time when personal resources may be at their lowest level. The therapist will experience many of the same emotional reactions as their patients. In particular, there may be guilt at abandoning patients and resentment for feeling obligated to them at a time when complete self-absorption may be necessary. Only those therapists using work to help them deny the reality of their impending death will wish to continue long after learning of the terminal illness. Most will make arrangements to stop clinical practice at the earliest possible time. This is necessary to enable them to tend to their personal affairs and family concerns.

Summary and Discussion

The very nature of the therapeutic relationship, with its inherent promise of therapist stability, reliability, and predictability, will make it difficult for all parties involved to face the inevitability of the therapist's impending death. Yet in order to ensure adequate continuation of care, this issue must be directly confronted and openly discussed as soon as possible. In some cases there will be adequate time for a manageable transfer of patients to a skilled colleague. This will bring about a regrettable but satisfactory transition for continuation of care and the resolution of feelings about the event. In other case, there will only be enough time for a few essential steps to be taken. Bellak (1981) cites the example of a therapist friend caught in this dilemma. "After his second coronary he realized that he did not have long to live. He spent his last days in an oxygen tent dictating progress notes on his patients" (p. 233).

As discussed previously regarding therapist disability, it will be helpful for the therapist to make detailed arrangements for the transfer of patient records to an experienced colleague to allow for continuation of care, should there be a need to refer to past treatment notes, testing results, or clinical summaries, or to provide them at the request of future therapists (Cohen, 1983). The more complete the charts, the more helpful they will be for future use.

The impact of terminal illness on the life and work of the therapist is profound. These admittedly brief remarks understate its significance, perhaps appropriately so.

Sudden Death of the Therapist

The tragedy of sudden death has a severe impact on surviving loved ones. Among those most profoundly affected will be the patients of the deceased psychotherapist. The shock of the sudden and complete disruption of treatment will likely have a marked influence on their feelings, thoughts, and behaviors which may require further professional assistance in order to bring about adequate resolution and closure.

Hopefully, the therapist took the steps outlined previously prior to his or her sudden death. If the deceased made prior arrangements with a colleague to have access to patient records if need arose, he or she will likely step in at this time and make contact with patients, referral sources, and creditors. Unfortunately, as mentioned previously, only about half of practicing psychotherapists make such arrangements in advance (Guy, Stark, & Poelstra, 1987). If this was not done, two or three colleagues may be enlisted at the request of a spouse or family member (Bellak, 1981). In the absence of spouse or family, and if no other prior arrangements were made, it may be necessary for the professional organization to which the therapist belonged to provide notice and assistance to current patients in the event of the therapist's unexpected death.

Patient Reactions

In an interesting study of 27 psychoanalysis patients whose analysts died before the completion of treatment, Lord, Ritvo, and Solnit (1978) documented the variety of reactions which resulted. One-third of the patients studied experienced the expected mourning reactions and uncomplicated bereavement. Nearly two-thirds had either pathological mourning reactions (complicated or prolonged) or had no reaction whatsoever—in some cases a problem in itself. "Early loss and deprivation appeared to be the most important factors associated with pathological mourning reactions" (p. 196). Those patients with more disturbed backgrounds reacted most pathologically, while those who had not sustained early loss or deprivation tended to have more realistic reactions to the death. Older patients experienced the most difficult and prolonged mourning, while younger analysands reacted with less disturbance. Factors which appeared to be unrelated to the degree and type of mourning reaction included sex of the patient, relative ages of patient and therapist, and the phase of treatment at the time of death.

Bellak (1981) notes that, in addition to these mourning reactions, therapy patients are likely to react with intense rage as a result of being deserted by the deceased. The sudden death is a "violation" of the therapeutic alliance with its implicit promise of permanence and stability. Surviving patients may find it difficult to "trust" another therapist, and resist forming a dependent relationship during a subsequent treatment. The therapist's death may confirm their belief that the world is a dangerous, unpredictable place, making it safer to remain detached and invulnerable to further hurt. On the other hand, as Bellak notes, an event as dramatic as the death of a therapist is likely to have positive fallout for some patients as well. New insights, increased inner strength, and a deeper appreciation for present life and relationships may bring benefits to surviving patients.

Summary

It is very troubling to note the profession's virtual silence on this issue (Cohen, 1983; Lord et al., 1978). Cohen suggests that "the anxiety-provoking nature of contemplating, let alone actively planning for death, as well as the experience of separateness and timelessness that can be an integral aspect of the practice of psychotherapy, are factors that contribute to the denial of death" (p. 225). Yet, as has been noted, the many complicated issues surrounding this event and the need for advanced preparation to ensure adequate patient care should a crisis arise make it necessary for the responsible therapist to give careful consideration to these issues. Perhaps, in this way, the deceased therapist can have a continuing impact on his or her patients even following his or her death; by having sufficiently prepared for this event, he or she is able to facilitate the provision of care provided by other colleagues to those patients who are likely to be in need. In this manner, true caring and concern are demonstrated. In effect, the therapist is saying, "Even now that I am gone, you will be aware of my desire to promote your growth and well-being."

DISCUSSION

The world of the psychotherapist is a strange mixture of fantasy and reality, a universe of dreams, hidden meanings, underlying motivations, and a spectrum of emotions. The blend of the personal and professional life of the therapist results in a blurring of boundaries, causing one existence to flow into the other. Over time there often appears to be less and less distinction between roles and persona, with the therapist becoming increasingly "clinical" and less real. Life is lived vicariously, and the therapist becomes an observer rather than participant in the events and experiences of everyday living. This process is like an ocean current: strong, silent, and relentless. All therapists struggle to swim against it, regardless of theoretical orientation, years of experience, or individual personality. For some, this has become a manageable task, sometimes difficult but not impossible. Others are eventually swept away, surrendering themselves to the "world" of psychotherapy, losing meaningful contact with family, friends, and their own individuality.

It is only at times of significant events in the life of the psychotherapist that it becomes apparent to everyone that the therapist is indeed alive, with an existence totally apart from his or her clinical work. Perhaps this is what makes such events so unsettling to both the therapist and client. In order to provide a stable, unchanging environment which encourages the client to rely on the strength and dependability of the therapist, a fantasy is often perpetuated which portrays the therapist as somehow exempt from the stresses, changes, and unexpected problems of life. It may be a rude shock to both therapist and patient to realize that nothing, not even the treatment relationship, is invulnerable to the vicissitudes of human existence. Despite a tendency for the therapist to appear to be a mere observer of life, these life events make it clear that he or she is very much a participant, sometimes a victor and occasionally a victim.

Therapists often get married, have children, and sometimes get divorced. They may relocate to new offices, cities, and states. They will frequently suffer the loss of loved ones, fall victim to illness and accident, and face the impact of aging on their life and work. Despite their seeming invulnerability to the tragedies of life, they may become terminally ill, and certainly all will die at some point. Neither the needs of patients nor the hopes of psychotherapists can change this reality. The therapist is simply not the permanent "object" that he or she may wish to appear.

Of course, this is as it must be. In order for therapists to enable others to face life's many exigencies, they must themselves be alive and experience life fully. Regardless of their level of training and expertise, it is out of this commonality of human experience that clinicians are able to share empathically in the tragedies and successes of patients. It is the very vulnerability of the therapist that makes it possible for him or her to understand, accept, and heal patient wounds and injuries. The motif of the wounded healer is once again pertinent to the discussion. The fact that the therapist can live a relatively satisfying, stable life despite the impact of various life events gives hope and comfort to clients who struggle with feelings of hopelessness and futility. It is for this reason that it is most unfortunate when therapists become too withholding concerning information about significant events in their lives. Regardless of the theoretical orientation employed, patients need to know that the therapist is alive, vulnerable, and affected by life events, and yet able to survive and live a meaningful life. If this is not the case, there is no reason to hope that the labors of the psychotherapist, and participation in psychotherapy, will result in the desired changes.

This means that the therapist who is not comparatively satisfied with life will find it difficult to be helpful to those in search of meaning and fulfillment. Those who become overwhelmed by the significant events of life may need to take a leave of absence until balance and stability can be restored. On the other hand, the therapist who maintains stability but attempts to keep his or her humanness and needs a complete secret neutralizes the potential for patients to believe in his or her ability to guide them to more successful living. While self-disclosure should never be indulged in to meet the needs of the therapist, it may be absolutely essential for the success of the treatment endeavor. While it is not always necessary for the therapist to be a victor in life, it is imperative that patients know that he or she is a participant to the fullest extent.

As the therapist journeys through the life cycle, the developmental changes and challenges associated with adult living will present a variety of issues and concerns which may disrupt the stability and predictability of their life and relationships. Many significant events in the life of the therapist have been shown to have an impact on the practice of psychotherapy. They influence the inner world of the therapist in a manner that frequently becomes apparent to patients during the course of treatment. As a result, a forthright discussion of the particular event may not only be helpful, but is often crucial in order to maintain the integrity of the therapy relationship.

In Chapter 6, consideration will be given to the onset of emotional impairment in the psychotherapist. Rather than being an expected life event in the experience of psychotherapists, such an occurrence seems to be a tragic anomaly that can sabotage the personal and professional life of the clinician. Ironically, its obvious relevance to the work of the mental health professional may actually mask its impact on the functioning of the therapist.

CHAPTER 6

Impairment Among Psychotherapists

The personality of the psychotherapist is the primary tool used in the practice of psychotherapy. Regardless of theoretical orientation or level of expertise, the personality of the therapist is one of the most important factors in the treatment. Bugental (1964) explains that

> there can be little doubt that the prime variable affecting psychotherapy (outside of the patient, himself, of course) is the psychotherapist. Psychotherapy may in time take forms which reduce the essential significance of the individual psychotherapist, but at least as of today the personality, sensitivity, and skills of the therapist are of crucial importance. (p. 272)

This observation still remains true after more than two decades of advancement in the practice of psychotherapy. It is the personality of the psychotherapist which impacts that of the patient, bringing intimate and meaningful encounter between two individuals intent on promoting growth and change in the client. Regardless of the techniques utilized, it is the optimism, integrity, and enthusiasm of the therapist that create the context within which successful therapy is conducted. Even more important, it is the emotional stability and maturity of the therapist that provide an essential foundation for the relationship and point of reference for the treatment.

If the psychotherapist has sufficient personal insight and has achieved a relatively advanced level of emotional maturity, he or she will facilitate rather than hinder the psychological growth and development of their patients. While this is not to imply that psychotherapists are necessarily more stable and mature than other individuals, it is largely self-evident that they must possess a level of wholeness and personal integration sufficient to enable them to serve as "guides" to those in search of deeper fulfillment and personal meaning.

The wounded healer motif clarifies this point by suggesting that it is both the transcendence and vulnerability of the healer that give validity and credibility to his or her ministrations (Henry, 1966). Psychotherapists remain very human, falling prey to personal tragedy, discouragement, and fears. Yet they have hopefully achieved a sense of resolution and peace about their mortality, having learned to accept and integrate the good with the bad, resulting in a sense of personal stability and satisfaction. Their deep empathy for and understanding of the pain and suffering of others comes from having personally experienced life's various assaults. Their own resultant "wounds" serve to inform and sensitize them to the problems of others.

Farber (1983a) notes that therapists typically value their own "craziness" as an important asset to clinical work. He states:

> Craziness, or more precisely the ability to be in touch with and utilize regressive and primitive thoughts and feelings, is a state that can be used in the service of empathy and insight. In the shamanic traditions as well, it is the knowledge of his own wounds that enables the shaman to heal the patient. Perhaps that is why psychotherapists, rather than vehemently denying the accusation of craziness, have in several instances promoted this view of themselves. (p. 111)

In this manner, psychotherapists seem to use their own emotional difficulties as a means of achieving insight and empathy in dealing with the variety of problems experienced by their patients.

Despite the potential value of the therapist's human vulnerabilities to increase understanding and sensitivity, it remains important for the therapist to possess an advanced level of emotional stability and wholeness, free as much as possible from "blind spots" and personal needs which might hinder his or her ability to conduct therapy in a helpful, effective manner. If this is not the case, for whatever reason, the therapist may be unable to practice. In other words, since the personality of the therapist is the primary tool of psychotherapy, it must be healthy enough to promote rather than hinder the emotional growth of therapy clients.

DEFINING IMPAIRMENT

It is difficult to arrive at a satisfactory definition of impairment. In recognition of the important role which the personality of the psychotherapist plays in the treatment relationship, most definitions of impairment focus on emotional deficits or problems in the personality of the therapist which hinder or sabotage effective treatment. Laliotis and Grayson (1985) define impairment as "interference in professional functioning due to chemical dependency, mental illness, or personal conflict" (p. 85).

To clarify this conceptualization of impairment, it is necessary to distinguish it from incompetency. This is a complex task in which concrete distinctions are lacking. As Kutz (1986) points out, impairment typically implies a deterioration or diminishment from a previously higher level of functioning. Thus the onset of chemical dependency might result in "impairment" in this sense, decreasing clinical judgment and lessening therapeutic skill from formerly acceptable levels. Incompetence, on the other hand, usually pertains to a lack of ability that may or may not be the result of impairment. Thus inadequate training and experience may be the source of clinical incompetence rather than the diminishing effects of mental illness or chemical dependency. In addition it is possible for impairment to occur which does not result in incompetency. In other words, although there is a deterioration of ability, it may be insufficient to reduce skills and performance to the level of incompetency. Furthermore, impairment in an individual may result in incompetency in some situations while not in others. Thus it is possible for varying levels of impairment and incompetency to result from mental illness, chemical dependency, and personal conflict.

While it is difficult to make clear delineations, some basic distinctions are evident. In order for deterioration of clinical ability to be of critical concern, it must approach incompetency. While all psychotherapists have the ethical obligation to function at their highest, most effective levels, the exigencies and problems of life will result in varying degrees of personal stability and therapeutic effectiveness. Quite simply, everyone will have an occasional "bad day." While regrettable, this is little cause for alarm. Of real concern, however, is when the deterioration of clinical skill and judgment approaches incompetency, increasing the potential of harm to patients. In some cases this will be a temporary condition, while in others it may become chronic. In either instance, if the personality of the therapist has become sufficiently affected to result in a level of impairment which increases the potential of incompetency, serious problems may arise.

For the purposes of this discussion, impairment will be defined as a diminution or deterioration of therapeutic skill and ability due to factors which have sufficiently impacted the personality of the therapist to result in potential clinical incompetence. Thus the therapist is no longer able to conduct psychotherapy effectively due to problems affecting his or her personality. While the impairment may be due to physical factors such as advancing age or illness, the present discussion will focus on other sources or types of emotional impairment which directly affect the personality of the therapist.

EXAMPLES OF IMPAIRMENT

Obviously it is a difficult task to determine the incidence of emotional impairment among psychotherapists. First, to do so requires agreement as to what constitutes sufficient evidence of this impairment. Typically, mental illness, suicide, chemical dependency, and sexual misconduct with patients are regarded as proof of emotional impairment sufficient enough to result in clinical incompetence or questionable therapeutic skill and ability (Laliotis & Grayson, 1985; Scott & Hawk, 1986; Wood, Klein, Cross, Lammers, & Elliot, 1985). As will be seen in the discussion that follows, in each of these categories psychotherapists appear to experience these difficulties at rates similar to (and sometimes surpassing) that found among the general population.

Mental Illness Among Psychotherapists

While it is difficult to determine the actual incidence of mental illness among psychotherapists, several studies suggest that it may be quite high. For example, Looney et al. (1980) surveyed 263 psychiatrists nationwide and found that 73% reported having experienced moderate to incapacitating anxiety during the early years of professional practice, while 58% experienced serious depression. In another survey of psychiatrists, Bermak (1977) found that more than 90% reported that they and their colleagues experienced a wide variety of mental illness. In a survey of 264 psychotherapists representing various disciplines, Deutsch (1985) reports that they experienced significant personal problems related to relationship difficulties (82%), depression (57%), substance abuse (11%), and suicide attempts (2%). In a survey of 507 psychologists, Thoreson, Budd, and Krauskopf (1986) found that 69% reported being personally aware of cases of mental illness among colleagues serious enough to result in impaired work performance, suggesting that the overall incidence may be very high. In another recent study, 4% of those psychotherapists surveyed admitted to suffering from personal "mental illness" during the previous three years (Guy, Stark, & Poelstra, 1987). Finally, Laliotis and Grayson (1985) note that, according to existing literature, the incidence of mental illness and chemical dependence among therapists ranges from 5 to 15%.

There appear to be other more indirect indications of a high rate of mental illness among psychotherapists. For example, Guggenbuhl-Craig (1979) states that his clinical experience has led him to conclude that therapists are more prone to mental illness than nontherapists due to a variety of factors related to both the personality of the therapist and the nature of clinical practice. Farber (1983a) suggests that the surprisingly high rate of suicide among psychotherapists is further proof of a "disproportionate prevalence of psychological disturbance" (p. 111). Tedesco (1982) found that emotional instability or personality disorder were cited as the main reasons for the premature termination of clinical psychology interns by over half of the intership centers surveyed. These psychotherapists-in-training evidently suffered from mental illness severe enough to impair their ability to practice significantly. Finally, Pfifferling's (1986) comprehensive review of the literature has led him to conclude that health care professionals, including psychotherapists, experience various forms of mental illness at a rate higher than that of the general population.

Unfortunately, these articles are based largely on data gathered by means of surveys, self-reports, and general clinical experience. The results are likely to have been affected by subject self-selection bias, questionable diagnostic validity and reliability, under- or overreporting, and interviewer bias. However, while these studies do not arrive at an exact estimate of the actual incidence of mental illness among practicing therapists, they do provide evidence which suggests that diagnosable psychopathology does occur at a rate similar to, if not greater than, that of the general population. Given the importance of the therapist's emotional stabilty and mental health for successful clinical practice, and the likelihood of incompetent clinical care resulting from emotional disturbance significant enough to impair the skill and judgment of the therapist, the occurrence of mental illness among clinicians is cause for serious concern.

Depression

The results of existing research suggest that psychotherapists are vulnerable to all types of mental illness. However, one of the most common forms reported to occur among therapists is depression (Freudenberger & Robbins, 1977). For example, in one survey of 167 training directors in psychiatric clinics and hospitals nationwide, Wood et al. (1985) reported that 75% felt that impaired practitioners whose work had been affected by depression and burnout were becoming a serious problem. Furthermore, 63% indicated that they were personally aware of colleagues who were affected by this problem to the point of noticeable impairment. Finally, 32% reported that they had experienced depression and burnout significant enough to interfere with their clinical work. In another study, Deutsch (1985) reports that 57% of those psychotherapists she surveyed indicated that they were experiencing significant problems related to depression.

A fascinating book entitled *Wounded Healers: Mental Health Workers' Experiences of Depression* (1985), edited by Rippere and Williams, contains several first-person accounts of therapist's who experienced debilitating depression while practicing psychotherapy. In addition to providing some of the most striking phenomenological descriptions of the experience of depression in print today, this book presents documentation of the presence of moderate to debilitating depression among psychotherapists in clinical practice. It also describes the many different reactions which those impaired practitioners received from colleagues, ranging from support and understanding to denial, harrassment, and open hostility. These sensitively presented accounts of the experiences of these impaired psychotherapists clearly demonstrate the potentially serious impact of depression on the ability to conduct psychotherapy.

Impairment Due to Mental Illness

While all psychotherapists struggle with varying levels of emotional difficulty, if the constellation of symptoms result in the level of distress, disability, and disadvantage required for a *Diagnostic and Statistical Manual of Mental Disorders— Third Edition (DSM-III)* (American Psychiatric Association, 1980) diagnosis, impairment of clinical ability is likely to result, increasing the possibility of eventual incompetency and harm to patients. Certainly in the case of active psychosis, debilitating anxiety or depression, or pronounced personality disorders such an occurrence seems highly probable. It is difficult for the mentally ill therapist to focus adequately on the needs and problems of patients when personal psychopathology clouds his or her attention and judgment. Furthermore, emotional impairment associated with mental illness is likely to undermine the stability and predictability necessary for effectively conducting therapy. Finally, emotional depletion and preoccupation with personal concerns will make it nearly impossible to assist adequately clients in distress.

Patients who recognize increasing impairment related to mental illness in their therapist will hopefully terminate treatment in order to seek assistance from another clinician. Unfortunately, this may not always be the case. Recent malpractice suits have documented the incredible abuse and mistreatment that some clients willingly endure over a period of months or even years. Furthermore it is not unusual for some clients to attempt to comfort or "treat" the impaired psychotherapist, knowingly providing nurturance, support, and guidance to the clinician in distress (Chiles, 1974). In this way they attempt to "take care of mother so she will take care of me." Thus while it may be hoped that patients will discontinue treatment before being harmed in some manner by the mentally impaired therapist, this will not always be the case. It is possible that such individuals will actually be hindered from making therapeutic gains and progress, or worse, be emotionally victimized by their impaired therapist.

Suicide

It is a widely held belief that psychotherapists commit suicide at a rate higher than that of the general population (Farber, 1983a; Guy & Liaboe, 1985). Such behavior suggests the presence of prior emotional impairment sufficient enough to have increased the likelihood of incompetent and inadequate patient care, at least during the time immediately prior to this occurrence. As a result, suicide is typically included in the list of examples of impairment among psychotherapists.

Several studies have attempted to document the rate of suicide among practicing psychotherapists. Among psychiatrists, reports of the incidence of suicide vary widely. For example, some researchers report that psychiatrists commit suicide at a rate which is four to five times greater than that of the general population (Blachly, Disher, & Roduner, 1969; DeSole, Singer, & Aronson, 1969; Freeman, 1967). This results in an incidence of approximately 50 per 100,000 as compared to 11 per 100,000 among the general population (Farber, 1983a). On the other hand, more recent studies have arrived at a suicide rate among psychiatrists which is similar to the norm (Kelly, 1973; Rosen, 1971). Part of this discrepancy may result from underreporting and the subjectivity involved in determining the cause of death from obituary notices found in the Journal of the American Medical Society, the source of information typically used in these studies (Gopplet, 1968). As a result, the conservative conclusion can only be that the suicide rate among psychiatrists appears to be equal to or somewhat higher than that of the general population. To what extent this is true remains to be determined.

Only one study could be found which assessed the suicide rate among psychologists. Steppacher and Mausner (1973) obtained the death certificates of members of the American Psychological Association who died between 1960 and 1970. The rate of suicide among male psychologists was actually slightly below that of males in the general population. However, female psychologists committed suicide at a rate which was nearly three times that of their counterparts in the general population. Once again the obituaries and death certificates utilized may be unreliable sources for determining the actual cause of death, and it is very possible that the rate of suicide may actually have been higher in both cases.

Unfortunately studies could not be found which focused on the suicide rates of other disciplines represented in the field of psychotherapy such as social work and marriage and family counseling. However, the incidence of suicide among physician groups (which include psychiatrists) has received considerable attention. Again, the results suggest that the rate of suicide among male physicians is equal to (Craig & Pitts, 1968; Kelly, 1973) or higher than (Ross, 1973) that of males in the general population. More startling is the finding that the rate of suicide among female physicians is three to four times as high—the highest reported for any female occupational group (Craig & Pitts, 1968; Ross, 1971; Steppacher & Mausner, 1973).

The rate of attempted suicide among 264 practicing psychotherapists surveyed by Deutsch (1985) was a full 2%. This figure suggests that the risk of suicide among psychotherapists, and its likely impact on psychotherapy patients, is a serious problem.

Impairment Due to Suicide

Since suicide is typically regarded as a desperate and irrational act, Farber's (1983a) conclusion that the disproportionately high rate of suicide among psychotherapists reflects the presence of debilitating emotional impairment seems warranted. If this is true, it is likely that this emotional impairment impacted the therapist's ability to practice in a competent, effective manner. In-depth studies of patients whose therapist committed suicide during the course of treatment suggest that this was indeed the case (Ballenger, 1978; Chiles, 1974). Patients reported being aware of the increasing depression and/or agitation of the therapist during the weeks and months prior to the suicide. Furthermore, some noted that their therapist seemed increasingly unable to focus on patient needs due to his or her preoccupation with personal difficulties, some of which were shared openly with clients during therapy sessions. This suggests that therapists who are distressed enough to consider (and perhaps eventually commit) suicide seriously are unlikely to be able to conduct therapy in an acceptable manner during this time. Such a degree of impairment increases the possibility of incompetent care and patient harm.

Patients have a variety of reactions to this occurrence. Some who sense the increasing distress of the therapist appropriately terminate treatment and seek help elsewhere. Others admit to remaining in therapy, attempting to "help" and support the impaired psychotherapist at their own emotional and financial expense (Chiles, 1974). As can well be imagined, feelings of fear, guilt, and anger were common among those who decided to remain with the distressed therapist out of a sense of caring or obligation. Following the suicide of their therapist, patients reported anger at having been abandoned, increased depression, renewed suicidal ideation, guilt due to the belief that they were partially responsible, and fear about their own ability to cope with life's problems (Ables, 1974; Ballenger, 1978; Chiles, 1974). Some experienced a more predictable pattern of denial, followed by despair and grief, which eventually led to resolution and acceptance. Undoubtedly, a therapist suicide results in trauma for most patients. Yet it is amazing to note that some were able to integrate even this event into their experience in an ultimately helpful manner.

Substance Abuse

Alcoholism and drug abuse among psychotherapists is being recognized as an increasing problem. While there is little documentation of their effect on the professional functioning of the therapist, they are widely regarded as examples of emotional impairment likely to have a sufficient enough impact on the personality of the therapist to increase the risk of clinical incompetency and patient harm (Laliotis & Grayson, 1985).

Incidence of alcoholism among psychotherapists remains largely a topic of speculation. Conservative estimates cite a rate of 6 to 10%, similar to that of the general population (Thoreson et al., 1986; Thoreson, Nathan, Skorina, & Kilburg, 1983). Others suggest that it may be 10% or more (Laliotis & Grayson, 1985). Estimates of drug abuse or addiction are even more troubling, with some estimating the rate to be as high as 50 to 100 times that of the general population (Pfifferling, 1986). Particularly in the case of physicians (including psychiatrists), the misuse of mood-altering drugs is thought to be at least twice as high as that of other professional groups. Deutsch (1985) found that 11% of those practicing therapists surveyed reported experiencing significant personal problems associated with substance abuse. In a survey of clinical psychologists practicing psychotherapy, over 50% indicated that they believed that impairment due to drug and alcohol abuse among psychotherapists had become a serious problem (Wood et al., 1985). Furthermore, they estimated that 18% of their colleagues were experiencing problems related to substance abuse serious enough to constitute impairment. Finally, slightly over 4% of the group surveyed admitted to personal drug and/or alcohol abuse serious enough to affect their clinical work. In a similar study by Thoreson et al. (1986), 33% of the psychologists surveyed were personally aware of psychotherapists who were experiencing alcohol-related impairment.

Although these studies are somewhat speculative and lacking in precise measurements, they do suggest that the incidence of substance abuse appears to be as great or greater than that found among the general population. The implications of these findings are extremely disturbing.

Impairment Due to Substance Abuse

The therapist who is abusing alcohol or mind-altering drugs is likely to experience emotional impairment sufficient enough to have a detrimental impact on his or her ability to conduct psychotherapy effectively (Laliotis & Grayson, 1985; Thoreson et al., 1983). This is not only due to the level of psychopathology which is typically associated with substance abuse, but may also result from the effects of the psychological and physical addictions which may occur. Those active in chemical abuse are unlikely to be able to attend to the emotional and physical demands of working with equally troubled therapy patients.

As in the case of mental illness and suicide, patients of psychotherapists who are active alcoholics or drug abusers may recognize the emotional impairment of the clinician and its effects on the efficacy of their treatment. Particularly intuitive and observant clients may even recognize the existence of alcoholism or drug abuse in the demeanor and behavior of the therapist. This may result in a variety of patient reactions such as anger, guilt, anxiety, doubts concerning the efficacy of therapy, fears concerning their own adequacy to face problems, and a cynicism regarding the competency of all mental health professionals. In such cases patients will hopefully discontinue therapy with the impaired practitioner and make arrangements to work with someone else. Unfortunately such an occurrence may actually prevent them from seeking further treatment. Even worse, some may choose to remain with the impaired therapist out of a sense of obligation, guilt, or the wish to provide assistance. There may also be a masochistic reenactment of past experiences with alcoholic parents which can make it difficult to discontinue treatment. It is unlikely that such a situation will result in any lasting benefit to the patient.

Patient Exploitation: Sexual Misconduct

A less well-defined group of examples suggesting emotional impairment of a therapist falls under the category of patient exploitation. The list of such occurrences typically includes sexual misconduct, emotional or financial exploitation, unhealthy dual-role relationships, unethical advertising or media presentations, and clinical practice outside of one's area of specialty (Laliotis & Grayson, 1985). Such a diverse and ill-defined list raises a number of issues which warrant consideration. For example, rather than being the result of emotional impairment, some occurrences (such as dual-role relationships) may be due to poor judgment and incompetence. Furthermore, some ethical violations (such as inappropriate media presentation or advertising) may be more the result of ignorance or greed than emotional impairment.

Because of the complexities involved in distinguishing between impairment and incompetence due to inexperience or poor judgment, most discussions of these issues focus primarily on psychotherapist sexual misconduct. There is widespread agreement that such behavior represents emotional impairment significant enough to result in incompetent practice and patient harm (Wood et al., 1985). Rather than being an example of poor judgment, most agree that sexual involvement with a patient is an expression of the emotional needs of the therapist which are being acted out in the treatment relationship in a manner which is unlikely to be in the patient's best interest.

In order to arrive at accurate estimates of the incidence of sexual misconduct among therapists it is first necessary to define what is meant by this term. Virtually all of the disciplines and professional groups represented in the field of psychotherapy agree that any kind of sexual intimacy between a therapist and client is unethical, inappropriate, and constitutes sexual misconduct. Holroyd and Brodsky (1977) define sexual intimacy as any physical contact between a therapist and patient which intends to lead to arousal or satisfaction of sexual desire. This includes passionate kissing, petting, oral–genital contact, mutual masturbation, anal intercourse, and/or genital intercourse. While some would maintain that there is too much ambiguity in such a broad definition, favoring one which centers on genital stimulation alone, the majority of researchers continue to regard the more inclusive definition as the most useful and appropriate (Scruggs, 1986).

Another difficulty in arriving at an acceptable definition of sexual misconduct involves the issue of time. Most researchers have focused on sexual intimacies which occurred concurrent with ongoing treatment or within three months of termination (Bouhoutsos, Holroyd, Lerman, Forer, & Greenberg, 1983; Holroyd & Brodsky, 1977; Pope, Keith-Speigel, & Tabachnick, 1986). It is generally agreed that sexual intimacy begun immediately after termination implies a prior "sexualization" of the treatment relationship, already regarded as inappropriate by the previously discussed definitions. On the other hand, others have suggested that any sexual intimacy with a former patient, regardless of the passage of time, constitutes sexual misconduct since the power differential of the former treatment relationship is never fully resolved, leaving the former patient vulnerable to later therapist exploitation (Langs, 1973). While this will likely remain a topic of debate, all parties agree that sexual intimacy between therapist and patient during ongoing treatment or immediately after termination constitutes sexual misconduct on the part of the therapist.

Given these definitions, estimates regarding the incidence of sexual misconduct among psychotherapists vary widely. Kardner, Fuller, and Mensh (1973) found that 13% of the 460 California physicians (includes psychiatrists) surveyed engaged in "erotic behavior" with patients while 5% engaged in sexual intercourse. Among psychologists practicing psychotherapy, 11% of the males and 2% of the females admitted to engaging in erotic contact with clients, while 5.5% of the males and .6% of the females admitted to sexual intercourse, during the course of ongoing therapy (Holroyd & Brodsky, 1977). When those engaging in sexual intercourse within three months of termination were included, the totals jumped to 8% of the males and 1% of the females surveyed. These findings were replicated by Bouhoutsos et al. (1983) who found that 4.8% of the males and .8% of the females had engaged in sexual misconduct with patients during the course of psychotherapy. Finally, Pope, Levenson, and Schover (1979) cite somewhat higher totals, with 12% of the males and 3% of the females reporting that they had engaged in sexual contact with patients.

Impairment Due to Sexual Misconduct

Due to the potential for the therapist to exploit clients to satisfy his or her own sexual needs and desires, it is generally regarded that therapists engaging in sexual misconduct are unable to provide competent care to that client. In part this is due to the belief that in order for a therapist to engage in a behavior so universally condemned by the profession, he or she would need to be experiencing emotional distress severe enough to cloud judgment and reduce impulse control (Wood et al., 1985). Furthermore, the effects of the sexual intimacy itself on the personality of the therapist may further hinder his or her ability to provide competent care. For example, guilt over potential negative effects of the misconduct (as well as fear of discovery and professional and legal censure) are likely to distort the clinician's judgment, making it nearly impossible for decisions to be made based solely on the best interests of the client involved.

The manipulation, intimidation, and blatant exploitation of the patient which may occur in such situations will probably render treatment ineffective. The research findings of Bouhoutsos et al. (1983) suggest that this appears to be the case. For example, among therapists surveyed who had worked with patients involved in sexual misconduct with a previous therapist, 34% reported that this occurrence adversely affected the patient's personality, 29% stated that the patient had lasting negative feelings about the experience, and 26% reported that the patient's other intimate relationships suffered as a result. Furthermore, 37% indicated that this occurrence resulted in the termination of the subsequent treatment, while 40% reported that it had a negative impact on the treatment sufficient enough to interfere with further progress. Finally, 48% reported that this experience made it difficult for the patient to recommence treatment with another psychotherapist.

While some have maintained that sexual intimacy between a therapist and client resulted in several patient benefits, such as an increase in self-esteem and knowledge about sexuality (McCartney, 1966; Shepard, 1971), most researchers have found that it tended to increase anxiety, depression, anger, suicidal behavior, general psychic distress, sexual dysfunction, mistrust and suspicion, and guilt (Bouhoutsos, 1985; Bouhoutsos et al., 1983; Butler, 1975; D'Addario, 1977; Pope et al., 1986; Zelen, 1985). These reactions ranged from moderately distressing to debilitating severely, with a duration of several years in some cases. In addition, because of the violation of trust involved, some patients regarded this occurrence as a type of incest, causing them to experience many of the same feelings of rage and shame common among incest victims.

Summary

The potential for clinical incompetency and patient harm due to an emotionally impaired therapist is evident. Regardless of whether it takes the form of a diagnosable mental illness, eventual suicide, identifiable substance abuse, or sexual misconduct, in each case there is evidence of emotional disturbance sufficient enough to impact the personality of the therapist in a manner which is likely to result in inadequate clinical performance. Thus the designation "impaired" is warranted. Considered together as a group, the total number of impaired psychotherapists take on surprising proportions. Using very conservative estimates of 10% for diagnosable mental illness, .5% for successful suicide, 8% for substance abuse, and 8% for sexual misconduct, the total incidence of therapist impairment begins to seem substantial. While some overlap is likely to reduce the total somewhat, difficulties concerning underreporting and mislabeling probably result in a total incidence rate even higher than that derived from adding together all of the aforementioned categories. The number of practicing therapists experiencing impairment sufficient enough to increase the likelihood of incompetency could include many thousands, perhaps even tens of thousands of clinicians. This is a very sobering prospect indeed.

ETIOLOGY OF PSYCHOTHERAPIST IMPAIRMENT

Given the potentially high incidence of impairment among psychotherapists and its significant impact on their ability to provide clinical services in a competent, effective manner, it seems important to consider the possible etiological factors which contribute to its development. While there are likely to be differences related to each individual occurrence, there appear to be several identifiable patterns which may precipitate impairment.

Mental Illness in the Psychotherapist

It would be unreasonable to assume that all of the factors leading to the onset of mental illness in psychotherapists could be correctly identified and presented in this discussion. However, an assortment of research findings do suggest that personality predisposition, factors related to the practice of psychotherapy itself, and the impact of life events may contribute to the onset of mental illness and emotional impairment in the psychotherapist.

Predisposition

As was discussed in detail in Chapter 1, some individuals who decide to enter the field of psychotherapy are motivated to do so out of the desire to bring about their own psychic healing (Chessick, 1978; Ford, 1963; Henry, 1966). Such individuals may already have been suffering from a diagnosable form of mental illness, and they chose to enter the field of psychotherapy in order to find ways of eliminating or reducing their own emotional symptoms and problems. As a result they experienced psychopathology prior to entering the field of mental health. In some cases such individuals were found to be unsuited for the role of psychotherapist and were denied admission, graduation, or licensure. Others were able to overcome this handicap sufficiently to permit them to enter professional practice. This may have resulted from self-analysis, personal therapy, or discussions with other students and faculty. Unfortunately a few may "slip through the cracks" unidentified and unremediated, entering the field of psychotherapy while still experiencing diagnosable mental illness.

Obviously those with a prior history of emotional distress may suffer a reoccurrence of symptoms during their work as therapists. While this may have been inevitable, it may also have been exacerbated somewhat by the impact of the emotional depletion, isolation, stress, and difficulties often associated with psychotherapeutic practice. Thus a predisposition toward mental illness may interact with various hazards of the profession to bring about a reoccurrence of identifiable symptomatology. However, while these professional hazards may have been sufficient to result in psychopathology, the predisposition toward mental illness serves as the "necessary" factor leading to the reoccurrence of psychopathology in such individuals during their career.

Work-Related Factors

There are a number of occupational hazards associated with the practice of psychotherapy which have the potential to affect negatively the personality of the therapist. In some cases their impact may be sufficient enough to result in emotional impairment. These factors may even occasionally lead to the onset of mental illness in a therapist with no prior history of diagnosable psychopathology. Some of these hazards are related to factors associated with clinical practice, while others seem to be the direct result of patient contact.

As discussed in Chapters 3 and 4, there are a number of liabilities involved in the practice of psychotherapy which can have a detrimental impact on the personality of the psychotherapist. If these hazards are not identified and steps taken to mitigate their impact on the therapist, they may result in personality changes which impair interpersonal functioning in both personal and professional encounters. Several authors have suggested that these hazards may be sufficient enough to precipitate the onset of mental illness, such as in the case of debilitating depression.

While the impact of liabilities associated with clinical practice may bring about emotional impairment in isolated cases, several authors have suggested that it is actual contact with patients that can lead to the onset of eventual psychopathology in the therapist. Ever since Jung (1966) spoke of an "unconscious infection" which can result from work with emotionally disturbed patients, many have speculated about the risks that psychotherapists face as a result. For example, Farber (1985a) maintains that "the practice of psychotherapy serves to continually reactivate therapists' early experiences, memories, and emotions" (p. 173). Storr (1979) goes further when he suggests that

> however balanced the therapist may be, he (she) is likely to encounter a few patients whose material is both particularly disturbing and fascinating, so that his own equilibrium is threatened. I am not referring to the danger of falling in love with the patient . . . what I have in mind is something to do with unconscious areas within the therapist's own psyche which, in ordinary life, might never have been stirred up, or even seen the light of day in his own personal analysis. (p. 184)

Thus work with particular patients may strike at hidden or unresolved personal issues in a way which results in their intensification or reawakening. Freudenberger and Robbins (1979) describe this process by noting that "the therapist's old scars and injuries are constantly being rubbed anew, particularly by the borderline patient" (p. 287). Henry (1966) also notes that "therapeutic practice itself provides continual reactivation of personal inner states" (p. 54). Thus one way in which the therapist may undergo emotional impairment due to mental illness is because contact with certain patients awakens or reactivates unresolved issues, problems, and needs.

More intriguing is the suggestion that there can be an actual "transfer of pathology" from the patient to the therapist (Farber, 1983a). It is as though the psychotherapist "catches" mental illness from emotionally disturbed clients. For example, Chessick (1978) speculates that a condition of depression and despair which he terms "soul sadness" is quite contagious. He states, "after laboring for long hours for many years with chronically anguished patients, psychiatrists (psychotherapists) tend to take the anguish to bed with them at night and grieve about it in their dreams; it remains like a gnawing theme in the back of their minds" (p. 5). Freudenberger and Robbins (1979) also warn that there may be a cumulative impact to continual contact with psychopathology and what they term "raw libido," endangering the very sanity of the therapist. Fine (1980) agrees, noting that "the depth therapist spending years at restoration of selves mostly more fragile and tentative than his or her own self gradually feels an erosion of will" (p 393). These authors suggest that close contact with troubled patients can "wear down" the therapist, leaving him or her vulnerable to the onset of personal psychopathology.

Will (1979) warns that the therapist can easily become emerged in the world of patient madness, in effect by following patients down the road to insanity. "Normal" life is abandoned as the therapist focuses all of his or her energy on understanding the inner experience of the disturbed client. This understanding of madness can lead to an acceptance which acts to normalize it, making the real world less relevant to the clinician who begins to think and feel like the patient. As Will describes it:

> the therapist may discover that his (her) patient's behaviors have become so familiar that they are no longer very distressing. They do not invite, then, much curiosity, or even require change as they have become so natural in their appearances. Then the real world is seen as insane while the therapist identifies with his patient who thus becomes "natural," an outcome more likely to be destructive than in any way beneficial. (p. 568)

This situation can lead to a distortion of judgment and perception on the part of the therapist which begins to take on the appearance of irrationality. The distinction between sanity and madness becomes blurred and the therapist gradually loses his or her grasp on reality.

Although there is a rather bizarre tone to warnings concerning the possibility of developing diagnosable psychopathology as a result of coming into contact with mentally ill patients, depending on one's view of personality theory and the etiology of emotional disturbance, it is hard to dismiss such considerations entirely. Although such claims are difficult to assess by objective means, they make intuitive sense. One cannot help but wonder about the impact of spending literally tens of thousands of hours with emotionally disturbed clients. Perhaps, as some have suggested, an erosion of the therapist's stability and judgment sufficient enough to lead to the onset of mental illness can result.

Impact of Life Events

In Chapter 4, consideration was given to the impact of several significant life events on the personality of the psychotherapist. As was discussed at that point, changes in the therapist's life have the potential to affect profoundly the functioning and work of the clinician. In particular, those accompanied by significant stress or distress may result in the onset of a diagnosable form of psychopathology, such as Adjustment Disorders, Affective Disorders, Anxiety Disorders, and several more severe forms of mental illness (American Psychiatric Association, 1980). The impact of these events may lead to the development of symptoms sufficient enough to warrant a psychiatric diagnosis of mental illness. In addition, the physiological sequelae associated with some of these events (such as in the case of illness or accident) may promote the onset of psychopathology as well.

It seems possible that regardless of predisposition toward mental illness or the impact of the hazards associated with the practice of psychotherapy, some therapists may develop identifiable psychopathology solely as the result of the impact of a significant life event on their personality and emotional functioning. In such cases the effects may be profound enough to bring a level of emotional impairment sufficient to result in professional incompetence and patient harm.

While each of the aforementioned three factors may in themselves precipitate the development of mental illness in a practicing psychotherapist, it seems more likely that they will interact to bring this result (Farber, 1983a). For example, the therapist's prior history of mental illness may make him or her vulnerable to the development of psychopathology during a time of crisis, such as may be associated with one or more significant life events. Furthermore, the underlying personality structure of the individual may interact with the pressures and hazards of clinical practice in a manner which promotes eventual emotional distress. Finally, as was discussed in the last chapter, the interaction between factors unique to a career in psychotherapy and the impact associated with certain life events can result in a level of stress and distress sufficient enough to impact the personality and well-being of the therapist.

Rather than attempting to isolate individual factors which can promote the appearance of psychic distress in the practicing psychotherapist, it seems more useful to address their interactive effects. In this manner, comprehensive interventions can be designed which are more inclusive and effective in reducing the likelihood of this occurrence.

Psychotherapist Suicide

The suggestion that the suicide rate of psychotherapists is equal to or surpasses that of the general population makes the issue of etiology an important one. What factors can be identified which increase the potential for a practicing therapist to resort to this act of personal violence? Again, predisposition, work-related factors, and the impact of significant life events seem to be among the most prominent causes. In addition, their interaction may also precipitate the decision to commit suicide.

Predisposition

It has been established previously that there is often a link between mental illness and suicide (Kolb & Brodie, 1982). Thus a predisposition toward certain forms of mental illness in the psychotherapist may increase the potential for eventual suicide. Recurrent psychosis, agitation, or despair may lead to the taking of one's life if the severity of the distress is great enough. The therapist who experiences a reoccurrence of acute or debilitating mental illness while practicing may lose the ability to exercise sound judgment and consequently resort to suicide. Thus a predisposition to mental illness may somewhat increase the likelihood of suicide in certain extreme situations. Even in cases where there has been no history of diagnosable psychopathology, basic personality structure may predispose the individual to consider suicide as an option during times of excessive distress or despair.

It is interesting to consider at this point the results of several studies of suicidal psychotherapists. Psychiatrists who eventually committed suicide were described by family, friends, colleagues, and patients as typically distant, aloof, detached, depressed, low in self-esteem, and lonely (Ballenger, 1978; Chiles, 1974; Pasnau & Russell, 1975). Physicians committing suicide (the largest portion of whom were psychiatrists) were characterized as self-seeking, self-indulgent, impulsive, possessing poor frustration tolerance, prone to substance abuse, and suffering from pronounced mood swings (Blachly, Disher, & Roduner, 1969; Ross, 1971 & 1973). Suicidal psychiatry residents were noted to be prone toward drug abuse, lacking in personal relationships, in the midst of an identity crisis, and experiencing marital discord (Pasnau & Russell, 1975). While a number of factors contribute to this pattern, a major one is likely to be the underlying personality structure of the psychotherapist which predisposed him or her toward eventual suicide.

Other factors unrelated to the practice of psychotherapy or the impact of life events may also serve to predispose the practitioner toward eventual suicide. For example, recurrent suicidal ruminations, a history of one or more successful suicides among family members, the influence of suicidal parents, the onset of substance abuse, or a history of previous personal attempts may increase the likelihood of such an occurrence at some point. In most cases these factors are likely to be present prior to the decision to enter the field of psychotherapy. Thus they can predispose the appearance of suicidal behavior during later adult years, after the individual has begun to practice.

It is unlikely that a simple predisposition toward suicide is sufficient to bring about its occurrence. While it may provide the "necessary" proclivity toward such action, it is not likely to be sufficient to cause this outcome. Instead, the predisposition toward suicide becomes an important factor when considering the interactive effects among the hazards associated with clinical practice and the impact of personal crisis associated with certain traumatic life events. In such cases, the aforementioned factors which tend to predispose an individual toward the act of suicide take on new relevance.

Work-Related Factors

In addition to basic personality stucture and underlying predispositions, a number of work-related factors may increase the likelihood of suicide in certain situations. For example, the hazards associated with the practice of psychotherapy may have a cumulative impact on the therapist. The physical and psychic isolation, self-denial, loneliness, lack of genuine relatedness, and emotional suppression sometimes resulting from clinical practice may reduce the therapist's sense of resolve and will to live (Guy & Liaboe, 1985). Furthermore, feelings of despair, futility, depletion, and "burnout" experienced by some therapists as a result of years of conducting psychotherapy may further increase the likelihood of eventual suicide (Chessick, 1978; Farber, 1983a; Fine, 1980; Freeman, 1967; McCarley, 1975).

In addition to the factors often associated with the practice of psychotherapy, several authors have suggested that frequent contact with suicidal patients increases the potential for the psychotherapist to eventually commit suicide. For example, Blachly et al. (1969) speculate that psychotherapists learn that suicide is an acceptable way of solving problems as a result of frequent and intense contact with suicidal patients. Farber (1983a) also notes that therapists may be prone to suicide as a result of the influence of spending so much time with other suicidal individuals. This harkens back to the idea that certain forms of patient despair or mental illness may be "contagious," engendering similar feelings in the therapist. In this regard, it is interesting to note that therapists committing suicide were found to have a significantly larger number of suicidal patients under their care than the average practitioner (Ballenger, 1978; Chiles, 1974).

It may be that working with suicidal patients, rather than subjecting the psychotherapist to a "contagious" condition, increases personal stress and tension to a point which makes suicide a likely course of action. Farber (1983b) notes that suicidal statements and ideation among patients are the most stressful aspects of clinical practice. In his study most psychotherapists reported that suicidal threats and action constituted the greatest source of distress in their professional work. Litman (1965) notes that therapists suffer a great deal of anguish and personal distress as a result of the suicidal actions of their patients. Perhaps the cumulative impact of working with suicidal patients over a course of years, even decades, results in a level of despair which increases the likelihood of therapist suicide.

The Impact of Life Events

The impact of certain events in the life of the therapist may be sufficient to increase the potential for suicide. For example, divorce, loss of a loved one, or the onset of terminal illness may result in a level of profound distress or despair which makes suicide an attractive option. While it is not likely that this will be sufficient in and of itself to prompt the therapist to take his or her life, it may combine with other factors to bring the individual to the point of complete desperation and irrationality. It is interesting to note that among female physicians, whose rate of suicide is three to five times that of the female general population, it has been suggested that life events such as pregnancy and parenthood, and the resultant role conflicts, contribute to the tendency for these individuals to resort to suicide (Guy & Liaboe, 1985).

Rather than fall prey to the limitations of either/or approaches to questions concerning the cause of suicide among psychotherapists, it is more useful to recognize the likelihood of the interactive effects among factors related to the personality of the individual, the hazards associated with the profession, and the impact of certain life events on the emotional stability of the therapist. A truly comprehensive analysis must consider all three factors and their interrelationships in order to arrive at a useful formulation of the problem. Thus, for example, it is likely that the hazards of the profession or the impact of crisis associated with certain life events result in the suicide of those therapists predisposed toward such action due to the presence of certain personality dynamics or previous experiences.

This conclusion seems to be supported by the findings of existing research. Pfifferling (1986) notes that factors found to correlate most highly with suicides among physicans are a sense of hopelessness, depression, drug dependency, chronic disease, the impact of aging and retirement, and professional success with personal failure. This diverse list clearly portrays the interactive effects of the personality of the therapist, the hazards of the profession, and the impact of certain life events, leading to eventual suicide.

Therapist Substance Abuse

The incidence of alcoholism and drug abuse among psychotherapists is alarmingly high, according to even the most conservative estimates. The impact of this problem on the life and work of the therapist has the potential to be profound. While this problem is likely to be the result of many causes, again, factors related to predisposition, hazards of the profession, and the impact of certain life events warrant consideration.

Predisposition

The gradual accumulation of research regarding predisposing factors related to substance abuse is relevant to this discussion about alcoholism and drug abuse among practicing therapists. A wide variety of personality variables, previous life experiences, physical vulnerabilities, and genetic predispositions have been identified as potential factors leading to alcohol or drug abuse (Kolb & Brodie, 1982). It is likely that some of these factors existed long before the individual decided to enter the mental health profession. Thus they constitute a predisposition toward substance abuse not directly related to the hazards associated with the practice of psychotherapy or the impact of life events. Instead, any of these factors may contribute necessary, and sufficient catalysts leading to the development of serious drug or alcohol abuse.

Work-Related Factors

Factors related to the practice of psychotherapy may contribute to the onset of substance abuse in the therapist. Increasing isolation, withdrawal, emotional depletion, and despair can have a cumulative impact which increases personal vulnerability to the development of alcoholism or drug abuse.

Thoreson et al. (1983) present a very enlightening profile of the psychotherapist vulnerable to substance abuse, focusing on factors directly related to professional practice. The desire for heightened personal insight and discovery motivates some to experiment with mind-altering drugs, occasionally leading to their use on a regular basis. The sense of grandiosity resulting from clinical practice can promote a denial and avoidance of the risks associated with potential or actual substance abuse. The relative freedom of practice, with its lack of supervision and observation by colleagues, further facilitates this denial by allowing the therapist to hide its presence and impact from others. The actual threat of job loss is nearly nonexistent for those in independent practice, permitting a greater degree of impairment to occur before professional sanctions are imposed. Work-related obsessiveness and overachievement often mask the actual impact of substance abuse on the personality and ability of the clinician. Past successes and accomplishments further distort the psychotherapist's judgment regarding the impact of substance abuse on present performance.

These work-related factors combine to make the practicing psychotherapist vulnerable to the development of substance abuse. Denial and avoidance of this potential problem are not limited to the individual, however. The entire profession has been guilty of "looking the other way" while ostracizing those whose gross impairment resulted in highly visible incompetency leading to legal action by injured or disgruntled clients (Laliotis & Grayson, 1985; Thoreson et al., 1986). A proactive stance with an emphasis on prevention, identification, and remediation has only recently emerged.

Impact of Life Events

It is difficult to isolate the impact of certain life events on the psychotherapist which have the potential to precipitate the development of alcoholism or drug abuse. Certainly stress related to marriage, parenthood, relocation, divorce, departing children, loss of a loved one, illness or accident, aging and retirement, or the onset of terminal illness may be sufficient enough to increase vulnerability to substance abuse. This seems particularly likely in cases where the associated psychic or physical pain and suffering is profound enough to create a sense of desperation, making the relief or escape offered through substance abuse attractive and even physically and/or psychologically addicting.

Thoreson et al. (1983) suggest that other "life events" may contribute to the potential of substance abuse as well. Socioeconomic changes resulting from increasing wealth and prestige may bring a host of unexpected hazards. For example, Thoreson et al. point out that "drinking is viewed as the hallmark of gracious living, and the cocktail party circuit is part and parcel of the life of most professional psychologists (psychotherapists). Thus psychologists find drinking to be not only socially acceptable but highly desirable in professional circles" (p. 672). Increased wealth may bring new opportunity for drug experimentation as well as the social pressure to participate in such activities. Relocation to a more prestigious neighborhood or job may bring new expectations and pressures concerning alcohol or drug use, sometimes to the detriment of the individual who sets aside personal prohibitions in order to "fit in." While this may result in substance abuse in only the most rare of circumstances, its potential impact should be considered.

It is apparent in Thoreson et al.'s (1983) description that there is typically an interaction among various personality, work-related, and environmental factors which contributes to potential substance abuse. While certain personality variables alone may be sufficient to precipitate the onset of alcoholism or drug abuse, such occurrences are more likely to be the result of a combination of variables related to the life and work of the psychotherapist. A comprehensive analysis is necessary in order to highlight fully the many factors contributing to substance abuse and the professional impairment and incompetency which often results.

Psychotherapist Sexual Misconduct

During the past decade there has been growing concern regarding the incidence of sexual misconduct among practicing therapists. As examples of sexual intimacy between therapist and client have been discovered and subjected to study, the impact of this behavior on the treatment relationship and the patient has been found to be profound, and typically negative and harmful. As a result, there is increasing interest in determining the contributing causes of this behavior.

Predisposition

While it is admittedly difficult to determine the role of the psychotherapist's personality structure and prior experiences in predisposing eventual sexual misconduct with patients, some tentative observations can be made. For example, Greenson (1967) suggests that early developmental experiences and traumas may later prompt the therapist to act out personal needs in the therapy relationship. This concept, typically referred to as "countertransference," is often given as a primary reason for sexual misconduct in the treatment relationship. Many theorists speculate that in most cases of sexual intimacy between therapist and patient, such actions are the result of the reactivation of unresolved needs and conflicts on the part of the therapist rather than the result of "real love" (Chesler, 1972; Dalberg, 1971; Pope et al., 1986; Tower, 1956). Thus, in the case of sexual misconduct, prior life experiences predispose the psychotherapist toward their reenactment in the treatment relationship.

Holroyd and Brodsky (1977, 1980) suggest that long-standing attitudes regarding power, status, and sex roles play a prominent part in the therapist's decision to get sexually involved with clients. Since this typically involves a male therapist and a female patient, they suggest that such behavior is often the expression of underlying hostility and sense of superiority on the part of the male toward the female. Chauvinistic attitudes which prompt this type of exploitation are likely to have existed prior to becoming a psychotherapist, thereby predisposing this type of inappropriate behavior.

Scruggs (1986) presents a list of predisposing personality characteristics that appear to contribute to the therapist's decision to become sexually intimate with one or more patients. These include the "Don Juan Syndrome," doubts concerning sexuality and sexual identity, curiosity about other's sexual performance, masochistic or sadistic tendencies, previous incestlike experiences, and a tendency to be exploitive.

Any combination of these underlying personality factors may motivate the therapist toward engaging in sexual misconduct with patients. Thus factors totally apart from the hazards of the profession and the impact of certain life events may prompt the therapist to initiate or submit to sexual activity with clients. These factors may not be sufficient in and of themselves, but are contributory in a significant way when considered in relationship to other factors.

Work-Related Factors

A number of variables related to the practice of psychotherapy may increase the potential for the therapist to engage in sexual misconduct with clients. Among these are the physical isolation of the therapy office, a schedule which often involves several late night appointments, repeated intense encounters with another human being which often stir up a host of desires and needs in both individuals, and the lack of supervision or monitoring of clinical work by a superior.

Several researchers have identified other work-related factors which may motivate sexually intimate behavior. For example, Pope et al. (1979) point out that the higher social status and prestige associated with the professional therapist gives him or her an advantage of influence and power over the patient. As noted previously, Holroyd and Brodsky (1977) and Bouhoutsos et al., (1983) also suggest that the power differential associated with being a male mental health professional contributes to this form of exploitation. Furthermore, Zelen (1985) notes that male therapists who tend to act out sexually with their patients are usually aware of this differential, and experience themselves as "father figures" in relationship to their patients. Thus the power and status associated with the role of psychotherapist in comparison to that of the patient increases the potential for the therapist to engage in sexual misconduct. Perhaps the sense of grandiosity and superiority which Marmor (1953) describes, resulting from years of patient idealization and admiration, further increases the tendency for the psychotherapist to act on his or her sexual urges or desires.

While certainly not justifying the therapist's behavior, a number of factors have been identified which prompt patients to participate in sexual misconduct with psychotherapists. Rather than being the expression of true, mature love based on an accurate assessment of the "real" relationship that exists between the therapist and patient, sexual intimacy is typically thought to be the expression of prior patient needs which have been reactivated in the treatment relationship. This of course is consistent with the concept of patient transference, a process whereby patient judgment and perception are distorted by the influence of past experiences and relationships (Hedges, 1983). The desire for intimacy, acceptance, friendship, comfort, and attachment are therefore expressed by means of sexual misconduct with the therapist (Belote, 1974; Chesler, 1972). In addition, the tendency for some individuals to reenact past incest experiences, and masochistically cooperate with the abusive and exploitive behavior of others, prompts them to engage in sexual intimacy with their therapist, even though it is unlikely to be in their best interests to do so. There may even be a tendency for some patients to wish to seduce the psychotherapist for a variety of reasons, thereby neutralizing his or her ability to be helpful in the treatment relationship. Once again, none of these possible motivations justify the inappropriate behavior of the psychotherapist who engages in sexual misconduct with a patient. Instead, they are presented merely to suggest that they sometimes contribute to the development of this form of therapist impairment.

Impact of Life Events

Several authors propose that sexual misconduct on the part of a psychotherapist may be at least partially the result of the impact of certain events in his or her life. Any of the life events discussed previously in Chapter 5 may engender a sense of need and desperation which could motivate the therapist to engage in sexual intimacy with a patient in order to receive comfort, reassurance, or pleasure. For example, Butler (1975) interviewed 20 psychotherapists who had engaged in sexual misconduct with their patients. Of this group, 90% reported feeling extremely vulnerable, lonely, or needy at the time when sexual intimacies were initiated.

In a later study, Butler and Zelen (1977) found that significant marital discord, recent separations, and/or divorce in the life of those therapists surveyed were significantly correlated with the start of sexual misconduct with patients. Scruggs (1986) also suggests that therapist marital dissatisfaction can be a contributing factor leading to the initiation of sexual intimacies with patients. While self-report bias may distort these findings considerably, it is interesting to note that most therapists admit that they turned to sexual misconduct with patients in order to meet personal needs resulting from the impact of events in their personal life.

The decision to engage in sexual intimacies with a patient is doubtless a complex one resulting from a combination of variables in the life and experience of both the patient and the therapist. However, there is widespread agreement that such behavior results primarily from emotional impairment of the psychotherapist and constitutes incompetent clinical practice. Thus, regardless of whatever patient variables may have entered in, this behavior is regarded as serious misconduct for which the psychotherapist is culpable.

At first glance, given the seriousness and complexity of this issue, one would expect that sexual misconduct is likely to be a rare experience in the life of a therapist deciding to initiate sexual intimacies with a client. In other words, one would expect that a unique and unusual blend of personality, work-related, and environmental factors prompted them to take such hazardous action on only one occasion during his or her career. Research findings verify that this is simply not the case. Instead, it appears that most therapists who engaged in sexual intimacies with patients were not responding to the unique variables and realities of the actual relationship. Instead, as Zelen (1985) points out, they "were engaged in self-serving, need-fulfilling behavior which had high reinforcement value for them" (p. 183), leading to an alarming rate of recidivism. Several researchers have discovered that those who engage in sexual behavior with patients tend to do so repeatedly. For example, Holroyd and Brodsky (1977) found that 80% of those admitting to sexual misconduct with a patient reported having done so on repeated occasions. In some cases, they engaged in sexual intimacy with the same patient over periods ranging from several weeks to years. Others reported becoming sexually involved with several patients for varying lengths of time during their career in psychotherapy. Butler (1975) reports similar findings, noting that 75% of those engaging in sexual misconduct with patients tended to repeat these contacts with the same and other patients.

This pattern would suggest that patient variables likely play a minor role in the etiology of sexual misconduct among psychotherapists. It is also difficult to determine the effect of significant events in the life of the therapist on the decision to engage in such behavior. It seems most likely that this occurrence results primarily from an interaction between personality variables and factors associated with the practice of therapy. Furthermore, it appears that once the pattern has been established, it is likely to repeat itself in subsequent treatment relationships.

It should be remembered that sexual misconduct was selected as representative of the broader fourth category of therapist impairment that being the general exploitation of patients. Many of the patterns and factors noted previously are likely to be found in other forms of patient exploitation such as emotional or financial exploitation, unhealthy dual-role relationships, unethical advertising or media presentations, and clinical practice outside of one's area of specialty. This is especially true when it is clear that the behavior is not simply the result of ignorance or poor judgment. In each case, the impairment and incompetence that occur are typically the result of an interaction among therapist personality predispositions, work-related factors, and the impact of significant life events.

Summary

Consideration has been given to the three primary factors which may contribute to the onset of emotional impairment of the psychotherapist. In each example, (i.e., mental illness, suicide, substance abuse, and sexual misconduct), variables like the underlying personality of the psychotherapist, work-related factors, and the effects of significant events in the life of the therapist interact to increase the potential for diminished clinical ability to result. While other factors can certainly influence the onset of emotional impairment, these three appear to be of primary importance.

Having reviewed the incidence, impact, and etiology of impairment among psychotherapists, it is now necessary to turn our attention toward identification, remediation, and prevention of this phenomenon. In the section that follows, the focus will be on the present and proposed responses of the psychotherapy profession to the debilitating effects of emotional impairment on the life and work of the psychotherapist.

INTERVENTION FOR PSYCHOTHERAPIST IMPAIRMENT

The previous discussion highlighted the incidence and etiology of emotional impairment among practicing psychotherapists. In view of its potential to result in patient harm and incompetent practice, it is disheartening to discover that the profession of psychotherapy has not admitted the reality of the problem, nor devised the means to deal with it. Ironically, other professional groups have taken a more proactive stance in implementing programs for the identification, remediation, and prevention of impairment among its practitioners. These include the professions of medicine, law, nursing, denistry, and pharmacy (Laliotis & Grayson, 1985; Wood et al., 1985). It has been only relatively recently that the disciplines of psychiatry and social work have designed programs for impaired clinicians, while psychologists continue to argue over definitions of impairment and issues related to jurisdiction (Turkington, 1984). What has caused the profession of psychotherapy to be so slow to respond to the needs of its impaired practitioners?

There may be several factors which increase denial and avoidance concerning the problem of emotional incompetence among psychotherapists. For practitioners, the widespread mistaken belief that therapists are nearly invulnerable to emotional impairment as a result of their training and experience may increase their tendency to overlook early indications of personal difficulty. This attitude may be strengthened by equating all emotional problems with incompetency, prompting secrecy, denial, and a refusal to seek help (Wood et al., 1985). Subtle tendencies toward grandiosity and feelings of omnipotence may also hinder acknowledgment of impairment. Finally, fears concerning potential loss of clients and referrals may motivate the therapist to delay seeking assistance, providing the opportunity for increased impairment.

Denial and avoidance of the problem of emotional impairment has existed at a broader level of the profession as well. There is a corporate investment in promoting the image of therapist invulnerability and superiority in order to instill public confidence in the efficacy of psychotherapy and the competence of its practitioners. Since it is in the arena of the emotions that the psychotherapist labors, there is likely to be a desire to portray him or her as perpetual victor rather than occasional victim. In addition, the very structure of the profession, with its many specialized disciplines, lack of centralized governance, minimal supervision and monitoring, and highly autonomous clinicians increases the potential for impairment to exist undetected.

As a result of these individual and corporate factors, the profession of psychotherapy has been very slow to acknowledge the problem of emotional impairment and formulate a plan of intervention (Claiborn, 1982; Laliotis & Grayson, 1985; Larsen, 1986; Thoreson et al., 1986; Wood et al., 1985). However, increased awareness and exposure have begun to prompt more organized attempts to identify, sanction, remediate, and prevent impairment on a broader scale.

Identification of Impaired Psychotherapists

The first step toward successful intervention concerning the problem of emotional impairment among therapists centers on the timely identification of those who are impaired. It is at this point that the profession experiences a major impediment. Overcoming the long-standing tendency to deny and avoid acknowledging the presence of impairment among practicing therapists was an important and relatively recent first step. Unfortunately this admission has not been sufficient to ensure that those experiencing emotional difficulties as evidenced by mental illness, suicide, chemical dependency, or patient exploitation are correctly identified.

The very nature of clinical practice, with its emphasis on the autonomous, independent, unsupervised work of the practitioner within a confidential treatment relationship, increases the potential for impairment to exist unnoticed. Regardless of whether the psychotherapist works in an institutional setting or in private practice, his or her work is largely unmonitored and conducted within the privacy of an office. The autonomy and independence of the therapist within the confines of the consulting office and the therapy hour are regarded as sacrosanct by other therapists. Thus the clinician is given authorization by state regulating bodies via licensure or certification to practice the healing art of psychotherapy free from interference and interruption. If he or she begins to experience impairment, it is likely to go unrecognized by colleagues during its early stages. As noted by Dlin (1984), there is a tendency for therapists to overlook symptoms of emotional distress in a colleague out of respect for individuality, privacy, and autonomy. Obviously there is also frequently a desire to remain uninvolved. The overworked clinician is usually hesitant to take on the additional burdens of colleagues, family and friends. Thus most tend to ignore the early signs of impairment among other therapists.

The isolation inherent in clinical practice prevents the early identification of emotional impairment. The onset of mental illness, suicidal risk, substance abuse, or patient exploitation may go unnoticed by both patients and colleagues. It is only when impairment begins to result in incompetence that the likelihood of identification increases. This is unfortunate, since the impairment is typically very serious by this point, and perhaps even chronic and entrenched. This pattern complicates later efforts toward remediation and restoration. Furthermore, even at this point, determining incompetency is a complex problem for many of the same reasons previously stated. The relative isolation associated with the practice of psychotherapy prevents the exposure of incompetency to public scrutiny, except in the case of gross mistreatment leading to professional and/or legal sanction. Until this level of incompetency has been reached, and appropriate action taken, inadequate clinical care and potential harm to patients are likely to result. Furthermore, the level of impairment required for gross incompetency to occur is likely to be significant enough to result in serious distress and suffering for the therapist over an extended period of time.

Admissions Screening

In order to overcome the tendency for impairment and incompetency among psychotherapists to exist unidentified, the profession of psychotherapy has begun to take steps to monitor its practitioners. Initially the emphasis was placed on determining suitability for clinical practice prior to entry into the field, as outlined in Chapter 2. Graduate programs assumed the responsibility for screening out those unsuited for the role of psychotherapist due to intellectual or emotional limitations. This intervention has proven to be an inadequate solution since, first, it is difficult to assess suitability at this stage of development. Second, this implies that suitability at the time of admission to graduate school eliminates the risk of later impairment. This is obviously not the case since personality predispositions can interact with work-related variables and the impact of later life events to result in emotional impairment sufficient enough to cause eventual incompetency. Therefore, the profession has been forced to confront the fact that rigorous admission screening does not preclude the need for later identification of impairment and incompetency.

Licensure/Certification

The second level of screening for emotional impairment and clinical incompetency occurs at the time of licensure or certification. As noted in Chapter 2, the focus of this evaluation is primarily on the adequacy and comprehensiveness of training and experience. While some attempts are made to address issues of clinical competency and personal suitability, the focus is typically on broader issues of readiness as reflected in academic and clinical experience. Furthermore, even if attempts to screen out impaired or incompetent clinicians are successful at this point (such as may result from an extended oral examination), this is of no help in identifying impaired individuals later on. Once the license has been granted, it is usually necessary only for the individual to pay a yearly renewal fee in order to remain authorized to practice without further supervision or evaluation. State licensing boards are not in a position to identify emotional impairment and associated incompetency after this point unless a complaint has been filed by a patient or colleague, an admittedly rare occurrence. Only if this occurs will action perhaps be taken to reevaluate the clinician's suitability and competency for continued practice. Short of this, licensure is a one-way door which grants authorization to practice until death. Thus it is not surprising that it has been largely ineffective in identifying impaired practitioners who have obtained certification and continue to send in their renewal fees. Added to this is the fact that a few states still do not regulate the practice of therapy whatsoever. In such locales anyone is free to provide therapy for a fee, and no regulatory body has the authority to prevent obviously impaired practitioners from offering their services to the public.

It is interesting to note the results of a nationwide study of psychology licensing boards conducted by Clairborn (1982). He found that licensure was largely unrelated to professional competence. Furthermore, he reports that fewer than half the states regarded professional negligence as sufficient grounds for investigative or punitive action by the licensing boards, while only 16 considered unprofessional conduct justification for state action. Fortunately, other disciplines such as psychiatry appear to be more closely regulated by state licensing boards (Laliotis & Grayson, 1985). Regardless of such varying policies or procedures, licensing boards continue to be ill-equipped for the task of correctly identifying most impaired practitioners.

Professional Organizations

The disciplines represented within the field of psychotherapy have attempted to address the issue of therapist impairment on a broader scale. For example, most have established "standards for providers" which outline issues of training and experience necessary for proclaiming an area of specialty. Furthermore, there are a variety of accrediting boards within the disciplines of social work, psychology, marriage and family counseling, and psychiatry which specify acceptable levels of performance for membership. These result in the assignment of various labels such as "board certified," diplomate, fellow, master clinician, or membership in the National Register of Health Care Providers. While some attempt is typically made to include competency-based criteria, most of the emphasis remains on the type and extent of prior training and experience. Furthermore, unless formal charges of incompetency or impropriety are instituted by colleagues or patients, continued membership is dependent solely on prompt periodic payment of membership fees. These professional organizations are unable to monitor their members on an ongoing basis in order to identify impaired or incompetent practitioners effectively.

Most of the disciplines in the field of psychotherapy sponsor some type of professional standards review committee which serves as an arbitrator for complaints regarding inadequate care initiated by patients or other professionals (Claiborn, 1982). These committees are typically associated with local, state, regional, or national associations (Larsen, 1986). Thus psychology, for example, has state psychological associations made up of psychologist members who have joined together for purposes of promoting the profession to the public. Each state association has a professional standards review committee which investigates charges of incompetence against its members (Laliotis & Grayson, 1985). However, this reactive stance does not permit early identification of impairment or incompetency prior to gross negligence typically resulting in a formal complaint or legal action.

Limitations

While each of the levels of evaluation described provide limited opportunities for screening out those lacking the training and experience necessary for competent clinical practice, none provide a means for actually evaluating professional performance and emotional stability. Furthermore, once membership or certification has been granted, there is no opportunity for ongoing evaluation or monitoring of competency and emotional health. The ability of such organizations to identify impaired practitioners is therefore dependent on the willingness of patients or colleagues to report evidences of incompetence or distress. Unfortunately, despite an increase in public awareness of malpractice actions against psychotherapists, it is very likely that insufficient reporting remains a serious problem in identifying those experiencing emotional impairment. Neither patients nor professional colleagues are reliable sources of such information.

It is unreasonable to expect the public to monitor the profession for signs of impairment or incompetency for several reasons. First, there are no widely known definitions of clinical competency (Clairborn, 1982). The average therapy patient is typically unaware of what constitutes acceptable standards of care and practice. As a result it may be difficult for him or her to distinguish between therapist innovations and quackery, enthusiasm and exploitation. Recent malpractice actions have documented the incredible abuse that some patients will endure out of ignorance or naivete. Even if a patient decides that the clinician is incompetent or impaired, he or she may continue in treatment, motivated by guilt, fear, obligation, or masochistic dependency. Those who wisely decide to terminate treatment may not realize that further action can be taken to report suspected incompetency or impairment. Very few individuals are aware of the existence or variety of appropriate licensing boards, professional guilds, and various review committess that are willing to investigate such charges. Unless an attorney is contacted, the disgruntled patient may decide that there is no recourse. Even among those who do learn of the myriad boards and committees which can be contacted in such an eventuality, few have the interest, motivation, patience, strength, or finances to initiate formal action against the clinician. As a result, despite a recent increase in malpractice action initiated by patients reporting sexual misconduct by therapists, most forms of incompetency and impairment probably remain unreported (Cummings & Sobel, 1985).

Relying on colleagues to report evidence of impaired or incompetent practitioners seems to be a questionable practice as well. For example, the relative isolation inherent in clinical practice denies colleagues a first hand look at the skills and practices of the suspected clinician. Thus concerned colleagues may lack sufficient evidence of impairment to warrant personal confrontation or formal reporting. A study by Wood et al. (1985) suggests that most therapists are extremely hesitant to report impaired or incompetent colleagues even when there is sufficient evidence. While 42% of 167 therapists surveyed admitted to offering help and/or a referral to an impaired practitioner, only 8% took steps to refer or report such a colleague to a regulatory agency. The rest decided that it was best to take no action at all. In addition, over 40% reported being aware of situations in which no action was taken by anyone to help a clearly identifiable, impaired colleague. Thoreson et al. (1986) found a similar pattern among psychologists who indicated that they were personally aware of impairment due to mental illness or alcoholism among their colleagues. Only 36% personally confronted the alcoholic colleague, while 53% spoke with those impaired by mental illness. The remainder chose to ignore the problem altogether. Reasons often given for this tendency to resist confrontation include fear of legal recourse, professional loyalty, dual-role concerns, reluctance to threaten a colleague's source of livelihood, and respect for individual privacy. Furthermore, no professional wants to be pegged as a "snitch" by his or her colleagues.

Insurance Review Committees

A more promising approach to determining clinical competency has been initiated by insurance companies and various third-party payers. A wide variety of "peer review," "utilization review," and "quality assurance" programs have been organized by the federal government, private industry, and independent insurers to monitor and evaluate the quality of care provided by practitioners being paid for rendering treatment (Clairborn, 1982). These programs typically involve the establishment of a review committee consisting of several senior therapists representing one or more disciplines who are assigned the task of reviewing requested records and interviewing practitioners when appropriate. It is intended that this type of review will screen out those engaging in incompetent practice. Unfortunately, monetary concerns can result in equating incompetent treatment with lengthy treatment, and the focus of action is usually centered on issues regarding reimbursement for future services rendered. Issues related to therapist impairment are rarely investigated and many aspects of incompetency are overlooked. Furthermore, even when there has been the identification of therapist impairment or incompetency, action is usually limited to the denial of reimbursement of services for the individual case under investigation. No further steps are typically taken against the incompetent practitioner. Thus, while insurance-related review committees have provided opportunities for monitoring and evaluating clinical competency, their purpose has been more to deny reimbursement to those who are inefficient or wasteful rather than identifying those who are emotionally impaired. This has had very little impact on attempts to identify and help psychotherapists in emotional distress.

Self-Referral

Self-referral remains the primary form of identification utilized for identifying impaired or incompetent practitioners in need of remediation. Obviously tendencies toward denial and avoidance make it unlikely that troubled clinicians will readily seek out help during the early stages of impairment. Fear of censure, ridicule, and loss of livelihood often cause psychotherapists to postpone seeking assistance when experiencing distress significant enough to impact clinical competency. For example, Wood et al. (1985) found that of the 167 psychotherapists surveyed,

4.2% admitted to problems with substance abuse, 0.6% acknowledged sexual misconduct with patients, and 32.3% experienced depression and burnout significant enough to interfere with clinical work. Of this group, nearly half refused to seek help or assistance in dealing with their problems.

In recognition of the difficulty that therapists have in admitting emotional impairment, virtually all of the individual disciplines in the field of psychotherapy have established voluntary programs for those desiring help in coping with mental illness, suicidal tendencies, substance abuse, and patient exploitation. Most of these guarantee confidentiality and freedom from professional censure for those presenting themselves voluntarily for assistance. Typically, only when an impaired professional refuses offers of help are steps taken to restrict practice (Larson, 1981). Admittedly, such programs are of limited value due to their reliance on self-referral. However, if the impaired individual is able to take this step, assistance and support are readily offered. Problems concerning jurisdiction, enforcement of recommended remediation, and supervision are complex with volunteer programs of this type. Yet a recent increase in the number of individuals presenting themselves for assistance indicates that this approach has potential to be a useful resource for those able to confront and admit their distress (Laliotis & Grayson, 1985; Larson, 1981).

Summary

In one recent study, therapists were asked how they would determine whether they were no longer competent to practice due to either physical or emotional disability (Guy, Stark, & Poelstra, 1987). The majority (57%) reported that their own self-assessment would be the primary source of such data, while 14% cited feedback from clients as the most important source of data to be considered. All other sources of information such as feedback from colleagues, friends, supervisors, family members, or personal therapist were regarded as relatively unimportant. Since the sources of feedback which therapists seem to value most are relatively unreliable, the problem of correctly identifying those who are impaired or incompetent remains a serious one for the profession. The need to rely on patient complaints, reports from other professionals, or self-referral greatly restricts the discipline's ability to monitor and evaluate clinicians effectively for evidence of personal distress and inadequate clinical performance. Furthermore, while the insurance industry's peer review programs provide some ongoing evaluation, their reliance on therapist self-report and the contaminating influence of the profit motive hinder their attempts to identify incompetent clinicians.

While each of these avenues provide some assistance in cases where there has been gross professional negligence, they are unlikely to help in the identification of those experiencing the early stages of emotional impairment. Furthermore, if the impairment has not resulted in highly visible incompetency, it is unlikely that it will be noticed. Several additional steps may need to be taken by the profession to improve the potential for correct and timely identification of emotional impairment among practicing therapists. For example, Wood et al. (1985) suggest that arriving at a clear definition of impairment and incompetency and presenting it to the public will educate both patients and therapists about the identifiable signs of impairment and incompetency which warrant reporting. Publicizing the appropriate agencies and committees that receive and process such complaints or reports will further facilitate the public's ability to take action when impairment is suspected. Removing the stigma associated with the presence of emotional distress in the life of the therapist will make it easier for self-referrals and reports by colleagues to be made. Increasing the visibility of therapist self-help and volunteer programs could also result in an increase in referrals (Thoreson et al., 1986).

Organized programs requiring periodic ongoing evaluation and supervision are also worthy of consideration. For example, it may be helpful to make licensure or certification more dependent on clinical performance rather than almost exclusively on academic credentials and general knowledge. This performance could be reevaluated periodically, such as at the time of license renewal. While this will not uncover less severe forms of impairment, it may identify those most likely to render inadequate care. Competency-based criteria could also be included in the qualifications for membership of certain professional organizations, with periodic reevaluations necessary for continued membership. At the present time evaluation programs such as these are typically regarded as too intrusive, expensive, and controlling by most professionals. In the survey conducted by Wood et al. (1985), 77% were opposed to a mandatory "mental health check-up" to be associated with licensure renewal, while 75% opposed mandatory supervision as a condition for licensure renewal. The vast majority (77%) preferred volunteer programs for impaired practitioners as a desirable alternative to mandatory evaluations. Perhaps if the problem of impairment or incompetency reaches more serious proportions or receives sufficient publicity, more aggressive measures such as those described previously will become increasingly acceptable to the profession. For the time being, however, the identification of distressed therapists will depend on self-referrals and the reports of patients and colleagues. Until efforts are made to require periodic evaluation in some fashion, unreported impairment and incompetency are likely to remain a recurrent problem.

Even when successful efforts for identifying impaired clinicians are finally instituted, this does not fully address the question of what is to be done in such cases. The issue of remediation for those so identified is an equally complex problem for the profession.

Remediation for the Impaired Psychotherapist

The correct and timely identification of an impaired therapist is only the first step to protecting the public and assisting the therapist in overcoming personal distress. Deciding what action is to be taken as a result opens up an entirely new issue with many of its own complicating factors and problems. Questions regarding censure versus rehabiltation, the efficacy of various possible intervention programs, and authority and enforcement remain obstacles to implementing programs of effective interventions.

Censure vs. Rehabilitation

The disinclination of psychotherapists to admit their impairment and the hesitation of other professionals to report an impaired colleague may result in part from fears of possible professional censure and restricted practice. While this may occur in the case of mental illness and substance abuse, it is even more likely to result if there has been evidence of patient exploitation such as sexual misconduct. Rather than risk disciplinary action, impaired psychotherapists often decide it is best to cope with their impairment alone, without the assistance of others. While the profession must deal directly with ethical violations and clinical incompetency, it is counterproductive to create an atmosphere of fear and distrust. The typical solution to this dilemma has been to offer amnesty to those voluntarily seeking assistance, reserving disciplinary actions for those who refuse help (Larson, 1981). In such cases, as long as the individual agrees to abide by the recommendations and directives of the committee concerned, no disciplinary action is usually taken.

It would be ironic indeed for a profession which espouses the potential for personality change to emphasize censure over rehabiltation. It is the belief that many cases of impairment can be remediated that prompts therapists to offer assistance to their impaired colleagues rather than resorting primarily to punishment. However, having favored rehabilitation over censure does not in and of itself suggest which forms of remediation are likely to be succesful. This is a separate issue.

Efficacy of Interventions

Typical interventions suggested for impairment and associated incompetency include personal psychotherapy, supervision, regular consultation, ongoing evaluation of work performance and competency, a reduction of work load when appropriate, and a variety of restrictions regarding the nature and scope of clinical responsibilities, depending on the type and severity of the impairment (Turkington, 1984). While comprehensive program evaluation is currently lacking, there are some early indications that such attempts at remediation have been successful.

For example, while based primarily on personal experience, both Freudenberger (1986) and Jaffe (1986) report that personal psychotherapy is often quite effective in treating impairment due to mental illness among practicing therapists. While there are several unique issues associated with a therapist entering treatment as a patient, these factors do not prevent therapy from being a relatively successful form of intervention for the impaired psychotherapist. Unfortunately, although many senior therapists maintain that psychotherapy has proven itself very useful in assisting therapists in emotional distress (Bermak, 1977; Chessick, 1978; Fleischer & Wissler, 1985; Ford, 1963), no published studies were found to document the rate of this success.

While no figures are available for therapists receiving treatment for substance abuse, several programs for physicians are reporting remarkable success rates which suggest that impaired health care professionals are more responsive to interventions of this type than the general population (Rosenberg, 1979). For example, success rates ranging from 50 to 83% have been reported for physicians attempting to overcome alcoholism and drug abuse (Laliotis & Grayson, 1985). While follow-up studies have discovered occasional relapses, the results are extremely encouraging. The vast majority of the impaired physicians were able to continue or resume medical practice, significantly improving the quality of both patient care and personal life. It would seem reasonable to assume that practicing psychotherapists seeking help are likely to be equally motivated and responsive to such treatment programs.

Given the primary underlying assumption of the mental health profession, namely that a variety of forms of psychotherapy are often effective in helping individuals overcome emotional impairment, it is reassuring to find indications that this is true for impaired psychotherapists as well. It appears that personal therapy and multimodal therapeutic programs such as those used for treating substance abuse are likely to be effective interventions for many impaired therapists. Unfortunately, there seems to be a pattern of underutilization of personal therapy by practicing therapists, even among those in distress, which prevents them from receiving help in this way.

While no data could be found to substantiate the efficacy of mandatory supervision and consultation for the recovery of the impaired therapist, this intuitively seems to be a useful intervention. Rather than resorting to extreme alternatives such as prohibiting further clinical practice or permitting continued unrestricted and unsupervised work, requiring the impaired therapist to submit to ongoing supervision and periodic review of clinical work seems to be a preferable option. In such cases restrictions regarding the number and type of clients to be seen can be imposed on an individual basis. A review committee could then determine when supervision and monitoring are no longer necessary. Of course in the case of severe impairment and incompetency it may be most appropriate to prohibit completely further practice indefinitely until there has been sufficient recovery.

Determining the forms of intervention most useful for the remediation and restoration of psychotherapists in distress does not guarantee that they will be utilized. Many questions remain regarding jurisdiction and enforcement.

Enforcement

Once an impaired therapist has been correctly identified and a program of intervention formulated, the problem of enforcement remains. This issue is very complex due to the variety of boundary and jurisdiction issues involved in the practice of psychotherapy by members of several professional disciplines. For example, the particular training program from which the individual has graduated no longer has authority or jurisdiction over the work of the therapist following the granting of the degree. Furthermore there is likely to be little opportunity for the faculty to observe impairment or incompetency among its alumni. Therefore, clinical training programs typically lack both the opportunity and authority to intervene in the emotional problems of its graduates.

Professional organizations and guilds lack the power to enforce rehabiltation programs for impaired members beyond the threat of expulsion from membership roles. Therefore, while complaints concerning emotional impairment, incompetency, and ethical violations filed by the public against association members will typically be investigated, little can be done to force the member to comply with recommended interventions. The results of the inquiry may be to recommend censure, expulsion, or required rehabilitation. The member is then free to either comply, resign from membership, or wait for the threatened dismissal. With the possible exception of psychiatry, membership in most professional guild associations is not required for obtaining the authorization of state boards to practice psychotherapy. For example, it is not necessary for a social worker to belong to the National Association of Social Work in order to receive state authorization to practice as a therapist. Therefore, being dropped from membership may not hinder future clinical practice. Thus such a threat may have little power in coercing a resistant therapist to cooperate with a program of remediation for emotional impairment.

While in reality professional organizations lack enforcement power beyond the threat of expulsion from active membership, it is possible that the results of such disciplinary action will be forwarded to state licensing boards by the professional association, resulting in further investigation by that board and possible revocation of licensure. Furthermore, publicity surrounding such investigations and formal action have the potential to damage significantly a psychotherapist's professional reputation (Larson, 1981). Thus the deliberations of ethics and professional practice committess are typically taken very seriously by those under investigation. However, one could speculate that growing liability risks associated with disciplinary action on the part of such committees may have the potential to limit further their authority and enforcement power in the future.

The public has the option to initiate legal action in the form of a civil suit against a therapist who has been incompetent, negligent, or unethical in his or her professional dealings. The malpractice action assumes that the therapist has breached his or her duty, resulting in loss or injury to the patient. The most frequent causes of malpractice action against psychotherapists are:

> faulty or negligent rendering of services, wrongful commitment, slander and libel, negligence leading to suicide or homicide, birth control or abortion counseling, electroshock or drug therapy, sex or other "sensuous" therapies, illegal search or violation of privacy, nude encounter groups, and failure to supervise a disturbed client. (Schwitzgebel & Schwitzgebel, 1980, p. 251)

The majority of malpractice charges center on the breach of professional duty, as evidenced by misdiagnosis, failure to refer or consult, physical contact during treatment, sexual misconduct, alienation of affection, undue influence, violation of confidentiality, and issues related to patient dangerousness to self or others. While such action can result in monetary fines and/or imprisonment, they may not in themselves prohibit further professional practice. Furthermore, unless a program of remediation is ordered by the court, the impaired therapist will receive little provocation to initiate a program of intervention. It is only when the state licensing board revokes the authorization to practice or mandates a program of rehabilitation as a result of such legal action that the practitioner is prohibited from practicing and/or forced to receive treatment for emotional impairment. Thus legal action is not necessarily an effective way of identifying and remediating impaired psychotherapists, particularly when there has not been gross, identifiable incompetence or negligence associated with the emotional distress.

Ultimately it is the state in which the therapist resides and practices that grants authorization to conduct psychotherapy via the process of licensure or certification. Therefore, it falls primarily on the state licensing board to determine whether the impaired practitioner should be prohibited from further clinical practice. Since a license or certification of some type is necessary to practice psychotherapy for a fee in many states, the threat of revocation resulting in loss of livelihood provides the necessary aspect of enforcement for those determined to be impaired and incompetent. Thus if the licensing board requires that the therapist undergo personal therapy and supervision in order to retain licensure, the impaired clinician has little choice but to comply. However, since such action is only likely to be taken as a result of an investigation in response to a formal complaint filed by a patient or colleague, most cases of impairment and incompetency remain unreported and unidentified. Therefore, the licensing board, while it has the jurisdiction and authority to require participation in a program of remediation and treatment, will have relatively few opportunities to intervene in this manner. Furthermore, in those states which do not regulate the practice of psychotherapy by means of licensure or registration, the local government has no authority whereby to require that an impaired therapist discontinue work or enroll in any type of treatment program for his or her own rehabilitation.

It is apparent that the impaired practitioner has the primary responsibilty to refer himself or herself for assistance. Unless severe disability has resulted in gross negligence or incompetence, most cases of impairment will go undetected by licensing boards, professional associations, and the general public. Therefore, unless the impaired clinician voluntarily pursues treatment, little is likely to be done. Even after having identified oneself as impaired, or having been so designated by others, it is still largely up to the therapist as to whether to cooperate with a program of intervention. With the exception of revocation of state authorization to practice psychotherapy, there is little that can be done to coerce an impaired therapist to submit to entering personal therapy and/or supervision. As Clairborn (1982) notes, the primary responsibility still lies with the distressed psychotherapist to pursue remediation and cooperate with the recommended intervention programs. While ultimately this may seem to be most appropriate, the tendency for denial and avoidance to cloud personal judgment in this situation may hinder the impaired practitioner from getting needed help. For example, Guy, Stark, and Poelstra (1987) found that less than half of those therapists who experienced personal distress during the previous three-year period obtained personal therapy, medication, or hospitalization as a result.

Further steps seem warranted to ensure that distressed therapists receive the assistance necessary to bring about their rehabilitation. In addition to the need to educate the public concerning definitions of professional competence versus incompetence, Clairborn (1982) suggests that there is a need to develop more effective detection mechanisms, ranging from reviews based on filed complaints to mandatory periodic review of competency. The profession must also develop a more effective adjudication procedure that is fair, open, efficient, and effective in addressing professional impairment and incompetency. Finally, there remains a need for a sanctioning system that has the authority and power to require an increase in professional competency and reduction of emotional impairment where necessary, or to remove the practitioner from clinical practice.

Prevention of Psychotherapist Impairment

While there is a need for better identification of impaired therapists and more effective implementation of programs for their rehabilitation, there is a greater need for the prevention of emotional distress and impairment before it reaches the level of disability or incompetence. A proactive stance that attempts to address the causes of impairment would be far more effective and efficient than a reactive stance that focuses on the results of distress. Furthermore, such measures could prevent unnecessary patient harm and therapist suffering. Among the many possible preventive steps, those most often recommended include continued education, personal therapy, periodic supervision, and peer interaction.

Continued Education

There appears to be a need to educate practicing therapists regarding emotional impairment and its early signs, typical modes of expression, and ultimate consequences (Laliotis & Grayson, 1985; Larsen, 1986). Alerting all therapists to their own potential to experience this problem may help to remove the stigma associated with it, making it easier for them to take steps to avoid its onset or confront its presence. This educational effort could take place by means of required seminars and workshops on this topic, both for therapists-in-training and those currently in practice. Furthermore, concentrated research in this area would be helpful in providing more precise information regarding the prevention, onset, and rehabilitation of the various forms of emotional impairment. Finally, the widespread distribution of the results of these studies in articles and books would maximize the profession's exposure to current information about this problem.

One important aspect of education regarding emotional impairment is the need to inform therapists about the role of prior personality and predisposition in increasing the potential for the onset of problems associated with psychic distress such as diagnosable mental illness, suicidal tendencies, substance abuse, and patient exploitation. While it might be assumed that most would have been exposed to such information during their graduate training, this is not necessarily the case. For example, Pope et al. (1986) report that most therapists have not received adequate training regarding the factors associated with sexual misconduct and how to deal with such issues in therapy relationships. In fact, issues of patient exploitation resulting from long-standing therapist personality dynamics may never have been discussed in graduate school. Furthermore, therapists-in-training may not have been encouraged to explore their own vulnerabilities to developing mental illness or substance abuse. Also, there may be a need for frequent reminders to encourage the practicing therapist to monitor his or her own tendencies toward impairment associated with the predisposition for such disabling problems.

The second area needing emphasis is that of the impact of work-related factors in the development of impairment and incompetence. As discussed previously, a host of variables related to clinical practice have the potential to promote the onset of mental illness, suicidal tendencies, substance abuse, or sexual misconduct in the psychotherapist. The practitioner needs to be taught about the potential hazards associated with psychic and physical isolation, patient idealization, analytic thinking, emotional exhaustion and depletion, vicarious living, conflicting priorities, and frantic schedules which can increase the likelihood of eventual impairment.

Likewise, there is a need to inform therapists about the potential impact of significant events in their life and the possible effects on clinical practice and personal relationships, as mentioned in Chapter 5. Alerting therapists to the disruptive potential of such events increases their chances of preventing the onset of impairment and incompetency.

Finally, educating practicing therapists about the likely interaction among all three of the preceding factors in precipitating emotional impairment will better equip them to monitor themselves and confront the early signs of distress before reaching the level of marked impairment and disability. Encouraging therapists to consider the role of personality predispositions, work-related factors, and the impact of life events in increasing the potential for the onset of mental illness, suicidal risk, substance abuse, and sexual misconduct is likely to assist in the prevention of emotional impairment and resultant incompetence.

Personal Psychotherapy

In a survey of female psychotherapists, counselors, and laypersons, Norcross and Prochaska (1986a) found that approximately 80% of the psychotherapists experienced at least one episode of high distress during the previous three years related to a host of factors such as relationship problems (28%), occupational problems (15.8%), family death (12.9%), family illness (9.9%), birth of children (7.6%), personal illness (5.3%), moving/relocation (2.3%), school-related problems (2.3%), death of a friend (1.8%), money problems (1.8%), legal problems (1.8%), and "other" (10.4%). Despite the potential for such events to precipitate emotional impairment, only 28% elected to enter personal psychotherapy (Norcross & Prochaska, 1986b) as compared to 43% of the female laypersons experiencing equivalent episodes of high distress. In another study, only 27% of those psychotherapists experiencing "high distress" life events obtained personal psychotherapy as a result, even though 37% admitted that the resultant distress was significant enough to impact patient care (Guy, Stark, & Poelstra, 1987). Deutsch (1985) found a similar pattern of underutilization among 264 psychotherapists representing various disciplines. Less than half of those reporting serious problems related to depression sought personal therapy. Furthermore, only 24% of those reporting substance abuse and 60% of those attempting suicide entered personal therapy as a result.

Although numerous authors suggest that personal therapy remains an extremely effective preventive method for coping with emotional distress and the potential of impairment (Bermak, 1977; Chessick, 1978; Farber, 1983a; Freudenberger & Robbins, 1979; Ford, 1963; Storr, 1979), there appears to be a curious pattern of underutilization among practicing psychotherapists (Guy & Liaboe, 1986b). Most therapists entering individual treatment only do so prior to entering professional practice (Greenberg & Staller, 1981; Wood et al., 1982). While there is a general acceptance of the usefulness of personal therapy as preparation for conducting therapy (Garfield & Kurtz, 1976), there seems to be a tendency for many therapists to resist entering treatment following graduation. For example, Prochaska and Norcross (1983b) found that, while psychotherapists recommended medication and facilitative relationships for patient distress, they tended to rely on cognitive self-help methods for dealing with their own emotional problems.

Several factors may account for the apparent underutilization of personal psychotherapy by practicing psychotherapists. Feelings of humiliation and embarrassment associated with identifying oneself as "patient" along with a general reluctance to assume a dependent role, may account for some of the resistance (McCarley, 1975). An uncomfortable split also occurs at times, whereby the therapist becomes both a patient and a therapist seeking consultation from a colleague regarding himself or herself, making it difficult to cope with the boundary issues which often arise (Grotjahn, 1970). Some therapists find it difficult to select a personal therapist, since those they trust most are typically colleagues who would be inappropriate to contact due to dual-role concerns and issues regarding confidentiality (Guy & Liaboe, 1986b).

Psychotherapists may overlook the value of treatment due to the mistaken belief that a previous training therapy is a completed act, as though it has permanently resolved any issues that might increase the potential for eventual emotional impairment. If reentering personal psychotherapy is regarded as a negative reflection on the previous therapist or oneself, this will most likely hinder attempts to assess objectively its appropriateness.

It is interesting to note that some therapists resist undergoing personal therapy because of secret doubts concerning the efficacy of treatment and their ability to benefit from the interventions of another therapist. While this may be the result of their own feelings of ineffectiveness as a therapist, it sometimes occurs because of previous unsuccessful therapy experiences. For example, Buckley, Karasu, and Charles (1981) reported that 21% of the psychotherapists they surveyed stated that their previous therapy had been harmful in some way.

Finally, few individuals realize more than psychotherapists the degree of financial and emotional commitment involved in entering personal treatment. This knowledge may prevent some individuals from initiating treatment due to hesitancy to begin such a substantial undertaking, particularly when this natural resistance is coupled with one or more of the aforementioned concerns.

In order for psychotherapists to benefit more fully from the very services which they provide for others, it is important that the issue of underutilization be addressed openly. Graduate students should be encouraged to regard personal treatment as a preventive measure as well as an intervention for potential emotional distress and impairment. Practicing therapists need to be encouraged to confront their hesitancies to enter psychotherapy in order to make it easier to normalize this preventive and remediative measure. More aggressive efforts could include requiring personal therapy for therapists-in-training and in practice. However, such extreme measures are typically rejected by members of the profession. For example, Wood et al. (1982) found that 46% of those therapists surveyed strongly opposed required psychotherapy for graduate students, while 77% opposed a "mental health check up" for those applying for license renewal. It is more likely that less aggressive measures such as well-publicized referral networks for therapists desiring personal treatment will increase the likelihood of their entering therapy before the actual onset of impairment.

Periodic Supervision

As in the case of personal therapy, several authors on the subject of therapist impairment suggest that periodic supervision and/or consultation is useful in reducing the potential of eventual emotional impairment (Farber, 1983a; Freudenberger & Robbins, 1979; Goldberg, 1986; Guy & Liaboe, 1986a). The reality testing, support, nurturance, and guidance provided by a respected colleague within the framework of formal or informal supervision can be very helpful in addressing the impact of personality predispositions, work-related factors, and fallout from significant life events on the practice and personal life of the therapist.

There may be a pattern of underutilization of personal supervision by practicing psychotherapists for many of the same reasons that explain their hesitancy to enter personal therapy. Factors related to time pressures, financial constraints, dual-role concerns, subtle superiority and grandiosity, fear of being seen as incompetent, and doubts concerning its usefulness may prevent the therapist from seeking assistance from a respected colleague. As a result, a surprisingly few psychotherapists may obtain regular supervision following licensure. For example, Wahl (1986) found that only 16% of the 153 practicing psychotherapists surveyed were currently receiving formal supervision, while an additional 17% were receiving only occasional "informal" supervision. The remaining 67% were not receiving any type of supervision at the time of the study. Given the potential benefits of supervision in reducing the likelihood of unrecognized impairment and incompetency, it is unfortunate that so few avail themselves of its advantages.

Once again, normalizing ongoing or periodic supervision would be a useful step toward encouraging psychotherapists to utilize this experience in order to prevent possible impairment. While most practitioners are opposed to requiring supervision following licensure or certification (Wood et al., 1982), it may be necessary to consider such aggressive measures in order to prevent incompetence and patient harm from occurring.

Peer Interactions

While not necessitating formal organization, opportunities for peer interaction are likely to be very helpful in preventing the onset and development of emotional impairment (Bellak, 1981; Farber, 1983a; Freudenberger & Robbins, 1979; Laliotis & Grayson, 1985). The freedom to discuss such issues openly with colleagues allows for the useful exchange of information and expressions of support, empathy, comfort, and caring. This is particularly helpful in overcoming the physical and psychic isolation inherent in clinical practice. While this can take place within seminars and workshops, it may also be useful for psychotherapists to meet informally to discuss such issues (Cray & Cray, 1977). As McCarley (1975) notes, therapists have a unique ability to understand the needs of other therapists, and the support and assistance provided during informal discussions can be invaluable in addressing factors that increase emotional distress. The opportunity to discuss candidly the impact of a recent divorce, emotional depletion, or personal depression with an understanding colleague may provide a valuable source of reality testing and direction for the therapist facing potential impairment.

Both the American Psychiatric Association and the American Psychological Association have provided opportunities for formal and informal discussions concerning the issue of impairment (Larsen, 1986; Larson, 1981). The response has been very encouraging, as a multitude of therapists have come together to discuss openly issues related to mental illness, suicide, chemical dependence, and patient exploitation within the profession. As a result of such meetings, numerous referral and volunteer help organizations have been formed to assist those in distress (Nathan, 1982). Furthermore, open dialogue has very likely served a preventive function as well, sensitizing psychotherapists to the issues involved in the development of impairment. Perhaps most important, the large number of psychotherapists attending open forums on this topic reflects a growing recognition of the extent of the problem, and an admission that it is one which is likely to be faced by each practitioner at some point during their career. Hopefully this groundswell of interest and support will result in the creation of prevention programs that are available and attractive to all practitioners.

Summary

Formulating a plan of intervention for psychotherapist impairment requires a comprehensive approach which addresses the problems of identification, treatment, and prevention of emotional distress and its debilitating impact on professional practice. For this to occur, there must be open dialogue concerning the many complex issues involved, a willingness to confront the full extent of the problem, and a readiness to take measures to implement an aggressive plan of rehabiltation and prevention. It would appear that the growing wave of concern regarding this issue signals a new readiness on the part of the profession to implement programs to restore impaired practitioners to their highest level of professional competency and personal satisfaction. It will be interesting to observe the improvements which are likely to result from current and future efforts in this area.

SUMMARY AND DISCUSSION

Despite many advancements and innovations in the practice of psychotherapy, the success or failure of the treatment endeavor continues to rely to a great extent on the stability and emotional well-being of the therapist. This may be difficult for mental health professionals to acknowledge since they are then faced with the temptation to imply that psychotherapists have overcome any personal vulnerability to emotional distress and impairment. To maintain this facade requires a substantial degree of denial and deception. However, to acknowledge the alternative—that psychotherapists do indeed fall victim to mental illness, suicide, substance abuse, sexual misconduct, spouse and child abuse, and a host of other tragic expressions of emotional impairment—requires an uncomfortable degree of humility and vulnerability. Such admissions reveal the true mortality of psychic healers who themselves occasionally suffer from the very afflictions that they seek to heal in others. Although they may wish for transcendence, psychotherapists remain very human.

Guggenbuhl-Craig (1979) suggests that therapists must accept their vulnerability to emotional impairment as the cost for their understanding and insight. Thus those most successful and talented in ameliorating psychic pain in others may be most vulnerable to the subtle onset of emotional distress and disability. While steeped in Jungian philosophy, this concept of the "shadow" is helpful to all practitioners. Rather than becoming immune to impairment as a result of the training and experience received in treating the emotional distress of others, the psychotherapist may be singularly vulnerable to its impact in his or her own personal life. If for no other reason, this may result in the psychotherapist's natural tendency to overlook and deny early evidences of psychic difficulty and failure to appreciate their potential to eventually result in severe impairment and incompetency.

It appears that the profession of psychotherapy is now ready to confront its own "shadow"—that of emotional impairment among its members. Recent efforts to investigate the incidence, etiology, and expression of impairment and incompetency suggest that the time has come to confront this problem openly by developing effective programs for the identification, rehabilitation, and prevention of emotional distress among practicing therapists. In the end, both patients and therapists will benefit from such endeavors.

Chapter 7 addresses the broader issue of job satisfaction and burnout among practicing psychotherapists in an attempt to identify those factors which lead to the decision to leave the field. While it is not unusual for individuals to have more than one career during a lifetime, the surprising number of psychotherapists who become dissatisfied with their work suggest that factors leading to burnout and job dissatisfaction warrant careful consideration.

CHAPTER 7

Career Satisfaction and Burnout

In view of the assortment of difficulties and hazards encountered by many therapists, it might be concluded that few individuals could possibly enjoy a long, satisfying career in psychotherapy. Fortunately this is not the case. As discussed in Chapter 1, there are a host of satisfactions associated with the practice of psychotherapy which seem to far outweigh the hazards and liabilities associated with this profession. For example, benefits such as professional independence, financial rewards, variety, recognition and prestige, intellectual stimulation, emotional growth and satisfaction, and personal enrichment and fulfillment are often cited as factors associated with the practice of psychotherapy which provide significant career satsifaction (Burton, 1975; Greben, 1975). Despite the emotional and interpersonal problems sometimes associated with the role of psychotherapist, most practitioners are very content with their career choice, even after many years of practice (Storr, 1979).

While it is encouraging to note that most psychotherapists find that the assets of professional practice outweigh the disadvantages, it is troubling to hear reports of career dissatisfaction among some practitioners (Prochaska & Norcross, 1983a). It appears that several factors associated with the practice of psychotherapy contribute to growing feelings of boredom, apathy, discouragement, and dissatisfaction in some therapists which prompt them to either leave the field entirely, or worse, to continue clinical practice while growing feelings of discontent impair their ability to provide adequate patient care. Recent research findings concerning the process and dimensions of burnout among psychotherapists also raise a host of questions regarding the likelihood of a long, satisfying career in psychotherapy for the typical practitioner (Farber, 1983a). It appears that burnout and job dissatisfaction are not necessarily unusual experiences among therapists.

This chapter examines the multitude of factors contributing to job satisfaction and dissatisfaction. The problem of burnout among therapists is also discussed, with special attention given to the incidence, symptoms, etiology, and treatment of this phenomenon. Finally, suggestions are provided for the prevention of career dissatisfaction and burnout.

CAREER SATISFACTION

While it is very encouraging to read the comments of well-seasoned professionals who have found psychotherapeutic practice to be personally satisfying and fulfilling (Bellak, 1981; Burton, 1975; Greben, 1975; Storr, 1979), this only serves to document the experience of a select few. These accounts have significant inspirational value for the clinician who occasionally feels discouraged and doubtful about his or her choice of career. Unfortunately such testimonials provide little information about the actual incidence of career satisfaction among psychotherapists as a group. However, several recent studies have attempted to assess the attitudes and opinions of large numbers of practicing therapists in order to determine whether most clinicians enjoy their work to the extent described by these authors.

Incidence of Career Satisfaction

The results of several studies suggest that as a group, psychotherapists are relatively satisfied with their choice of career. In some cases, those expressing satisfaction were a slim majority, a less than reassuring discovery. For example, Kelly, Goldberg, Fiske, and Kilkowski (1978) found that only 54% of those clinical psychologists surveyed indicated that they would reenter the field if they were to live their lives over again. Similarly, only 58% of the clinical psychologists surveyed by Norcross and Prochaska (1982) reported that they would become psychologists again if they were beginning life over. While these findings suggest that the majority of psychotherapists—or at least the majority of psychologists—are content with their choice of career, there does appear to be a substantial number who are not.

Fortunately, most investigators report even higher incidences of satisfaction among psychotherapists than those cited previously. Several studies found that therapists were overwhelmingly content with their choice of profession. For example, Walfish et al. (1985) found that 87% of the psychotherapists they surveyed indicated that they were satisfied with their choice of career. Similarly, Prochaska and Norcross (1983a) and Norcross and Prochaska (1983a, 1983b) found that over 90% of their sample of psychologists expressed satisfaction with their career choice. Other investigators report equally high levels of career satisfaction among practicing psychotherapists (Farber, 1985b; Jerrell, 1983; Peterson, Eaton, Levine, & Snepp, 1982).

Since these studies also focused primarily on clinical psychologists, little is known about satisfaction among the membership of the other disciplines represented in the field of psychotherapy. An important exception is an investigation conducted by Farber and Heifetz (1981) who found that among practicing psychotherapists, social workers reported the highest level of career satisfaction, followed by psychologists and then psychiatrists, in descending order of contentment. In addition, the majority of all three subgroups reported high levels of contentment with their career in psychotherapy. If this finding reflects a general trend, it seems reasonable to conclude that the large majority of all practicing psychotherapists are satisfied with their choice of career, regardless of their particular professional discipline or specialty.

Factors Contributing to Career Satisfaction

While it is heartening to learn of the high degree of career satisfaction among practicing psychotherapists, as reported by the majority of studies focusing on this issue, it is also helpful to identify those specific factors which contribute to this overall feeling of contentment. A number of investigators have attempted to isolate aspects of therapeutic practice that promote feelings of fulfillment, satisfaction, and pleasure in the therapist.

Tryon (1983b) surveyed 300 private practitioners and found that the satisfactions associated with clinical practice most often reported, in descending order of frequency, were professional independence, success, high income, flexible hours, relating to patients, variety, challenge of work, enjoyment of work, contacts with other professionals, serving humankind, and recognition. No sex-related differences were reported, with the exception of the tendency for female therapists to report deriving greater pleasure from "relating to patients" than did male respondents.

Farber and Heifetz (1982) found that psychotherapists derive the greatest amount of career satisfaction from helping patients to change, gaining an increased understanding of human nature, and experiencing a sense of intimate involvement in their lives. When these findings were subjected to factor analysis, further sources of satisfaction were identified (Farber & Heifetz, 1981). Pleasure derived from "promoting growth" included satisfaction resulting from increased self-knowledge, self-growth, and patient growth. The second major factor, "intimate involvement," included satisfactions related to learning intimate details of another's life, learning about many different types of people, achieving intimacy with patients, and experiencing oneself as socially useful. A third factor, "revered efficacy," was found to include pleasures derived from gaining and using therapeutic expertise, the "mystique" of being a therapist, the status of a professional career, and being valued by patients. While the pleasures derived from "intimate involvement" were unrelated to any of the subgroup variables, females reported gaining more satisfaction from "promoting growth" and "revered efficacy" than males. Furthermore, social workers derived more satisfaction from these two factors than either psychologists or psychiatrists.

In a later study, Farber (1985b) found that among the 93.5% of practicing therapists surveyed who expressed receiving moderate to significant satisfaction from psychotherapeutic work, several diverse aspects of practice were identified as contributing to this sense of contentment. These included a personal sense of having experienced suitable emotional rewards, relaxed work atmosphere, feelings of effectiveness and accomplishment, sense of personal commitment, opportunities for personal growth, and feelings of personal competence. In addition, Farber reports that greater amounts of clinical experience appeared to reduce perceived vulnerability to the stresses and sources of dissatisfaction associated with the practice of therapy.

Factors related to education and training have been found to have an impact on therapists' later career satisfaction. Those who felt the greatest degree of satisfaction with their graduate and clinical training tended to be more satisfied with their career in psychotherapy (Norcross & Prochaska, 1983a; Peterson et al., 1982; Tryon, 1983b). It would appear that those who felt most prepared by their training were able to derive the greatest degree of satisfaction from their practice. Conversely, those feeling that their preparation had been inadequate tended to find clinical work to be less personally satisfying. While it may be that other variables account for this relationship, such as differences in personality, motivation, and native ability, it is likely that adequate training does increase the potential for greater career satisfaciton.

Jerrell (1983) reports that doctoral level psychologists experienced greater job satisfaction than those with only master's level training. Furthermore, social workers with a masters degree reported being significantly more content with their work than those with only a bachelor's degree. While further training may increase the sense of preparedness (thus increasing contentment), it may also result in other sources of satisfaction such as career advancement, greater autonomy, and increased status and recognition. While Jerrell cautions the reader from concluding that increasing amounts of education and training always result in greater career satisfaction among psychotherapists, the findings of this study suggest that such a relationship may possibly exist. Further research is needed to examine more fully the impact of advanced education and training on career satisfaction.

Several factors related to the therapist's environment appear to affect career satisfaction. Psychotherapists practicing in urban areas reported more contentment with "community satisfactions," such as social and leisure opportunities and the adequacy of public services, than those living in rural areas (Freund & Sarata, 1983). Interestingly, there was no significant difference in measures of actual "work satisfaction." However, in a related study of urban versus rural psychotherapists, Eisenhart and Ruff (1983) found that the degree of job satisfaction was directly related to the type of community in which the therapist resided and how well community goals and expectations coincided with those of the individual mental health professional. Those most suited to rural life were more likely to be satisfied with their career in rural mental health, while those favoring urban environments were most likely to experience greater career satisfaction when working in an urban setting.

The relationship between career satisfaction and environmental variables is not limited to the surrounding community. On the contrary, as one would expect, factors related to the actual work setting also appear to impact the practitioner's sense of contentment. For example, Cherniss and Egnatios (1978) found that therapists working in community mental health centers were considerably less satisfied with their careers than a comparable group of highly educated workers in the general population. Reasons given for this finding included poor communication, lack of organization, ambiguity of roles, and inefficiency, all of which were reported to be characteristic of the work environment in community mental health centers. Farber (1985b) found a similar pattern of dissatisfaction among the psychologists he surveyed who worked in institutional settings. Given these findings, it is not surprising that there has been a dramatic increase in the number of psychotherapists entering part- or full-time private practice (Norcross & Prochaska, 1983b). Those doing so report greater career satisfaction than those remaining in the public sector. As reported by Norcross and Prochaska, independent practitioners experience higher levels of job satisfaction due to achieving greater professional autonomy, freedom to specialize, and financial incentives, as well as experiencing increased dissatisfaction with institutional care and bureaucratic red tape.

Some individuals have found that diversifying their clinical duties to include supervision, consultation, teaching, administration, writing, and research has resulted in a greater degree of overall career satisfaction (Ott, 1986). Those who enjoy the variety and stimulation resulting from working in multiple settings report being very satisfied with this arrangement. It seems that for these individuals the freedom to function in several roles and contexts reduces boredom and isolation while increasing energy and motivation. Tryon (1983b) found that those working in more than one clinical setting valued the resultant interaction with other colleagues, variety of work, educational opportunities, and financial rewards. On the other hand, those less suited for such an arrangement who were forced to diversify because of economic necessity were less satisfied with their careers. For these individuals, the need to "spread themselves" among several work sites served to increase stress and decrease feelings of competency.

Finally, the practice of psychotherapy has been found to promote significant personal growth in the practicing psychotherapist. Farber (1983b) reports that the therapists he surveyed experienced increases in assertiveness, self-assurance, self-reliance, introspection, self-disclosing ability, self-reflection, and expanded sensitivity as a result of clinical practice. These psychotherapists reported becoming more psychologically minded, self-assured, and self-aware. Burton (1975) found a similar pattern of personal growth associated with the practice of psychotherapy. He reports that psychotherapists found therapy to be intellectually and emotionally stimulating, resulting in the subjective experience of personality growth and greater emotional maturity over the years of clinical practice. Community recognition and prestige associated with the role of therapist brought an increase in self-respect among those surveyed. It would appear that the personal growth experienced by many psychotherapists serves to increase their overall satisfaction with their career.

The majority of psychotherapists enjoy and respect their work, valuing the emotional growth that it promotes both in themselves as well as in their patients (Farber, 1985b). The interpersonal encounters and variety of environmental factors promote a sense of satisfaction and fulfillment in the majority of therapists in clinical practice. While no occupation is without its shortcomings and frustrations, most psychotherapists appear to find their choice of career to be a worthwhile and satisfying endeavor. Certainly for these individuals the many benefits associated with the practice of therapy far outweigh the potential hazards and liabilities.

CAREER DISSATISFACTION

Despite the encouraging reports of high levels of career satisfaction among psychotherapists, there remains a sizable number of clinicians who do not find the practice of psychotherapy to be sufficiently fulfilling and satisfying. These individuals fall into two major groups. The first includes those who became disillusioned with their choice of career, prompting them to discontinue the practice of psychotherapy in favor of another occupation. The second group comprises those who express varying levels of dissatisfaction but who continue to practice nevertheless. While it is encouraging to note that the majority of psychotherapists report being satisfied with their work, those who feel otherwise cite several reasons worthy of consideration by all practitioners.

Incidence of Career Dissatisfaction

It is nearly impossible to determine the incidence of psychotherapists who leave the profession due to career dissatisfaction and disillusionment. The relative autonomy and diversification associated with clinical practice makes it difficult to track a practitioner's career over many years of labor. Furthermore, a lack of central governance or registration among the various disciplines represented in the field hinders attempts to document total rates of attrition. Therefore, one can only speculate, based on rumor and personal encounters, that a small but noteworthy number of psychotherapists eventually decide to discontinue clinical practice in order to pursue a different or related career which does not involve conducting therapy. Just how many do so remains to be determined.

While no data could be found regarding the actual number of those departing from the profession, several studies have investigated job satisfaction and dissatisfaction among therapists who continue to practice despite their discontent. Reports concerning the incidence of career dissatisfaction vary somewhat among those investigating this issue. For example, Kelly et al. (1978) found that 36% of those surveyed expressed dissatisfaction with their career in psychotherapy after 10 years of practice. This figure jumped to 46% after 25 years in the field. Prochaska and Norcross (1983a) report that over 40% of the psychotherapists they surveyed indicated that they would not make the same career choice if they had the opportunity to begin life over again. Similarly, Garfield and Kurtz (1976) found that 29% of those clinical psychologists surveyed reported being dissatisfied with their choice of profession. While Farber and Heifetz (1981) did not determine the actual percentage of psychotherapists who were primarily dissatisfied with their career, they do report that the psychiatrists surveyed reported receiving the least amount of satisfaction from their work, followed by psychologists and social workers, in that order.

Unfortunately these findings may not clearly delineate the actual incidence of career dissatisfaction among psychotherapists. The methodology used to evaluate career satisfaction varies widely among investigators. For example, those studies which question about alternative fantasy careers typically receive higher ratings of career dissatisfaction than those inquiring specifically about satisfaction with a present career (Prochaska & Norcross, 1983a). Even among the same individuals, expressions of dissatisfaction vary according to how the questions are presented. For example, while 42% of those surveyed by Norcross and Prochaska (1982) indicated that they would prefer a different career, nearly 90% of these same individuals expressed some degree of satisfaction with their present career. Thus attempts to assess actual levels of career dissatisfaction accurately may be undermined by such methodological problems.

Despite these inconsistencies, it would appear that some psychotherapists are not satisfied with their present career. While they have apparently elected to continue to practice rather than leave the profession, they report experiencing less pleasure and fulfillment from their work than those who indicate that they are satisfied with their choice of career. Although the precise incidence and nature of this dissatisfaction remains a topic of debate, the existence and etiology of such feelings among practicing psychotherapists warrant careful consideration.

Factors Contributing to Career Dissatisfaction

Psychotherapists cite a wide array of factors associated with clinical practice which contribute to general feelings of dissatisfaction, stress, and displeasure. While some of these are the direct result of patient contact, others are related to factors inherent in the practice of psychotherapy. In a survey of psychiatrists, psychologists, and social workers in clinical practice, Farber and Heifetz (1981) identified three primary sources of therapeutic stress. These were factors related to personal depletion, the therapeutic relationship, and working conditions. Each of these have the potential to undermine career satisfaction and reduce feelings of fulfillment and meaning.

Personal Depletion

As discussed extensively in Chapters 3 and 4, a variety of factors associated with the practice of psychotherapy can negatively impact the clinician's life and relationships. Various hazards resulting from physical and psychic isolation, emotional depletion and withdrawal, incessant psychological-mindedness, lack of spontaneity, vicarious living, conflicting priorities, physical exhaustion, and hectic work schedule can seriously deplete the therapist's emotional and psychic reserves. Conducting therapy is a very difficult endeavor which can significantly tax the therapist's personal strength and resolve. Unless steps are taken to minimize the impact of such factors, their cumulative effect can result in a growing sense of career dissatisfaction and overwhelming personal feelings of futility, despair, and discouragement (Burton, 1975; Chessick, 1978; Fine, 1980; Greben, 1975).

In Farber and Heifetz's (1981) study, the primary factor of "personal depletion" was found to include many of the aforementioned variables. The psychotherapists surveyed reported that interpersonal difficulties outside of work, emotional depletion, physical exhaustion, difficulty setting aside an "analytic perspective," inevitable need to relinquish patients, and constraints related to the "50 minute hour" contributed to their experience of work-related stress and dissatisfaction. Tryon (1983a) also reports that the therapists surveyed found problems related to isolation and personal depletion to be major sources of career dissatisfaction. Thus it would appear that the impact of conducting psychotherapy on the life of the therapist outside of the office has the potential to promote overall feelings of career dissatisfaction and displeasure. If the practicing therapist finds that clinical work has a negative effect on his or her personal life and relationships, this is likely to increase feelings of dissatisfaction which may eventually motivate a change in career.

Therapeutic Relationship

Intimate encounters with patients are often extremely meaningful and satisfying. However, there are times when the work involved can be stressful and difficult for the therapist. The difficulties associated with learning the art and science of psychotherapeutic practice are numerous. Recurring doubts about the efficacy of treatment and difficulties encountered when attempting to evaluate patient progress were found to be sources of considerable distress for practicing psychotherapists, particularly for those with less experience. Other factors such as the need to withhold personal information and opinions, emotional constraint, the need to set aside personal problems and concerns, distorted public stereotypes of therapists, one-way intimacy, patient devaluation and attack, and inevitable patient terminations and abandonment are all potential sources of therapist stress and discomfort. Furthermore, working with emotionally troubled patients is believed by some to be rather hazardous to the therapist's own mental health and well-being. Thus in addition to the potentially negative impact of clinical work on the therapist's personal life and relationships, the clinician's inner experience of therapeutic encounters may also promote feelings of career dissatisfaction.

Farber and Heifetz's (1981) factor analysis of their survey results revealed that the second primary factor of work-related stress—therapeutic relationship—included variables such as dissatisfaction associated with feeling responsible for patients' lives, the need to control one's emotions, the monotony of work, difficulty evaluating progress, difficulty in working with disturbed people, doubts regarding the efficacy of therapy, and a lack of gratitude from patients all contributed to increased stress and dissatisfaction. This is similar to the results obtained by Tryon (1983a) who reports that psychotherapists found problems associated with therapeutic relationships to be a major source of career dissatisfaction. Thus it would appear that therapists find some factors inherent in clinical practice to be quite stressful and dissatisfying. If these begin to outweigh the benefits of being a psychotherapist, a growing sense of career dissatisfaction may eventually prompt the individual to leave the profession altogether.

Working Conditions

There are a number of factors associated with the practical aspects of clinical practice which can become sources of considerable stress for the therapist. For example, the physical and psychic isolation associated with clinical practice has the potential to create feelings of alienation, competition, and misunderstanding among professional colleagues. Furthermore, the financial instability and risk associated with full- or part-time private practice, engaged in by as many as 90% of those psychotherapists surveyed (Norcross et al., 1985), was found to be another source of difficulty for some individuals. Also, the tendency towards overwork and overcommitment can have a detrimental impact on the life and relationships of some therapists. Finally, the organizational frustrations associated with working in the public sector were found to be a signficant source of career displeasure for some clinicians. Thus several factors directly related to the working conditions of the psychotherapist can create discontent and dissatisfaction.

Farber and Heifetz (1981) found that working conditions were identified by those psychotherapists surveyed as a third major source of stress and dissatisfaction. This factor was found to include frustrations related to organizational politics, excessive paperwork, excessive workload, and professional conflicts. Tryon (1983a) also reports that the psychotherapists whom she surveyed cited time pressures, economic and caseload uncertainties, business aspects, and lack of fringe benefits to be major sources of dissatisfaction among those in private practice. It would seem that some practical aspects associated with conducting therapy can be unsatisfying to the therapist. Again, if this dissatisfaction becomes significant enough, it may motivate the decision to pursue other career interests.

Summary

As with any career, the profession of psychotherapy has its share of associated pleasures and displeasures, benefits and hazards. However, the majority of therapists find that the assets far outweigh the liabilities, resulting in a sense of overall career satisfaction regardless of the difficulties encountered (Farber, 1985b). Why is it that some find the opposite to be true? It would appear that this is the result of individual and work-related differences perhaps largely independent of the actual practice of psychotherapy.

As discussed in Chapters 1 and 2, some individuals attracted to a career in psychotherapy are not suited for the role of therapist to begin with. It may be that the individual lacks—and seems unable to acquire—the personality characteristics which are necessary for conducting psychotherapy. Furthermore, personal interests, abilities, and attitudes may prove to be incompatible with those required for the role of therapist. If such an individual enters the profession, it is possible that he or she will find that the "fit" is not a good one, resulting in career dissatisfaction and disappointment. Even if there is a sufficient degree of compatibility between the personality and goals of the individual and the duties and responsibilities of the role of therapist, changing interests and outlook (and/or changes in the field) may lead to increasing incompatibility and dissatisfaction. Finally, the impact of significant events in the life of the therapist may result in profound changes which can reduce the goodness of fit, resulting in a decrease in overall career satisfaction. It would appear that a host of individual variables not directly related to liabilities inherent in the practice of psychotherapy can result in career dissatisfaction.

Work-related factors not directly associated with conducting psychotherapy have also been found to increase job dissatisfaction. As mentioned earlier, political disputes, competition, poor communication, bureaucractic red tape, and a host of business and financial concerns have all been identified as major sources of stress and displeasure. Since psychotherapists practice in a wide variety of environments and contexts, many factors related to the physical surroundings and collegial relationships have the potential to undermine job satisfaction independent of variables associated with the actual practice of therapy with patients.

It seems reasonable to conclude that the dissatisfaction reported by some practicing therapists is the result of an interaction among the personality of the individual, the characteristics of the work environment, and factors inherent in conducting psychotherapy. It appears that the practice of psychotherapy, in and of itself, is unlikely to promote lasting feelings of career dissatisfaction in the well-suited individual working in a favorable environment. While such a statement may at first seem naive, the relatively high level of job satisfaction reported among therapists suggests that most individuals entering the profession experience a sufficiently favorable interaction among these three variables to promote a sense of pleasure, contentment, and fulfillment. The right person in the right place is very likely to enjoy conducting psychotherapy. Perhaps a better way of stating it would be to acknowledge that an ill-suited individual or an unfavorable environment is sometimes sufficient to diminish whatever satisfactions are inherent in the practice of therapy. In such a case, career dissatisfaction will be the likely result.

BURNOUT AMONG PSYCHOTHERAPISTS

It is interesting how some of the most seemingly innocuous remarks or findings can result in revolutionary transitions in thought and practice. Freudenberger and Robbins (1979) suggest that an increase in career-related stress and dissatisfaction sometimes result in the psychotherapist "becoming burnt out as a person" (p. 285). With this simple statement, these authors applied Freudenberger's earlier work (about public health care workers whom he labeled "burned out") to the field of psychotherapy and its practitioners. Little did they realize at the time the lasting impact that this would have on the profession. During the past decade, there has been a growing wave of research into the process of burnout as it relates to the work of psychotherapists and human service professionals, as well as members of numerous other career groups in the "helping professions." While many issues are yet to be resolved, it appears that the profession of psychotherapy is beginning to confront the phenomenon of burnout among its membership.

History

Farber (1983a, 1983d) provides an excellent narrative of the developmental history of the concept of burnout which will be only briefly summarized here. Freudenberger (1974,1975) is credited with being the first individual to use the 1960s drug culture term "burned out" to describe the process of physical and emotional depletion resulting from a variety of detrimental work-related conditions which he observed among the staff of alternative health care agencies. As a trained psychoanalyst he went on to apply this concept to psychotherapists who evidenced similar physical and emotional symptoms associated with depletion and despondency. Meanwhile, Maslach (1976) and Pines (1980), social psychologists at the University of California at Berkeley, began to apply a more empirical conceptualization of burnout to a wide variety of occupational groups. Farber (1983d) notes that these three individuals pioneered early efforts to determine the etiology, course of development, treatment, and prevention of burnout among human service providers. As a result of their efforts, a substantial amount has been learned about this phenomenon and its impact on various occupational groups, including psychotherapists.

Definition

Over the years a variety of definitions have been given for the term burnout. Freudenberger and Richelson (1980) define burnout as a "state of fatigue or frustration brought about by devotion to a way of life, or relationship, that has failed to produce the expected reward" (p. 13). Pines and Maslach (1978) define it as "a syndrome of physical and emotional exhaustion, involving the development of negative self-concept, negative job attitudes, and loss of concern and feelings for clients " (p. 233). Perlman and Hartman (1982) define burnout as a response to chronic emotional stress characterized by emotional and/or physical exhaustion, lowered productivity, and excessuve depersonalization of clients and co-workers. Finally, Edelwich and Brodsky (1980) define it as a "progressive loss of idealism, energy, purpose, and concern as a result of conditions of work" (p. 14).

These various definitions of burnout demonstrate that it is considered to be both a process and a state or condition. In other words, while some prefer to emphasize the process of "burning out," others choose to focus on "burned out" as a separate entity or syndrome. Either way, the result appears to be the same. Work-related factors contribute to noticeable decline in job performance and a marked decrease in pleasure derived from interpersonal relationships both inside and outside of work.

Symptoms

In view of the scope of the various definitions of burnout, a review of the symptoms of burnout may be helpful for clarifying both the process and dimension of this phenomenon. Investigators have attempted to isolate those symptoms most characteristic of burnout. While some had hoped to reduce the list to a few well-defined and clearly observable traits, most researchers agree that the condition of burnout among psychotherapists is characterized by a wide array of symptoms. For clarity of presentation, these are typically categorized as cognitive, affective, behavioral, physical, and relational.

Cognitive

Individuals succumbing to burnout are likely to manifest a particular cognitive style. Freudenberger (1975) characterizes such individuals as increasingly intolerant, rigid, inflexible, and closed to new input. There is also likely to be a decrease in capacity for ambiguity and an increase in detachment, defensiveness, cynicism, pessimism, suspicion, depersonalization, boredom, omnipotence, and a hypercritical attitude (Patrick, 1979; Watkins, 1983). In more serious cases, there may even be blatant paranoia (Freudenberger, 1975). Such cognitive changes are considered by some to be attempts to regain a sense of personal control over life events and inner experience (Watkins, 1983). Therapists experiencing such symptoms are likely to find it increasingly difficult to be patient, tolerant, and accepting of patients. Furthermore, there may be renewed doubts concerning efficacy of treatment and personal competency (Farber, 1983a).

Affective

The emotional changes accompanying the onset of burnout can be very troubling and profound. Affective symptoms include an increase in depression and despondency, loneliness, fearfulness, emotional exhaustion and depletion, guilt, irritability, helplessness, tension, anger, loss of control, and self-doubt (Freudenberger, 1975; Watkins, 1983). Along with these feelings comes a desire to withdraw from and avoid both clients and colleagues. Psychotherapists undergoing such affective changes may find it increasingly difficult to experience care and concern for their clients. Instead, they are likely to withdraw by regarding them in an impersonal, highly clinical fashion. Furthermore, there may be an increase in emotional detachment and compartmentalization (Farber, 1983a).

Behavioral

The impact of burnout on the individual's behavior varies widely, depending on a host of personal and environmental variables. Some individuals evidence a decline in productivity, become bored and distractible, and wander around the work site aimlessly as though looking for something to catch their interest. There may also be an increase in complaining, arguing, and aggressive behavior at home and work. Some individuals increase their consumption of food, caffeine, alcohol, tobacco, medications, or illicit drugs. Finally, there may be a noticeable increase in risk-taking behavior and proneness to accidents (Carrol & White, 1982; Freudenberger, 1975). Psychotherapists exhibiting such tendencies sometimes dramatically alter their style of conducting therapy, regardless of its impact on particular patients. In addition, they may find therapeutic interactions to be increasingly dissatisfying, causing them to be easily distracted by movements, noises, or interfering thoughts.

Physical

Individuals experiencing burnout are likely to evidence several observable physical symptoms. These include chronic fatigue, exhaustion, sleep disturbance, muscle tension, and increased illness. There may also be the reoccurrence of preexisting medical disorders such as high blood pressure, insomnia, headaches, lower back pain, asthma, and allergies. Finally, there may be an increased susceptibility to a variety of gastrointestinal problems, muscular pain, and weight changes (Carrol & White, 1982; Patrick, 1979). Therapists experiencing these symptoms are likely to find it increasingly difficult to conduct psychotherapy due to a decrease in stamina and energy and an increase in personal physical discomfort and illness.

Relational

Psychotherapists experiencing burnout will begin to relate to individuals differently, both in and outside of the consulting office. There is likely to be a loss of pleasure associated with their relationships, making it difficult for them to communicate with others (Freudenberger & Robbins, 1979). As a result, he or she may begin to relate in a mechanical, highly contrived manner which leads to increasing withdrawal and isolation. An increase in interpersonal conflicts often occurs, since the individual tends to misperceive and misinterpret the motives and feelings of others (Freudenberger, 1975; Watkins, 1983). Consequently the psychotherapist experiencing burnout is likely to have a great deal of difficulty relating satisfactorily with patients, colleagues, family, and friends.

In view of the many symptoms and expressions of burnout, one might expect that it is a relatively easy process to identify individuals suffering from this syndrome. Unfortunately this is not the case. As Farber (1983a) notes:

> Despite the general unanimity of opinion regarding some of the characteristics of burnout, the determination of whether a worker is or is not burned out is not easily made. Burnout does not seem to lend itself to such clear dichotomies - in part, because burnout is a process rather than an event. Nor is burnout identical for each person. (p. 3)

It would appear that the various definitions of burnout and the wide array of symptoms associated with this complex phenomenon further complicate efforts to understand this syndrome. Rather than considering it to be a clearly identifiable state or condition, it seems most productive to view it as a process which is uniquely experienced by each individual as a result of a blend of personal and environmental factors. Consequently the phenomenon of burnout in a given individual is expressed by symptoms specific to the particular factors involved.

Incidence of Burnout Among Psychotherapists

Few studies could be found which set out to determine the actual incidence of burnout among psychotherapists. Most researchers preferred to investigate its causes and symptoms. However, Farber (1985b) reports that the overall incidence of burnout among the psychotherapists he surveyed, as reflected in their total scores on the Maslach Burnout Inventory (Maslach & Jackson, 1978), was approximately 6%. The Maslach Inventory assesses levels of emotional exhaustion, depersonalization, and personal accomplishment. When considering these particular variables individually, however, the subjective experience of burnout among those surveyed may have been somewhat higher than total scores and mean averages would suggest. For example, nearly 19% scored in the moderate range of the "emotional exhaustion" subscale, while an additional 6% scored in the high range. Those scoring in the moderate range on the "depersonalization" subscale comprised 24% of those surveyed, while 2.3% scored in the high range. Finally, those scoring in the moderate burnout range of the subscale "personal accomplishment" totaled nearly 37% while an additional 19% scored in the high range. Thus although psychotherapists as a group tended to score lower than other professional groups on the various burnout scales, a substantial percentage appeared to be experiencing at least moderate levels of burnout in each of the three individual dimensions.

As mentioned in Chapter 6, psychotherapists surveyed by Wood et al. (1985) reported that they believe therapists are experiencing burnout at a worrisome rate. When asked about impaired practitioners whose work has been affected by depression and burnout, 75% indicated that they believed this to be a "somewhat serious" to "very serious" problem. Sixty-three percent admitted that they knew of a colleague whose work had been impaired by this phenomenon. As a group, those surveyed estimated that approximately 26% of their colleagues were suffering from symptoms related to depression and burnout. Finally, over 32% acknowledged that they themselves had experienced burnout or depression serious enough to interfere with their ability to work. Because the label depression was regrettably combined with that of burnout in this survey, it is impossible to determine the incidence of either individual variable. However, it seems reasonable to conclude that these therapists believed burnout to be a phenomenom of substantial proportions.

It may be that the complexity of the symptoms and definitions associated with the concept of burnout has hindered efforts to determine its incidence among practicing therapists. As a result, one can only speculate as to the actual extent of the problem. If Freudenberger and Robbins (1979) are correct, an increasing number of psychotherapists are experiencing burnout serious enough to impact their professional work and their personal life and relationships.

Factors Contributing to Burnout

In view of the potentially debilitating effects of burnout on the life and work of the therapist, it is not surprising to learn that much of the research conducted in this area has focused on isolating the factors which contribute to this phenomenon. Certainly, if burnout is to be prevented and its victims rehabilitated, it is first necessary to determine its underlying causes. As can be imagined, the complexity of the various definitions and symptoms associated with burnout complicate efforts to clarify its etiology. Nonetheless, there is a growing body of literature which describes the many variables associated with the onset and therapist burnout.

Before discussing the specific factors found to contribute to the development of burnout, it is first necessary to consider its etiology and development in more general terms. As mentioned at the beginning of this chapter, Freudenberger and Robbins (1979) were the first to describe the process of burnout as it occurs among psychotherapists. They suggested that the impact of the various stresses associated with clinical practice can combine to create a burnt out individual who is no longer able to derive satisfaction and pleasure from interpersonal relationships with patients, colleagues, family, or friends. The implication of their comments seems to be that the same stressors which can create a sense of career dissatisfaction can also lead to the experience of burnout.

As Farber (1983a) notes, this conceptualization of burnout has been a very popular one, whereby the concept of stress is equated or confused with that of burnout. This is unfortunate since it distorts the meaning of both terms. While very similar in meaning, stress and burnout are not identical concepts. Stress, in an of itself, is not necessarily detrimental. As a result of the work of Selye (1956), it is now widely recognized that stress can have positive effects if it is not excessive. When an individual is not overwhelmed by the demands of the environment, stress can be motivating and exciting. Even when the stress is more aversive than energizing, if it occurs in tolerable amounts it may have little lasting impact on the individual's sense of well-being. Certainly some degree of stress is likely to be unavoidable in a career in psychotherapy. Even those who report being satisfied with their work as therapists acknowledge that they experience certain aspects of the job as stressful and aversive. However, stress and feelings of dissatisfaction do not create burnout in every case.

Rather than equating stress, a universal experience among psychotherapists, with burnout, a phenomenon experienced by a minority of practitioners, it is more accurate to view burnout as a result of unmediated, unrelenting stress and dissatisfaction (Farber, 1983a). In other words, if an individual's personal resources are chronically overwhelmed by environmental demands, it is likely that he or she will eventually experience burnout. Farber describes burnout as the "final step in a progression of unsuccessful attempts to cope with a variety of negative stress conditions" (1983a, p. 15). It is a state of utter despair and exhaustion resulting from the cumulative impact of a host of stressors and aversive aspects related to therapeutic practice. Thus job-related stress does not necessarily lead to burnout in all cases. Furthermore, feelings of career dissatisfaction do not automatically reflect the presence of burnout. Instead, it is the chronic experience of high levels of stress and dissatisfaction that is likely to result in eventual burnout if steps are not taken to bring relief and replenishment.

Given this conceptualization of the etiology of burnout, the discussion can now turn to highlighting the multitude of factors which have been found to contribute to burnout among practicing therapists. These include variables related to the personality of the therapist, patient characteristics, work-related factors, and societal attitudes.

Personality of the Psychotherapist

Several authors have identified personality factors which have been found to contribute to the potential for eventual burnout among psychotherapists. Once again, it is important to remember that no one factor "causes" burnout. Instead, it is typically the accumulation of stress and dissatisfaction resulting from one or more of these variables which can precipitate eventual burnout in the therapist.

Individuals who tend to be loners seem more prone to burnout than those who are able to utilize interpersonal relationships as sources of pleasure and replenishment (Farber, 1983a; Freudenberger, 1975; Freudenberger & Robbins, 1979). A tendency toward withdrawal and isolation outside of work seems to increase individual vulnerability towards work-related burnout and discouragement. Chessick (1978) notes that satisfying and intimate personal relationships outside of the consulting office are necessary in order to encourage, replenish, and strengthen the therapist's capacity for functioning within therapeutic relationships. As Farber (1983a) states, "satisfying relationships with family and friends produce a support network that mitigates the impact of work-related stresses" (p. 5). If the practitioner lacks sufficient opportunities to relax and unwind with others, he or she may be vulnerable to eventual burnout. Thus those who prefer to be more isolated and withdrawn in their personal life may be more susceptible to the effects of professional burnout.

Individuals who tend to be overly idealistic, dedicated, and people-oriented also seem to be vulnerable to eventual burnout (Freudenberger, 1975). Such individuals are likely to sacrifice their own needs and concerns for the benefit of others, even when this results in physical or emotional harm to themselves. It is not commitment that is the problem here; it is overcommitment and inappropriate levels of dedication that increase the chances of eventual burnout. Those who have a tendency to lose their own identity, immersing themselves in the lives and problems of their patients, may eventually find their inner resources depleted (Freudenberger & Robbins, 1979). The idealism, dedication, and enthusiasm present in earlier years begin to wane, leaving discouragement and despondency in their place. Individuals who were once willing to make great personal sacrifices for their patients may eventually find that their resources and "love" have been used up after years of practice, resulting in burnout and despair.

Related to excessive idealism and dedication is the tendency for some individuals to harbor excessively high self-expectations regarding their own clinical performance and abilities. They simply expect too much of themselves. When they are unable to meet these unrealistic expectations, burnout is the possible outcome. For example, Deutsch (1984) identified several irrational beliefs held by practicing psychotherapists which were found to be sources of significant stress. These included, in descending degree of stress experienced, the expectation to be able to work at a peak level of enthusiasm and competence at all times, handle effectively all client emergencies, help every client, assume personal blame for treatment failures, work without time off when clients are in need, consider the job to be one's "life," work with every client, serve as a perfect model of mental health, be on call 24 hours per day, place client needs before one's own, be the most important person in every client's life, assume personal responsibility for client behavior, and have the ability to control clients' lives. Individuals who harbor a sufficient number of these unrealistic personal expectations are likely candidates for eventual burnout. Failure to achieve these goals is a difficult experience for some individuals, particularly if such expectations are motivated by guilt, grandiosity, or personal need (Freudenberger, 1975).

Psychotherapists who tend to be authoritarian and controlling seem to be prone to the onset of burnout (Freudenberger, 1975; Pines, 1980). This personality characteristic is likely to motivate the person to attempt to "do everything" himself or herself, resisting the need to delegate responsibility to others. Such individuals may experience frustration and discouragement at their inability to control fully the lives and behaviors of their patients. It is difficult to accept the limitations inherent in the role of therapist if there is a personal need on the part of the therapist to assume full responsibility and control in the lives of clients. Furthermore, such individuals are likely to become increasingly discouraged and resentful as a result of the tendency for some patients to disregard their advice, suggestions, and directives regularly. Therapists who are authoritarian and controlling by nature may find that burnout eventually sets in as a result of the chronic frustration of such needs by therapy patients. Even when patients submit to the therapist's need to dominate and control, the rest of the world simply will not. The responsibility of sustaining the well-being of a caseload of clients soon becomes an overwhelming task in the face of the vicissitudes and randomness of life events.

Individuals who are driven by the need to give to others due to a longing for intimacy and closeness are also likely to experience growing discouragement and despondency, leading to eventual burnout (Farber, 1983a; Pines, 1980). This is a particular problem for some psychotherapists. In Chapter 1, it was noted that some individuals enter the profession of psychotherapy out of a desire to experience intimacy and closeness with others. These candidates are typically lonely and socially isolated, making the interpersonal encounters characteristic of the therapy relationship attractive. Following their entry into the profession, they often discover that the isolation, one-way intimacy, and distorted interactions associated with the practice of psychotherapy do not satisfy these longings and needs. To the contrary, they often exacerbate the underlying sense of aloneness, creating even greater alienation and social withdrawal. As discussed in Chapters

3 and 4, the very nature of the therapy relationship, with its emphasis on therapist abstinence and patient individuation and departure, can leave the therapist feeling increasingly detached and isolated from others over the course of professional practice. If the individual has not found other ways to satisfy the longing for intimacy which motivated this career choice, the experience of stress and dissatisfaction may reach a level sufficient enough to result in burnout.

Farber (1983a) suggests that "type A" personalities have a greater tendency to develop burnout than "type B" individuals. Therapists who tend to be aggressive, competitive, intense, moody, and driven are more likely to experience stress and anger when they perceive that their efforts to assist others are sometimes unsuccessful or ineffective. Also, the tendency for some patients to undermine or sabotage their own progress may be an additional source of distress for such therapists. If type A clinicians find that they are unable to achieve the level of success necessary for satisfaction and fulfillment, the resultant discouragement and frustration may precipitate eventual burnout. As Farber notes, it is often the expectations, attitudes, perceptions, and beliefs which differ between type A and type B individuals rather than the objective experience of stress. Burnout results from the manner in which the personality style interacts with the factors associated with professional practice, leaving type A individuals most vulnerable.

Finally, personality changes resulting from the impact of significant events in the life of the psychotherapist may produce burnout in individuals formerly immune to this problem (Farber, 1983a). The emotional impact of events such as divorce, loss of a loved one, personal illness or accident, or any one of a number of other misfortunes may be enough to shift the balance towards feelings of personal despondency, defeat, and despair. In such cases the previously satisfied and effective therapist may succumb to the effects of burnout. In addition, Farber notes that the typically stressful periods of transition and crisis resulting from predictable developmental changes during adult life as identified by Levinson (1978), may increase the potential for eventual burnout if sufficiently prolonged and intense. Thus during certain times of transition the practicing psychotherapist may be vulnerable to the onset of burnout if associated conflicts and problems are not effectively resolved in a timely manner.

There are a number of factors related to the personality of the individual which can increase the potential for burnout. While no particular variable can be identified as the "cause" of burnout among psychotherapists, the presence of one or more of these personality characteristics increases the potential for the onset of burnout if the resultant job-related stress and dissatisfaction reach sufficient levels. Nor are personality characteristics alone likely to "cause" burnout. Instead, they merely increase the potential for its onset.

Patient Characteristics

In addition to the contributing factors associated with the personality of the psychotherapist, several patient variables have been identified as sources of stress sufficient enough to increase the potential for burnout if their impact remains unmediated and intense (Farber, 1983c). Among a long list of patient characteristics contributing to therapist stress are suicidal threats, aggression and hostility, premature termination, and various symptoms associated with more serious forms of psychopathology.

Psychotherapists typically rate patient suicidal threats as the most stressful client behavior encountered in clinical practice (Deutsch, 1984; Farber, 1983c; Hellman et al., 1986). In one survey (Farber & Heifetz, 1981) 85% of the therapists surveyed indicated that suicidal statements were at least moderately stressful. This factor typically includes patient suicidal statements, gestures, and ideation. More than any other patient variable, it is the risk of suicide that is the source of greatest distress and worry for the clinician. The complicated moral, ethical, emotional, and legal aspects of this issue seem to weigh heavily on the minds of clinicians, contributing to high levels of stress or anxiety when one or more patients exhibit suidical tendencies. Consistent with previous formulations regarding the etiology of burnout, one would assume that practitioners working with large numbers of such patients over an extended period of time will be most likely to develop eventual burnout.

Patient expressions of hostility and aggression were reported to be the second greatest source of personal stress among psychiatrists, psychologists, and social workers surveyed by Farber and Heifetz (1981). A total of 70% of those questioned by Farber and Heifetz indicated that such behavior was experienced to be at least moderately stressful by the therapist. This finding was replicated by Deutsch (1984) who reports that expressions of anger toward the therapist was the second greatest source of stress among psychotherapists surveyed. It would appear that clinicians find it difficult to endure verbal attacks of patients and hostile and aggressive actions. This experience of stress is not limited to overt patient anger or aggression. Hellman et al. (1986) found that covert, passive–aggressive behavior on the part of patients was one of five major sources of stress reported by the therapists participating in their investigation. More subtle forms of anger and aggression found to be stressful included defensive withholding and withdrawal, passive–aggressive behaviors directed at the therapist, and statements overly idealizing the clinician. A second major factor, labeled "resistances," was found by Hellman et al. to be a significant source of therapist stress. This included such patient behaviors as missed appointments, tardiness, erratic payment of fees, reluctance to leave at the end of the hour, phone calls to places other than the therapist's office, and denial. All of these behaviors have been identified as typical indirect expressions of patient anger and aggression. Thus it would appear that psychotherapists find patient aggression and hostility, in both overt and covert forms of expression, to be very stressful. Once again, if this patient variable results in sufficient stress over a prolonged period of time, the psychotherapist is likely to experience the onset of burnout.

Farber (1983c) reports that patient premature termination was the third greatest source of therapist stress cited by those practitioners surveyed. This finding was again replicated by Deutsch (1984), who found that those she interviewed ranked premature termination as the fifth greatest source of work-related frustration and stress. Therapists apparently find the untimely departure of patients to be a very difficult experience. Whether this is due to resultant feelings of failure, abandonment, disappointment, hurt, rejection, or betrayal remains to be determined. It is easy to imagine that therapists who find client attrition to be stressful are likely to experience burnout if it occurs too frequently.

Factor analysis of 25 patient behaviors identified by practicing psychotherapists as significant sources of therapist stress, conducted by Farber and Heifetz (1981), revealed that 36.4% of the total variance was accounted for by the factor labeled "overt psychopatholgy." This variable included agitated anxiety [cited as the fourth greatest source of stress in Farber's (1983c) study], apathy and depression (cited as the fifth major source of therapist stress), and other assorted variables including impulsive behavior, compulsive behavior, psychopathic behavior, paranoid delusions, hypersensitivity, and schizoid detachment. Hellman et al. (1986) report a similar finding, noting that these very same symptoms comprised the third major source of stress among those surveyed in their investigation. This pattern was also confirmed by Deutsch (1984) who noted that severe depression and apparent apathy or lack of motivation were the third and fourth major sources of therapist stress reported by practicing psychotherapists.

As nearly all therapists will readily admit, working with emotionally troubled patients can at times be a difficult experience. It is not unusual for the practitioner to wonder, at times of particular frustration, why clients can't be more reasonable, considerate, patient, and grateful. This complaint is usually followed by an insightful smile as the therapist realizes that it is for this very reason that they have presented themselves for assistance and treatment. However, while unavoidable, such interactions can take their toll on the well-being of the therapist. If the stress associated with certain patient behaviors becomes sufficiently frequent, intense, or chronic, therapist burnout can result.

As was the case with psychotherapist personality variables found to be contributing factors in the etiology of burnout, individual patient characteristics and behaviors are not likely alone to precipitate the onset of burnout in most practicing therapists. In the same manner, patient variables as a group may not be sufficient to result in therapist burnout. However, the interaction between certain patient variables and therapist personality characteristics can result in levels of stress and dissatisfaction sufficiently intense and prolonged to increase the potential of eventual burnout. Yet other additional factors are likely to contribute to this unfortunate outcome as well.

Work-Related Factors

Farber (1983a) presents a comprehensive summary of work-related factors which have been found to promote burnout among various groups of human service providers. He identifies four major factors: role ambiguity, role conflict, role overload, and inconsequentiality. Each of these variables have the potential to increase psychotherapist stress and career dissatisfaction to levels which increase the likelihood of burnout.

Role ambiguity is associated with a "lack of clarity regarding a worker's rights, responsibilities, methods, goals, status, or accountability" (Farber, 1983a, p. 6). Additional factors found to contribute to role ambiguity include rapid organizational change and increasing complexity of tasks and technology. Psychotherapists typically encounter a high degree of role ambiguity in their work. There is widespread disagreement over what is entailed in the practice of psychotherapy (Schlicht, 1968). Furthermore, complex decisions regarding choice of discipline, degree, theoretical orientation, speciality, and work site further blur role definition. It is not unusual for a psychotherapist-in-training to receive a graduate degree and still experience confusion regarding what factors bring about successful therapeutic change. This may cause the neophyte clinician to feel like a fraud or charlatan when conducting psychotherapy. Therapists typically work without receiving adequate feedback regarding professional performance and competency (Marston, 1984). They also often harbor secret doubts about the efficacy of treatment. The lack of role definition encountered by practicing psychotherapists has the potential to be a major source of stress. In addition, conducting psychotherapy is often a complex, very slow moving process which is difficult to monitor and evaluate. This serves to increase therapist ambiguity regarding his or her role in the ongoing therapeutic process. Hellman et al. (1986) also found that the factor labeled "professional doubt" was the third greatest source of stress among those therapists surveyed. This variable included such factors as doubts about the efficacy of psychotherapy, difficulty evaluating personal competency, frustrations with insufficient success, and slow and erratic work pace.

Role conflict is reported by Farber (1983a) to occur "when inconsistent, incompatible, or inappropriate demands are placed onan individual" (p. 6). This can express itself in several ways. For example, within the therapeutic encounter the clinician may experience the impulse to relate to a client in a variety of contradictory or conflicting ways such as parent, friend, lover, sibling, employer, employee, mentor, or judge. Role ambiguity only serves to increase the potential of such conflicts, as the therapist attempts to determine which approach will be most appropriate and helpful for the client. Negotiating these role conflicts (both internally and in cooperation with individual clients) can be a stressful experience for some psychotherapists. Role conflicts can also be experienced outside of the therapeutic encounter. For example, the practicing therapist may be forced to serve as administrator, teacher, supervisor, mentor, business executive, investor, landlord, or team player, depending on the work environment. Each of the multiple roles can be incompatible at times, with that of psychotherapist/ humanitarian. For example, being forced to terminate treatment with a patient due to lack of sufficient funds may make perfect business sense but feel traumatic to the sensitive therapist. Role conflicts can also occur as a result of political and territorial disputes, as often occur among psychotherapists representing various disciplines who strive to carve out areas of jurisdiction and clarify self-definition (Farber, 1983a). The potential for role conflicts to arise is further increased by conflicting individual, familial, social, and patient-related needs and priorities which confront the therapist. In view of these potential role conflicts, it is not surprizing that Hellman et al. (1986) found several of those examples mentioned previously to be sources a significant stress among those psychotherapists surveyed. Certainly if the experience of stress resulting from role conflicts becomes intense and chronic enough, burnout may result.

Role overload involves both quantitative and qualitative factors which have the potential to create significant stress. While having too much to do is an obvious example of role overload, it is possible for increasingly complex tasks which require skills or abilities not possessed by the individual in question to precipitate burnout as well. Psychotherapists are prone to overwork, increasing the potential for many to experience role overload. For these individuals there are simply too many patients and too little time. Ever increasing administrative duties crowd in on those working in institutional settings. The constant stream of new referrals and former patients who return for further treatment tax the therapist's energy and abilities. This is a particular problem for those who find it difficult to say "no" to patients requesting additional sessions and valued referral sources requesting that the practitioner find time to squeeze in "just one more patient." Helpers find it difficult to stop offering to "help," even after their ability to do so has long since been exhausted. Yet there can be a qualitative aspect to role overload as well. The complexity of the psychotherapeutic task seems overwhelming to many psychotherapist-in-training who, despite their fears to the contrary, eventually become proficient in a particular treatment modality. The real overload comes with the need to update clinical knowledge and techniques in response to the ongoing advances in the field. For example, those trained in psychoanalytic approaches may find it too difficult to broaden their clinical armamentarium to include biofeedback, cognitive therapy, short-term treatment modalities, and behavioral techniques. Rapid innovations have given rise to the widespread belief that advances in the field of psychotherapy make information learned more than eight years ago obsolete.

Hellman et al. (1986) report that factors labeled as "scheduling" and "work overinvolvement" account for nearly 19% of the variance in the ratings of sources of therapist stress. These factors included variables associated with quantitative and qualitative aspects of role overload, as described previously. In another study by Farber and Heifetz (1982), a heterogeneous sample of psychotherapists reported that "excessive workload" was the single most stressful aspect of clinical work. Thus practicing psychotherapists appear to be vulnerable to both the quantitative and qualitative aspects of role overload. If this factor contributes sufficient stress, burnout can result.

Finally, Farber (1983a) identifies feelings of inconsequentiality as a fourth major source of work-related factors contributing to burnout. Farber describes this experience as

a feeling on the part of professionals that no matter how hard they work, the payoffs in terms of accomplishment, recognition, advancement, or appreciation, are not there . . .

individuals feel that their actions can no longer effect desired changes in the environment and that, therefore, there is no point in continuing to try. (p. 6)

As mentioned previously, the practice of psychotherapy is difficult, slow work. While it sometimes results in dramatic, highly evident changes, most therapists admit that they have had to accept the fact that few therapy patients will experience significant changes over a short period of time, if ever (Bugental, 1964). This leaves some struggling with feelings of inconsequentiality. As Garfield and Bergin (1978) note, some therapy patients experience only marginal growth or change. Others experience no benefits at all. Unfortunately a few even become more troubled as a result. The practicing therapist may unwittingly become discouraged, as he or she takes the blame for treatment failures and yet is hesitant to claim responsibility for apparent successes. Farber and Heifetz (1982) report that 74% of psychotherapists surveyed cited a lack of therapeutic success as one of the most stressful aspects of clinical practice. It would appear that many therapists occasionally question the efficacy and importance of their efforts. It is not surprising that psychotherapists struggle with such feelings of inconsequentiality in view of research reports which suggest that some patients experience a greater reduction of symptoms without treatment (Hellman et al., 1986). If such feelings become prominent enough, the therapist is likely to experience burnout and a profound sense of futility (Kottler, 1986).

In addition to the four primary work-related factors which Farber suggests contribute to the onset of burnout, several other aspects of clinical practice have been identified as sources of therapist stress. The potentially negative impact of physical and psychic isolation, nonreciprocated attentiveness, emotional constraint, physical inactivity, personal abstinence, growing feelings of omnipotence, incessant psychological-mindedness, vicarious living, emotional withdrawal and depletion, physical exhaustion, and financial instability associated with the practice of psychotherapy are additional sources of therapist stress with the potential to precipitate eventual burnout in the practicing psychotherapist.

Societal Attitudes

Variables related to the personality of the psychotherapist, patient characteristics, and work-related factors which contribute to the development of burnout occur within a larger context of societal values and attitudes. Farber (1983a) suggests that the impact of capitalism and the increase in competitive individualism serves to alienate American workers from their communities. Furthermore, he maintains that there is a growing insistence on attaining personal fulfillment and gratification from one's career which reflects a rather narcissistic, self-absorbed orientation. These pervasive societal values seem to interact with several factors directly related to the practice of psychotherapy, increasing the potential for the development of burnout. For example, psychotherapists derive much of their sense of accomplishment from the success of their treatment. However, progress is usually slow and somewhat unpredictable, often depending on a host of patient-related variables beyond the direct control of the practitioner. Dramatic, remarkable treatment successes are a rare occurrence. Thus the sense of career fulfillment and gratification valued by society may occur less frequently than desirable, leaving the therapist increasingly vulnerable to discouragement, dissatisfaction, and eventual burnout. If the therapist works in isolation, without the benefit of a sense of community support and encouragement, the risk of disillusionment is even greater. While such speculations are difficult to prove, they are thought-provoking. Perhaps American society's emphasis on individualism, personal achievement, and competition is not conducive to the practice of psychotherapy. Rather than facilitating this endeavor, perhaps such attitudes hinder good career adjustment or even increase the likelihood of eventual burnout.

Societal attitudes related to public stereotypes concerning the role of psychotherapists may further contribute to eventual disillusionment and burnout. As mentioned in Chapters 3 and 4, psychotherapists are viewed in a variety of ways which sometimes distort and sabotage their participation in and enjoyment of interpersonal relationships outside of the office. For example, some individuals view therapists in an unrealistically positive light. They consider them to be "special" people who are saint-like and self-sacrificing. Those who view psychotherapists in this manner expect them to be able to bear the psychic pain of society with little or no difficulty. Furthermore, their expectations of emotional stability and professional competency are often highly unrealistic. Added to this orientation is society's assorted expectations concerning the "human service professional," which emphasize the giving, altruistic, and zealous qualities characteristic of the Peace Corps (Farber, 1983a). These attitudes combine to portray the therapist in a highly idealized manner which has the potential to become burdensome and overwhelming to the clinician who secretly harbors many of the same expectations and a messiahlike desire to help others. The potential for discouragement and burnout increases for those who are unable to remain realistic about their own abilities and the limitations of their profession. Therapists who come to believe that they have been called to be society's "psychic saviour" are highly vulnerable to eventual despair. The isolation and interpersonal alienation which sometimes results can imprison the psychotherapist in a profound sense of loneliness and disillusionment.

In much the same way, those who view psychotherapists in an unfairly negative and derogatory manner increase their potential for discouragement and burnout. The marginal status of the profession reflects the tendency for some to consider therapists to be opportunists who prostitute their caring, earning an income off the vulnerability and emotional pain of others. This perspective portrays them as voyeurs who breed dependency and exploit unsuspecting clients. Furthermore, the profession of psychotherapy is regarded by such individuals as harmless quackery at best, and dangerous mind control at worst. These negative societal attitudes fuel therapists' secret doubts regarding the efficacy of treatment and the adequacy of their personal competency. As a result, psychotherapists who are unable to maintain a balanced perspective about their abilities and the value of their profession become vulnerable to burnout and career dissatisfaction. The tendency to become apologetic and embarrassed about one's career makes it even more difficult to cope with occasional public criticisms and media attacks regarding its usefulness and value.

Summary

Once again, it seems best to avoid either/or conceptualizations regarding the etiology of burnout. No one factor is likely to be sufficient by itself to cause psychotherapist burnout. Instead, it is most useful to consider the host of causes which seem to contribute to this outcome. Furthermore, as Cherniss (1980) points out, burnout is most likely the result of a complex interaction among individual, organizational, and societal factors. Thus the continued emphasis on work-related factors as the primary cause of burnout is destined to be inadequate and superficial (Farber, 1983a). It appears that it is most appropriate to suggest that burnout results from an interaction among the personality traits of the therapist, patient characteristics, work-related factors, and societal attitudes. Therapist stress and dissatisfaction associated with these factors precipitate the eventual onset of burnout when they have reached levels sufficiently aversive and chronic to destroy the therapist's motivation and sense of commitment to the therapeutic endeavor.

Fortunately, only a relative minority of psychotherapists seem to experience burnout serious enough to render them incapacitated or impaired. However, the lines of demarcation between therapist stress, dissatisfaction, burnout, and impairment are often very blurred. Since it is useful to view burnout as a process as well as an identifiable syndrome or condition, psychotherapists are likely to fall at a variety of points along a continuum, with some being more burned out than others. As a result, programs for its prevention and treatment are considered to be increasingly important for the well-being of all those practicing psychotherapy.

PREVENTION AND TREATMENT OF BURNOUT

Due to confusion regarding definitions of burnout, its actual incidence, and variety of causes, efforts to isolate interventions most helpful for its prevention and treatment have been less than successful. However, the research and experience of several in the field have resulted in the utilization of a variety of interventions which have met with varying degrees of success. For the most part, these efforts have focused on reducing levels of therapist stress and dissatisfaction in both professional and personal life.

Education

As in the case of the other forms of therapist impairment or disability, alerting practicing therapists to the symptoms and risks associated with the development of burnout is a critical first step towards its prevention and early treatment (Freudenberger, 1975). Increased self-awareness and self-monitoring allow the clinician to assess past, current, and future levels of stress and dissatisfaction in order to motivate further steps toward remediation and rehabilitation. Since burnout seems to be the result of unmediated stress and discouragement (Farber, 1983a), efforts to alert clinicians to its early signs and symptoms are likely to decrease the likelihood of their overlooking its impact. Recent publicity and exposure of the phenomenon of burnout have made it a somewhat trendy, overused concept in popular vernacular. Nonetheless, some psychotherapists continue to underestimate its potential to sabotage their personal and professional functioning insidiously. As a result, increased efforts to educate practitioners seem warranted.

Ideally, training programs preparing individuals for the practice of therapy will include classes or seminars concerning the phenomenon of burnout in their curriculum (Farber & Heifetz, 1982). This would provide future therapists with the ability to identify its onset and take appropriate steps to neutralize its impact. However, since this is not likely to occur in all (or even perhaps most) graduate programs, it may be necessary for the profession of psychotherapy to expose its practitioners to this information by means of journal articles, bulletins, seminars, and workshops. Ongoing continuing education programs would do well to include an emphasis on the identification and remediation of burnout among psychotherapists.

Continuing education need not be limited to the topic of burnout to be of use in combating career-related discouragement and dissatisfaction. On the contrary, regular continuing education on a variety of subjects related to the practice of psychotherapy is likely to provide stimulation and renewal to clinicians, thereby decreasing the potential for disillusionment and burnout to develop (McCarley, 1975). While psychiatry has adopted an aggressive continuing education requirement for its practitioners, the other disciplines represented in the profession of psychotherapy have been slow to require regular ongoing training for its practitioners. As a result many therapists fail to avail themselves to the benefits of ongoing continuing education. For example, Guy, Stark, and Poelstra (1987) found that over 42% of those therapists surveyed had failed to participate in any form of approved continuing education during the previous year. It may be necessary to establish more stringent requirements in order to ensure that all therapists receive exposure to recent advances in the field on a regular basis. In addition to improving competency, such a program would be useful in reducing the potential for burnout.

Personal Psychotherapy and Supervision

It is not surprising to find that personal psychotherapy and/or supervision are frequently recommended as effective interventions for the prevention and treatment of therapist burnout (Farber, 1983a). Personal therapy provides an opportunity for self-awareness, self-assessment, rejuvenation, reality testing, and replenishment. With the help of a skilled psychotherapist, the clinician is likely to have a opportunity to identify the onset of burnout and take appropriate steps to eliminate its negative impact on his or her work and relationships. A wide variety of forms of psychotherapy have been used to treat burnout successfully. For example, Freudenberger (1981) suggests that short-term, goal-specific treatment is a useful form of intervention. Edelwich and Brodsky (1980) report that a more directive, "reality" oriented approach is helpful in assisting psychotherapists to overcome this phenomenon. Treatments designed to reduce therapist stress sometimes focus on cognitive–behavioral and stress-reduction techniques such as systematic desensitization, biofeedback, progressive relaxation training, and meditation (Farber, 1983a). Group therapy has also been identified as a useful intervention for burnout-prone psychotherapists, providing both support and feedback to those experiencing discouragement and dissatisfaction with their life and career (Farber, 1983a). Finally, more long-term, psychodynamic approaches remain a favorite form of treatment to enable the clinician to identify personal vulnerabilities toward discouragement and disillusionment (Ford, 1963).

While personal therapy is helpful in sorting through stresses associated with patient characteristics, work-related factors, and societal attitudes, it is most useful for assisting the therapist to confront and resolve personality traits which predispose him or her toward the development of burnout. For example, if the therapist has tendencies toward social withdrawal, excessive idealism, unrealistic self-expectations, authoritarianism, unmet longings for intimacy, "type A" drivenness, or dysfunctional personality changes related to the impact of a recent life event—all of which were discussed as factors related to the onset of burnout—it may be very helpful to explore and resolve these issues in personal psychotherapy. A personal therapist knowledgable in the process of burnout can be an invaluable resource in its prevention and treatment.

Supervision has also been identified as a useful intervention for therapist burnout (Farber, 1983a). Both individual and group supervision have been found to be a source of support, reality testing, and feedback for the practicing therapist. As a result supervision provides an opportunity to monitor and reduce sources of stress and dissatisfaction associated with a variety of patient characteristics, work-related factors, and societal attitudes (Savicki & Cooley, 1982).

Self-Care

In recognition of the fact that burnout seems to impact all physical and emotional aspects of individual functioning, several authors have suggested that a well-designed program of self-care is perhaps the best intervention for preventing and treating burnout. Pines, Aronson, and Kafry (1981) suggest that the practitioner must develop an attitude of detached concern which provides a degree of objectivity and distance from client problems in order to allow for the exercise of sound professional judgment and adequate self-care. The practitioner must also remain cognizant of his or her potential to lose this perspective, increasing the chance for burnout to develop. Finally, by establishing clear boundaries and taking responsibility for one's actions and feelings, the therapist is able to monitor and correct tendencies toward discouragement and burnout. Thus the way in which clinicians think about their work, and their attitudes and feelings about their role, must be characterized by this sense of perspective in order to reduce the potential for dissatisfaction and disillusionment. If a therapist is unable to alter personal attitudes or expectations sufficiently on their own, personal therapy and/or supervision may be needed to help accomplish this task.

Another aspect of effective self-care involves the importance of physical health and exercise. Adequate opportunities for rest and relaxation are essential for maintaining a sense of well-being and stability (Freudenberger & Robbins, 1979; Shinn, Rosario, Morch, & Chestnut, 1984). Leighton and Roye (1984) suggest that a regular program of exercise for mental health professionals interested in combating professional burnout include aerobic conditioning, flexibilty exercises, and muscle strength and endurance conditioning, as well as a balanced diet. This is certainly no surprise to the sophisticated therapist who often recommends such a regimen to his or her own patients. However, it is encouraging to note that adequate exercise and relaxation do appear to be very effective in reducing burnout among therapists as well. For example, Hoeksema (1986) found that those psychotherapists who regularly participated in various leisure activities consistently scored lower on the Maslach Burnout Inventory (Malsach & Jackson, 1978). Those who appeared to enjoy a well-balanced program of entertainment and exercise tended to report experiencing less burnout.

Other self-care interventions designed to assist therapists in reducing the potential for burnout might include learning time management techniques, the development of interests, hobbies, and activites unrelated to psychotherapy, and integrating adequate time for vacation into the ongoing work schedule. Activities such as these allow the clinician to set aside the role and responsibilities of professional practice in order to rest, recuperate, and replenish depleted resources (Farber, 1983a; Freudenberger & Robbins, 1979; Guy & Liaboe, 1986a). Furthermore, the need for solitude and privacy must also be recognized as an important aspect of an adequate self-care program. Finally, therapists need to provide sufficient periods of unstructured time to allow for the deeper dimension of relaxation to occur, such as that which comes from "pausing" and doing nothing for a few moments.

Interpersonal Involvement

Several authors have suggested that interpersonal involvement with a wide variety of individuals is an important intervention for the prevention and treatment of burnout among psychotherapists (Freudenberger, 1975; Guy & Liaboe, 1986a; Shinn et al., 1984). As mentioned in Chapter 4, it is important that this circle of friends and acquaintances include individuals unrelated to the field of psychotherapy in order to provide a balanced perspective and accurate feedback to the practitioner. Since isolation has been cited as a major source of stress for the therapist (see Chapter 3), the importance of spending time with others cannot be overstated.

Farber (1983a) suggests that social support networks are among the most promising interventions for burnout among human service professionals. Social support has been found to reduce emotional exhaustion, allow for useful venting of feelings, provide for the learning of effective coping skills, reduce the psychological effects of physical stress, and increase a sense of personal adequacy. In addition to combating the debilitating effects of isolation, social support networks appear to be one of the most important interventions for combating therapist burnout.

Professional Involvement

In addition to pursuing personal therapy or supervision, the therapist desiring to prevent burnout may also find it useful to seek out opportunities for interaction with other colleagues in discussion groups designed to provide an environment conducive to mutual support and guidance. This is somewhat different from the aforementioned need for an adequate social support network. In the former case, the emphasis was on establishing and maintaining relationships with individuals outside of the profession, focusing on activities unrelated to the practice of psychotherapy. In the latter case, the emphasis is on the need to create a network of support among other psychotherapists who will be able to provide a dimension of feedback impossible for those outside of the profession. Bellak (1981) suggests that such discussion groups allow for the informal exchange of information, advice, and encouragement among practitioners who well understand the pressures and stresses encountered by their colleagues. Open sharing among peers concerning the limitations of the profession, personal mistakes or shortcomings, and common problems confronted in practice can greatly reduce the stress and dissatisfaction experienced by many therapists.

Reducing Stress Related to Clinical Practice

Since one important factor in the development of burnout involves the unmediated and chronic impact of stress associated with work-related factors and patient characteristics, several steps may be required to minimize their potentially negative impact on the therapist. For example, therapists may find it very helpful to balance their caseloads as much as possible, in order to avoid being inundated with those types of patients found to be the most frequent sources of therapist stress. In view of existing research, it would appear wise to limit the number of patients seen who are actively suicidal, aggressive, or suffering from more severe forms of psychopathology. In this manner the therapist is able to take an active role in monitoring and regulating the potential for patient-related stress within the limitations of the job setting. Regardless of whether the individual practices psychotherapy in a public or private setting, there must be some control exerted over the types of patients treated in order to avoid the eventual development of burnout.

In addition to exerting some control over patient-related variables, therapists desiring to avoid or reduce burnout are also well-advised to attempt to reduce work-related factors found to contribute to the onset of burnout. For example, concerns regarding role ambiguity, role conflict, role overload, and inconsequentiality need to be addressed openly and extensively by those in both public and private practice. The number of direct service hours provided, speciality to be practiced, administrative responsibilities assumed, and supervisory functions performed will need to reflect personal abilities, limitations, and interests. In the case of those working in the public sector, these issues will need to be discussed forthrightly with superiors, supervisors, colleagues, and associates. Individuals practicing in the private sector may need to seek out the advice and counsel of a respected peer in order to gain a balanced perspective on issues of personal concern. Once again, it is necessary for the practitioner to exercise some degree of control over work-related factors that can contribute to therapist burnout. For example, this may be accomplished by diversifying professional responsibilities to include a wide variety of vocational roles and experiences. As mentioned previously, dividing professional time among psychotherapy, supervision, consultation, research, teaching, writing, and other nonpsychotherapeutic activities provides renewal and refreshment to some practitioners seeking to avoid burnout (Kottler, 1986; Tryon, 1983a; 1983b).

Summary

Obviously it is impossible to eliminate all dissatisfying and stressful aspects of psychotherapeutic practice. Some would even maintain that it would be undesirable to do so since some degree of stress is necessary to energize and challenge the practitioner. Rather, it appears that the most useful approach to the prevention and treatment of burnout is to reduce stress and dissatisfaction while taking active steps to replenish and refresh clinicians on an ongoing basis. As suggested, this necessitates a proactive rather than reactive stance, which appreciates the potential for burnout to develop in any practitioner, given the right interaction among various personal and environmental factors. As a result, the interventions suggested in this chapter reflect an attempt to eliminate as many sources of stress as possible while reducing those which are inevitable, given the various constellation of factors involved.

Just as there appears to be no single cause of psychotherapist burnout, there does not seem to be one primary means of effective prevention or treatment. Consequently, it is most useful for the clinician to implement a many faceted intervention program that addresses the variety of factors contributing to burnout in a comprehensive manner. While therapists may be less prone to burnout than members of other career groups (Farber, 1985b), the potential for such an occurrence is great enough to warrant that serious consideration be given to its prevention and treatment.

THERAPIST DYSFUNCTION IN PERSPECTIVE

The last several chapters have provided documentation of the many potential hazards and risks associated with the practice of psychotherapy that are often encountered by psychotherapists. These included a wide variety of personal and environmental factors which were shown to have the potential to impact significantly the professional and private life and relationships of the clinician. It may appear to the reader by this point that a career in psychotherapy is fraught with difficulties which undermine the personal adjustment and professional satisfaction of most, if not all, of its practitioners. Furthermore, it may seem that few are likely to choose willingly to remain in this career, in view of its many potential liabilities and hazards. Yet the vast majority of psychotherapists report experiencing significant personal satisfaction from their career. In addition, only a minority seem to experience impairment or burnout sufficient enough to noticeably interfere with their clinical work or private life. Finally, many indicate that their personal lives and relationships are greatly enriched by their work with patients. While a quick review of these research results provide reassurance that most psychotherapists regard their career in a favorable manner, one is left wondering about the risks and hazards previously described. In view of their potential seriousness and prevalence, why do the majority of practitioners remain in clinical practice throughout their lifetime?

Certainly the practice of psychotherapy is a difficult, challenging undertaking. Yet despite the liabilities associated with the role of psychotherapist, the benefits resulting from clinical practice far outweigh the hazards. The intellectual stimulation, emotional growth, and satisfying encounters often associated with conducting therapy provide the practitioner with many rewards. Most therapists would choose to enter this profession again if they were to begin life over, in spite of the difficulties and frustrations encountered. Few other careers offer the rich satisfactions, variety, autonomy, and challenge of a career in psychotherapy. By and large, it is a privilege to practice psychotherapy.

Given the many benefits and rewards of this career, one might wonder why the dysfunctional aspects of psychotherapeutic practice have been examined in such detail. This was done for several important reasons. First, psychotherapists need to be aware of the seemingly inevitable liabilities associated with clinical practice. Some stresses and problems come with the territory and cannot be completely avoided. Regardless of a therapist's intentions or efforts to the contrary, there are likely to be some personality variables, patient characteristics, work-related factors, and life events which occasionally promote career dissatisfaction and stress. This is obviously true of all vocations, as well as life in general. Therefore, therapists must be prepared to cope with these difficulties as best as possible, utilizing the suggested interventions presented earlier in this chapter. They must be willing and able to react effectively to these problems as soon as they appear. Steps can often be taken ahead of time to increase the available resources and coping skills of the practitioner in preparation for when such problems are most likely to be confronted. Discussions regarding isolation, interpersonal dysfunction, impairment, and burnout have attempted to elucidate factors which are frequently encountered by practitioners, in order to increase understanding and effective coping.

The major emphasis of the previous chapters has been on the hazards and liabilities associated with the role of psychotherapist which can often be avoided or eliminated. Rather than intending to portray psychotherapy to be the "impossible profession" that some suggest (see Malcolm, 1980), an effort has been made to demonstrate that a career as a therapist is indeed a rewarding, "possible" profession for those who take adequate measures to safeguard their well-being. Thus previous discussions have attempted to highlight the wide array of problems resulting from clinical practice which can be lessened, avoided, or eliminated altogether. Furthermore, suggested intervention strategies have stressed preventative measures demonstrated to be effective in reducing the potential for the onset of therapist dysfunction.

Rather than encouraging a vigilant, reactive stance, the emphasis has been on maintaining a proactive perspective which motivates psychotherapists to take aggressive measures to ensure a balanced, healthy existence. Perhaps this has been the real tragedy of the profession—the failure of therapists to take adequate steps to satisfy their physical, emotional, and spiritual needs, while at the same time attempting to do so for others. Not unlike the physician who continues to smoke three packs of cigarettes a day while treating patients with lung cancer, many therapists fail to take care of their own psychological needs. In some cases this seems to be the result of ignorance or naivete. In others it is associated with a subtle grandiosity and omnipotence which fools some therapists into feeling invulnerable to emotional problems. Regardless of the reason for such neglect, psychotherapists must attend to their personal well-being in order to function effectively in their role. As McCarley (1975) notes, "it must be recognized that the psychotherapist uses his (her) feelings, his self, to a degree that is unique. And that self has to be adequately cared for to function well" (p. 224). Unless adequate preventative measures are taken, the potential hazards associated with conducting therapy are likely to impact increasingly both the professional and personal life and relationships of the therapist. As a result, those failing to appreciate the need for adequate self-care will often fall victim to many of the same debilitating problems experienced by patients who have also failed to adequately take care of their personal needs. The problem is not that a career in psychotherapy is fraught with hazards and serious liabilities. Instead, the danger is that some psychotherapists fail to take aggressive measures to eliminate avoidable stresses and adequately prepare for those likely to be inevitable. For this reason, the previous chapters have sounded a warning to practitioners to encourage them to take seriously the potentially negative impact of clinical practice on their life and relationships. Those who do are likely to enjoy a long, satisfying career as a psychotherapist. Those who do not increase their potential to develop burnout, impairment, and interpersonal dysfunction.

The wounded healer motif has been useful for portraying the mortality and personal vulnerability of the therapist to the very afflictions that he or she attempts to heal in others. Yet it is not solely the fact that psychotherapists have been "wounded" that provides them with the insights and skills to heal others' wounds. Instead, it is because their personal wounds have been adequately "healed" that they are able to offer hope and comfort to patients seeking treatment. Therefore, it is not the fact that psychotherapists are also prone to impairment and dysfunction that gives them credibility with the general public. On the contrary, it is because many psychotherapists apparently take adequate steps to prevent and change those personal and environmental factors which have the potential to precipitate eventual interpersonal dysfunction, impairment, and burnout that they are able to increase patients' confidence and hope.

With this in mind, it is easier to understand the recent public outcry regarding mounting evidence of emotional disability among therapists. It is not primarily because of an insistence that psychotherapists be invulnerable to mental illness or psychic distress. Instead, public impatience is most likely due to a recognition that psychotherapists, of all people, should know how to prevent, avoid, decrease, or eliminate many of those personal and environmental stresses which can lead to the eventual onset of emotional disability. Regardless of their fantasies or wishes, most patients do not expect their therapist to be invulnerable to psychological difficulties. However, with few exceptions, they do expect him or her to be relatively successful in remediating their impact. Even more importantly, they demand that psychotherapists regularly utilize their expertise in order to assure their own self-care and well-being. Neglect of personal emotional needs by psychotherapists will no longer be tolerated by an informed, consumer-minded public. Just as it would be difficult to respect a surgeon general who continues to smoke heavily while insisting that advertizers warn consumers of the many health risks associated with smoking, psychotherapists are living proof of the efficacy of their treatment. Again, it is not necessary that they be stable and mature at all times. Instead, it is essential that they regularly use all that they know in order to achieve the highest possible degree of personal wholeness and emotional health. This results in better patient care as well as a more satisfying life.

The time has come for the profession to make similar demands of its practitioners in an open and forthright manner. It is not helpful to avoid discussion or deny the existence of impairment, burnout, and dysfunction among therapists. Nor is it useful to throw up one's hands and call psychotherapy the "impossible profession." Rather, the time has come for therapists to recognize their need to prepare for and directly confront those hazards which appear to be inevitable in the practice of psychotherapy. Even more importantly, it is necessary for therapists to take aggressive, measures to decrease or eliminate personal and environmental stresses which have the potential to impact negatively their professional and personal life and relationships. Such preventative and rehabilitative measures, applied in a responsible and timely fashion, are likely to be very successful in reducing therapist dysfunction and resultant patient harm. Hopefully the discussions and analyses presented in this book will increase insight and understanding regarding these concerns, enabling psychotherapists to experience greater career-related growth and satisfaction as a result.

SUMMARY AND DISCUSSION

In this chapter, factors contributing to career dissatisfaction and eventual burnout were examined in order to identify those variables which promote therapist discouragment and disillusionment. It was found that a wide variety of personal and environmental factors are often involved, necessitating a comprehensive, multifaceted intervention program for the successful prevention and treatment of burnout. Despite the hazards associated with the practice of psychotherapy, it was again stressed that this profession is a satisfying, fulfilling one for most practitioners, particularly for those who take steps to ensure their own self-care and well-being.

The focus of Chapter 8 will take the reader in a new direction. Having examined the impact of practicing psychotherapy on the personal and professional life and relationships of the psychotherapist, it is now appropriate to consider likely future trends and developments in the profession. While still rather embryonic in its formation, the profession of psychotherapy is already undergoing significant changes and facing formidable challenges which have the potential to impact greatly on the life and work of psychotherapists.

CHAPTER 8

Future Trends in the Practice of Psychotherapy

The profession of psychotherapy is a relatively new specialty in the health care field. Most of its major developments have occurred within the past 50 years, while many of its particularly important innovations have appeared during the last two decades. There are currently over 200 different types of psychotherapy being practiced in the United States, and ongoing research and treatment innovations are likely to increase this number substantially during the years ahead (Prochaska, 1984). Rapid changes in training and service delivery are resulting in a metamorphosis which will continue to alter the life and work of the practicing therapist in the future. The thoughtful clinician often finds himself or herself pausing to consider the implications of potential future trends in the field in order to facilitate personal adaptation and adjustment. In this chapter, several of these major trends will be examined, and their likely impact on the life and practice of the therapist will be discussed, in order to assist psychotherapists in their attempts to anticipate the significance of these possible changes.

THE CONTEXT OF PROFESSIONAL PRACTICE

Most experts in the field suggest that the "Golden Era" of psychotherapy is over (Cummings, 1984). At one time it seemed as though there would always be an endless flow of clients. This no longer appears to be the case. Despite advances and progress in service delivery, it is now apparent to the general public that psychotherapy is not going to cure society's ills, nor is it going to be helpful to everyone in personal distress. Among some individuals, this has lead to a sense of disillusionment and cynicism regarding it's utility and effectiveness. Furthermore, it is no longer considered fashionable to enter psychotherapy in some circles, while it continues to be regarded as unacceptable and a source of embarrassment in others. Finally, there has been a dramatic decrease in third-party reimbursements for psychotherapy, increasing the out-of-pocket expense of the consumer. As a result of these and other factors, there has been a noticeable drop in the number of individuals seeking psychotherapy, particularly in the case of those selecting private practitioners whose services are typically more expensive (Cummings, 1984).

Along with this decrease in the number of clients, there has been a rapid increase in the number of practitioners, resulting in intense competition in some regions of the country. Indeed, in areas such as New York City and southern California, it seems as though a member of every third household practices some sort of "psychotherapy." Not only are there more individuals entering the profession, but there has been a dramatic increase in the number of psychotherapists entering private practice (Norcross et al., 1985). This has resulted in the need for rather aggressive marketing strategies and advertising by therapists who often find such activites uncomfortable and foreign to their nature and training (Zimet, 1981).

Also, the changing political climate has brought a marked decrease in governmental support and financing of psychotherapy services. Less state and federal money is being appropriated for the training and practice of therapists, resulting in staff and facility cutbacks in government-supported outpatient and inpatient mental health programs (Cummings, 1984; Kovacs, 1982). There is decreasing willingness on the part of government leaders to underwrite any portion of the cost of psychotherapy for individuals unable or unwilling to pay for such services themselves.

These trends have resulted in a number of changes in the delivery of psychotherapy by professionals in the field. Over the past two decades, therapists have steadily migrated from government-supported community mental health centers and public psychiatric hospitals to the private sector. As mentioned, the most frequent undertaking has been to open a private practice in psychotherapy. This has often involved a solo practice in which the psychotherapist rents an office and works alone. The many benefits associated with independent practice, and growing disillusionment with the changes and cutbacks in the public sector, are likely to make this an attractive option in the future as well. As a result, this trend will probably continue, with most psychotherapists electing to maintain an independent practice in addition to other possible career involvements.

Despite the growing tendency for therapists to enter private practice, increased competition, rapid innovations, rising consumerism, and a decrease in the number of patients have led some to conclude that solo ir dependent clinical practice will be extinct before the turn of the century (Cummings, 1984). In order to keep pace with increasing professional demands and rapid changes in the field, many psychotherapists may elect to join together into group practices that allow for specialization and intergroup referrals. Indeed, it appears that this trend is already beginning. Bellak (1981) suggests that there is an increase in the number of private practitioners who are forming multidisciplinary group practices, a pattern which he feels is likely to continue in the future. As will be discussed, the formation of group cooperative practices will put the psychotherapist in a better position to offer services to private industry Employee Assistance Programs (EAPs) and Preferred Provider Insurance Plans in the coming years. As a result, it is likely that psychotherapists will continue to form group practices in the future at an increasing rate.

In addition to entering private group or solo practice, therapists are practicing in other contexts as well. Rather than limiting the practice of psychotherapy to mental health centers, psychiatric hospitals, or private offices, therapists are now also offering their services to business and industry (Zimet, 1981). In addition to direct clinical service, these individuals are frequently engaged in "preventive" activities such as providing seminars concerning stress management, child rearing, self-esteem, assertiveness training, and retirement to interested employees. Some therapists actually assume permanent staff positions within a company in order to provide ongoing consultation and personal therapy for employees. In other cases, business firms contract with local group practices to provide clinical services to their employees on a direct referral basis. Such EAPs are becoming increasingly popular, and this trend is likely to continue in the future. Thus psychotherapists are finding that private business and industry may be willing to utilize their services on a regular basis.

The broader health care industry is embracing the work of psychotherapists with new enthusiasm as well. Therapists are assuming staff positions in university medical centers, private medical hospitals, and health clinics, working closely with physicians and nurses in order to provide more comprehensive, holistic care for patients suffering from cancer, cardiac or neurological problems, psychosomatic illnesses, and a wide variety of physical disabilities (Cummings, 1984; Zimet, 1981). Psychotherapists are also being employed in increasing numbers by health maintenance organizations (HMOs), multidisciplinary health care firms sponsored by private insurance companies. Future advances in the health care field are likely to include the services of psychotherapists whose contribution to holistic medicine grows in significance with each passing year. Psychotherapists will probably experience an increasing demand for their services from allied health care professionals in the future.

While psychotherapists have begun to establish themselves in the fields of medicine, industry, and business, the future frontiers may lie in other disciplines such as law, mass media, education, public policy and government, international diplomacy, law enforcement, and penal reform (Peterson, 1984). While some encouraging inroads are being made into these fields, there is much yet to be accomplished as psychotherapists continue to find new contexts and environments for their practice. In order to keep pace with the rapid advancements and changes in the field, it will be important for therapists to think creatively regarding ways to make their services available to the public.

Shifting economic and political forces will continue to shape the context within which therapy is offered to clients. It will be necessary for psychotherapists to be flexible and innovative in order to adjust to these changes. Practitioners who are able to offer their services in a manner which is responsive to shifting community demands and societal needs will enjoy a long, satisfying career. Those who are unable to do so may find that there is increasingly less demand for their services.

Increased competition and a constantly shifting job market may be a source of considerable anxiety for future practitioners. This may cause some to question their motivation for entering this career and reexamine the wisdom of this vocational choice should it become sufficiently difficult to obtain gainful and satisfying employment. It is ironic that future psychotherapists may find that their sincere desire to help others will not necessarily result in a busy clinical practice. Furthermore, some individuals may become discouraged when they discover that the many years of preparation and the great financial cost involved in training to become a therapist will not guarantee suitable employment or an adequate income, at least immediately after graduation. However, despite such possibilities, it is encouraging to remember that although the context of service delivery may change, the need for such services will likely continue in the future. There will almost certainly be future requests for help from those suffering from mental illness and emotional distress. As a result, the services of psychotherapists will continue to be in demand regardless of funding cutbacks and shifting economic and political priorities. Future therapists will continue to find ways to apply their expertise in a increasing variety of contexts.

While past and present patterns of service delivery provide a point of reference for predicting future trends in clinical practice, both neophyte and veteran therapists are likely to find that the nature and context of their professional endeavors may change dramatically over the course of a career in psychotherapy. Resiliency and flexibility will be necessary to facilitate personal adjustment and redirection in response to changing patterns in service delivery. Therapists who are convinced of the usefulness and value of their skills, and who remain committed to practicing the art and science of psychotherapy, will likely possess the confidence and resourcefulness needed to find profitable employment and satisfying contexts for future professional practice.

THE TYPE OF THERAPY OFFERED

While it is encouraging to note that there is very likely to be an ongoing demand for the services of future psychotherapists, a raging controversy continues regarding the efficacy and efficiency of the very assistance which they are offering. Since Eysenck's (1952) charge that psychotherapy is largely ineffective, there have been innumerable studies which have attempted to determine whether it is, indeed, effective in ameliorating emotional distress. While the results have been somewhat equivocal, the preponderance of evidence suggests that a wide variety of forms of psychotherapy are, by and large, helpful in treating mental illness (Garfield & Bergin, 1978). At first glance, such findings would seem to guarantee the practitioner's future security. Psychotherapists are often effective and helpful in reducing emotional pain and increasing personal adjustment.

Current controversy is no longer focused primarily on whether psychotherapy is effective, however. On the contrary, most informed individuals acknowledge its potential usefulness and benefits. Yet,there are over two hundred forms of psychotherapy currently being practiced in the United States, involving a wide variety of treatment techniques and expenses. This leads to a crucial question which remains unanswered. That is, which specific form of therapy is most effective. The rising costs of psychotherapy, the reduced insurance coverage being provided for it, and growing consumer demands regarding efficacy and efficiency combine to heighten the controversy over which type of treatment should be offered by therapists in the future.

The Question of Efficacy

Government policy during the Carter administration outlined that no form of health intervention or treatment—physical or mental—should be supported through third-party payments and publicly funded training programs if it has not been found to be both safe and effective (Klerman, 1983). This prompted the Office of Technology Assessment (OTA), an agency of the U. S. Congress, to investigate the wide array of psychotherapies currently practiced in order to determine which type was the most effective in treating mental illness—an ambitious undertaking, to be sure. As one might suspect, this investigation discovered that almost any recognized brand of psychotherapy is effective in treating emotional distress. Furthermore, no single type was found to be superior to the rest (McGuire & Frisman, 1983). Much to everyone's disappointment, little empirical evidence could be found to isolate those specific therapeutic techniques which are most effective in the treatment of various forms of mental illness.

Such setbacks are not likely to stop efforts permanently to determine which of the many forms of psychotherapy are most effective in treating patient emotional distress. Increased sophistication has resulted in a new generation of psychotherapy outcome research projects which "explore the relative advantages and disadvantages of alternative treatment strategies for patients with different specific psychological and behavioral difficulties" (VandenBos, 1986, p. 111). While the results of such investigations are still forthcoming, early evidence indicates that certain forms of therapy may indeed be more effective in treating particular forms of mental illness. For example, a large project sponsored by the National Institute of Health has announced preliminary findings which suggest that cognitive behavior therapy and interpersonal psychotherapy are as effective in reducing the symptoms associated with depression as standard drug treatment (Gelman, 1986). Research projects attempting to determine which type of therapy is most effective for a particular form of emotional distress are likely to increase in number during the years ahead.

If it can eventually be determined that some forms of psychotherapy are more effective for treating a particular type of psychopathology, it seems likely that psychotherapists will be pressured by professional organizations, consumer groups, and third-party payers to offer that form of treatment to such individuals. Indeed, the American Psychiatric Association has already begun the groundwork for the drafting of a Psychiatric Treatment Manual, a companion to *DSM-III*, which is to provide detailed treatment recommendations for various psychiatric disorders (Klerman, 1983). Subpanels are currently investigating which forms of therapy are most effective in treating schizophrenia, anxiety disorders, and depression by comparing outcome studies utilizing such treatment modalities as long- and short-term psychodynamic, interpersonal, cognitive, behavioral, and drug therapies. The time may well come when therapists are forced to adopt several treatment approaches from which to choose the one demonstrated to be the most effective for treating the specific disorder presented by the patient. The growing emphasis on efficacy in the practice of psychotherapy is likely to continue.

The Question of Efficiency

While most experts agree that psychotherapy is effective in treating mental illness, the issue of efficiency has become a more prominent concern during recent years. In view of government funding cutbacks for publicly supported mental health care as well as the increasing hesitancy of insurance companies to underwrite even partially the cost of psychotherapy, the present growing concern for efficient, cost-effective treatment is not surprising. Among the many treatment modalities currently in existence, the length and cost of treatment vary widely. While some forms of therapy offer a course of treatment lasting six to eight sessions, other types involve three to five sessions per week for several years. Furthermore, while some psychotherapists charge as little as $15 per session, others may charge $125 or more for each 50 minute hour.

In view of such variation, the recent NIMH findings concerning the efficacy of cognitive behavior therapy for the treatment of depression have generated a great deal of controversy. Since this and other forms of time-limited or brief psychotherapy typically involve 25 sessions or less to complete a course of treatment, the issue of efficiency and cost-effectiveness becomes a major consideration (Mann, 1982). If it can be conclusively demonstrated that brief psychotherapy is as good, if not better than, more traditional longer forms of treatment, psychotherapists in the future may be forced to develop expertise in such treatment modalities regardless of their personal preferences or beliefs. The issue of efficiency is likely to be a continual source of controversy and concern during the years ahead.

The Rise of Consumerism

No longer is the psychotherapist regarded as a mysterious figure to be revered and blindly obeyed. The contemporary informed and educated client comes to the therapist with a host of questions, demands, and expectations. While some of these beliefs may be the result of distortions or mistaken impressions, others are not. Certainly, at the very least, it must be acknowledged that therapy patients now knowingly have the right to expect results. For many patients, it is no longer acceptable to be kept in the dark and told to "trust the process." Instead, psychotherapists are faced with increasingly informed clients who often wish to participate actively in goal setting and ongoing evaluation of treatment progress. While the practitioner remains unable to offer any guarantees regarding a successful outcome, it may be increasingly necessary for him or her to provide a thoughtful and convincing rationale to patients regarding the type of treatment to be offered and the likelihood of success.

The recent astounding rise in malpractice lawsuits against psychotherapists (Cummings & Sobel, 1985; *NASW News*, 1986; Turkington, 1986) suggests that consumers are becoming more aggressive in demanding satisfactory service delivery from clinicians. This trend is very likely to continue during the years ahead. The demystification of the practice of psychotherapy has resulted in an increased examination of its usefulness. Therapists will likely be required in the future to justify the effectiveness and efficiency of their treatment to vigilant consumers to an even greater extent than is now the case (Klerman, 1983).

Summary

It would seem that psychotherapists will be increasingly challenged in the future to demonstrate that the form of treatment that they offer will effectively and efficiently ameliorate the type of psychopathology presented by each particular patient. If current research does eventually single out certain forms of treatment as more effective than others, therapists will be forced to acquire the necessary expertise to offer these types of treatment to suitable patients. Furthermore, if research findings suggest that some effective forms of psychotherapy are more cost-effective and efficient than others, these, too, will need to be adopted by psychotherapists wishing to remain in practice. Some suggest that short-term therapies are likely to be among those found to be most effective and efficient, when all factors are taken into consideration, requiring that expertise in such approaches may be necessary for future professional survival (Kovacs, 1982).

While at first glance this might seem to be a reasonable and easily met expectation, further reflection suggests that some psychotherapists may find it difficult to develop an armamentarium of several theoretical orientations and treatment modalities. While many therapists are exposed to more than one set of treatment techniques during graduate training, over the course of a career most tend to narrow their work to include only one or two "favorite" forms of psychotherapy with which they feel compatible and content (Norcross & Prochaska, 1983a). As outlined in Chapter 2, the adoption of a particular theoretical orientation and treatment modality is often the result of an interaction among a set of highly complex personal and environmental factors. As this process of narrowing continues, the favored modality begins to shape the therapist's personal and professional perspectives on human behavior. It becomes an integral part of his or her inner experience. It often shapes how the world is perceived and understood by the practitioner, and it represents a very personal choice. As a result, only one or two theoretical orientations are typically favored and maintained throughout the practitioner's career, with very little change or adaptation.

Given this pattern, the need to adopt several new theoretical orientations and treatment modalities may be a difficult undertaking for some therapists. Being forced to alter one's personal and professional view of psychopathology and treatment because of the latest research results and reimbursement policies of third-party payers may be distasteful and offensive to some clinicians. Actually, it may also be very threatening to be confronted with the inadequacy or inefficiency of one's favorite treatment modality. Furthermore, the increasing need to justify the efficacy of one's treatment techniques and approach to consumers and insurance companies may put some clinicians on the defensive. Rather than regarding such inquiries as a personal insult, it will be useful for future therapists to recognize that responsible clinical practice will require that such questions be adequately addressed. It will be important for psychotherapists to be as informed and aware as possible of the latest data regarding treatment outcome studies in order to guarantee that their mode of treatment is informed and enhanced by current research findings. This will increase the practitioner's confidence and sense of personal competence, making it easier to respond to challenges and questions regarding the efficacy and efficiency of his or her treatment techniques. Rather than regarding the need for adaptation and updating of clinical skills as a personal affront, it will be helpful to recognize that these changes are primarily intended to improve the overall quality of patient care.

Future therapists who are able to adopt a wide array of contemporary clinical skills, techniques, and treatment modalities will most likely find it easier to maintain a "general" practice, accepting a wide variety of patients representing various diagnostic groups. The gradual move towards eclecticism will likely continue for those who desire the greatest amount of professional freedom. On the other hand, those who are unable or unwilling to practice a variety of therapeutic forms may find it necessary to specialize in one or two forms of treatment, seeing only those patients for whom this modality has been demonstrated to be most effective. For such individuals, the trend towards specialization will likely increase, allowing them to practice the one form of psychotherapy with which they feel most compatible and competent but limiting the number of patients for whom their treatment techniques will be appropriate. One thing is certain: future research findings will eventually make it impossible for a psychotherapist to insist legitimately on providing only one form of treatment for all emotional disorders represented by patients presenting in a general psychotherapy practice.

ISSUES CONCERNING REIMBURSEMENT

Having considered issues regarding the context of practice and type of psychotherapy to be offered in the future, it is time to turn to the ongoing controversy regarding reimbursement for such services. Three factors exist which complicate the question of reimbursement for psychotherapy services. First, the cost of therapy has steadily risen to its present levels of $50 to $125 per session (Gelman, 1986). As with other escalating health costs, this trend is likely to continue in the future. Second, government's willingness to underwrite all or part of the cost for such services (e.g., by means of Medicare and federal employee insurance coverage) has decreased with the current administration (Cummings, 1984; McGuire & Frisman, 1983). Finally, following the federal government's lead, many private insurance companies have dramatically reduced benefits for outpatient psychotherapy services, lowering both the precentage of reimbursement and total number of therapy sessions covered by their policies during a calender year (Kovacs, 1982, 1986; McGuire & Frisman, 1983). As a result, there has been growing controversy regarding who is to pay for treatment and at what expense.

Patient Payments

It comes as no surprise that, as a result of these factors, most individuals have had to assume directly a greater portion of the cost for psychotherapy. Not only has this meant that the final "out-of-pocket" expense has been greater for clients, but fewer therapists in private practice are willing to allow insured patients to pay for only their portion of the expense. Instead, they are increasingly requiring that patients pay their fees in full at the time of each session and then wait for their insurance companies to reimburse them directly, freeing the clinician from long and anxious waits for payment. Thus some clients are also assuming a greater portion of the total "up-front" costs for their treatment as well. If these trends continue, individuals may eventually be forced to pay for outpatient psychotherapy without any assistance from governmental or private insurance policies.

HMOs and PPOs

While some insurance companies are curtailing or greatly restricting the amount of coverage provided for psychotherapy, others have chosen to pursue rather creative alternatives. For example, some have formed health maintenance organizations (HMOs) which provide a variety of health care services, including psychotherapy, to their members for little additional cost beyond the policy premiums. Such services are provided by staff members who are employed exclusively by the HMO. There are currently over 250 HMOs across the nation that service close to ten million individuals (Cheifetz & Salloway, 1984). The HMOs require that policyholders consult only their staff members for psychotherapeutic services. Reimbursement will not be provided for the services of therapists who do not work for the HMO. If at intake the staff member decides that psychotherapy is not warranted, the individual seeking treatment will have to obtain it in the community at his or her own expense. If, however, therapy is thought to be necessary, the number of sessions will typically be limited to twenty or less per year (Gelman, 1986). Since most HMOs seek to reduce expenses in order to make a profit, some individuals complain that adequacy of patient care may not always be an overriding concern when treatment-related decisions are made. At any rate, while such insurance programs provide a predetermined salary for psychotherapists employed by the HMO, they do not provide any reimbursement for the services of therapists outside of their organization. As a result, HMOs do not provide financial support for the majority of psychotherapists practicing in the public or private sector today. If the impressive growth in HMO membership continues in the future, psychotherapists may well feel its impact on their clinical practice.

Preferred provider plans (PPOs) are another alternative being pursued by insurance programs. Modeled after the federal government's Civilian Health and Medical Program of the Uniformed Services (CHAMPUS), Medical, and Medicare Programs, PPOs attempt to control the amount of reimbursement offered for psychotherapy services by placing a ceiling or cap on the cost regarded as acceptable by the company. Thus, rather than simply reducing or eliminating the percentage of reimbursements allowed, the insurance company exerts control over the fee to be charged to the consumer and then pays a predetermined percentage of this amount. Psychotherapists who agree to accept this cap as payment in full for services rendered, and who satisfy the minimum credential requirements, are allowed to "join" the referral network. Policyholders are usually reimbursed at a higher percentage for services provided by such "preferred providers" than for those not appearing on this list. Furthermore, for both member and nonmember psychotherapists, the percentage of reimbursement typically drops quite dramatically for therapy which extends beyond 15 to 20 sessions. While this may result in satisfactory levels of reimbursement for individuals seeking short-term treatment from approved "preferred providers," it often results in little or no coverage for those pursuing more long-term treatment or those preferring to work with a nonmember psychotherapist. The PPOs are rapidly spreading across the nation, and they are likely to have an increasing impact on the practices of psychotherapists who decline membership.

Prospective Payment and DRGs

Another attempt to control the amount of insurance reimbursement for health care is the development of the prospective payment system. Patients are classified according to diagnosis related groups (DRGs), and hospitals are paid a set fee for their care based on the average nationwide cost for medical care for a particular diagnosis (Weiss, 1986). Thus, regardless of the actual cost of the medical care, the hospital is paid a predetermined amount for that patient's treatment. Presently, prospective payment and DRG programs are being utilized primarily by Medicare and Veterans Administration hospitals for medically related problems (Binner, 1986). However, Congress is now considering extending the current Medicare prospective payment system to include inpatient psychiatric services (Leff & Bradley, 1986). Speculation abounds regarding its eventual use by all insurance companies for reimbursement for both inpatient and outpatient psychiatric care (Binner, 1986).

While some suggest that prospective payment systems are appropriate for reimbursement for surgical procedures, few endorse its use for the treatment of mental illness (Nightingale, 1986). There is simply too much variability among patients and their response to various treatment techniques to allow for such standardization. It is difficult to regulate or predict how many sessions will be required to treat depression, anxiety disorders, or psychosis effectively. As Uyeda and Moldawsky (1986) note, "diagnostic related groups have minimal value as a predictor of resource need and therefore are a poor basis for setting reimbursement payment levels" for the treatment of psychiatric disorders (p. 63). Furthermore, the blatant profit incentive prominent in such programs seems incongruent with the underlying philosophy of health care, making it distasteful and offensive to many psychotherapists.

Regardless of their inappropriateness or limitations, DRGs and prospective payment programs are gaining support in the insurance industry as an effective means of controlling rising health care costs. As a result, in the future psychotherapists may find that reimbursements for psychotherapy services are dependent on DRG-type guidelines. It remains to be seen whether prospective payment systems will be used for both inpatient and outpatient mental health care. What is certain is that unlimited reimbursement for psychiatric treatment is a thing of the past. Most insurance companies already limit the number of outpatient sessions for which they are willing to offer reimbursement annually, regardless of the diagnosis or seriousness of the patient's condition. Furthermore, some limit the number of days of psychiatric hospitalization considered to be reimbursable during a calendar year. While psychotherapists currently remain free to decide how much treatment they deem appropriate for a given condition, insurance companies are exerting increasing control over how much they are willing to pay for such services. Thus, with the exception of those wealthy enough to pay for their own care, in most cases it will be third-party payers who determine how long an individual is to remain in treatment for a particular psychiatric diagnosis, despite the therapist's possible opinions to the contrary. This trend is very likely to continue in the future.

Peer Review

As discussed in Chapter 7, several government and private insurance organizations have instituted peer review programs to evaluate the quality and cost-effectiveness of treatment services rendered by psychotherapists seeking reimbursement (Young, 1982). In addition, most public and private inpatient and outpatient psychiatric programs have adopted some type of Professional Standards Review Organizations (PSRO) to monitor the quality and efficiency of psychotherapy services provided by their employees. Such review programs require that psychotherapists periodically complete extended questionnaires and reports concerning the diagnosis, treatment methods and goals, and probable date of termination for a particular patient. This plan is then evaluated by the appropriate review committee (made up of senior psychotherapists from one or more disciplines in the field) to determine whether it represents both effective and efficient treatment.

While most psychotherapists working in the public sector accept the need for PSROs to guarantee adequate patient care given limited resources, few practitioners are enthusiastic about insurance of these committees. This is understandable since insurance companies using peer review systems base their reimbursements on the decisions of such review committees. While there has been heated controversy regarding resultant violations of patient confidentiality and a fear that insurance companies may value company profit over the quality of patient care, most agree that peer review programs are here to stay and will become even more pervasive during the years ahead (Dall & Claiborn, 1982; Stricker & Cohen, 1984; Young, 1982).

In the future psychotherapists will probably be asked to justify and document their treatment services to an even greater extent if they wish to continue to receive third-party reimbursements. In an effort to cut expenses and ensure the quality of patient care, those underwriting the costs for such services are likely to become increasingly intrusive and controlling regarding the type and duration of treatment provided. Rising medical costs have made third-party payers unwilling to underwrite rapidly increasing expenses passively. Instead the present initiative to gain control over escalating costs is likely to become permanent policy. As a result, psychotherapists will need to get used to having someone "watching over their shoulder" if they wish to receive reimbursement from insurance companies in the future.

Summary

As mentioned previously, one of the reasons given for the exodus of psychotherapists from the public to the private sector has been the decrease in funding for therapy services, and the resultant restrictions on the type and duration of treatment permitted as a result. Psychotherapists forced to terminate clients before they feel it's appropriate, due to the decisions of PSRO committees or organizational policies regarding mandatory short-term treatment, may decide that entering private practice will ensure their freedom to base treatment decisions solely on the needs of the patient.

While this is true in principle, the economic factors which have led to such restrictions in the public sector have now fully impacted the private sector as well. As a result, those in private practice must contend with many of the same problems regarding funding and control over the type and duration of treatment. Future psychotherapists will continue to struggle to balance economic realities with patient needs. Entry into private practice will not render the therapist immune to such dilemmas.

Since psychotherapists earn their livelihood primarily from reimbursement for delivering services provided to their patients, issues concerning payment for these services are of great importance to most practitioners. The constantly changing climate of reimbursement policies is likely to continue during the years ahead. It will be important for therapists to keep abreast of new developments regarding insurance programs and regulations. On this basis, knowledgeable decisions can then be made regarding how to ensure continued payment for future services. At this time, several options are worthy of consideration.

First, given the trends toward greater control exerted by third-party payers, future psychotherapists will be faced with the need to either cooperate or go it alone. In view of possible accusations regarding restraint of trade infractions associated with PPOs and HMOs, who might otherwise attempt to monopolize health care services completely, nonparticipating psychotherapists will probably always be eligible for some type of insurance reimbursement, however inadequate it may be. Nonetheless, increasing restrictions and controls will present a challenge to the therapist who wishes to practice in a manner which ensures both an adequate livelihood and superior quality of patient care for the greatest number and variety of patients possible. Those is part- or full-time private practice must decide whether they are willing to cooperate with the policies and practices of insurance companies utilized by their patients for full or partial reimbursement for psychotherapy services. If the practitioner decides affirmatively, it will be necessary to allow sufficient office time for the many forms and questionnaires that may be required. Furthermore, it will be necessary to document thoroughlsy treatment techniques and goals in order to demonstrate the quality and efficiency of the care provided. The clinician will need to wait through the extended delays in processing and reimbursement payments typical of large organizations. Finally, the practitioner will need to accept the limitations imposed by insurance companies regarding acceptable fees and duration of treatment. Cooperation with peer review procedures, DRGs, PPO programs, and so forth, will be necessary to satisfy the various requirements leading to partial or full reimbursement by third-party payers. A nondefensive attitude of openness and collaboration will be helpful, along with patience and a sense of humor. The frustrations inherent in increasing bureaucracy will present a formidable challenge to those wishing to receive insurance payments for services provided to patients in the future.

Psychotherapists in clinical practice who decide that they do not wish to participate in the wide variety of insurance programs likely to develop during the years ahead will face several difficult decisions. Their refusal to cooperate with peer review committees, PPOs, prospective payment programs, or DRGs may result in no insurance reimbursement for psychotherapy services which they have rendered to a given patient. This will mean that the entire cost will have to be borne by the individual client. Since present standard fees for therapy are expensive for the average person, therapists will find that only a relative few will be able to afford their services. Consequently, therapists will either be forced to limit their practices to those wealthy enough to afford such fees, or reduce their professional fees substantially in order to make them more affordable to the average individual. Not only is this likely to be a sound business practice in such cases, but the most ethical and socially responsible course of action as well.

Such difficult decisions may force psychotherapists to reconsider their reasons for entering this profession in the first place. If therapists are motivated to choose this career primarily by a desire to help others, then there will be a need to balance this source of satisfaction thoughtfully with the need to earn a sufficient personal income. It will be incumbent on future therapists to ensure that all individuals have access to adequate treatment regardless of shifting economic and political priorities. This may prompt some clinicians to offer their services to a number of individuals at a reduced fee, while it will cause others to cooperate fully with all requirements and policies of third-party payers, regardless of how time-consuming or frustrating. Changing reimbursement policies are likely to force therapists to find innovative ways to provide services to the broad spectrum of individuals seeking treatment. Rather than limiting these services to the privileged few, those experiencing the greatest amount of personal satisfaction will find ways to balance personal income needs with socially responsive fee structures and payment policies that allow a greater number of individuals to receive help.

It may be that decreasing third-party reimbursement will lead to a reorganization among psychotherapists providing services to the public. One group of practitioners will include those remaining in the public sector such as in mental health centers and psychiatric hospitals supported by government funding. These individuals willl continue to earn paid salaries rather than "commissions" based on client fees. At the present time this group is apparently shrinking in size due to funding cutbacks. (However, a change in political philosophy at the national level could alter this trend in the future.) A second group will be made up of those who join the staffs of HMO-type programs, who will also receive salaries for psychotherapy services independent of client fees. At the present time, this group is growing in size, causing some to predict that all therapists in private practice will be employed by HMOs in the future. Time will tell whether this movement will continue to gain momentum. Finally, the third group will be comprised of those who enter private practice, whose income is based primarily on insurance reimbursement and client fees. Although this group also continues to grow in number, many predict that this trend will change as private practice becomes less lucrative in the future.

FUTURE TRENDS IN THE TRAINING OF PSYCHOTHERAPISTS

The many changes impacting the field of psychotherapy will continue to shape the manner in which psychotherapists are trained. While the controversy regarding whether psychotherapy is a science or an art is likely to continue during the years ahead, other issues are becoming important areas of concern as well. For example, there is a growing trend for programs training psychotherapists to deemphasize the scientific aspects of the profession, such as formal research and statistical design (Fox et al., 1985; Henry, 1984; Peterson, 1985). Instead, there is a growing emphasis on professional issues more directly related to service delivery and the practice of psychotherapy. The previous theoretical emphasis is being increasingly replaced by a more focused, practical one which attempts to expose trainees to a wide array of treatment techniques and approaches. Rather than specializing in one particular theoretical orientation or treatment modality, the faculty of clinical training programs are becoming more willing to teach a variety of skills and models. In view of the aforementioned changes in service delivery, such trends are likely to continue, as psychotherapy training programs attempt to equip graduates for increased competition in the marketplace. Trainees will need to acquire a host of treatment techniques and modalities in order to satisfy the increasingly diverse demands of consumers and employers. As psychotherapists enter new fields such as holistic health care, forensics, and the media, innovative training will be necessary to enable trainees to adapt treatment techniques to new contexts. While tensions may increase between traditionalists and innovators as training programs continue to undergo change and adaptation, it seems likely that future trends in training will include an increased emphasis on professional practice and a decreased stress on theoretical concerns.

In view of shrinking public and private funding for mental health services and increased competition among practitioners, there is growing concern regarding the large number of psychotherapists who continue to enter the field annually. This has led some to assert that the profession has become saturated, and fears of overproduction of new psychotherapists by the hundreds of training programs now operating nationwide are being expressed (Cummings, 1984; Zimet, 1981). While therapists are finding new contexts for their services, the fact remains that many are beginning to recognize that employment opportunities are becoming increasingly limited and competitive. Yet, even as these concerns are being expressed, new psychotherapy training programs are forming across the country, and the number of graduates continues to increase dramatically. Because of the lack of central governance among the various disciplines represented in the field of psychotherapy, there is as yet no organized way to regulate the number of incoming students and outgoing graduates. If anything, interdisciplinary rivalry may motivate each of the disciplines to attempt to enroll increasing numbers of students in the hopes that greater political clout will result. If such trends continue, which appears likely, the time may come when there is clearly an overabundance of psychotherapists who will find it difficult to obtain suitable employment. Some suggest that the profession of psychotherapy will soon experience the same problem of saturation currently confronting the legal profession (Cummings, 1984). If so, psychotherapy training programs nationwide will need to cooperate to control the number of individuals entering the field in the future.

As growing concern is expressed regarding the possibility of eventual saturation, there has been a trend to implement stricter standards to limit the number of practitioners in the field. Despite evidence which suggests that experienced masters-level therapists are often as effective as doctoral-level practitioners (Klerman, 1983), some masters-level clinicians are finding it increasingly difficult to obtain employment, licensure, and further training in the field of psychotherapy (Cummings, 1984; Perlman, 1985). Furthermore, third-party payers are becoming increasingly reluctant to underwrite therapy conducted by masters-level psychotherapists in some geographical regions, despite their lower fee schedules. As competition increases, such individuals may find themselves squeezed out of the field by doctoral-level practitioners with more education and training.

Should this pattern continue, it is possible that psychotherapy training programs will eventually eliminate terminal masters degree tracts, admitting only those students desiring doctorates. While social work and marriage and family counseling programs are set up primarily for masters-level training, making such a trend seem rather unlikely at this time, the discipline of psychology is already contemplating the elimination of the masters degree in favor of the doctorate. In view of the fact that most states will not license masters level psychologists to practice independently without supervision, there are increasing doubts about the usefulness of this degree. Furthermore, since less than 1 in 40 are later admitted to doctoral programs, there is little hope for most of obtaining the credentials necessary for eventual independent clinical practice (Cummings, 1984). It seems likely that this pattern will spread to the other disciplines, as increased competition results in stricter standards and higher requirements.

Training programs preparing individuals for entry into the profession of psychotherapy in the future will continue to adapt to the changing demands and requirements of an increasingly competitive and specialized field. Programs that are able to respond to these trends will likely be successful in their endeavors, while those unable to keep pace will find it increasingly difficult to attract talented students. Until some uniformity and cooperation takes place among the various disciplines in the field (ensuring quality control and a balanced market) students will have primary responsibility for selecting a program which will most adequately prepare him or her for a long, satisfying career as a psychotherapist. Unfortunately, this will be an increasingly difficult task.

THE NEED FOR INTERDISCIPLINARY UNITY

There is, at times, significant animosity among the various disciplines in the field of psychotherapy. Territorial disputes among psychiatrists and psychologists are legendary, and recent years have brought social workers and marriage and family counselors into the controversy as well (Cattell, 1983). At first glance, one might be surprised to learn of the intense competition among groups of professionals possessing such a wide variety of skills. Each discipline has at least one area of specialty not provided by the others. For example, psychologists are able to conduct psychological testing. Psychiatrists prescribe medication. Social workers typically possess expertise in community resources and systems. Marriage and family counselors are adept at conceptualizing problems from a family perspective. However, regardless of their individual areas of expertise, practitioners from the various disciplines end up functioning in nearly identical roles following graduation (Henry et al., 1971). Most are trained to conduct psychotherapy, and all are employed by public and private psychiatric clinics and hospitals to provide treatment services to patients. Furthermore, in many states all are eligible for certification for the independent practice of psychotherapy. As a result, there is an ongoing battle for parity and public recognition (Cattell, 1983; Klerman, 1983; Morin,

1986; Resnick, 1985; Zimet, 1981). As competition for funding and referrals grows, it seems inevitable that interdisciplinary disputes will continue.

As mentioned previously, it is unfortunate that there is no central governance for the profession of psychotherapy. Instead, each discipline operates in a highly autonomous, and often self-serving, manner. The public would be far better served if the present "survival of the fittest" mentality was replaced by a commitment towards cooperation and a pooling of resources among psychiatrists, social workers, marriage and family counselors, and psychologists. At the present time, huge sums of money are being spent to wage political battles within the profession regarding insurance reimbursement eligibility, hospital admitting and discharging priviledges, and licensure. In contrast, Peterson (1984) presents an encouraging scenario which depicts the benefits of mutual collaboration and teamwork among the various disciplines which could result in greater advances in patient care. The increase in competition among psychotherapists has the potential to result in refined techniques, superior treatment services, and quality training if the present trends toward political factions and rivalries can be turned around. Admittedly, such hopes are idealistic and naive. Yet, psychotherapists wishing to focus their energy and resources on providing quality care for their patients will find that interdisciplinary cooperation significantly facilitates this endeavor. Hopefully this desire will eventually lead to greater collaboration and less confrontation in the future among those psychotherapists able to see beyond the present sources of controversy.

Perhaps unity and cooperation must first be accomplished at the individual level before it can occur on a larger scale. Psychotherapists entering the profession may initially be surprised at the animosity and rivalry that exists among the various disciplines in the field. It may be these individuals, who have not yet begun to engage in such political disputes, that have the greatest potential to embrace their colleagues in a spirit of cooperation and respect. Rather than following in the pattern of their predecessors, future therapists who are able to transcend such rivalries will faciltate the eventual coming together of psychologists, counselors, psychiatrists, and social workers, resulting in more satisfying professional relationships and better patient care.

DISCUSSION

As can be seen by the preceding discussion, psychotherapists will most likely be faced with a number of challenges and changes during the years ahead. Changes in the context of professional practice, type of therapy offered, and patterns of reimbursement will require ongoing adaptations in the manner in which psychotherapists are trained for later entry into the field. Furthermore, such changes will make it necessary for practicing psychotherapists to alter the way in which they conduct their work in order to keep abreast of shifting needs and requirements. However, it is also useful to consider briefly the potential trends which represent more proactive than reactive changes in the practice of psychotherapy. These will shape the practitioner's professional future as well.

One of the more exciting trends in the field of psychotherapy is in the area of research focusing on the underlying causes of mental illness. Each passing year seems to bring new information regarding the various factors related to the etiology of depression, anxiety, and psychosis. It is likely that such advancements will continue, as researchers examine further the biological, environmental, and intrapsychic forces leading to the development of psychopathology. As theories regarding the etiology of various psychiatric disorders are updated and refined, the practice of psychotherapy will no doubt be significantly impacted. Efforts will need to be made to formulate effective treatment methods that reflect these discoveries. In the future, accumulating evidence regarding the etiology of various forms of psychopathology will change the nature of the treatment interventions provided by psychotherapists.

A related area of research likely to impact the practice of psychotherapy centers on outcome studies which evaluate the efficacy of various treatment modalities for the wide array of diagnostic categories. As mentioned earlier in this chapter, there has been a veritable revolution in the manner in which such research is being conducted, resulting in a greater sophistication and refinement of investigatory procedures and theoretical conceptualizations. The results of such research studies are very likely to change the types of treatment modalities included in psychotherapy training programs, as attempts are made to equip future therapists with those techniques demonstrated to be most effective. While the complexity of this task has delayed such an outcome, it is reasonable to anticipate that the time will come when certain treatment programs will be shown to be more effective than others. At that point, the manner in which psychotherapy is taught and practiced will undoubtably change to reflect such conclusions. While some may continue to diversify and maintain a "general practice" in psychotherapy, others will likely favor increased specialization, restricting their clinical work to highly specific patient groups and treatment modalities. The psychotherapist of the future will find that this specialization permits greater expertise in a more focused area. As has already occurred in the field of medicine, the profession of psychotherapy will probably splinter into narrowly defined speciality groups that share a common core of knowledge while possessing skills and techniques specific to each particular speciality.

While advancements in knowledge regarding the etiology and treatment of psychopathology will bring exciting and significant changes to the profession of psychotherapy, other forces may alter future practice as well. For example, some have speculated that the forms of psychopathology expressed in a given society change as a result of shifting environmental influences. While Freud is said to have found a predominance of neurotic and hysterical forms of mental illness in Victorian Europe, factors related to twentieth-century western society seem to promote an increase in the number of characterological disorders, such as narcissism (Kohut, 1977). It is interesting to speculate about the possible transformations which may result from societal and technological changes occurring as we enter the twenty-first century. For example, how will the increasing nuclear threat and environmental pollution alter our society's forms of mental illness? How will overpopulation, toxic waste, and depleted natural resources impact future patterns of psychopathology? If there is a third World War, how will its outcome affect those prone toward mental illness? Will the therapist of the future find more cases of narcissism, or will there be an increase in the number of individuals suffering from depression or anxiety disorders? It might be said that psychotherapists treat society's pathology as it is expressed in its individual's members. Time will tell what future therapists will encounter as they seek to bring relief from the psychic distress of their patients. Perhaps this is why so many psychotherapists admit to a passion for science fiction books. It may be that such speculations foretell the nature of future psychotherapeutic practice more than we realize.

The years ahead hold many challenges for psychotherapists who are able to continue to grow and adapt in response to new information and insights. Remaining personally flexible and open to change will enable practitioners to embrace future innovations with a sense of excitement and discovery. In addition to improving the quality, effectiveness, and efficiency of patient care, future developments and advancements in the practice of psychotherapy will hopefully include a greater emphasis on adequate self-care for clinicians as well. Assisting therapists to cope more effectively with the impact of clinical practice on their personal life and relationships, while finding better ways to reduce the incidence of therapist burnout and impairment, will greatly improve the likelihood of quality patient care as well as increasing the overall personal satisfaction of practitioners. This, too, must be a priority in future developments in the field of psychotherapy if there is to be meaningful progress for both patients and clinicians. Hopefully, neglect in this area will be replaced by renewed concern for the personal well-being of practicing psychotherapists and their relationships with family and friends.

The lasting power of the archetypal figure of the shaman or healer suggests that there will always be psychotherapists of one sort or another. Regardless of future changes in psychotherapy training and practice, selected individuals will no doubt continue to bring relief to individuals in psychic distress. Perhaps in addition to an increase in knowledge regarding the etiology and treatment of psychopathology, future events and experiences will deepen therapists' understanding of the spiritual, transcendent aspects of human beings. As the future therapist seeks a deeper sense of personal meaning and relationship with the divine, he or she may be better able to address those same issues and concerns among patients experiencing a sense of alienation and insignificance in the midst of a chaotic existence. This spiritual evolution, on both an individual and corporate level, has the potential to impact the practice of psychotherapy during the years ahead significantly. With an increase in understanding what it means to be human will come meaningful progress in attempts to restore wholeness to those whose humaness has been fragmented. Like the shaman of the past, this will continue to be the primary task for the psychotherapist of the future.

CHAPTER 9

Closing Comments on a Career in Psychotherapy

Who will do the hard thing?
Those who can.
And who will do the impossible thing?
Those who care.

—Japanese Proverb

The decision to become and remain a psychotherapist reflects a commitment to more than a set of theoretical suppositions and clinical techniques. It also involves more than the adoption of a narrowly defined professional role. Instead, the life of the psychotherapist expresses a unique interplay between "becoming" and "being," as the practitioner commits himself or herself to the lifelong task of personal growth and the ongoing development of self and others. This striving for actualization reflects both a sense of duty and an inner passion, a calling and destiny. The truly gifted clinician understands and accepts this task with a resolve and dedication which transcend the limitations and liabilities inherent in the role of psychotherapist. Despite potential problems which may result, the mature practitioner remains a reasonably content individual throughout an entire lifetime, both in and out of the consulting office. In a unique way, his or her life becomes an expression of both a sense of obligation and privilege, much as the shaman who cannot escape, nor would ever choose to surrender, his or her assigned societal role. Those most suited for the practice of psychotherapy appear to have this sense of being both assigned, and yet having also assumed, the task of being a healer of psychic pain (Goldberg, 1986). They can do nothing else, nor would they ever wish to.

It may be that the force behind this rather mysterious sense of calling can be found in the Japanese proverb quoted earlier. Researchers have conclusively demonstrated that nearly any individual who is sufficiently intelligent and motivated can learn the basic techniques, theories, and treatment methods necessary for the practice of psychotherapy. In this way, they can learn to do the "hard thing." Such individuals are often able to obtain admission to graduate training, advanced degrees in one of the mental health disciplines, licensure or registration for independent practice, and gainful employment as psychotherapists. As a result, these average clinicians enter the profession and often achieve acceptable levels of competence and success.

However, the truly outstanding clinician has something in addition to skill and expertise. He or she possesses a deep sense of caring and compassion that results in a level of empathy and sensitivity that touches others in very extraordinary ways. This underlying experience of caring remains throughout an entire career in psychotherapy, and it may in fact grow stronger as higher levels of personal growth and maturity are achieved. Such individuals are able to integrate comfortably their own needs with those of their patients. They are free of the sense of reckless drive, on the one hand, or defensive withholding, on the other, often characteristic of those possessing the technical skills but lacking the necessary personal balance. There is a resultant transcendence which enables these special individuals to accomplish the "impossible thing." They are able to combine the role of therapist with their personal pilgrimage through life in a natural, comfortable manner which seems to eliminate many potential role conflicts, stresses, and sources of impairment. For such individuals, the blend of being and becoming is a gratifying experience which is spontaneously shared with patients, family, and friends. Whether in session or on vacation, the fully integrated therapist constantly shares his or her sense of perspective and worldview. A personal passion for psychic wholeness is incorporated into nearly every encounter, not because of an uncontrollable drive, but due to a genuine sense of mutuality and caring.

How does one acquire this transcendent perspective which separates the ordinary psychotherapist from the exceptional one? For a few individuals, it seems to be an almost innate characteristic, as though the capacity to care and empathize in a healthy, balanced fashion is woven into the very fabric of their being. For others, it appears to be an acquired trait, perhaps resulting from life experiences that expand personal horizons beyond the immediate concerns of self, such as that which may accompany the healing of deep personal wounds by way of a meaningful interpersonal relationship or profound religious experience. Whatever the source, the result is an ability to care for both self and others, neglecting neither, enabling the fully integrated practitioner to maintain a sense of perspective which sees beyond immediate concerns to more ultimate issues.

The wounded healer motif which has been referred to throughout this book is relevant once again. It is not simply the presence of personal wounds that equips some uniquely talented psychotherapists to be helpful to others. Instead, it is the fact that such therapists have been both wounded and healed which enables them to offer assistance to others in psychic distress (Augsburger, 1986). Yet this wounded/healed cycle is an ongoing process which requires that therapists possess several personal healing relationships in their own private lives. As discussed previously, friends and family typically serve this function for the practitioner whose longings for intimacy must be satisfied in order for emotional growth to continue. In addition, there may be an ongoing sense of healing or purpose derived from a personal religious experience or identification with meaningful social, political, or philosophical causes. These healing experiences and relationships provide the exceptional clinician with the energy, determination, and perspective necessary for empowering the sincere caring and empathy which characterizes his or her interpersonal style of relating with others.

It is also true that the healer is sometimes deeply impacted by those to whom he or she ministers. Just as the shaman who gladly receives the sincere gifts and expressions of caring provided by members of the community, the fully integrated psychotherapist learns to appreciate and accept the personal challenge, encouragement, and support offered by his or her patients. In short, he or she learns how to enjoy the people and work involved in conducting therapy fully. Rather than being uncomfortable with the realization that patients are sometimes important sources of caring and satisfaction, the mature therapist recognizes that a certain amount of pleasure and fulfillment is an appropriate outcome of the intimacy involved in such genuine encounters.

As a result of learning how to enjoy therapeutic endeavors, regardless of the difficulty and stress periodically associated with clinical practice, the actualized therapist is able to remain relatively optimistic, energetic, committed, and fulfilled. In a manner which is free of manipulation or exploitation of patients, he or she is able to experience personal growth and development, in part, as a result of intimate encounters with clients. To a large extent, the work is good for him or her, promoting wholeness, well-being, and maturity. Not only is the wounded healer able to assist in the healing of the psychic wounds of others, but he or she is able to experience ongoing personal healing partly as a result of these special relationships.

It is important to note that it is not an underlying sense of need which motivates the mature psychotherapist to continue conducting psychotherapy, as though he or she is compelled to pursue the potential benefits of intimate encounters with patients. The possibility of eventual therapist impairment or burnout would be high and inadequate patient care likely in such a case. Instead, the fully integrated therapist continues to work and live "therapeutically" out of a sense of gratitude, anticipation, and respect for the dignity and mutuality of human experience. In short, it is a sense of deep caring which engenders the spontaneous feeling of warmth and optimism often experienced both in and out of the therapy office. Herein lies the source of the lasting commitment that such practitioners feel throughout their lifetime of clinical practice. Despite occasional periods of discouragement or stress, the mature therapist enjoys his or her work and gladly receives the personal benefits which are derived from intimate encounters with patients.

Psychotherapy is a noble profession, and its practitioners are ordinary mortals who have moments of genuine transcendence during which time they are able to promote the healing and wholeness of others who are in psychic distress with remarkable success. While their mortality requires that they attend to the potential negative impact of their work on personal relationships and emotional well-being, the transcendence achieved by mature psychotherapists allows them to both express and experience satisfying intimacy with patients, friends, and family. Rather than resulting in burnout or impairment, such encounters promote emotional growth and actualization of the highest order.

This book has been an attempt to take a serious look at the impact of conducting psychotherapy on the life and relationships of the practitioner. Certainly, the discussion has at times been sobering, as consideration was given to the negative impact of the many potential liabilties associated with clinical practice. Yet, despite the gravity of such concerns, it is also important not to lose sight of the many personal benefits which are often derived from this profession. It is hoped that this discussion will enable the reader to become more balanced in his or her attempts to integrate personal needs with those of psychotherapy patients, promoting full actualization of the ability to assist in the healing of psychic pain in a manner which is growth-enhancing for all concerned.

The mature psychotherapist who expresses his or her caring and commitment to others in a manner informed by the concerns summarized in this book will hopefully be able to do "the impossible thing" by promoting growth in both oneself and others throughout an entire professional career and beyond.

References

Abend, S. M. (1982). Serious illness in the analyst: Countertransference considerations. *Journal of the American Psychoanalytic Association, 30,* 365–379.

Ables, B. S. (1974). The loss of a therapist through suicide. *Journal of the American Academy of Child Psychiatry, 13,* 143–152.

American Psychiatric Association. (1980). *Diagnostic and statistical manual of mental disorders. (Third edition). (DSM-III).* Washington, DC: American Psychiatric Association.

Anonymous (1978). The essence of being stuck: It takes one to think you know one—or—work on the therapist's own family. *International Journal of Family Counseling, 6,* 36–47.

Aronson, D. E., Akamatsu, T. J., & Page, H. A. (1982). An initial evaluation of a clinical psychology practicum training program. *Professional Psychology, 13,* 610–619.

Ashway, J. A. (1984). A therapist's pregnancy: An opportunity for conflict resolution and growth in the treatment of children. *Clinical Social Work, 121,* 3–17.

Augsburger, D. (1986). *Wound speaks to wound, healing to healing.* Unpublished manuscript.

Ballenger, J. C. (1978). Patients' reaction to the suicide of their psychiatrist. *Journal of Nervous and Mental Disease, 166,* 859–867.

Balsam, A., & Balsam, R. (1974). The pregnant therapist. In A. Balsam & R. Balsam (Eds.), *Becoming a psychotherapist* (pp. 265–288). Boston: Little, Brown.

Barron, J. (1978). A Prolegomenon to the personality of the psychotherapist: Choices and changes. *Psychotherapy: Theory, Research, & Practice, 15,* 309–313.

Baum, O. E., & Herring, C. (1975). The pregnant psychotherapist in training: Some preliminary findings and impressions. *American Journal of Psychiatry, 132,* 419–422.

Baxter, J. C., Brock, B., Hill, P. C., & Rozelle, R. M. (1981). Letters of recommendation: A question of value. *Journal of Applied Psychology, 66,* 296–301.

Bellak, L. (1981). *Crises and special problems in psychoanalysis and psychotherapy.* New York: Brunner-Mazel.

Belote, B. (1974). *Sexual intimacy between female clients and male therapists: Masochistic sabotage.* Unpublished doctoral dissertation, California School of Professional Psychology, San Francisco.

Bermak, G. E. (1977). Do psychiatrists have special emotional problems? *American Journal of Psychoanalysis, 37,* 141–146.

Binner, P. R. (1986). DRGs and the administration of mental health services. *American Psychologist, 41,* 64–69.

Blachly, P. H., Disher, W., & Roduner, G. (1969, December). Suicide by physicians. *Bulletin of Suicidology,* pp. 1–18.

Bolles, R. N. (1977). *What color is your parachute?* Berkeley, CA: Ten Speed Press.

Bouhoutsos, J. C. (1985). Therapist–client sexual involvement: A challenge for mental health professionals and educators. *American Journal of Orthopsychiatry, 55*, 177–182.

Bouhoutsos, J. C., & Brodsky, A. M. (1985). Mediation in therapist–client sex: A model. *Psychotherapy, 22*, 189–192.

Bouhoutsos, J. C., Holroyd, J., Lerman, H., Forer, B. R., & Greenberg, M. (1983). Sexual intimacy between psychotherapists and patients. *Professional Psychology: Research & Practice. 14*, 185–196.

Boxley, R., Drew, C. R., & Rangel, D. M. (1986). Clinical trainee impairment in APA approved internship programs. *Clinical Psychologist, 39*, 49–52.

Bradley, J. R., & Olson, J. K. (1980). Training factors influencing felt psychotherapeutic competence of psychology trainees. *Professional Psychology, 11*, 930–934.

Breen, D. (1977). Some differences between group and individual psychotherapy in connection with the therapist's pregnancy. *Journal of Group Psychotherapy, 27*, 499–506.

Brenner, D. (1982). *The effective psychotherapist: Conclusions from practice and research.* New York: Pergamon.

Buckley, P., Karasu, T. B., & Charles, E. (1981). Psychotherapists view their personal therapy. *Psychotherapy: Theory, Research, & Practice, 18*, 299–305.

Bugental, J. F. T. (1964). The person who is the psychotherapist. *Journal of Consulting Psychology, 28*, 272–277.

Burt, C. E. (1985). Reflections on interviewing for internship. *Clinical Psychologist, 38*, 91–92.

Burton, A. (1970). The adoration of the patient and its disillusionment. *American Journal of Psychoanalysis, 24*, 494–498.

Burton, A. (1972). *Twelve therapists.* San Francisco: Jossey-Bass.

Burton, A. (1975). Therapist satisfaction. *American Journal of Psychoanalysis, 35*, 115–122.

Butler, S. (1975). *Sexual contact between therapists and patients.* Unpublished doctoral dissertation, California School of Professional Psychology, Los Angeles.

Butler, S., & Zelen, S. L. (1977). Sexual intimacies between therapists and patients. *Psychotherapy: Theory, Research, & Practice, 14*, 139–145.

Cantor, D. W., & Moldawsky, S. (1985). Training for independent practice: A survey of graduate programs in clinical psychology. *Professional Psychology: Research & Practice, 16*, 768–772.

Carkhuff, R. R. (1969). *Helping and human relations.* New York: Holt, Rinehart, & Winston.

Carrol, J. F., & White, W. L. (1982). Theory building: Integrating individual and environmental factors within an ecological framework. In W. S. Paine (Ed.), *Stress and burnout in the human service professions.* New York: Praeger.

Cattell, R. B. (1983). Let's end the duel. *American Psychologist, 38*, 769–776.

Charness, N. (1985). *Aging and human performance.* New York: Wiley.

Cheifetz, D. I., & Salloway, J. C. (1984). Patterns of mental health services provided by HMOs. *American Psychologist, 39*, 495–502.

Cherniss, C. (1980). *Professional burnout in human service organizations.* New York: Praeger.

Cherniss, C., & Egnatios, E. (1978). Is there job satisfaction in community mental health? *Community Mental Health Journal, 14,* 309–318.

Chesler, P. (1972). *Women and madness.* New York: Avon.

Chessick, R. D. (1978). The sad soul of the psychiatrist. *Bulletin of the Menninger Clinic, 42,* 1–9.

Cheifetz, D. I., & Salloway, J. C. (1984). Patterns of mental health services provided by HMOs. *American Psychologist, 39,* 495–502.

Chiles, J. A. (1974). Patient reactions to the suicide of a therapist. *American Journal of Psychiatry, 130,* 463–468.

Clairborn, W. L. (1982). The problem of professional incompetence. *Professional Psychology, 13,* 153–158.

Cogan, T. (1977). *A study of friendship among psychotherapists.* (Doctoral Dissertation, Illinois Institute of Technology, 1977). Dissertation Abstracts International, 78, 859.

Cohen, J. (1983). Psychotherapists preparing for death: Denial and action. *American Journal of Psychotherapy, 37,* 222–226.

Cole, D. S. (1980). Therapeutic issues arising from the pregnancy of the therapist. *Psychotherapy: Theory, Research, & Practice, 17,* 210–213.

Cole, M. A., Kolko, D. J., & Craddick, R. A. (1981). The quality and process of the internship experience. *Professional Psychology, 12,* 570–577.

Colon, F. (1973). In search of one's past: An identity trip. *Family Process, 12,* 429–438.

Coombs, R. H., & Fawzy, F. I. (1982). The effect of marital status on stress in medical school. *American Journal of Psychiatry, 139,* 1490–1493.

Cottle, M. (1980). An accident and its aftermath: Implications for therapy. *Psychotherapy: Theory, Research, & Practice, 17,* 184–191.

Craig, A. G., & Pitts, F. N. (1968). Suicide by physicians. *Diseases of the Nervous System, 29,* 763–772.

Cray, C., & Cray, M. (1977). Stresses and rewards within the psychiatrist's family. *The American Journal of Psychoanalysis, 37,* 337–341.

Cuca, J. M., Sakakeeny, L. A., Johnson, D. G. (1976). *The medical school admissions process: a review of the literature,* 1955–1976. Washington, DC: Association of American Medical Colleges.

Cummings, N. A. (1984). The future of clinical psychology in the United States. *Clinical Psychologist, 37,* 19–20.

Cummings, N. A., & Sobel, S. B. (1985). Malpractice insurance: Update on sex claims. *Psychotherapy, 22,* 186–188.

Curtis, J. M. (1981). Effect of therapist's self-disclosure on patient's impressions of empathy, competence, and trust in an analogue of a psychotherapeutic interaction. *Psychological Reports, 48,* 127–136.

D' Addario, L. (1977). *Sexual relations between female clients and male therapists.* Unpublished doctoral dissertation, California School of Professional Psychology, Los Angeles.

Dalberg, C. C. (1971). Sexual contact between patient and therapist. *Medical Aspects of Human Sexuality, 5,* 34–56.

Dall, O. B., & Claiborn, W. L. (1982). An evaluation of the AETNA pilot peer review project. *Psychotherapy: Theory, Research, & Practice, 19,* 3–8.

Dent, J. K. (1978). *Exploring the psycho-social therapies through the personalities of effective therapists.* (p. 73), U.S. Department of Health, Education, and Welfare, National Institute of Mental Health, Baltimore, Maryland.

DeSole, E. E., Singer, P., & Aronson, S. (1969). Suicide and role strain among physicians. *International Journal of Social Psychiatry, 15,* 294–301.

Deutsch, C. J. (1984). Self-reported sources of stress among psychotherapists. *Professional Psychology: Research & Practice, 15,* 833–845.

Deutsch, C. J. (1985). A survey of therapists' personal problems and treatment. *Professional Psychology: Research & Practice, 16,* 305–315.

Deutsch, H. (1944). *The psychology of women: A psychoanalytic interpretation.* New York: Grune & Stratton.

Dewald, P. A. (1982). Serious illness in the analyst: Transference, countertransference, and reality responses. *Journal of the American Psychoanalytic Association, 30,* 347–363.

Dlin, B. M. (1984). Masking the call for help: Encounters with colleagues in the corridor. *Psychosomatics, 25,* 25–29.

Drabman, R. S. (1985). Graduate training of scientist–practitioner-oriented clinical psychologists: Where we can improve. *Professional Psychology: Research & Practice, 16,* 623–633.

Eber, M., & O'Brien, J. M. (1982). Psychotherapy in the movies. *Psychotherapy: Theory, Research, & Practice. 19,* 116–120.

Edelwich, J., & Brodsky, A. (1980). *Burnout: Stages of disillusionment in the helping professions.* New York: Human Services Press.

Eisenhart, M. A., & Ruff, T. C. (1983). The meaning of doing a good job: Findings from a study of rural and urban mental health centers in the south. *Journal of Community Psychology, 11,* 48–57.

Eissler, K. R. (1977). On the possible effects of aging on the practice of psychoanalysis. *Psychoanalysis Quarterly, 46,* 182.

Erikson, E. (1968). *Identity: Youth and crisis.* New York: Norton.

Eysenck, H. (1952). The effects of psychotherapy: An evaluation. *Journal of Consulting Psychology, 16,* 319–324.

Farber, B. A. (1983a). Dysfunctional aspects of the psychotherapeutic role. In B. A. Farber (Ed.), *Stress and burnout in the human service professions* (pp. 97–118). New York: Pergamon.

Farber, B. A. (1983b). The effects of psychotherapeutic practice upon psychotherapists. *Psychotherapy: Theory, Research, & Practice, 20,* 174–182.

Farber, B. A. (1983c). Psychotherapists' perceptions of stressful patient behavior. *Professional Psychology: Research and Practice, 14,* 697–705.

Farber, B. A. (1983d). Introduction: A critical perspective on burnout. In B. A. Farber (Ed.), *Stress and burnout in the human service professions* (pp. 1–20). New York: Pergamon.

Farber, B. A. (1985a). The genesis, development, and implications of psychological-mindedness in psychotherapists. *Psychotherapy, 22,* 170–177.

Farber, B. A. (1985b). Clinical psychologists' perceptions of psychotherapeutic work. *Clinical Psychologist, 38,* 10–13.

Farber, B. A., & Heifetz, L. J. (1981). The satisfactions and stresses of psychotherapeutic work: A factor analytic study. *Professional Psychology, 12,* 621–630.

Farber, B. A., & Heifetz, L. J. (1982). The process and dimensions of burnout in psychotherapists. *Professional Psychology, 13,* 293–301.

Fine, H. J. (1980). Despair and depletion in the therapist. *Psychotherapy: Theory, Research, & Practice, 17,* 392–395.

Flaherty, J. A. (1979). Self-disclosure in therapy: Marriage of the therapist. *American Journal of Psychotherapy, 38,* 442–452.

Fleischer, J. A., & Wissler, A. (1985). The therapist as patient: Special problems and considerations. *Psychotherapy, 22,* 587–594.

Ford, E. S. C. (1963). Being and becoming a psychotherapist: The search for identity. *American Journal of Psychotherapy, 17,* 472–482.

Fox, R. E., Kovacs, A. L., & Graham, S. R. (1985). Proposals for a revolution in the preparation and regulation of professional psychologists. *American Psychologist, 40,* 1042–1050.

Frank, H. (1975). After the fall: The re-evaluation of self. *Journal of Family Counseling, 3,* 52–54.

Freeman, W. (1967). Psychiatrists who kill themselves: A study in suicide. *American Journal of Psychiatry, 124,* 154–155.

Freud, A. (1954). The widening scope of indications for psychoanalysis: Discussions. *Journal of the American Psychoanalytic Association, 2,* 607.

Freud, S. (1912). Recommendations to physicians practicing psychoanalysis. In *Standard Edition of the Complete Psychological Works* (Vol. 12). London: Hogarth.

Freud, S. (1949). *An outline of psycho-analysis.* New York: Norton.

Freudenberger, H. J. (1974). Staff burnout. *Journal of Social Issues, 30,* 159–165.

Freudenberger, H. J. (1975). The staff burn-out syndrome in alternative institutions. *Psychotherapy: Theory, Research, & Practice, 12,* 73–82.

Freudenberger, H. J. (1981). *The burned out professional: What kind of help?* Paper presented at the First National Conference on Stress and Burnout, Philadelphia.

Freudenberger, H. J. (1986). The health professional in treatment: symptoms, dynamics, and treatment issues. In C. D. Scott & J. Hawk (Eds.), *Heal thyself: The health of health care professionals* (185–194). New York: Brunner/Mazel.

Freudenberger, H. J., & Richelson, G. (1980). *Burnout: The high cost of high achievement.* Garden City, NY: Anchor Press.

Freudenberger, H. J., & Robbins, A. (1979). The hazards of being a psychoanalyst. *Psychoanalytic Review, 66,* 275–295.

Freund, C. M., & Sarata, B. (1983). Work and community satisfactions of psychologists in rural and nonrural areas. *Journal of Rural Community Psychology, 4,* 19–28.

Friedman, E. H. (1971). The birthday party: An experiment in obtaining change in one's own extended family. *Family Process, 10,* 345–359.

Fromm-Reichmann, F. (1960). *Principles of intensive psychotherapy.* Chicago: University of Chicago Press.

Gaitz, C. M. (1977). Planning for retirement: Advice to physicans. *Journal of the American Medical Association, 238,* 149–151.

Garfield, S. L., & Bergin, A. E. (Eds). (1978). *Handbook of psychotherapy and behavioral change*. New York: Wiley.

Garfield, S. L., & Kurtz, R. (1976). Personal therapy for the psychotherapist: Some findings and issues. *Psychotherapy: Theory, Research, & Practice, 13*, 188–192.

Gelman, D. (May 26, 1986). Quick fix therapy. *Newsweek*, pp. 74–76.

Gitelson, M. (1952). The emotional positions of the analyst in the psychoanalytic situation. *International Journal of Psychoanalysis, 33*, 1.

Givelber, F., & Simon, B. (1981). A death in the life of a therapist and its impact on the therapy. *Psychiatry, 44*, 141–149.

Glaser, R. D., & Thorpe, J. S. (1986). Unethical intimacy: A survey of sexual contact and advances between psychology educators and female graduate students. *American Psychologist, 41*, 43–51.

Glazer, M. (1981). Anonymity reconsidered. *Journal of Contemporary Psychotherapy, 12*, 146–153.

Goldberg, C. (1986). *On being a psychotherapist: The journey of the healer*. New York: Gardner.

Goplerud, E. N. (1980). Social support and stress during the first year of graduate school. *Professional Psychology, 11*, 283–290.

Gopplet, J. W. (1968). Psychiatrists who kill themselves: Uncertainty of sources. *American Journal of Psychiatry, 124*,1471.

Granet, R. B., & Kalman, T. P. (1982). Anniversary reactions in therapists. *American Journal of Psychiatry, 139*, 1599–1601.

Greben, S. E. (1975). Some difficulties and satisfactions inherent in the practice of psychoanalysis. *International Journal of Psycho-Analysis, 56*, 427–433.

Greenberg, R. P., & Staller, J. (1981). Personal therapy for therapists. *American Journal of Psychiatry, 138*, 1467–1471.

Greenson, R. (1967). *The technique and practice of psychoanalysis*. New York: International Universities Press.

Grotjahn, M. (1970). Psychiatric consultations for psychiatrists. *American Journal of Psychiatry, 125*, 56–61.

Guggenbuhl-Craig, A. (1979). *Power in the helping professions*. Irving, TX: Spring Publications.

Guy, J. D., Guy, M. P., & Liaboe, G. P. (1986). First pregnancy: Therapeutic issues for both female and male psychotherapists. *Psychotherapy, 23. 297–302.*

Guy, J. D., & Liaboe, G. P. (1985). Suicide among psychotherapists: Review and discussion. *Professional Psychology: Research & Practice, 16*, 470–472.

Guy, J. D., & Liaboe, G. P. (1986a). The impact of conducting psychotherapy on the psychotherapists' interpersonal functioning. *Professional Psychology: Research & Practice, 17*, 111–114.

Guy, J. D., & Liaboe, G. P. (1986b). Personal therapy for the experienced psychotherapist: A discussion of its usefulness and utilization. *Clinical Psychologist, 39*, 20–23.

Guy, J. D., & Souder, J. K. (1986, August). *The aging psychotherapist*. Paper presented to the American Psychological Association Convention, Washington, DC.

Guy, J. D., & Souder, J. K. (in press). The impact of therapist illness or accident upon psychotherapeutic practice: Review and discussion. *Professional Psychology: Research & Practice.*

Guy, J. D., Souder, J. K., Baker, R. N., & Guy, M. P. (in press). Husband and wife psychotherapists: A discussion of unique issues and concerns. *Voices.*

Guy, J. D., Stark, M., & Poelstra, P. (1987). *National survey of psychotherapists' attitudes and beliefs.* Unpublished manuscript.

Hafner, J. L., & Fakouri, M. E. (1984). Early recollections of individuals preparing for careers in clinical psychology, dentistry, and law. *Journal of Vocational Behavior, 24,* 236–241.

Halgin, R. P. (1985). Teaching integration of psychotherapy models to beginning therapists. *Psychotherapy, 22,* 555–563.

Halleck, S. C., & Woods, S. M. (1962). Emotional problems of psychiatric residents. *Psychiatry, 25,* 339–346.

Halloran, D. F. (1985). The retirement identity crisis—and how to beat it. *Personnel Journal, 64,* 38–40.

Halpert, E. (1982). When the analyst is chronically ill or dying. *Psychoanalytic Quarterly, 51,* 372–389.

Hammer, M. (1972). *The theory and practice of psychotherapy with specific disorders.* Springfield, IL: Charles C. Thomas.

Harris, B. M. (1976). *Recalled childhood experiences of effective child psychotherapists.* Unpublished Doctoral Dissertation, California School of Professional Psychology, San Francisco.

Hedges, L. (1983). *Listening perspectives.* New York: Aronson.

Hellman, I. D., Morrison, T. L., & Abramowitz, S. I. (1986). The stresses of psychotherapeutic work: A replication and extension. *Journal of Clinical Psychology, 42,* 197–204.

Henry, B. (1984). The future of clinical training: Forward into the past. *Clinical Psychologist, 37,* 25–26.

Henry, W. E. (1966). Some observations on the lives of healers. *Human Development, 9,* 47–56.

Henry, W. E., Sims, J. H., & Spray, S. L. (1971). *The fifth profession.* San Francisco: Jossey-Bass.

Henry, W. E., Sims, J. H., & Spray, S. L. (1973). *Public and private lives of psychotherapists.* San Francisco: Jossey-Bass.

Herbsleb, J. D., Sales, B. D., & Overcast, T. D. (1985). Challenging licensure and certification. *American Psychologist, 40,* 1165–1178.

Hoeksema, J. H. (1986). *Burnout and leisure time activities among clinical psychologists.* Unpublished Doctoral Dissertation, Rosemead School of Psychology, La Mirada, CA.

Holroyd, J. C., & Brodsky, A. M. (1977). Psychologists' attitudes and practices regarding erotic and nonerotic physical contact with patients. *American Psychologist, 32,* 843–849.

Holroyd, J. C., & Brodsky, A. M. (1980). Does touching patients lead to sexual intercourse? *Professional Psychology, 11,* 807–811.

Holt, R. R. (1959). Personality growth in psychiatry residents. *AMA Archives of Neurology & Psychiatry, 81*, 203–215.

Holt, R. R., & Luborsky, L. (1958). *Personality patterns of psychiatrists.* New York: Basic Books.

Howe, H. E., & Neimeyer, R. A. (1980). Job relevance in clinical training: Is that all there is? *Professional Psychology, 11*, 305–313.

Hutt, C. H., Scott, J., & King, M. (1983). A phenomenological study of supervisees' positive and negative experiences in supervision. *Psychotherapy: Theory, Research, & Practice, 20*, 118–123.

Ingram, R. E., & Zurawski, R. (1981). Choosing clinical psychologists: An examination of the utilization of admissions criteria. *Professional Psychology, 12*, 684–689.

Jaffe, D. T. (1986). The inner strains of healing work: Therapy and self-renewal for health professionals. In C. D. Scott & J. Hawk (Eds.), *Heal thyself: The health of health care professionals* (pp. 194–209). New York: Brunner/Mazel.

Jasnow, A. (1978). The psychotherapist—artist and/or scientist? *Psychotherapy: Theory, Research, & Practice, 15*, 318–323.

Jerrell, J. M. (1983). Work satisfaction among rural mental health staff. *Community Mental Health Journal, 19*, 187–200.

Jung, C. J. (1966). Psychology of the transference. *The Practice of Psychotherapy. Volume 16, Bollingen Series.* Princeton, NJ: Princeton University Press.

Kardner, S. H., Fuller, M., & Mensh, I. N. (1973). A survey of physicians' attitudes and practices regarding erotic and nonerotic contact with patients. *American Journal of Psychiatry, 130*, 1077–1081.

Kaslow, N. J., & Rice, D. G. (1985). Developmental stresses of psychology internship training: What training staff can do to help. *Professional Psychology: Research & Practice, 16*, 253–261.

Kelly, E. L., Goldberg, L. R., Fiske, D. W., & Kilkowski, J. M. (1978). Twenty-five years latter: A follow-up study of trainees assessed in the VA selection research project. *American Psychologist, 33*, 746–755.

Kelly, W. A. (1973). Suicide and psychiatric education. *American Journal of Psychiatry, 130*, 363–468.

Kernberg, O. (1965). Notes on countertransference. *Journal of the American Psychoanalytic Association, 13*, 38–56.

Kimmel, D. C. (1974). *Adulthood and aging.* New York: Wiley.

Kingsley, K. (1985). Reflections on internship year. *Clinical Psychologist, 38*, 93–94.

Klerman, G. L. (1983). The efficacy of psychotherapy as the basis for public policy. *American Psychologist, 38*, 929–934.

Knesper, D. J., Pagnucco, D. J., & Wheeler, J. R. (1985). Similarities and differences across mental health service providers and practice setttings in the United States. *American Psychologist, 40*, 1352–1369.

Kohut, H. (1977). *The restoration of the self.* New York: Universities Press.

Kohut, H. (1985). *How does analysis cure?* Chicago: University of Chicago Press.

Kolb, L. C., & Brodie, H. K. (1982). *Modern clinical psychiatry.* Philadelphia: Saunders.

Kottler, J. A. (1986). *On being a therapist.* San Francisco: Jossey-Bass.

Kovacs, A. L. (1982). Survival in the 1980s: On the theory and practice of brief psychotherapy. *Psychotherapy: Theory, Research, & Practice, 19*, 142–146.

Kovacs, A. L. (1986). Outpatient care confronts the future. *APA Monitor, 17*, 2.

Kutz, S. L. (1986). Defining "impaired" psychologist. *American Psychologist, 41*, 220.

Laliotis, D. A., & Grayson, J. H. (1985). Psychologist heal thyself. *American Psychologist, 40*, 84–96.

Lamb, D. H., Baker, J. M., Jennings, M. L., & Yarris, E. (1982). Passages of an internship in professional psychology. *Professional Psychology, 13*, 661–669.

Langs, R. (1973). *The technique of psychoanalytic psychotherapy* (vol. 1). New York: Aronson.

Larsen, R. C. (1986). State medical societies: Their perceptions and handling of impairment. In C. D. Scott & J. Hawk (Eds.), *Heal thyself: the health of health care professionals* (228–235). New York: Brunner/Mazel.

Larson, C. (1981). Psychologists ponder ways to help troubled colleagues. *APA Monitor, 12*, 16, 50.

Layne, C. (1978). Harmful effects of clinical training upon students' personalities. *Perceptual & Motor Skills, 47*, 777–778.

Lax, R. F. (1969). Some considerations about transference and countertransference manifestations evoked by the analyst's pregnancy. *International Journal of Psychoanalysis, 50*, 363–372.

Leff, H. S., & Bradley, V. J. (1986). DRGS are not enough. *American Psychologist, 41*, 73–78.

Leighton, S. L., & Roye, A. K. (1984). Prevention and self-care for professional burnout. *Family & Community Health, 12*, 44–55.

Levinson, D. J. (1978). *The seasons of a man's life.* New York: Ballantine.

Levinson, D. J. (1986). A conception of adult development. *American Psychologist, 41*, 3–13.

Lewis, J. M. (1982). Dying with friends: Implications for the psychotherapist. *American Journal of Psychiatry, 139*, 261–266.

Liaboe, G. P., & Guy, J. D. (in press). Assessing the current stereotypes of the psychotherapist's family of origin relationships. *Psychotherapy in Private Practice.*

Lindner, H. (1984). Therapist and patient reactions to life-threatening crises in the therapist's life. *International Journal of Clinical & Experimental Hypnosis, 32*, 12–27.

Litman, R. E. (1965). When patients commit suicide. *American Journal of Psychotherapy, 19*, 570–576.

Looney, J. G., Harding, R. K., Blotcky, M. J., & Barnhart, F. D. (1980). Psychiatrists' transition from training to career: Stress and mastery. *American Journal of Psychiatry, 137*, 32–35.

Lord, R., Ritvo, S., & Solnit, A. J. (1978). Patients' reactions to the death of the psychoanalyst. *International Journal of Psycho-Analysis, 59*, 189–197.

Malcolm, J. (1980). *Psychoanalysis: The impossible profession.* New York: Knopf.

Mann, J. (1982). *Time-limited psychotherapy.* Cambridge, MA: Harvard University Press.

Marmor, J. (1953). The feeling of superiority: An occupational hazard in the practice of psychotherapy. *American Journal of Psychiatry, 110*, 370–376.

Marmor, J. (1968). The crisis of middle age. *Psychiatry Digest, 29,* 17–21.

Marston, A. R. (1984). What makes therapists run? A model for analysis of motivational styles. *Psychotherapy, 21,* 456–459.

Maslach, C. (1976). Burned-out. *Human Behavior, 5,* 16–22.

Maslach, C., & Jackson, S. (1978, April). *A scale measure to assess experienced burnout: The Maslach Burnout Inventory.* Paper presented at Western Psychological Association, San Francisco.

Maurice, W. L., Klonoff, H., Miles, J. E., & Krell, R. (1975). Medical student change during a psychiatry clerkship: Evaluation of a program. *Journal of Medical Education, 50,* 181–189.

McCarley, T. (1975). The psychotherapist's search for self-renewal. *American Journal of Psychiatry, 132,* 221–224.

McCartney, J. L. (1966). Overt transference. *Journal of Sex Research, 2,* 227–237.

McConnell, S. C. (1984). Doctor of psychology degree: From hibernation to reality. *Professional Psychology: Research & Practice, 15,* 362–370.

McGuire, T. G., & Frisman, L. K. (1983). Reimbursement policy and cost-effective mental health care. *American Psychologist, 38,* 935–947.

Menninger, K. A. (1957). Psychological factors in the choice of medicine as a profession. *Bulletin of the Menninger Clinic, 21,* 99–106.

Merklin, L., & Little, R. B. (1967). Beginning psychiatry training syndrome. *American Journal of Psychiatry, 124,* 193–197.

Miller, A. (1981). *Prisoners of childhood.* New York: Basic Books.

Morin, S. (1986). Division I: Heading off the AMA. *California State Psychologist, 20,* 6.

Nadelson, C., Notman, M., Arons, E., & Feldman, J. (1974). The pregnant therapist. *American Journal of Psychiatry, 131,* 1107–1111.

Naparstek, B. (1976). Treatment guidelines for the pregnant therapist. *Psychiatric Opinion, 13,* 20–25.

NASW News. (1986). How to cope with malpractice migraines. January, 11–12.

Nathan, P. E. (1982). Psychologists need psychologists, too. *APA Monitor, 13,* 5.

Nevid, J. S., & Gildea, T. J. (1984). The admissions process in clinical training: The role of the personal interview. *Professional Psychology: Research & Practice, 15,* 18–25.

Newman, A. S. (1981). Ethical issues in the supervision of psychotherapy. *Professional Psychology, 12,* 690–695.

Nightingale, E. J. (1986). Experience with prospective payment in the Veterans Administration. *American Psychologist, 41,* 70–72.

Norcross, J. C., & Prochaska, J. O. (1982). A national survey of clinical psychologists: Views on training, career choice, and APA. *Clinical Psychologist, 35,* 2–6.

Norcross, J. C., & Prochaska, J. O. (1983a). Clinicians' theoretical orientations: Selection, utilization, and efficacy. *Professional Psychology: Research & Practice, 14,* 197–208.

Norcross, J. C., & Prochaska, J. O. (1983b). Psychotherapists in independent practice: Some findings and issues. *Professional Psychology: Research & Practice, 14,* 869–881.

Norcross, J. C., & Prochaska, J. O. (1986a). Psychotherapist heal thyself-I. The psychological distress and sel-change of psychologists, counselors, and laypersons. *Psychotherapy, 23,* 102–114.

Norcross, J. C., & Prochaska, J. O. (1986b). Psychotherapist heal thyself-II. The self-initiated and therapy-facilitated change of psychological distress. *Psychotherapy, 23,* 155–168.

Norcross, J. C., Nash, J. M., & Prochaska, J. O. (1985). Psychologists in part-time independent practice: Description and comparison. *Professional Psychology: Research & Practice, 16,* 565–575.

Norcross, J. C., Stevenson, J. F., & Nash, J. M. (1986). Evaluation of internship training: Practices, problems, and prospects. *Professional Psychology: Research & Practice, 17,* 280–282.

Ott, D. B. (1986). *Factors related to job satisfaction among psychotherapists.* Unpublished doctoral research paper, Rosemead School of Psychology, La Mirada, CA.

Paluszny, M., & Pozanski, E. (1971). Reactions of patients during pregnancy of the psychotherapist. *Child Psychiatry & Human Development, 1,* 226–275.

Pasnau, R. O., & Bayley, S. (1971). Personality changes in the first year of psychiatry training. *American Journal of Psychiatry, 128,* 79–84.

Pasnau, R. O., & Russell, M. C. (1975). Psychiatric resident suicide: An analysis of five cases. *American Journal of Psychiatry, 132,* 402–405.

Patrick, P. K. (1979, November). Burnout: Job hazard for health workers. *Hospitals,* pp. 87–90.

Perlman, B. (1985). Training and career issues of APA-affiliated master-level clinicians. *Professional Psychology: Research & Practice, 16* 753–767.

Perlman, B., & Hartman, E. A. (1982). Burnout: Summary and future research. *Human Relations, 35,* 283–305.

Perlman, G. (1972). Change in self and ideal self-concept congruence of beginning psychotherapists. *Journal of Clinical Psychology, 28,* 40–48.

Peterson, D. R. (1984). Komos and Targos in the future of clinical psychology. *Clinical Psychologist, 37,* 21–22.

Peterson, D. R. (1985). Twenty years of practitioner training in psychology. *American Psychologist, 40,* 441–451.

Peterson, D. R., Eaton, M. M., Levine, A. R., & Snepp, F. P. (1982). Career experience of doctors of psychology. *Professional Psychology, 13,* 268–277.

Pfifferling, J. H. (1986). Cultural antecedents promoting professional impairment. In C. D. Scott & J. Hawk (Eds.), *Heal thyself: the health of health care professionals* (pp. 3–19). New York: Brunner/Mazel.

Pines, M. (1980). Psychological hardiness: The role of challenge in health. *Psychology Today, 14,* 34–44.

Pines, A. M., & Maslach, C. (1978). Characteristics of staff burnout in mental health settings. *Hospital and Community Psychiatry, 29,* 233–237.

Pines, A. M., Aronson, E., & Kafry, D. (1981). *Burnout.* New York: Free Press.

Pion, G. (1986). Job focus shifts to service. *APA Monitor, 17,* 25–26.

Pope, K. S., Levenson, H., & Schover, L. R. (1979). Sexual intimacy in psychology training: Results and implications of a national survey. *American Psychologist, 34,* 682–689.

Pope, K. S., Schover, L. R., & Levenson, H. (1980). Sexual behavior between clinical supervisors and trainees: Implications for professional standards. *Professional Psychology, 11,* 157–162.

Pope, K. S., Keith-Spiegel, P., & Tabachnick, B. G. (1986). Sexual attraction to clients: The human therapist and the (sometimes) inhuman training system. *American Psychologist, 41*, 147–158.

Prochaska, J. O. (1984). *Systems of psychotherapy.* Homewood, IL: Dorsey Press.

Prochaska, J. O., & Norcross, J. C. (1983a). Contemporary psychotherapists: A national survey of characteristics, practices, orientations, and attitudes. *Psychotherapy: Theory, Research, & Practice, 20*, 161–173.

Prochaska, J. O., & Norcross, J. C. (1983b). Psychotherapists' perspectives on treating themselves and their clients for psychic distress. *Professional Psychology: Research & Practice, 14*, 642–655.

Racusin, G. R., Abramowitz, S. I., & Winter, W. D. (1981). Becoming a therapist: Family dynamics and career choice. *Professional Psychology, 12*, 271–279.

Raskin, N. J. (1978). Becoming—a therapist, a person, a partner, a parent. *Psychotherapy: Theory, Research, & Practice, 15*, 362–370.

Resnick, R. J. (1985). The case against the blues: The Virginia challenge. *American Psychologist, 40*, 975–983.

Rickard, H. C., & Miller, H. L. (1983). Procedures and students' rights in the evaluation process. *Professional Psychology: Research & Practice, 14*, 830–835.

Rickard, H. C., & Rahaim, G. L. (1982). Retrospective responses to an interview procedure by accepted and rejected clinical applicants. *Professional Psychology, 13*, 443.

Rippere, V., & Williams, R. (1985). *Wounded healers: Mental health workers' experiences of depression.* New York: Wiley.

Robiner, W. N. (1982). Role diffusion in the supervisory relationship. *Professional Psychology, 13*, 258–267.

Robinson, W. L., & Reid, P. T. (1985). Sexual intimacies in psychology revisted. *Professional Psychology: Research & Practice, 16*, 512–520.

Rogers, C. R. (1951). *Client-centered therapy.* Boston: Houghton Mifflin.

Rogers, C. R. (1961). *On becoming a person.* Boston: Houghton Mifflin.

Rogers, C. R. (1980). *A way of being.* Boston: Houghton Mifflin.

Rosen, D. (1971). Suicide rates among psychiatrists. *Journal of the American Medical Association, 224*, 246–247.

Rosenberg, C. L. (1979, April). Doctor rehabilitation: It is working. *Medical Economics.* pp. 114–122.

Ross, M. (1971). Suicide among physicians. *Psychiatry in Medicine, 2*, 189–198.

Ross, M. (1973). Suicide rates among physicians. *Diseases of the Nervous System, 34*, 145–150. Salholz, E. (1986, March 31). A mother's choice. *Newsweek, 108*, 46–59.

Sanders, C. M. (1984). Therapists, too, need to grieve. *Death Education, 8*, 27–35.

Savicki, V., & Cooley, E. J. (1982). Implications of burnout research and theory for counselor educators. *Personnel & Guidance Journal, 60*, 415–419.

Schafer, R. (1979). On becoming a psychoanalyst of one persuasion or another. *Contemporary Psychoanalysis, 15*, 345–360.

Schlicht, W. J. (1968). The anxieties of the psychotherapist. *Mental Hygene, 52*, 439–444.

Schofield, W. (1964). *Psychotherapy: The purchase of friendship.* Englewood Cliffs, NJ: Prenctice-Hall.

Schultz, D. (1981). *Theories of personality.* Monterey, CA: Brooks-Cole.

Schwartz, M. C. (1986). Know when to drop the work-shop talk. *NASW News, 31,* 7.

Schwitzgebel, R. L., & Schwitzgebel, R. K. (1980). *Law and psychological practice.* New York: Wiley.

Scott, C. D., & Hawk, J. (1986). *Heal thyself: The health of health care professionals.* New York: Brunner/Mazel.

Scruggs, S. (1986). *Sexual intimacy in psychotherapy: A review and analysis of the empirical literature and theoretical assumptions.* Unpublished doctoral research paper, Rosemead School of Psychology, La Mirada, CA.

Searles, H. F. (1979). *Countertransference and related subjects.* New York: International Press.

Seligmann, J. (1984, October 15). The mental state of the union. *Newsweek, 104,* 113.

Seyle, H. (1956). *The stress of life.* New York: McGraw-Hill.

Sharaf, M. R. (1960). *An approach to the theory and measure of intraception.* Unpublished doctoral dissertation, Harvard University.

Shepard, M. (1971). *The love treatment: sexual intimacy between patients and psychotherapists.* New York: Wyden.

Shinn, M., Rosario, M., Morch, H., & Chestnut, D. E. (1984). Coping with job stress and burnout in the human services. *Journal of Personality & Social Psychology, 46,* 864–876.

Silver, A. S. (1982). Resuming the work with a life-threatening illness. *Contemporary Psychoanalysis, 18,* 314–326.

Solway, K. S. (1985). Transition from graduate school to internship: A potential crisis. *Professional Psychology: Research & Practice, 16,* 50–54.

Steiner, G. L. (1978). A survey to identify factors in the therapists' selection of a therapeutic orientation. *Psychotherapy: Theory, Research, & Practice, 15,* 371–374.

Steppacher, R. C., & Mausner, J. S. (1973). Suicide in professionals: A study of male and female psychologists. *American Journal of Epidemiology, 98,* 436–445.

Stevenson, J. F., Norcross, J. C., King, J. T., & Tobin, K. G. (1984). Evaluating clinical training programs: A formative effort. *Professional Psychology: Research & Practice, 15,* 218–229.

Stiles, W. B., Shapiro, D. A., & Elliot, R. (1986). "Are all psychotherapies equivalent?" *American Psychologist, 41,* 165–180.

Storr, A. (1979). *The art of psychotherapy.* New York: Methuen.

Stricker, G., & Cohen, L. (1984). APA/CHAMPUS peer review project: Implications for research and practice. *Professional Psychology: Research & Practice, 15,* 96–108.

Stricker, L. J. (1981). The role of noncognitive measures in medical school admissions. *Applied Psychological Measurement, 5,* 313–323.

Strupp, H. H. (1955). The effect of the psychotherapist's personal analysis upon his techniques. *Journal of Consulting Psychology, 19,* 197–204.

Szalita, A. B. (1985). On becoming a psychoanalyst: Education or experience? *Contemporary Psychoanalysis, 21,* 130–142.

Taggart, M. (1980). Salvete et valete: On saying goodbye to a deceased former parent. *Journal of Marital & Family Therapy, 14,* 117–122.

Tedesco, J. F. (1982). Premature termination of psychology interns. *Professional Psychology, 13*, 695–698.

Thoreson, R. W., Budd, F. C., & Krauskopf, C. J. (1986). Perceptions of alcohol misuse and work behavior among professionals: Identification and intervention. *Professional Psychology: Research & Practice, 17*, 210–216.

Thoreson, R. W., Nathan, P. E., Skorina, J. K., & Kilburg, R. R. (1983). The alcoholic psychologist: Issues, problems, and implications for the professional. *Professional Psychology: Research & Practice, 14*, 670–684.

Tower, L. E. (1956). Countertransference. *Journal of the American Psychoanalytic Association, 4*, 224–255.

Tremblay, J. M., Herron, W. G., & Schultz, C. C. (1986). Relationship between therapeutic orientation and personality in psychotherapists. *Professional Psychology: Research & Practice, 17*, 106–110.

Truax, C. B., & Carkhuff, R. R. (1967). *Toward effective counseling and psychotherapy.* Chicago: Aldine.

Tryon, G. S. (1983a). The pleasures and displeasures of full-time private practice. *Clinical Psychologist, 36*, 45–48.

Tryon, G. S. (1983b). Full-time private practice in the United States: Results of a national survey. *Professional Psychology: Research & Practice, 14*, 685–696.

Turkington, C. (1984). Volunteer effort proposed to help troubled colleagues. *APA Monitor, 15*, 25.

Turkington, C. (1986). Response to crisis: Pay up or go naked. *APA Monitor, 17*, 6–8.

Tyler, J. D., & Steven, H. W. (1981). Evaluating the clinical supervisee: A survey of practices in graduate training programs. *Professional Psychology, 12*, 434–437.

Underwood, M. & Underwood, E. (1976). Clinical observations of a pregnant therapist. *Social Work, 21*, 512–517.

Uyeda, M. K., & Moldawsky, S. (1986). Prospective payment and psychological services: What difference does it make? *American Psychologists, 41*, 60–63.

Van Hoose, W. H., & Worth, M. R. (1982). *Adulthood in the life cycle.* Dubuque, IA: Brown.

VandenBos, G. R. (1986). Psychotherapy research: Special issue. *American Psychologist, 41*, 111–112.

Wahl, W. K. (1986). *Conducting psychotherapy: impact upon the psychotherapist's martial satisfaction.* Unpublished doctoral dissertation, Rosemead School of Psychology, La Mirada, CA.

Walfish, S., Polifka, J. A., & Stenmark, D. E. (1985). Career satsfaction in clinical psychology: A survey of recent graduates. *Professional Psychology: Research & Practice, 16*, 576–580.

Walton, D. E. (1978). An exploratory study: Personality factors and theoretical orientations of therapists. *Psychotherapy: Theory, Research, & Practice, 15*, 390–395.

Wampler, L. D., & Strupp, H. H. (1976). Personal therapy for students in clinical psychology: A matter of faith? *Professional Psychology, 7*, 195–201.

Watkins, C. E. (1983). Burnout in counseling practice: Some potential professional and personal hazards of becoming a counselor. *Personnel & Guidance Journal, 61*, 304–308.

Weiner, M. F. (1972). Self-exposure by the therapist as a therapeutic technique. *American Journal of Psychotherapy, 26,* 42.

Weiss, T. (1986). A legislative view of Medicare and DRGs. *American Psychologist, 41,* 79–82.

Wheelis, A. (1958). *The quest for identity.* New York: Norton.

Will, O. A. (1979). Comments on the professional life of the psychotherapist. *Contemporary Psychoanalysis, 15,* 560–575.

Wood, B., Klein, S., Cross, H. J., Lammers, C. J., & Elliot, J. K. (1985). Impaired practitioners: Psychologists' opinions about prevalence, and proposals for intervention. *Professional Psychology: Research & Practice, 16,* 843–850.

Worden, J. W. (1982). *Grief counseling and grief therapy.* New York: Springer.

Young, H. H. (1982). A brief history of quality assurance and peer review. *Professional Psychology, 13,* 9–13.

Zelen, S. L. (1985). Sexualization of therapeutic relationships: The dual vulnerability of patient and therapist. *Psychotherapy, 22,* 178–185.

Zimet, C. N. (1981). The clinical psychologist in the 1980's: Entitled or untitled. *Clinical Psychologist, 35,* 12–14.

Author Index

Subject Index